AVENGERS
THE INITIATIVE
SECRET INVASION

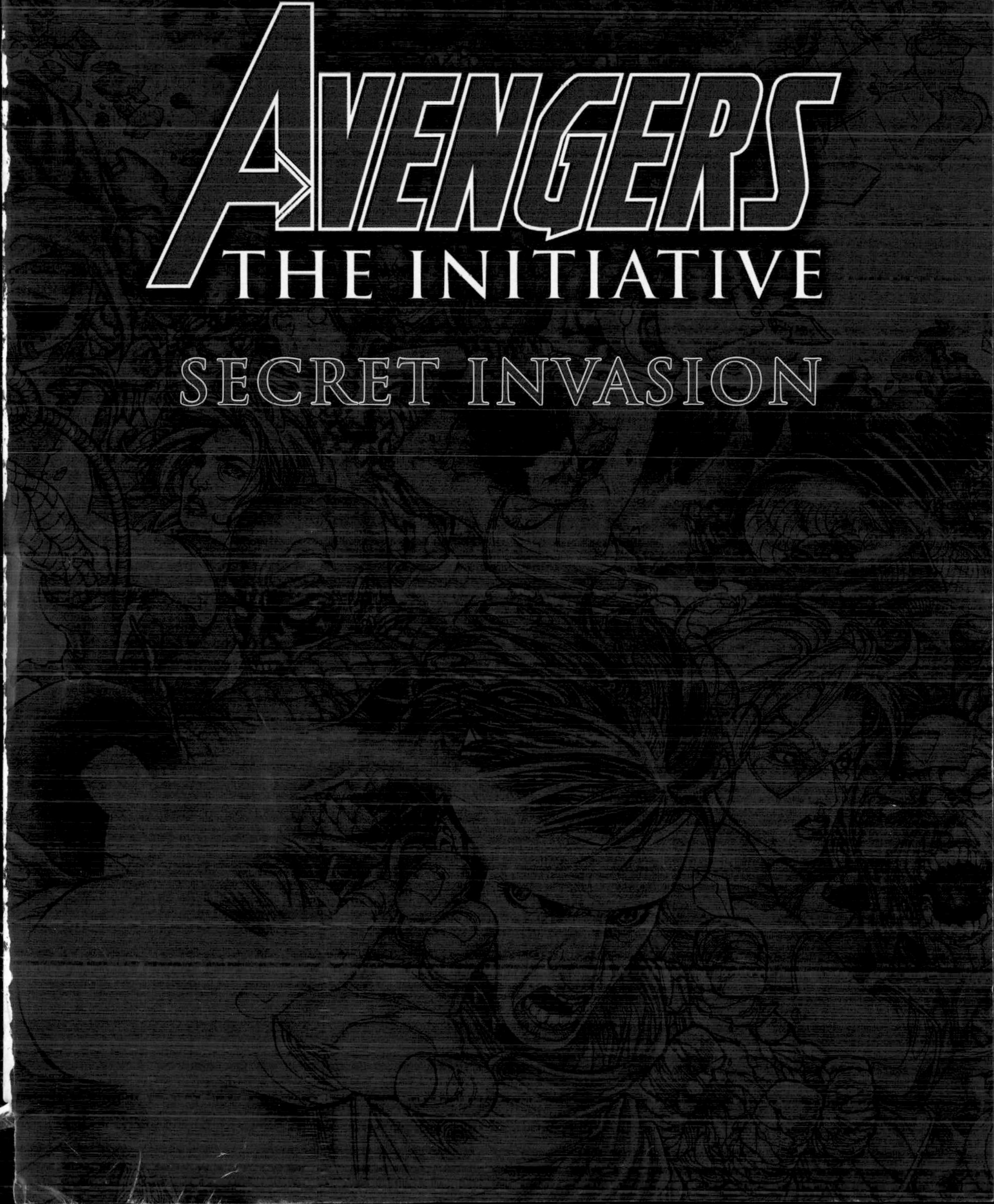

AVENGERS
THE INITIATIVE
SECRET INVASION

WRITERS: DAN SLOTT & CHRISTOS N. GAGE
ARTISTS: STEFANO CASELLI (ISSUES #14 & 16)
& HARVEY TOLIBAO (ISSUES #15, 17 & 19)
WITH BONG DAZO (ISSUE #19)
PENCILS (ISSUE #18): STEVE KURTH
INKS (ISSUE #18): DREW HENNESSY
COLOR ART: DANIELE RUDONI (ISSUE #14),
JAY DAVID RAMOS (ISSUES #15, 17 & 19), LUCA MALISAN (ISSUE #16)
& MATT MILLA (ISSUE #18) WITH CHRIS SOTOMAYOR (ISSUE #19)
COVER ART: MARK BROOKS & CHRISTINA STRAIN

LETTERER: VIRTUAL CALLIGRAPHY'S JOE CARAMAGNA
WITH CHRIS ELIOPOULOS
ASSISTANT EDITORS: MOLLY LAZER & TOM BRENNAN
ASSOCIATE EDITOR: JEANINE SCHAEFER
EDITOR: TOM BREVOORT

COLLECTION EDITOR: JENNIFER GRÜNWALD
EDITORIAL ASSISTANT: ALEX STARBUCK
ASSISTANT EDITORS: CORY LEVINE & JOHN DENNING
EDITOR, SPECIAL PROJECTS: MARK D. BEAZLEY
SENIOR EDITOR, SPECIAL PROJECTS: JEFF YOUNGQUIST
SENIOR VICE PRESIDENT OF SALES: DAVID GABRIEL
VICE PRESIDENT OF CREATIVE: TOM MARVELLI

EDITOR IN CHIEF: JOE QUESADA
PUBLISHER: DAN BUCKLEY

AVENGERS: THE INITIATIVE VOL. 3 — SECRET INVASION. Contains material originally published in magazine form as AVENGERS: THE INITIATIVE #14-19. First printing 2009. ISBN# 978-0-7851-3150-2. Published by MARVEL PUBLISHING, INC., a subsidiary of MARVEL ENTERTAINMENT, INC. OFFICE OF PUBLICATION: 417 5th Avenue, New York, NY 10016. Copyright © 2008 and 2009 Marvel Characters, Inc. All rights reserved. $19.99 per copy in the U.S. (GST #R127032852); Canadian Agreement #40668537. All characters featured in this issue and the distinctive names and likenesses thereof, and all related indicia are trademarks of Marvel Characters, Inc. No similarity between any of the names, characters, persons, and/or institutions in this magazine with those of any living or dead person or institution is intended, and any such similarity which may exist is purely coincidental. **Printed in the U.S.A.** ALAN FINE, CEO Marvel Toys & Publishing Divisions and CMO Marvel Characters, Inc.; JIM SOKOLOWSKI, Chief Operating Officer; DAVID GABRIEL, SVP of Publishing Sales & Circulation; DAVID BOGART, SVP of Business Affairs & Talent Management; MICHAEL PASCIULLO, VP Merchandising & Communications; JIM O'KEEFE, VP of Operations & Logistics; DAN CARR, Executive Director of Publishing Technology; JUSTIN F. GABRIE, Director of Publishing & Editorial Operations; SUSAN CRESPI, Editorial Operations Manager; ALEX MORALES, Publishing Operations Manager; STAN LEE, Chairman Emeritus. For information regarding advertising in Marvel Comics or on Marvel.com, please contact Mitch Dane, Advertising Director, at mdane@marvel.com. For Marvel subscription inquiries, please call 800-217-9158.

10 9 8 7 6 5 4 3 2 1

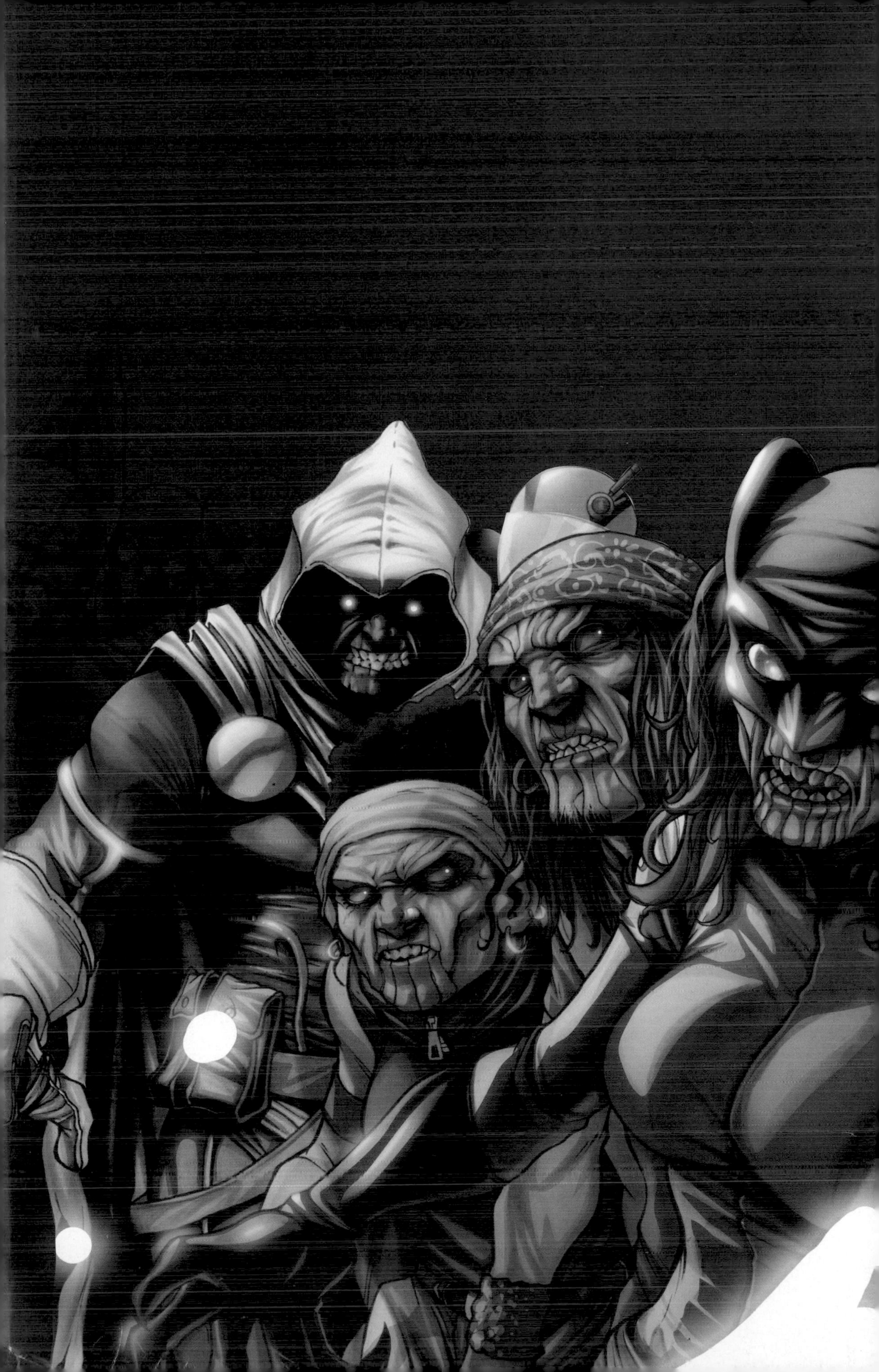

AVENGERS THE INITIATIVE

AFTER STAMFORD, CONNECTICUT WAS DESTROYED DURING A TELEVISED FIGHT BETWEEN THE NEW WARRIORS AND A GROUP OF DANGEROUS VILLAINS, A FEDERAL SUPERHUMAN REGISTRATION ACT WAS PASSED. ALL INDIVIDUALS POSSESSING PARANORMAL ABILITIES MUST NOW REGISTER WITH THE GOVERNMENT. TONY STARK, A.K.A. IRON MAN, HAS BEEN APPOINTED DIRECTOR OF S.H.I.E.L.D., THE INTERNATIONAL PEACEKEEPING FORCE. HE HAS SET IN MOTION THE INITIATIVE, A PLAN FOR TRAINING AND POLICING SUPER HEROES IN THIS BRAVE NEW WORLD, INTENDED TO POSITION A LOCAL SUPER HERO TEAM IN EACH OF AMERICA'S FIFTY STATES.

YELLOWJACKET
DIRECTOR

ANT-MAN
CADET

TRAUMA
COUNSELOR

3-D MAN
GRADUATE

CRUSADER
CADET

Skrulls — an alien race with shape-shifting abilities and an envious eye towards earth. For years, they've been infiltrating our planet, replacing our citizens with spies loyal to their cause. With the recent advancement of the Fifty State Initiative, the Skrulls have manipulated the United States government into helping them place agents across the country — and tighten their grasp on Earth.

SECRET INVASION

The newest recruits of Camp Hammond have taken the base, butting heads with their instructors and learning the ropes. They'd better learn fast, however, as Earth is under siege — Skrulls from across the galaxy have infiltrated our world with their eyes on taking Earth. They've sent their spies into every facet of Earth's defenses — including the Initiative itself. Hank Pym, a.k.a. Yellowjacket, the director of Camp Hammond, is secretly a Skrull impostor, and plans to take the base down from the inside...

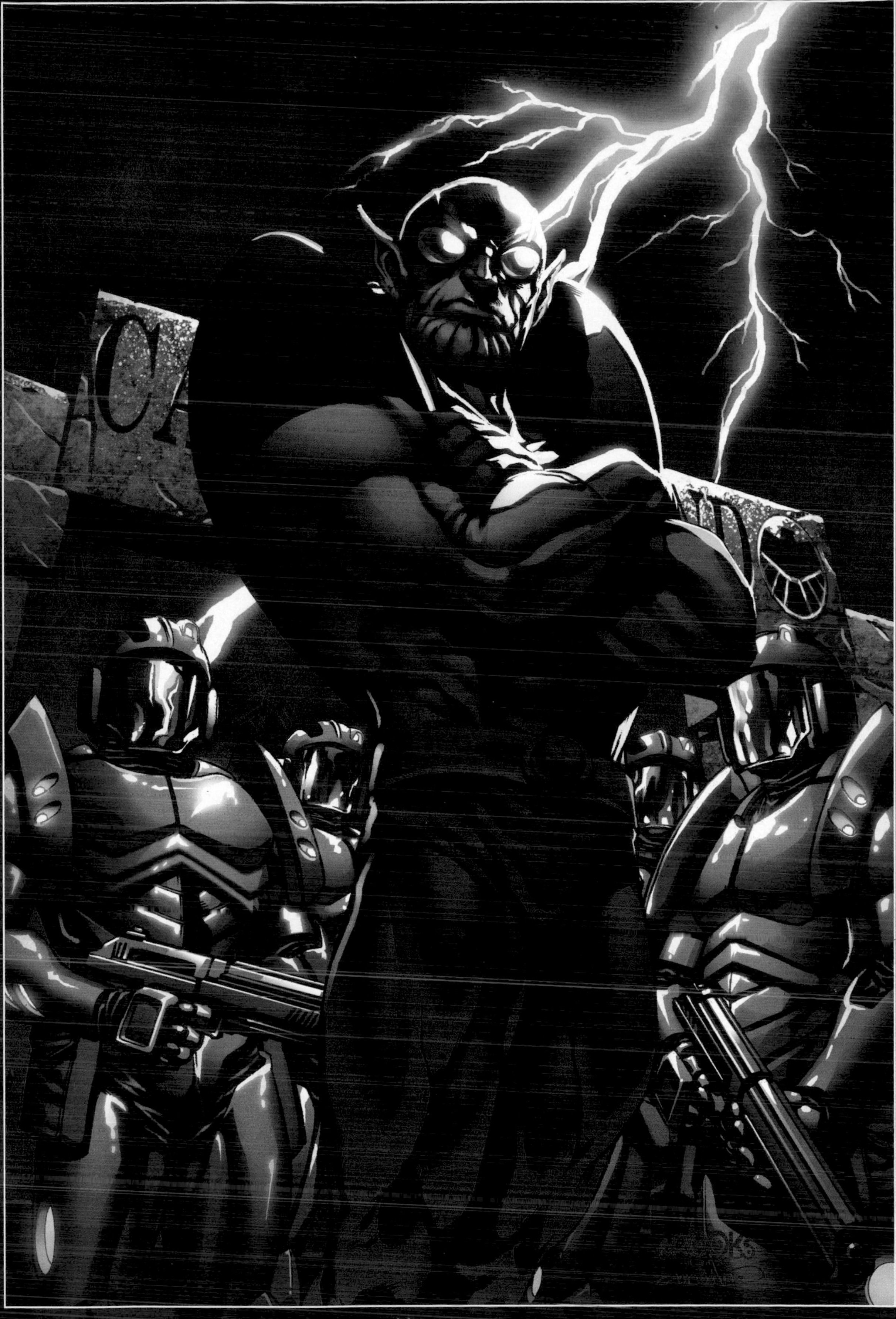

#14

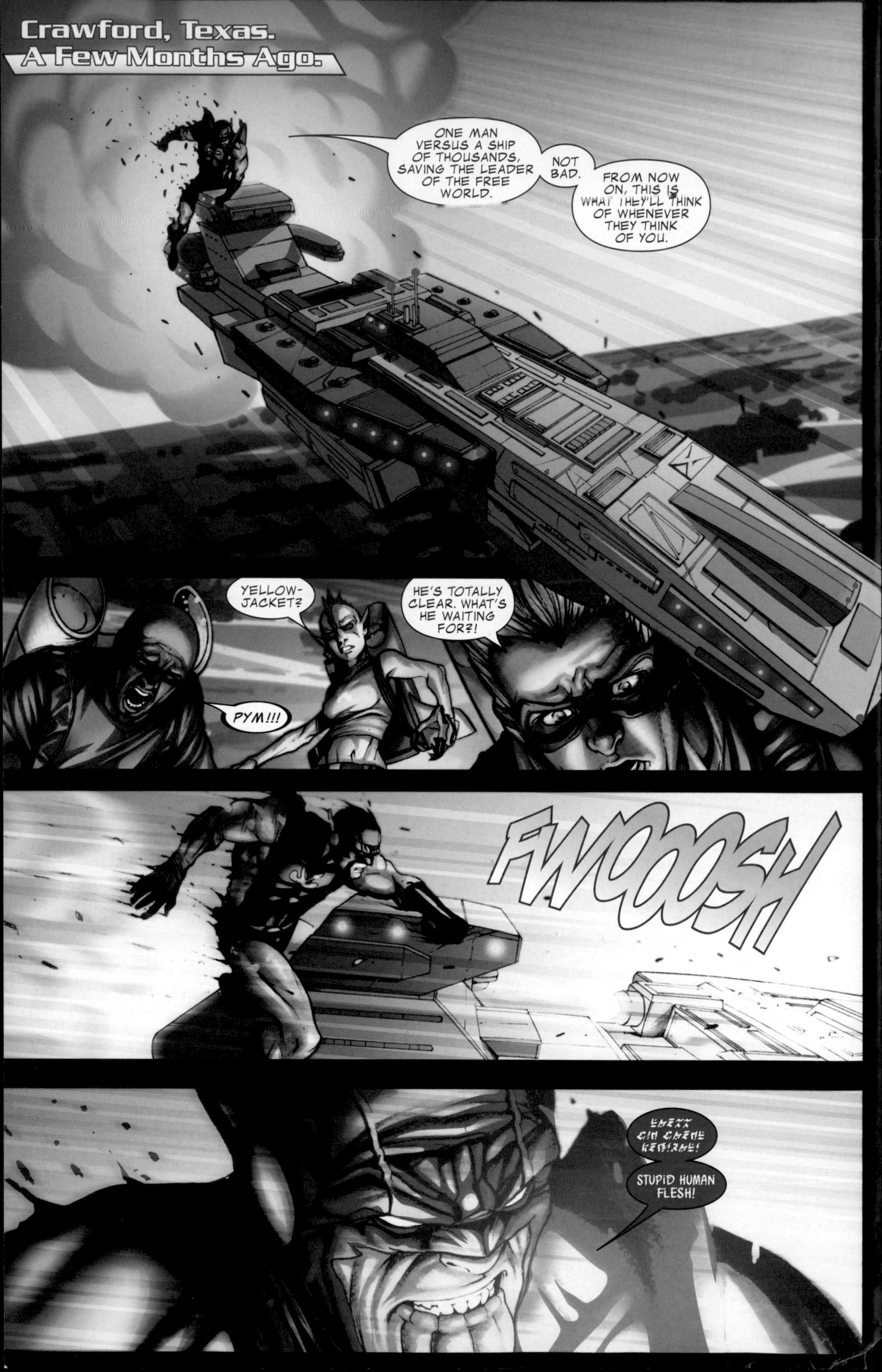
Crawford, Texas. A Few Months Ago.
ONE MAN VERSUS A SHIP OF THOUSANDS, SAVING THE LEADER OF THE FREE WORLD.
NOT BAD.
FROM NOW ON, THIS IS WHAT THEY'LL THINK OF WHENEVER THEY THINK OF YOU.
YELLOW-JACKET?
HE'S TOTALLY CLEAR. WHAT'S HE WAITING FOR?!
PYM!!!
FWOOOSH
STUPID HUMAN FLESH!

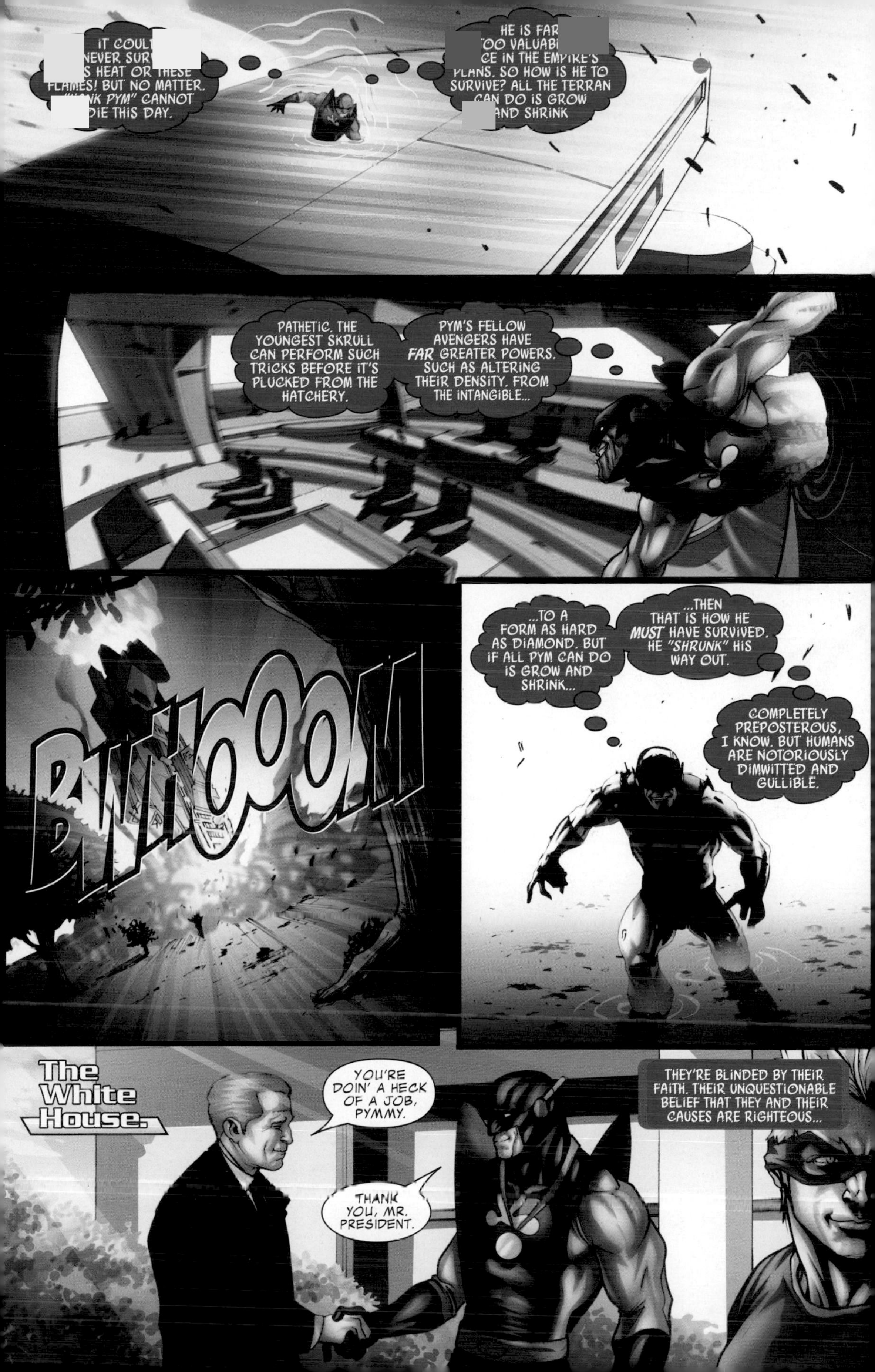
IT COUL NEVER SUR S HEAT OR THESE FLAMES! BUT NO MATTER. NK PYM" CANNOT DIE THIS DAY.
HE IS FAR OO VALUAB CE IN THE EMPIRE'S PLANS. SO HOW IS HE TO SURVIVE? ALL THE TERRAN CAN DO IS GROW AND SHRINK
PATHETIC. THE YOUNGEST SKRULL CAN PERFORM SUCH TRICKS BEFORE IT'S PLUCKED FROM THE HATCHERY.
PYM'S FELLOW AVENGERS HAVE FAR GREATER POWERS. SUCH AS ALTERING THEIR DENSITY. FROM THE INTANGIBLE...
BWHOOOM
...TO A FORM AS HARD AS DIAMOND. BUT IF ALL PYM CAN DO IS GROW AND SHRINK...
...THEN THAT IS HOW HE MUST HAVE SURVIVED. HE "SHRUNK" HIS WAY OUT.
COMPLETELY PREPOSTEROUS, I KNOW. BUT HUMANS ARE NOTORIOUSLY DIMWITTED AND GULLIBLE.
The White House.
YOU'RE DOIN' A HECK OF A JOB, PYMMY.
THANK YOU, MR. PRESIDENT.
THEY'RE BLINDED BY THEIR FAITH. THEIR UNQUESTIONABLE BELIEF THAT THEY AND THEIR CAUSES ARE RIGHTEOUS...

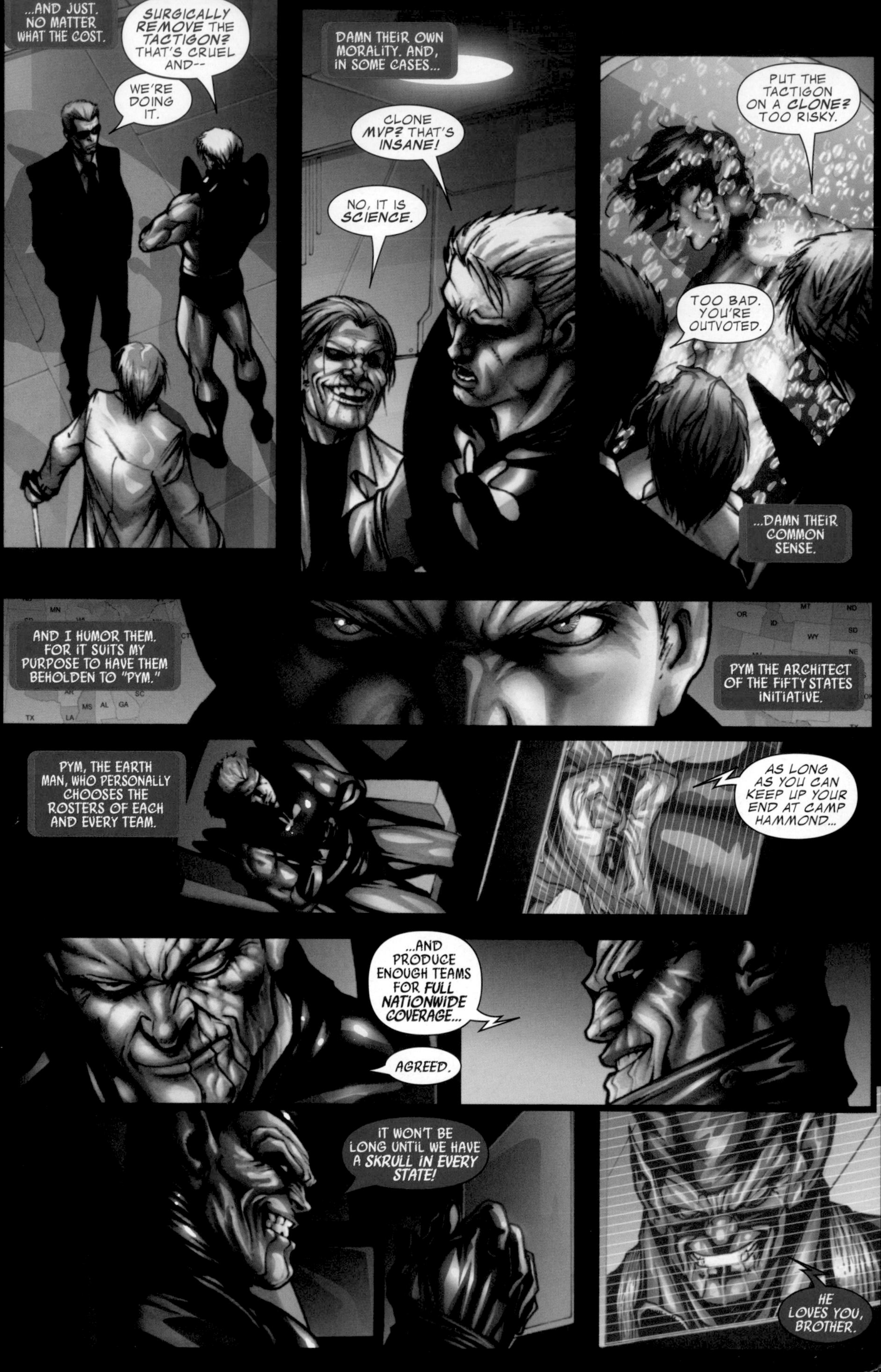

...AND JUST. NO MATTER WHAT THE COST.
SURGICALLY REMOVE THE TACTIGON? THAT'S CRUEL AND--
WE'RE DOING IT.
DAMN THEIR OWN MORALITY. AND, IN SOME CASES...
CLONE MVP? THAT'S INSANE!
NO, IT IS SCIENCE.
PUT THE TACTIGON ON A CLONE? TOO RISKY.
TOO BAD. YOU'RE OUTVOTED.
...DAMN THEIR COMMON SENSE.
AND I HUMOR THEM. FOR IT SUITS MY PURPOSE TO HAVE THEM BEHOLDEN TO "PYM."
PYM THE ARCHITECT OF THE FIFTY STATES INITIATIVE.
PYM, THE EARTH MAN, WHO PERSONALLY CHOOSES THE ROSTERS OF EACH AND EVERY TEAM.
AS LONG AS YOU CAN KEEP UP YOUR END AT CAMP HAMMOND...
...AND PRODUCE ENOUGH TEAMS FOR FULL NATIONWIDE COVERAGE...
AGREED.
IT WON'T BE LONG UNTIL WE HAVE A SKRULL IN EVERY STATE!
HE LOVES YOU, BROTHER.

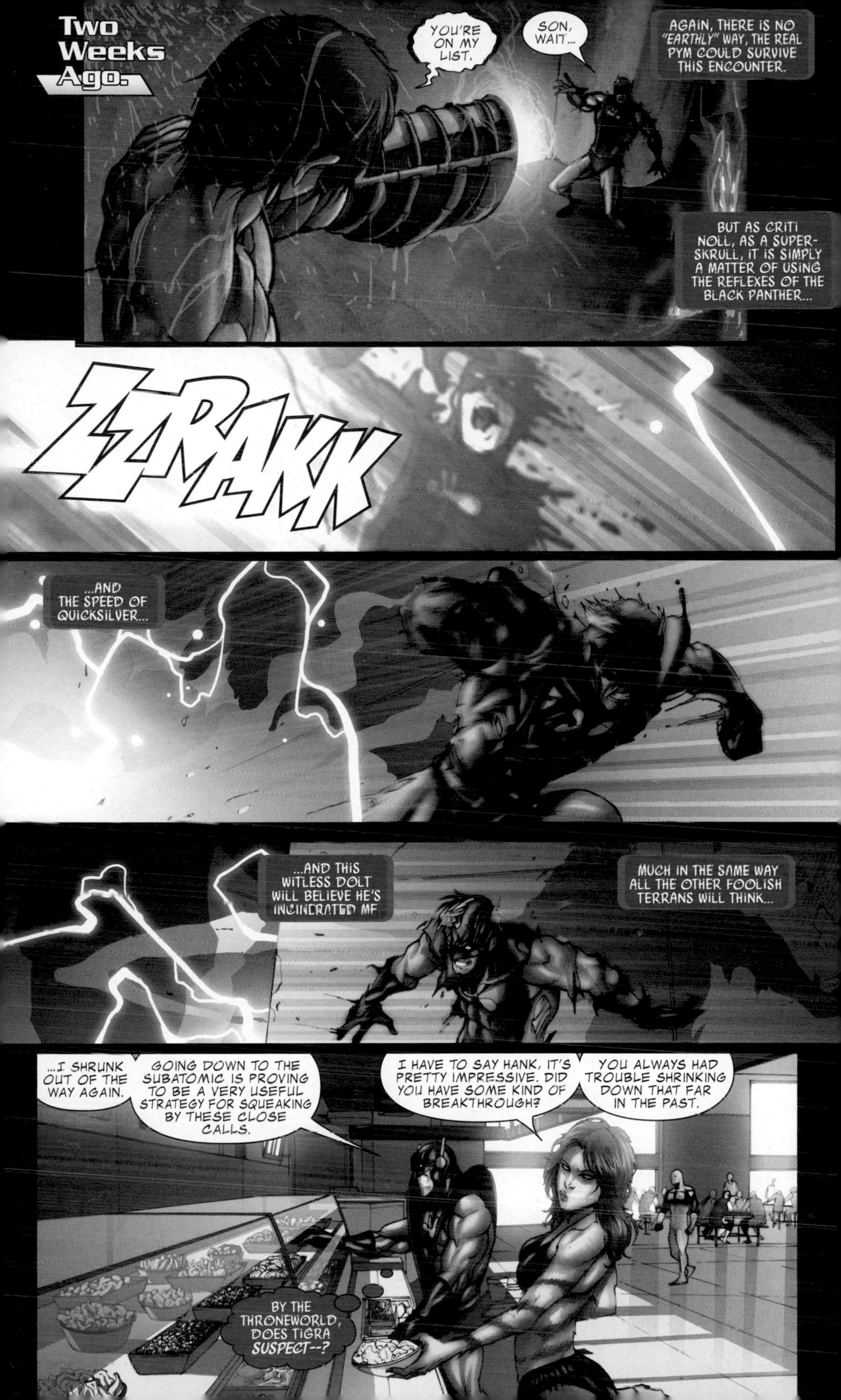
Two Weeks Ago.
YOU'RE ON MY LIST.
SON, WAIT...
AGAIN, THERE IS NO "EARTHLY" WAY, THE REAL PYM COULD SURVIVE THIS ENCOUNTER.
BUT AS CRITI NOLL, AS A SUPER-SKRULL, IT IS SIMPLY A MATTER OF USING THE REFLEXES OF THE BLACK PANTHER...
ZZRAKK
...AND THE SPEED OF QUICKSILVER...
...AND THIS WITLESS DOLT WILL BELIEVE HE'S INCINERATED ME
MUCH IN THE SAME WAY ALL THE OTHER FOOLISH TERRANS WILL THINK...
...I SHRUNK OUT OF THE WAY AGAIN.
GOING DOWN TO THE SUBATOMIC IS PROVING TO BE A VERY USEFUL STRATEGY FOR SQUEAKING BY THESE CLOSE CALLS.
I HAVE TO SAY HANK, IT'S PRETTY IMPRESSIVE. DID YOU HAVE SOME KIND OF BREAKTHROUGH?
YOU ALWAYS HAD TROUBLE SHRINKING DOWN THAT FAR IN THE PAST.
BY THE THRONEWORLD, DOES TIGRA SUSPECT--?

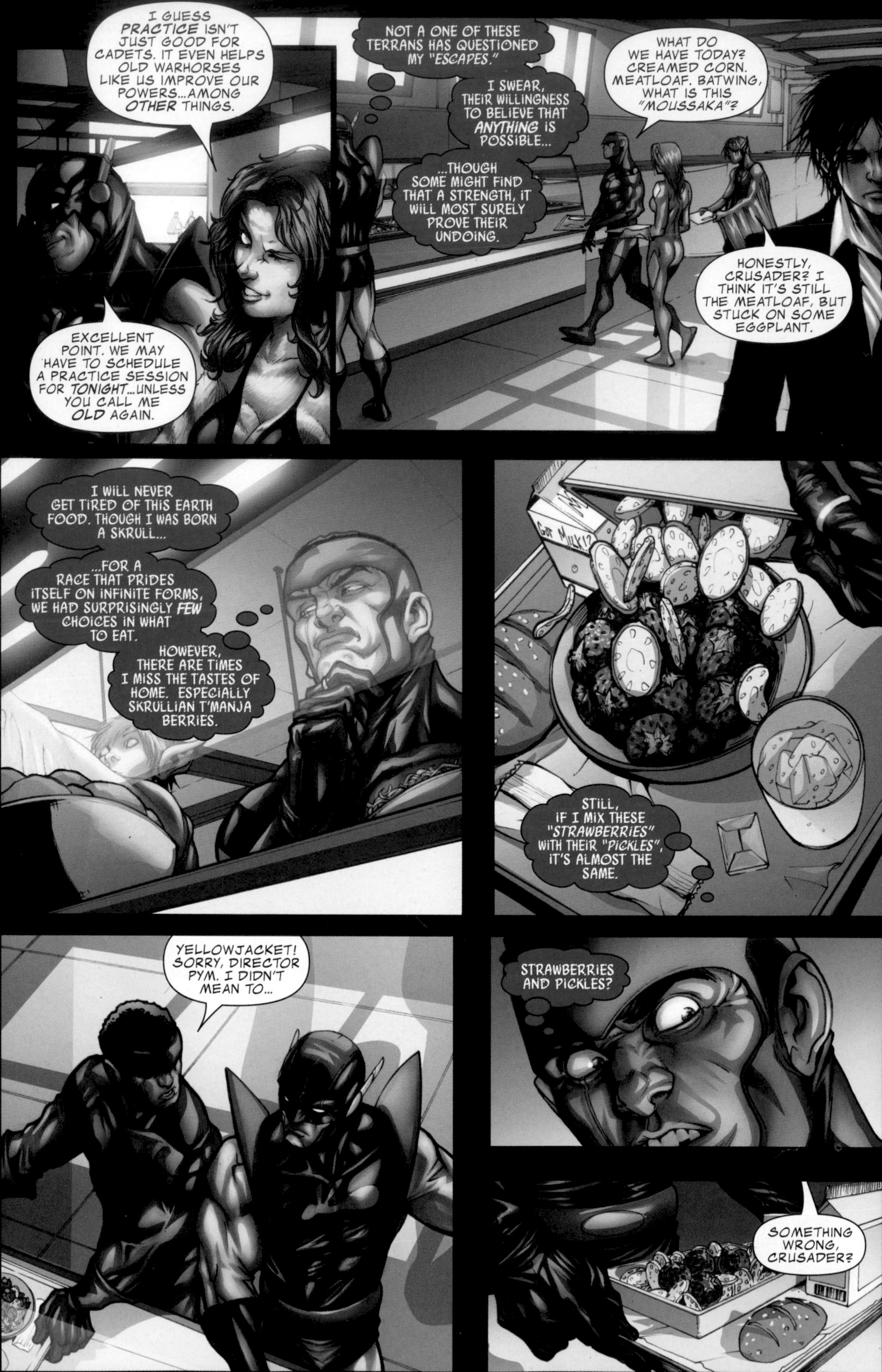

I GUESS PRACTICE ISN'T JUST GOOD FOR CADETS. IT EVEN HELPS OLD WARHORSES LIKE US IMPROVE OUR POWERS...AMONG OTHER THINGS.
EXCELLENT POINT. WE MAY HAVE TO SCHEDULE A PRACTICE SESSION FOR TONIGHT...UNLESS YOU CALL ME OLD AGAIN.
NOT A ONE OF THESE TERRANS HAS QUESTIONED MY "ESCAPES."
I SWEAR, THEIR WILLINGNESS TO BELIEVE THAT ANYTHING IS POSSIBLE...
...THOUGH SOME MIGHT FIND THAT A STRENGTH, IT WILL MOST SURELY PROVE THEIR UNDOING.
WHAT DO WE HAVE TODAY? CREAMED CORN. MEATLOAF. BATWING, WHAT IS THIS "MOUSSAKA"?
HONESTLY, CRUSADER? I THINK IT'S STILL THE MEATLOAF, BUT STUCK ON SOME EGGPLANT.
I WILL NEVER GET TIRED OF THIS EARTH FOOD. THOUGH I WAS BORN A SKRULL...
...FOR A RACE THAT PRIDES ITSELF ON INFINITE FORMS, WE HAD SURPRISINGLY FEW CHOICES IN WHAT TO EAT.
HOWEVER, THERE ARE TIMES I MISS THE TASTES OF HOME. ESPECIALLY SKRULLIAN T'MANJA BERRIES.
GOT MILK!?
STILL, IF I MIX THESE "STRAWBERRIES" WITH THEIR "PICKLES", IT'S ALMOST THE SAME.
YELLOWJACKET! SORRY, DIRECTOR PYM. I DIDN'T MEAN TO...
STRAWBERRIES AND PICKLES?
SOMETHING WRONG, CRUSADER?

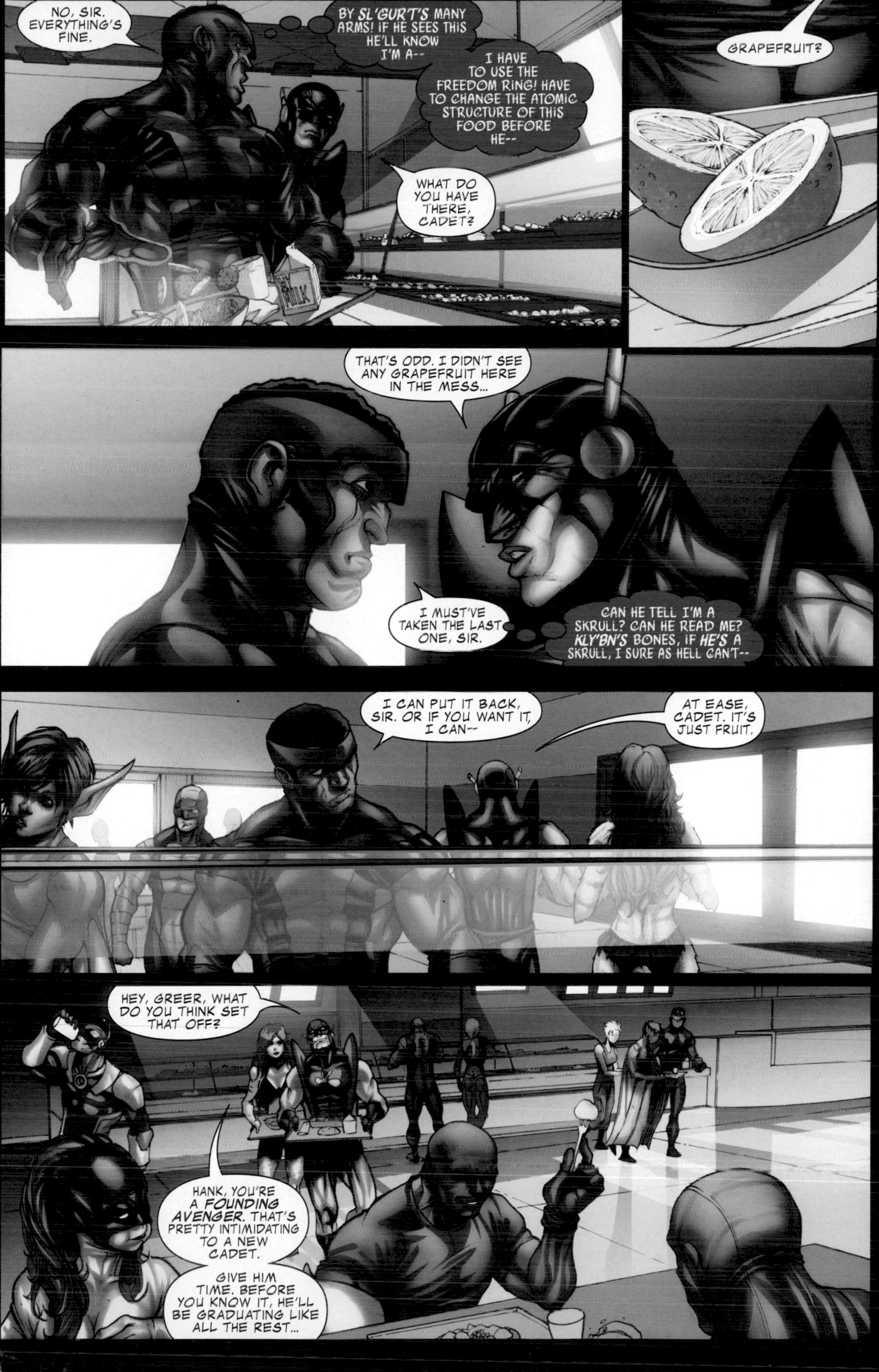
NO, SIR. EVERYTHING'S FINE.
BY SL'GURT'S MANY ARMS! IF HE SEES THIS HE'LL KNOW I'M A--
I HAVE TO USE THE FREEDOM RING! HAVE TO CHANGE THE ATOMIC STRUCTURE OF THIS FOOD BEFORE HE--
WHAT DO YOU HAVE THERE, CADET?
GRAPEFRUIT?
THAT'S ODD. I DIDN'T SEE ANY GRAPEFRUIT HERE IN THE MESS...
I MUST'VE TAKEN THE LAST ONE, SIR.
CAN HE TELL I'M A SKRULL? CAN HE READ ME? KLY'BN'S BONES, IF HE'S A SKRULL, I SURE AS HELL CAN'T--
I CAN PUT IT BACK, SIR. OR IF YOU WANT IT, I CAN--
AT EASE, CADET. IT'S JUST FRUIT.
HEY, GREER, WHAT DO YOU THINK SET THAT OFF?
HANK, YOU'RE A FOUNDING AVENGER. THAT'S PRETTY INTIMIDATING TO A NEW CADET.
GIVE HIM TIME. BEFORE YOU KNOW IT, HE'LL BE GRADUATING LIKE ALL THE REST...

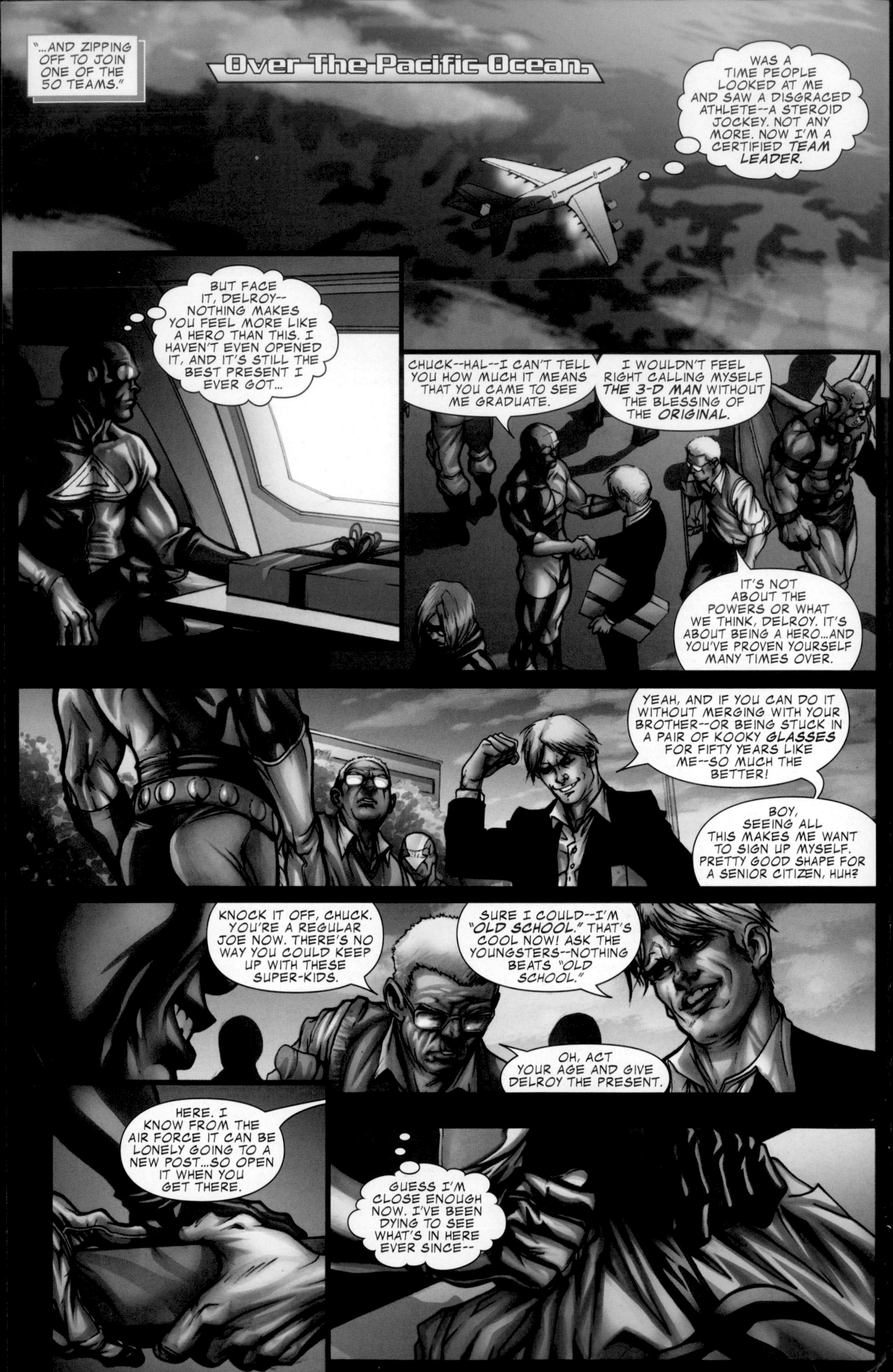
"...AND ZIPPING OFF TO JOIN ONE OF THE 50 TEAMS."
Over The Pacific Ocean.
WAS A TIME PEOPLE LOOKED AT ME AND SAW A DISGRACED ATHLETE--A STEROID JOCKEY. NOT ANY MORE. NOW I'M A CERTIFIED TEAM LEADER.
BUT FACE IT, DELROY--NOTHING MAKES YOU FEEL MORE LIKE A HERO THAN THIS. I HAVEN'T EVEN OPENED IT, AND IT'S STILL THE BEST PRESENT I EVER GOT...
CHUCK--HAL--I CAN'T TELL YOU HOW MUCH IT MEANS THAT YOU CAME TO SEE ME GRADUATE.
I WOULDN'T FEEL RIGHT CALLING MYSELF THE 3-D MAN WITHOUT THE BLESSING OF THE ORIGINAL.
IT'S NOT ABOUT THE POWERS OR WHAT WE THINK, DELROY. IT'S ABOUT BEING A HERO...AND YOU'VE PROVEN YOURSELF MANY TIMES OVER.
YEAH, AND IF YOU CAN DO IT WITHOUT MERGING WITH YOUR BROTHER--OR BEING STUCK IN A PAIR OF KOOKY GLASSES FOR FIFTY YEARS LIKE ME--SO MUCH THE BETTER!
BOY, SEEING ALL THIS MAKES ME WANT TO SIGN UP MYSELF. PRETTY GOOD SHAPE FOR A SENIOR CITIZEN, HUH?
KNOCK IT OFF, CHUCK. YOU'RE A REGULAR JOE NOW. THERE'S NO WAY YOU COULD KEEP UP WITH THESE SUPER-KIDS.
SURE I COULD--I'M "OLD SCHOOL." THAT'S COOL NOW! ASK THE YOUNGSTERS--NOTHING BEATS "OLD SCHOOL."
OH, ACT YOUR AGE AND GIVE DELROY THE PRESENT.
HERE. I KNOW FROM THE AIR FORCE IT CAN BE LONELY GOING TO A NEW POST...SO OPEN IT WHEN YOU GET THERE.
GUESS I'M CLOSE ENOUGH NOW. I'VE BEEN DYING TO SEE WHAT'S IN HERE EVER SINCE--

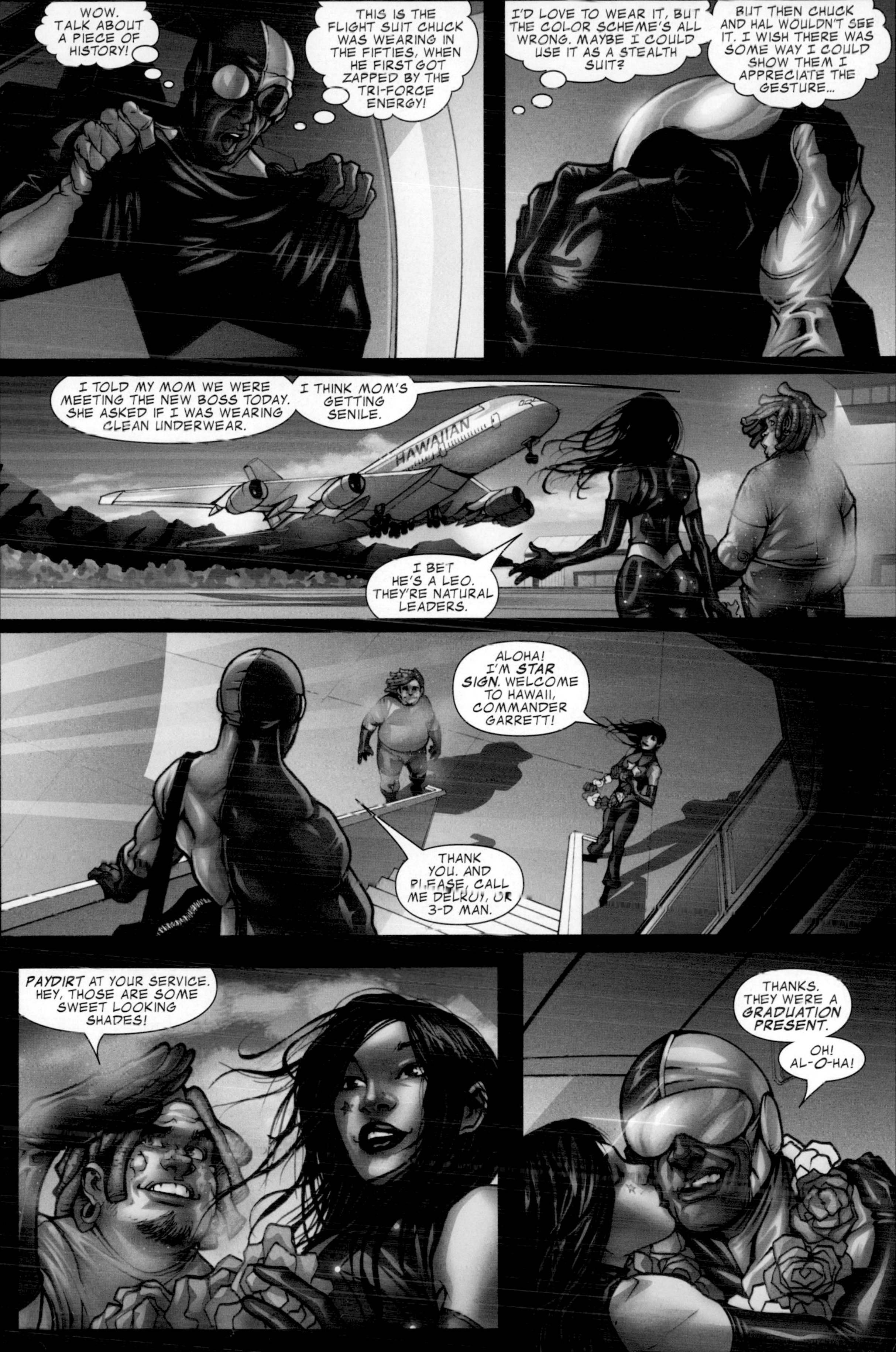
WOW. TALK ABOUT A PIECE OF HISTORY!
THIS IS THE FLIGHT SUIT CHUCK WAS WEARING IN THE FIFTIES, WHEN HE FIRST GOT ZAPPED BY THE TRI-FORCE ENERGY!
I'D LOVE TO WEAR IT, BUT THE COLOR SCHEME'S ALL WRONG. MAYBE I COULD USE IT AS A STEALTH SUIT?
BUT THEN CHUCK AND HAL WOULDN'T SEE IT. I WISH THERE WAS SOME WAY I COULD SHOW THEM I APPRECIATE THE GESTURE...
I TOLD MY MOM WE WERE MEETING THE NEW BOSS TODAY. SHE ASKED IF I WAS WEARING CLEAN UNDERWEAR.
I THINK MOM'S GETTING SENILE.
HAWAIIAN
I BET HE'S A LEO. THEY'RE NATURAL LEADERS.
ALOHA! I'M STAR SIGN. WELCOME TO HAWAII, COMMANDER GARRETT!
THANK YOU. AND PLEASE, CALL ME DELROY, OR 3-D MAN.
PAYDIRT AT YOUR SERVICE. HEY, THOSE ARE SOME SWEET LOOKING SHADES!
THANKS. THEY WERE A GRADUATION PRESENT.
OH! AL-O-HA!

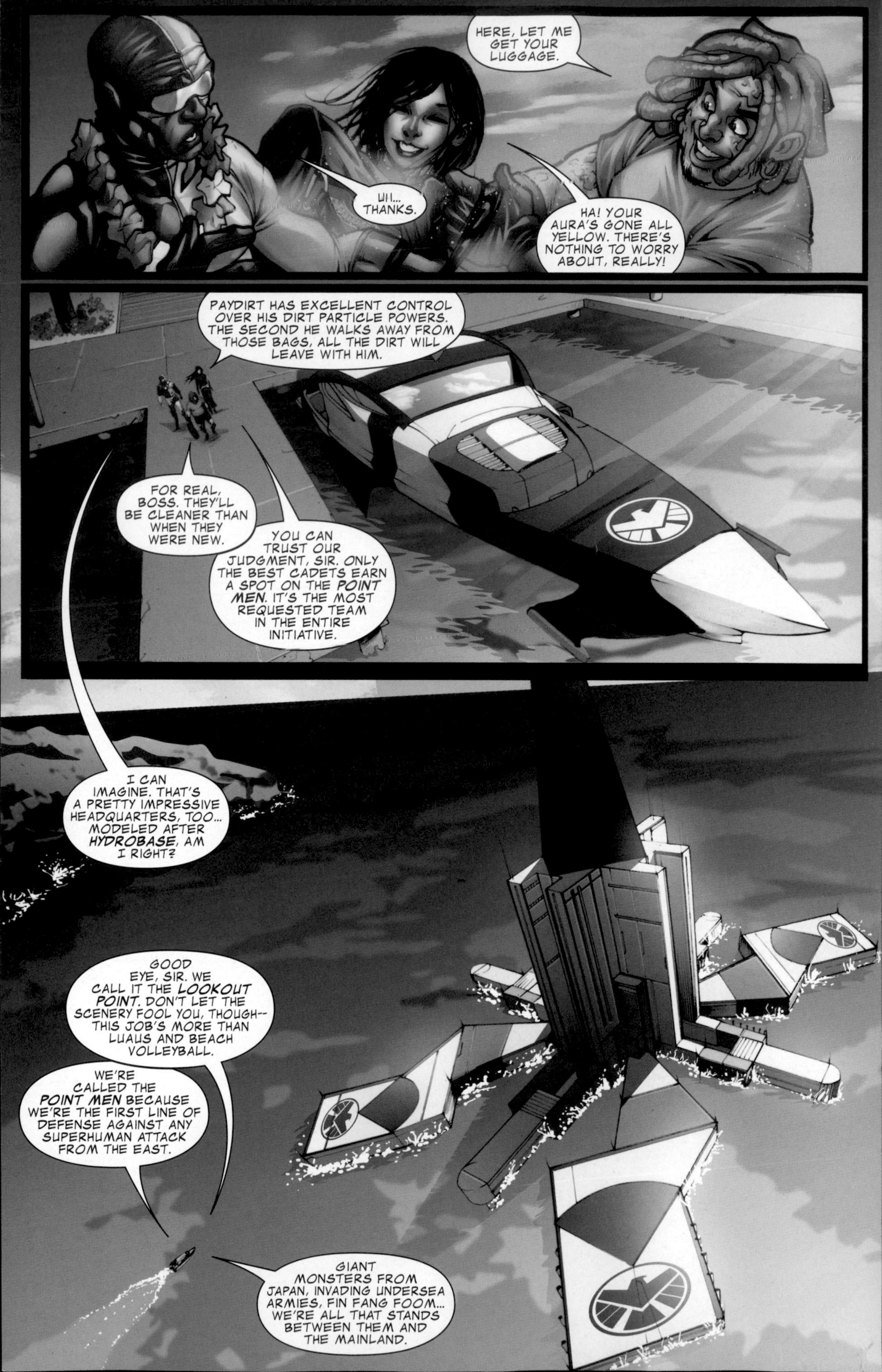
HERE, LET ME GET YOUR LUGGAGE.
UH... THANKS.
HA! YOUR AURA'S GONE ALL YELLOW. THERE'S NOTHING TO WORRY ABOUT, REALLY!
PAYDIRT HAS EXCELLENT CONTROL OVER HIS DIRT PARTICLE POWERS. THE SECOND HE WALKS AWAY FROM THOSE BAGS, ALL THE DIRT WILL LEAVE WITH HIM.
FOR REAL, BOSS. THEY'LL BE CLEANER THAN WHEN THEY WERE NEW.
YOU CAN TRUST OUR JUDGMENT, SIR. ONLY THE BEST CADETS EARN A SPOT ON THE POINT MEN. IT'S THE MOST REQUESTED TEAM IN THE ENTIRE INITIATIVE.
I CAN IMAGINE. THAT'S A PRETTY IMPRESSIVE HEADQUARTERS, TOO... MODELED AFTER HYDROBASE, AM I RIGHT?
GOOD EYE, SIR. WE CALL IT THE LOOKOUT POINT. DON'T LET THE SCENERY FOOL YOU, THOUGH-- THIS JOB'S MORE THAN LUAUS AND BEACH VOLLEYBALL.
WE'RE CALLED THE POINT MEN BECAUSE WE'RE THE FIRST LINE OF DEFENSE AGAINST ANY SUPERHUMAN ATTACK FROM THE EAST.
GIANT MONSTERS FROM JAPAN, INVADING UNDERSEA ARMIES, FIN FANG FOOM... WE'RE ALL THAT STANDS BETWEEN THEM AND THE MAINLAND.

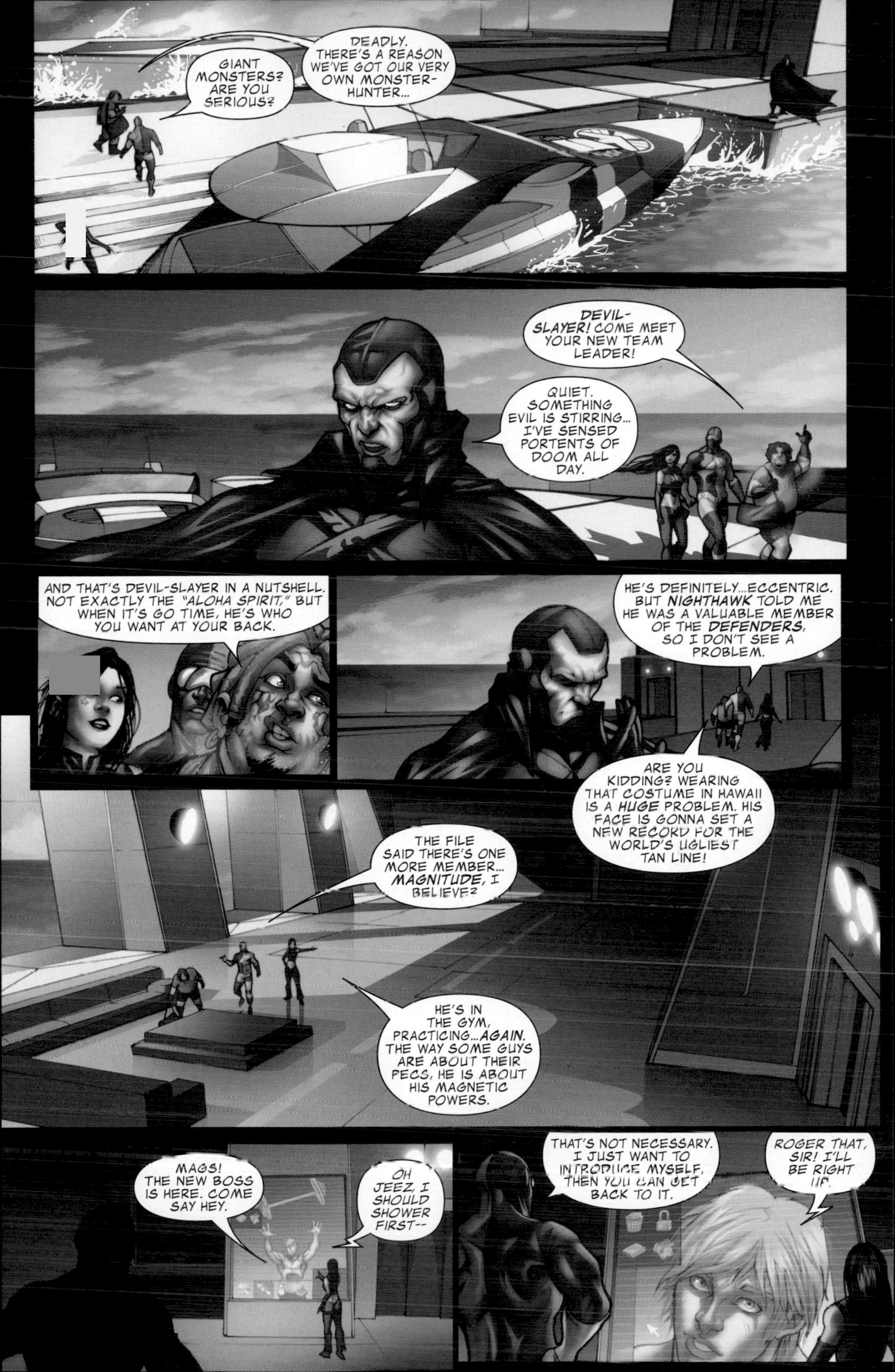
GIANT MONSTERS? ARE YOU SERIOUS?
DEADLY. THERE'S A REASON WE'VE GOT OUR VERY OWN MONSTER-HUNTER...
DEVIL-SLAYER! COME MEET YOUR NEW TEAM LEADER!
QUIET. SOMETHING EVIL IS STIRRING... I'VE SENSED PORTENTS OF DOOM ALL DAY.
AND THAT'S DEVIL-SLAYER IN A NUTSHELL. NOT EXACTLY THE "ALOHA SPIRIT," BUT WHEN IT'S GO TIME, HE'S WHO YOU WANT AT YOUR BACK.
HE'S DEFINITELY...ECCENTRIC. BUT NIGHTHAWK TOLD ME HE WAS A VALUABLE MEMBER OF THE DEFENDERS, SO I DON'T SEE A PROBLEM.
ARE YOU KIDDING? WEARING THAT COSTUME IN HAWAII IS A HUGE PROBLEM. HIS FACE IS GONNA SET A NEW RECORD FOR THE WORLD'S UGLIEST TAN LINE!
THE FILE SAID THERE'S ONE MORE MEMBER... MAGNITUDE, I BELIEVE?
HE'S IN THE GYM, PRACTICING...AGAIN. THE WAY SOME GUYS ARE ABOUT THEIR PECS, HE IS ABOUT HIS MAGNETIC POWERS.
MAGS! THE NEW BOSS IS HERE. COME SAY HEY.
OH JEEZ, I SHOULD SHOWER FIRST--
THAT'S NOT NECESSARY. I JUST WANT TO INTRODUCE MYSELF, THEN YOU CAN GET BACK TO IT.
ROGER THAT, SIR! I'LL BE RIGHT UP.

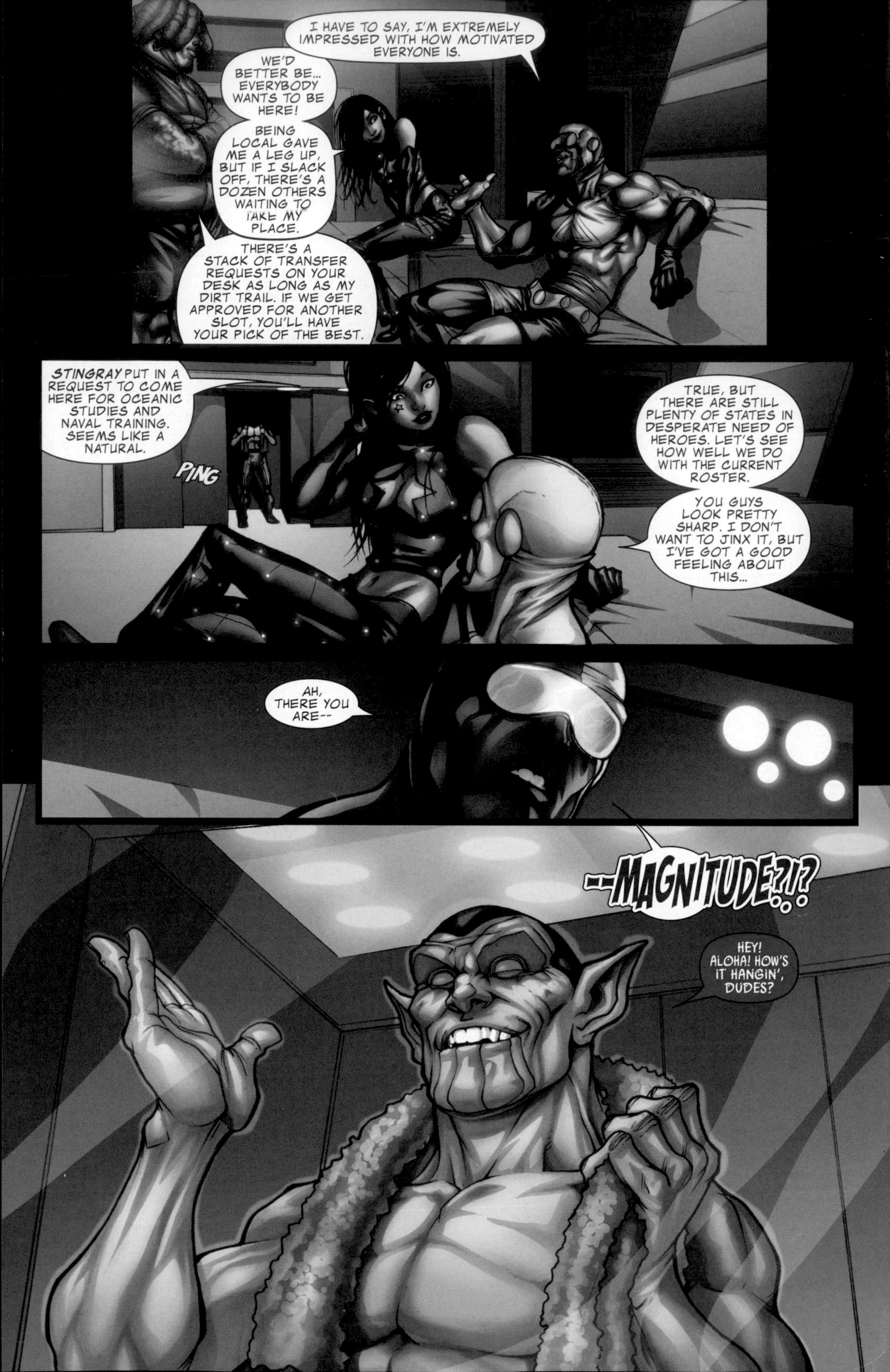

I HAVE TO SAY, I'M EXTREMELY IMPRESSED WITH HOW MOTIVATED EVERYONE IS.
WE'D BETTER BE... EVERYBODY WANTS TO BE HERE!
BEING LOCAL GAVE ME A LEG UP, BUT IF I SLACK OFF, THERE'S A DOZEN OTHERS WAITING TO TAKE MY PLACE.
THERE'S A STACK OF TRANSFER REQUESTS ON YOUR DESK AS LONG AS MY DIRT TRAIL. IF WE GET APPROVED FOR ANOTHER SLOT, YOU'LL HAVE YOUR PICK OF THE BEST.
STINGRAY PUT IN A REQUEST TO COME HERE FOR OCEANIC STUDIES AND NAVAL TRAINING. SEEMS LIKE A NATURAL.
TRUE, BUT THERE ARE STILL PLENTY OF STATES IN DESPERATE NEED OF HEROES. LET'S SEE HOW WELL WE DO WITH THE CURRENT ROSTER.
YOU GUYS LOOK PRETTY SHARP. I DON'T WANT TO JINX IT, BUT I'VE GOT A GOOD FEELING ABOUT THIS...
PING
AH, THERE YOU ARE--
--MAGNITUDE?!?
HEY! ALOHA! HOW'S IT HANGIN', DUDES?

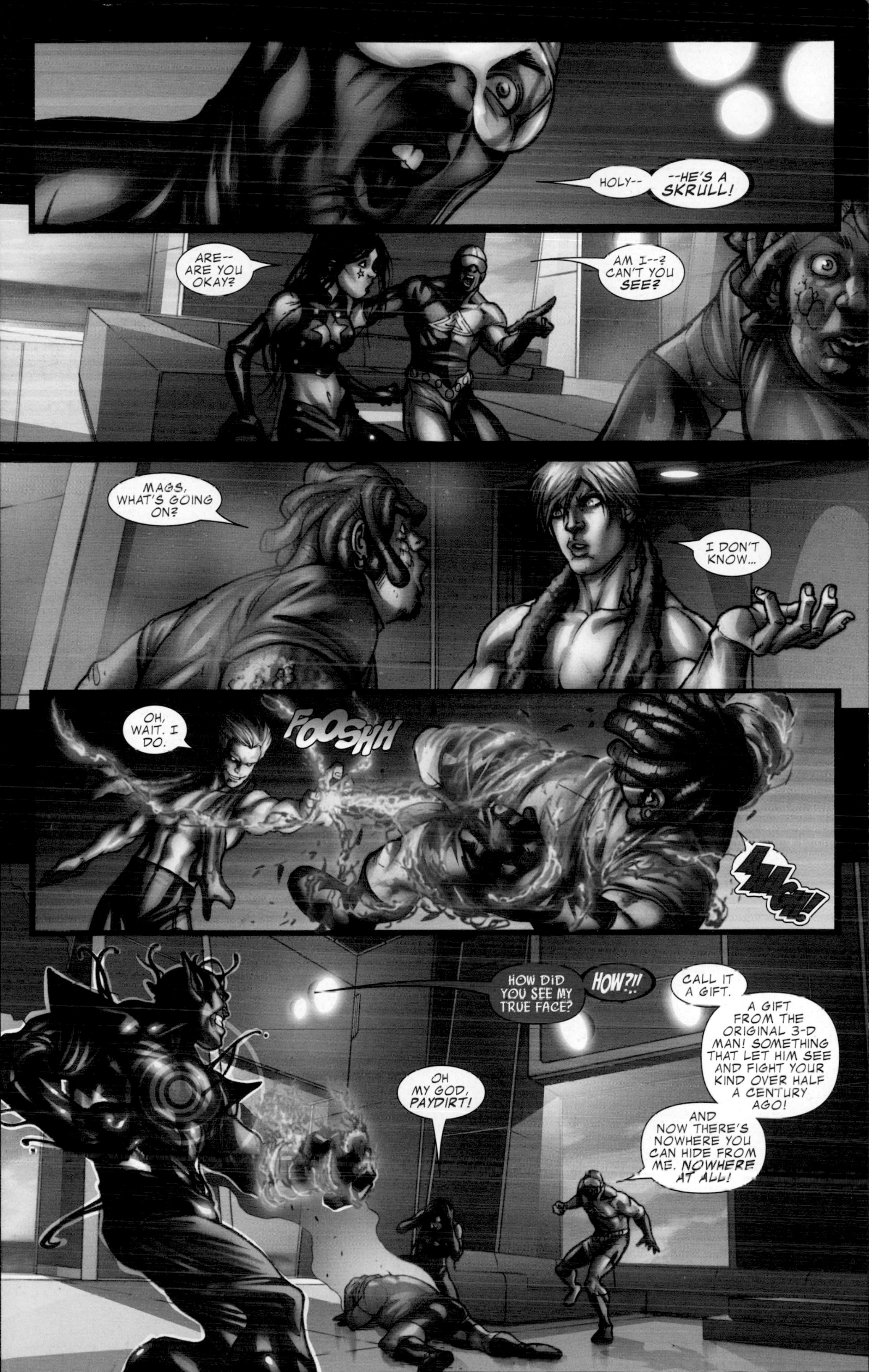

HOLY--
--HE'S A SKRULL!
ARE-- ARE YOU OKAY?
AM I--? CAN'T YOU SEE?
MAGS, WHAT'S GOING ON?
I DON'T KNOW...
OH, WAIT. I DO.
FOOSHH
HOW DID YOU SEE MY TRUE FACE?
HOW?!!
CALL IT A GIFT.
A GIFT FROM THE ORIGINAL 3-D MAN! SOMETHING THAT LET HIM SEE AND FIGHT YOUR KIND OVER HALF A CENTURY AGO!
OH MY GOD, PAYDIRT!
AND NOW THERE'S NOWHERE YOU CAN HIDE FROM ME. NOWHERE AT ALL!

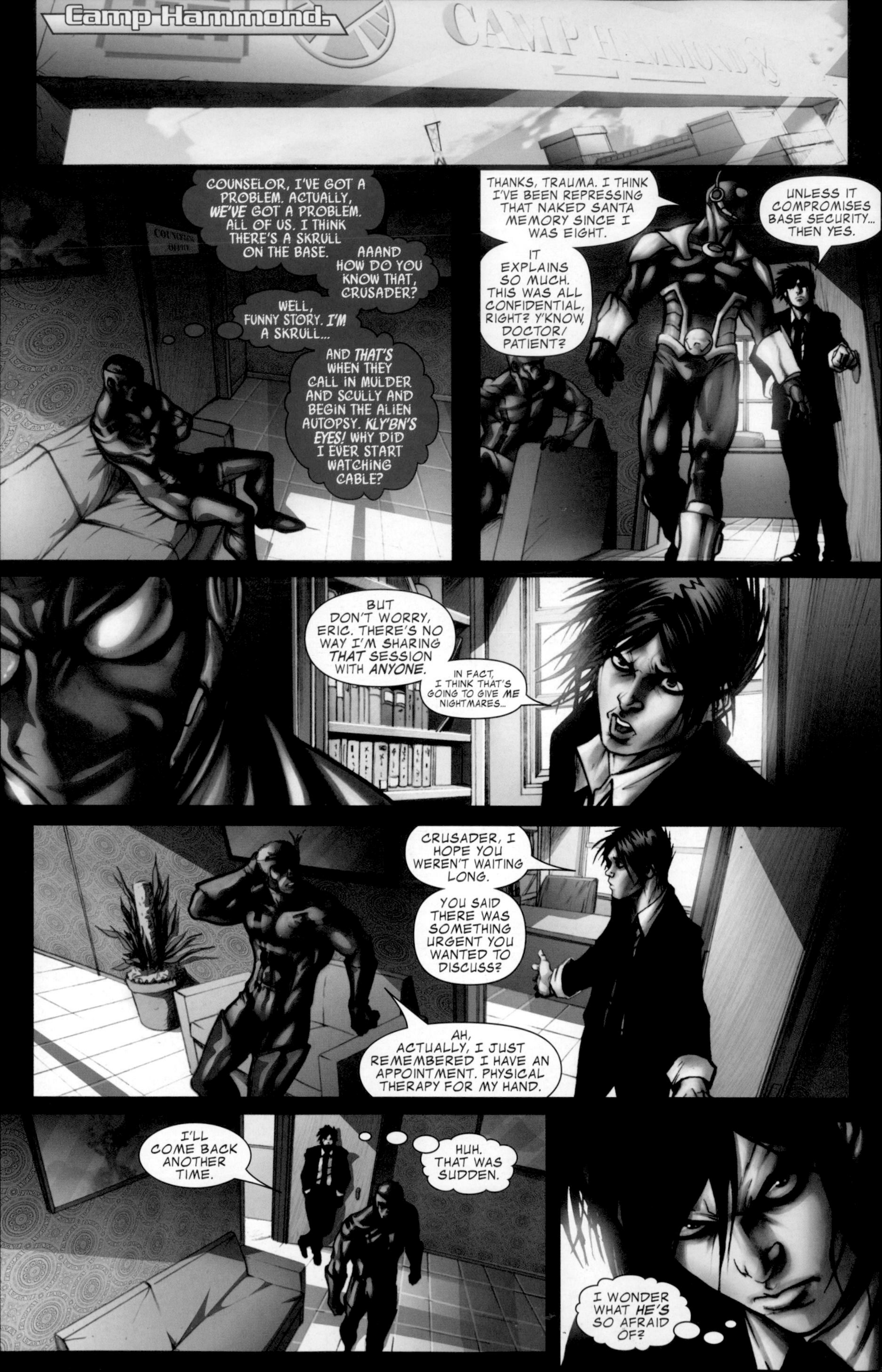
Camp Hammond.
CAMP HAMMOND
COUNSELOR, I'VE GOT A PROBLEM. ACTUALLY, WE'VE GOT A PROBLEM. ALL OF US. I THINK THERE'S A SKRULL ON THE BASE.
AAAND HOW DO YOU KNOW THAT, CRUSADER?
WELL, FUNNY STORY. I'M A SKRULL...
AND THAT'S WHEN THEY CALL IN MULDER AND SCULLY AND BEGIN THE ALIEN AUTOPSY. KLY'BN'S EYES! WHY DID I EVER START WATCHING CABLE?
THANKS, TRAUMA. I THINK I'VE BEEN REPRESSING THAT NAKED SANTA MEMORY SINCE I WAS EIGHT.
IT EXPLAINS SO MUCH. THIS WAS ALL CONFIDENTIAL, RIGHT? Y'KNOW, DOCTOR/PATIENT?
UNLESS IT COMPROMISES BASE SECURITY... THEN YES.
BUT DON'T WORRY, ERIC. THERE'S NO WAY I'M SHARING THAT SESSION WITH ANYONE.
IN FACT, I THINK THAT'S GOING TO GIVE ME NIGHTMARES...
CRUSADER, I HOPE YOU WEREN'T WAITING LONG.
YOU SAID THERE WAS SOMETHING URGENT YOU WANTED TO DISCUSS?
AH, ACTUALLY, I JUST REMEMBERED I HAVE AN APPOINTMENT. PHYSICAL THERAPY FOR MY HAND.
I'LL COME BACK ANOTHER TIME.
HUH. THAT WAS SUDDEN.
I WONDER WHAT HE'S SO AFRAID OF?

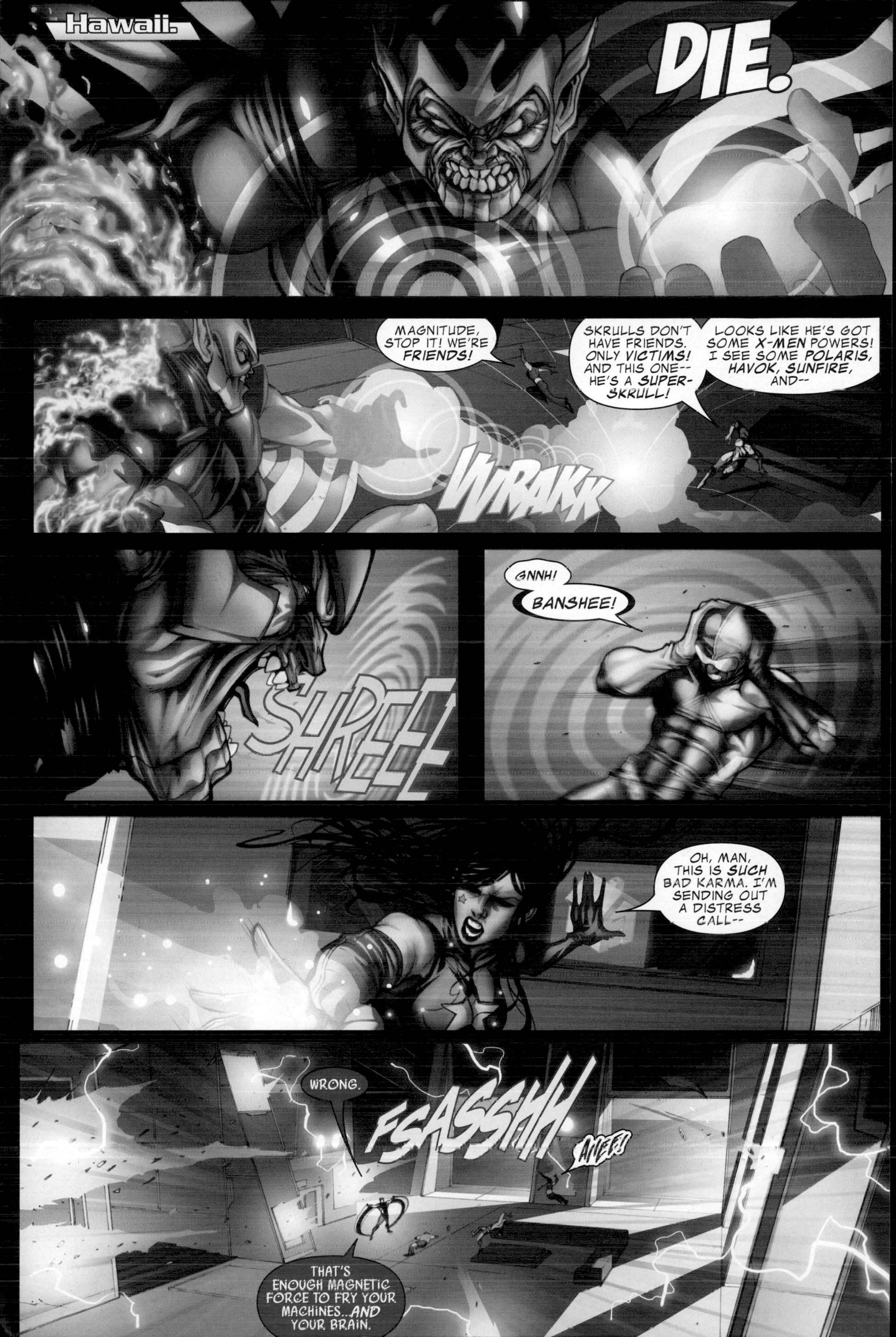
Hawaii.
DIE.
MAGNITUDE, STOP IT! WE'RE FRIENDS!
SKRULLS DON'T HAVE FRIENDS. ONLY VICTIMS! AND THIS ONE-- HE'S A SUPER-SKRULL!
LOOKS LIKE HE'S GOT SOME X-MEN POWERS! I SEE SOME POLARIS, HAVOK, SUNFIRE, AND--
WRAKK
SHREEE
GNNH!
BANSHEE!
OH, MAN, THIS IS SUCH BAD KARMA. I'M SENDING OUT A DISTRESS CALL--
WRONG.
FSASSHH
THAT'S ENOUGH MAGNETIC FORCE TO FRY YOUR MACHINES...AND YOUR BRAIN.

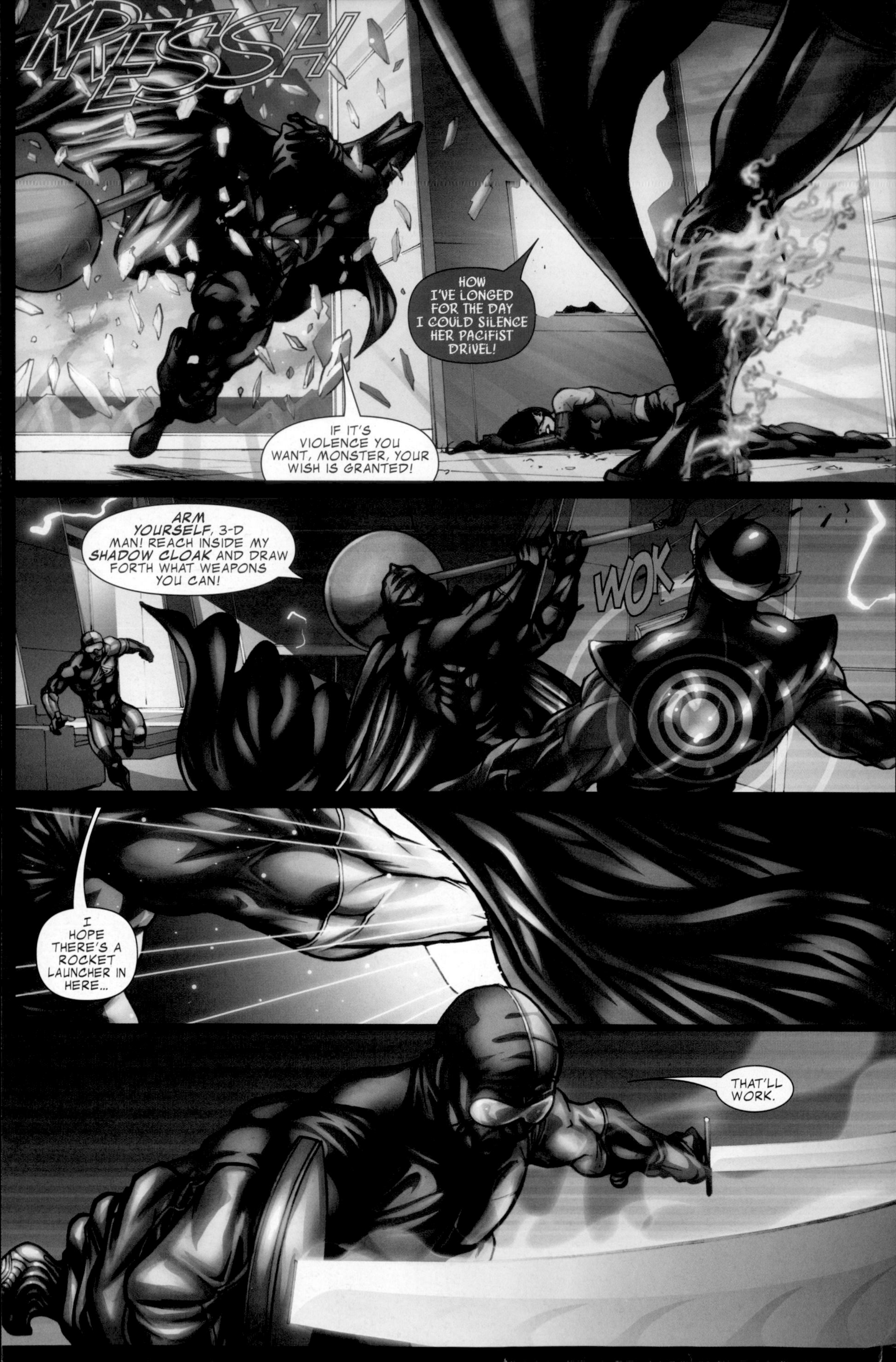
KRESSH
HOW I'VE LONGED FOR THE DAY I COULD SILENCE HER PACIFIST DRIVEL!
IF IT'S VIOLENCE YOU WANT, MONSTER, YOUR WISH IS GRANTED!
ARM YOURSELF, 3-D MAN! REACH INSIDE MY SHADOW CLOAK AND DRAW FORTH WHAT WEAPONS YOU CAN!
WOK
I HOPE THERE'S A ROCKET LAUNCHER IN HERE...
THAT'LL WORK.

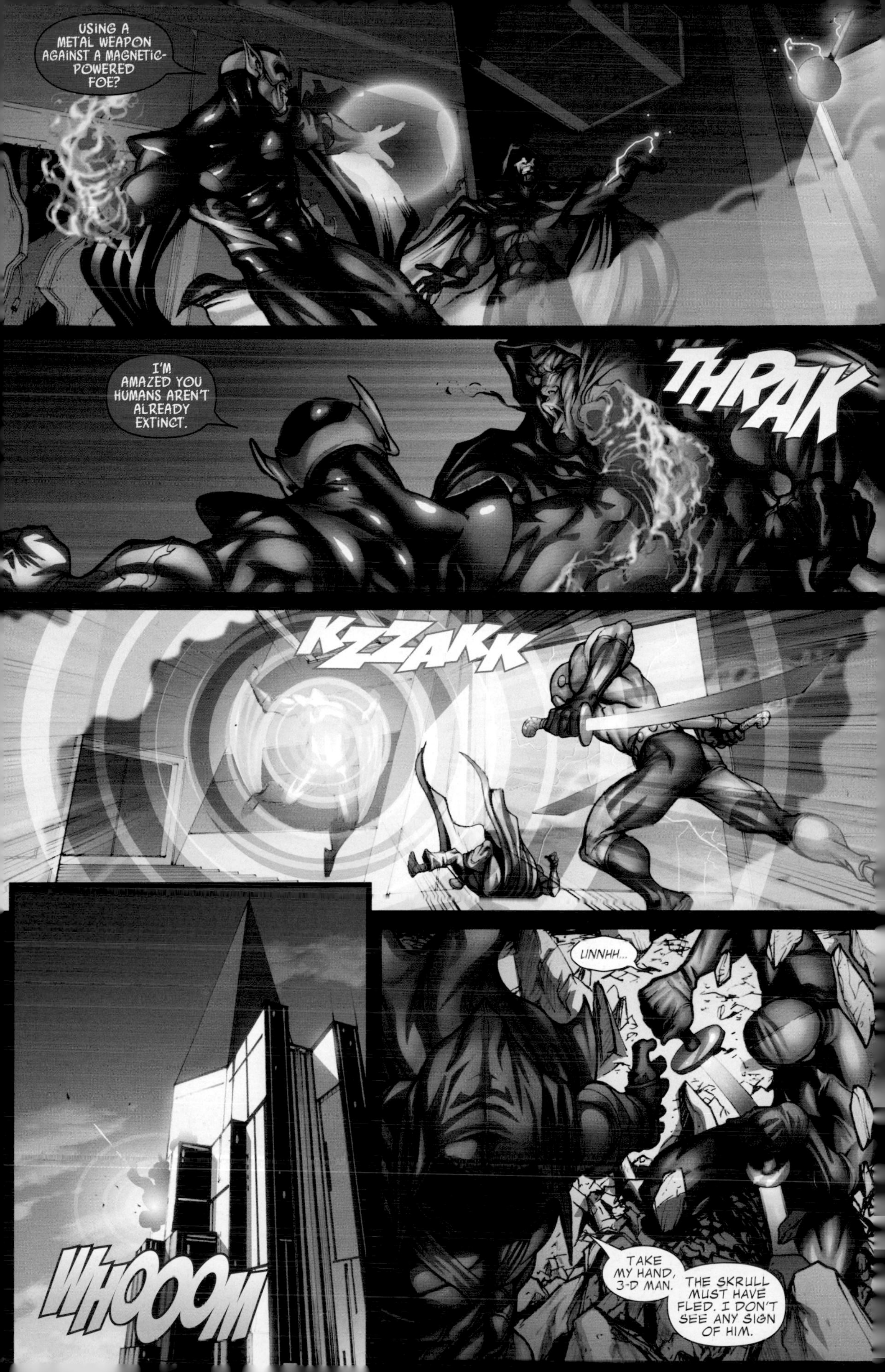
USING A METAL WEAPON AGAINST A MAGNETIC-POWERED FOE?
I'M AMAZED YOU HUMANS AREN'T ALREADY EXTINCT.
THRAK
KZZAKK
WHOOOM
UNNHH...
TAKE MY HAND, 3-D MAN.
THE SKRULL MUST HAVE FLED. I DON'T SEE ANY SIGN OF HIM.

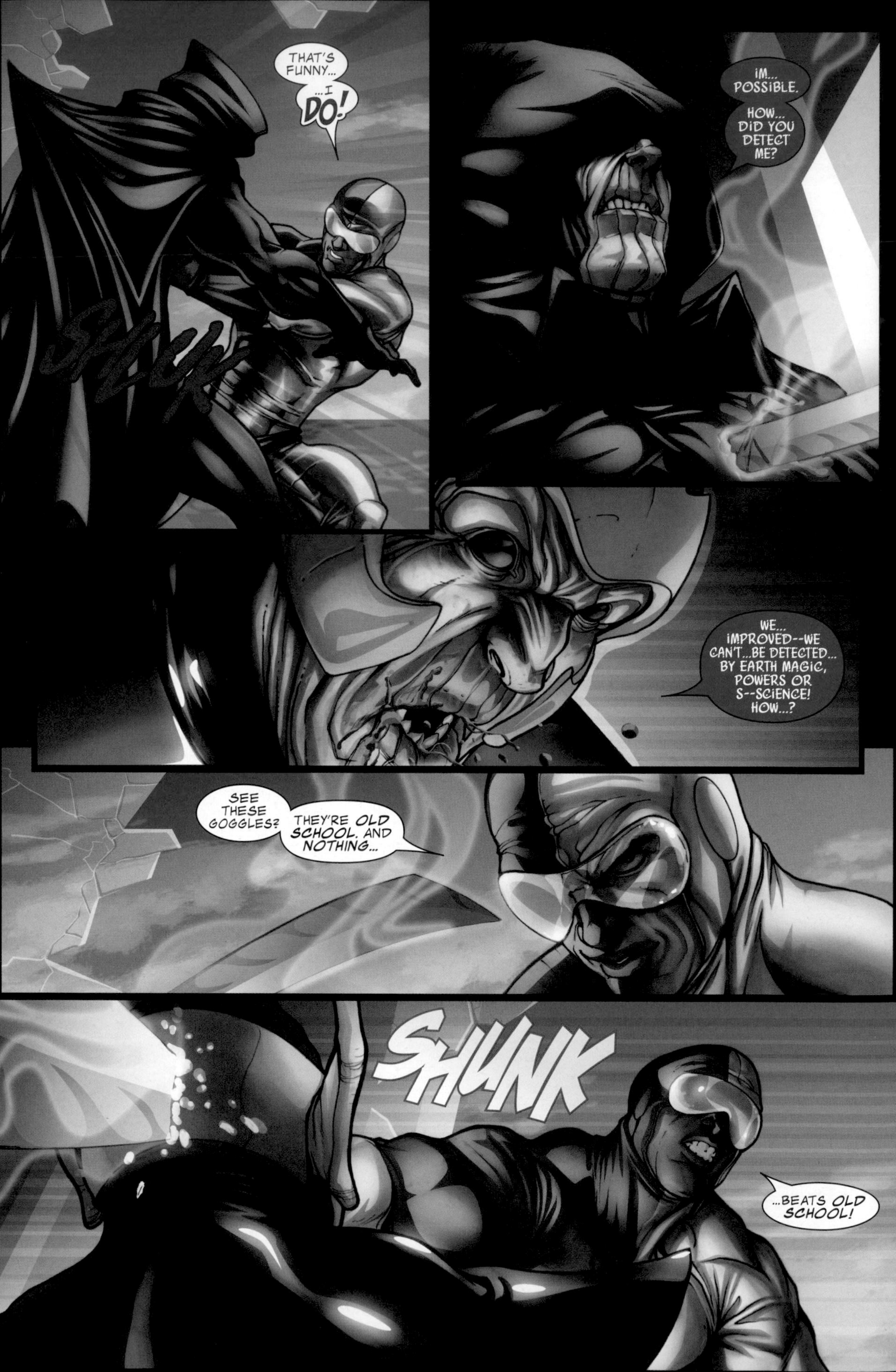
THAT'S FUNNY...
...I DO!
SPLCH
IM... POSSIBLE.
HOW... DID YOU DETECT ME?
WE... IMPROVED--WE CAN'T...BE DETECTED... BY EARTH MAGIC, POWERS OR S--SCIENCE! HOW...?
SEE THESE GOGGLES?
THEY'RE OLD SCHOOL. AND NOTHING...
SHUNK
...BEATS OLD SCHOOL!

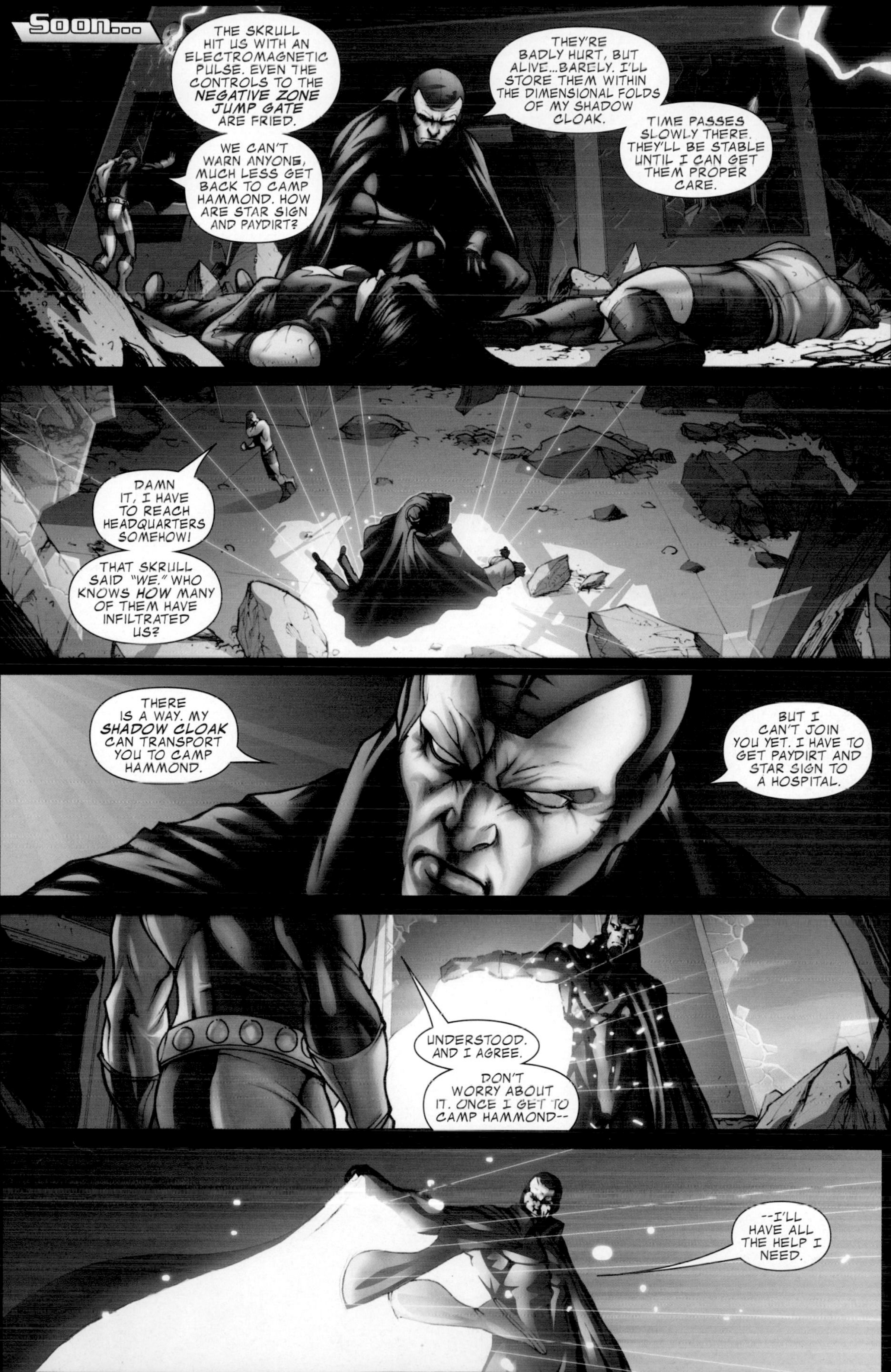
Soon...
THE SKRULL HIT US WITH AN ELECTROMAGNETIC PULSE. EVEN THE CONTROLS TO THE NEGATIVE ZONE JUMP GATE ARE FRIED.
WE CAN'T WARN ANYONE, MUCH LESS GET BACK TO CAMP HAMMOND. HOW ARE STAR SIGN AND PAYDIRT?
THEY'RE BADLY HURT, BUT ALIVE...BARELY. I'LL STORE THEM WITHIN THE DIMENSIONAL FOLDS OF MY SHADOW CLOAK.
TIME PASSES SLOWLY THERE. THEY'LL BE STABLE UNTIL I CAN GET THEM PROPER CARE.
DAMN IT, I HAVE TO REACH HEADQUARTERS SOMEHOW!
THAT SKRULL SAID "WE." WHO KNOWS HOW MANY OF THEM HAVE INFILTRATED US?
THERE IS A WAY. MY SHADOW CLOAK CAN TRANSPORT YOU TO CAMP HAMMOND.
BUT I CAN'T JOIN YOU YET. I HAVE TO GET PAYDIRT AND STAR SIGN TO A HOSPITAL.
UNDERSTOOD. AND I AGREE.
DON'T WORRY ABOUT IT. ONCE I GET TO CAMP HAMMOND--
--I'LL HAVE ALL THE HELP I NEED.

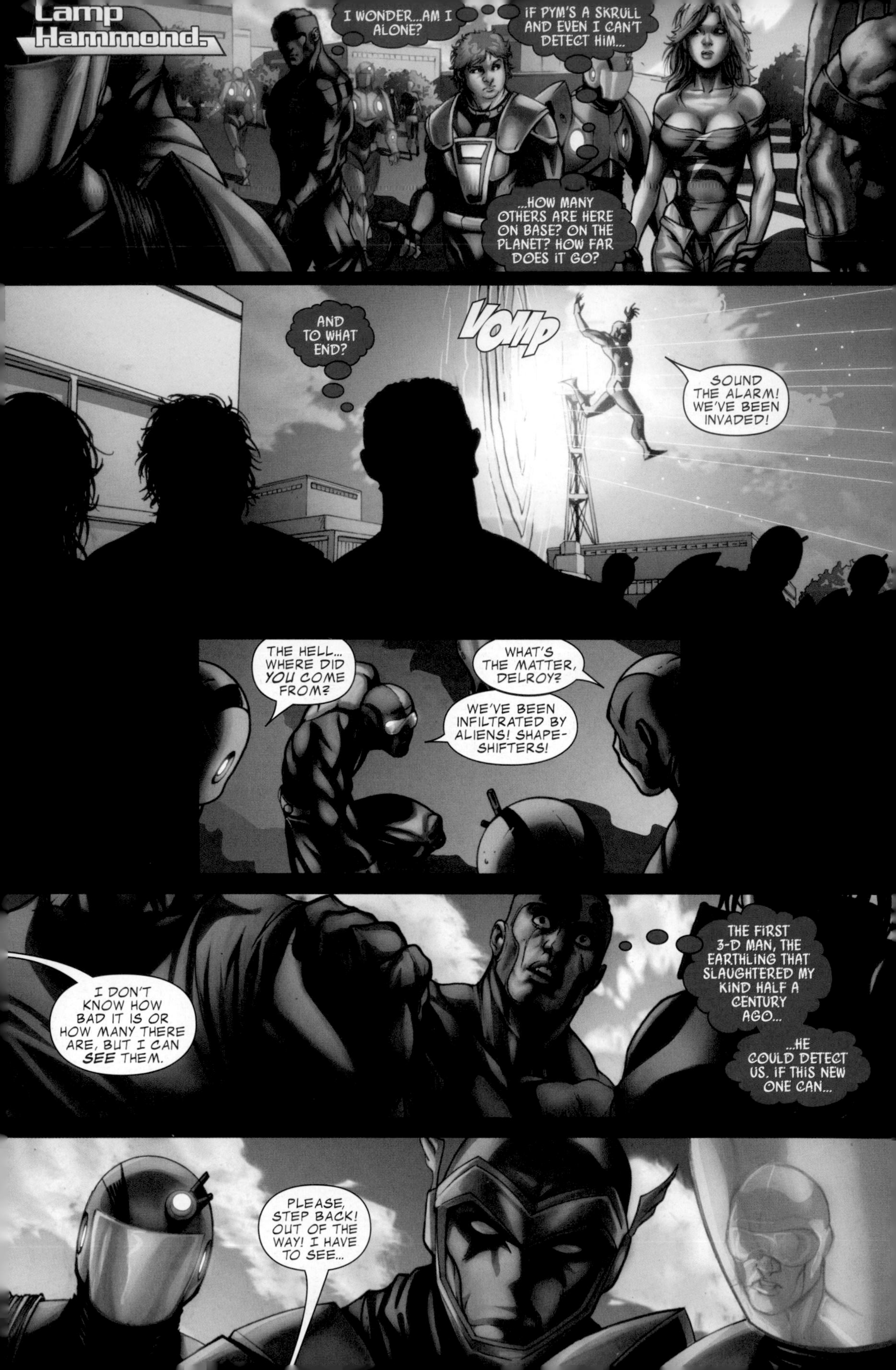
Camp Hammond.
I WONDER...AM I ALONE?
IF PYM'S A SKRULL AND EVEN I CAN'T DETECT HIM...
...HOW MANY OTHERS ARE HERE ON BASE? ON THE PLANET? HOW FAR DOES IT GO?
AND TO WHAT END?
VOMP
SOUND THE ALARM! WE'VE BEEN INVADED!
THE HELL... WHERE DID YOU COME FROM?
WHAT'S THE MATTER, DELROY?
WE'VE BEEN INFILTRATED BY ALIENS! SHAPE-SHIFTERS!
I DON'T KNOW HOW BAD IT IS OR HOW MANY THERE ARE, BUT I CAN SEE THEM.
THE FIRST 3-D MAN, THE EARTHLING THAT SLAUGHTERED MY KIND HALF A CENTURY AGO...
...HE COULD DETECT US. IF THIS NEW ONE CAN...
PLEASE, STEP BACK! OUT OF THE WAY! I HAVE TO SEE...

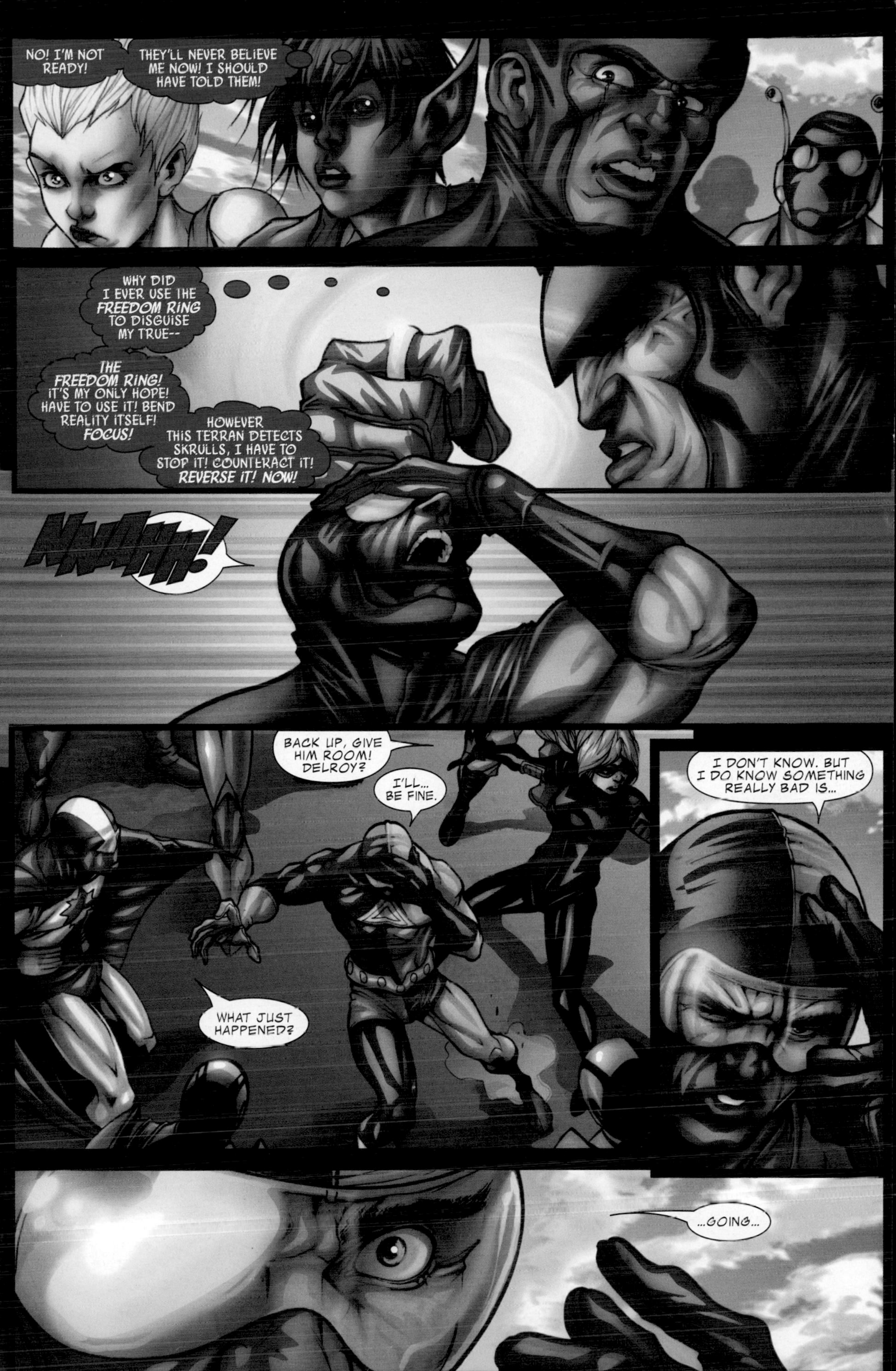
NO! I'M NOT READY!
THEY'LL NEVER BELIEVE ME NOW! I SHOULD HAVE TOLD THEM!
WHY DID I EVER USE THE FREEDOM RING TO DISGUISE MY TRUE--
THE FREEDOM RING! IT'S MY ONLY HOPE! HAVE TO USE IT! BEND REALITY ITSELF! FOCUS!
HOWEVER THIS TERRAN DETECTS SKRULLS, I HAVE TO STOP IT! COUNTERACT IT! REVERSE IT! NOW!
NNAAHH!
BACK UP, GIVE HIM ROOM! DELROY?
I'LL... BE FINE.
I DON'T KNOW. BUT I DO KNOW SOMETHING REALLY BAD IS...
WHAT JUST HAPPENED?
...GOING...

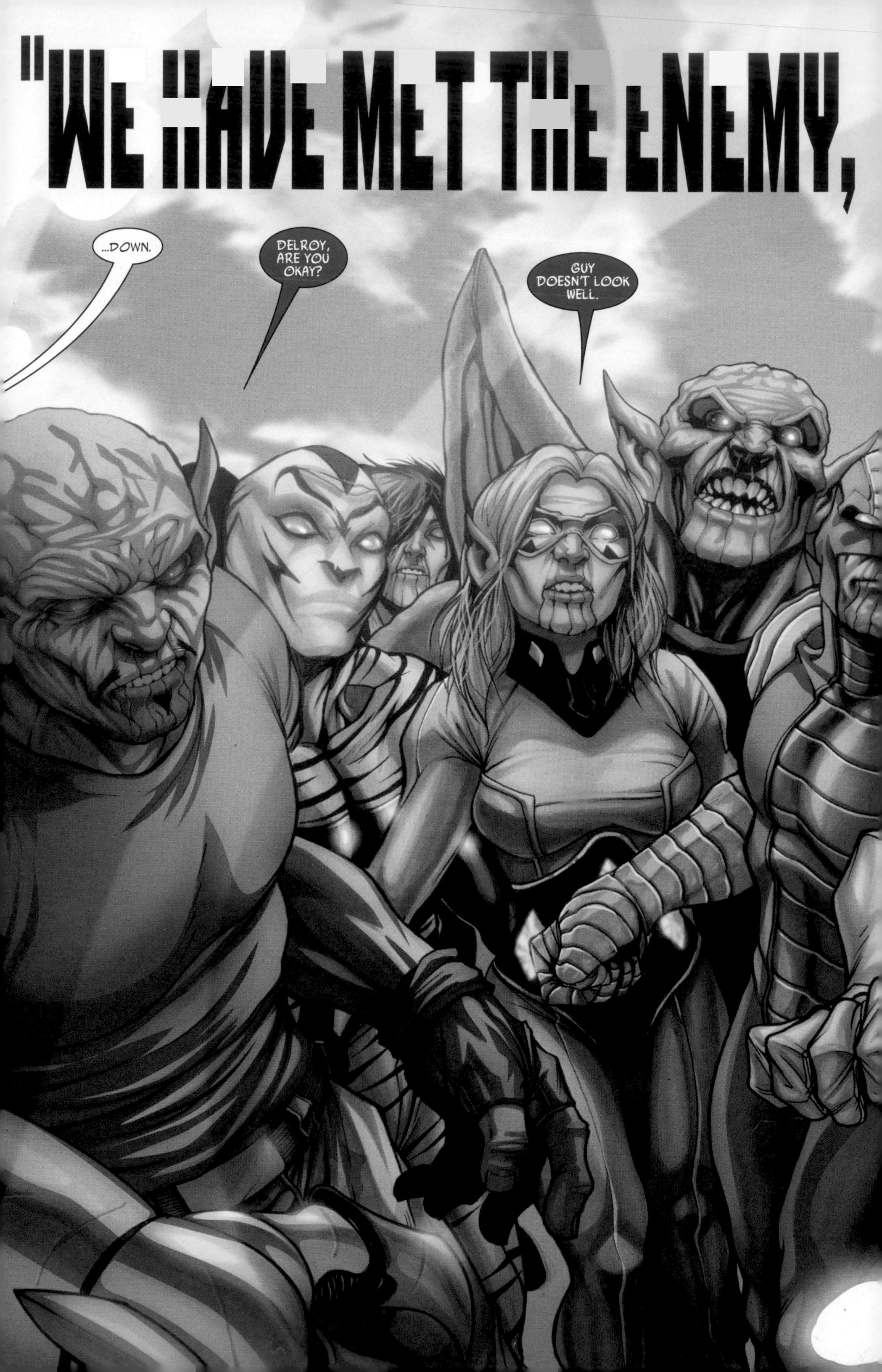
"WE HAVE MET THE ENEMY,
...DOWN.
DELROY, ARE YOU OKAY?
GUY DOESN'T LOOK WELL.

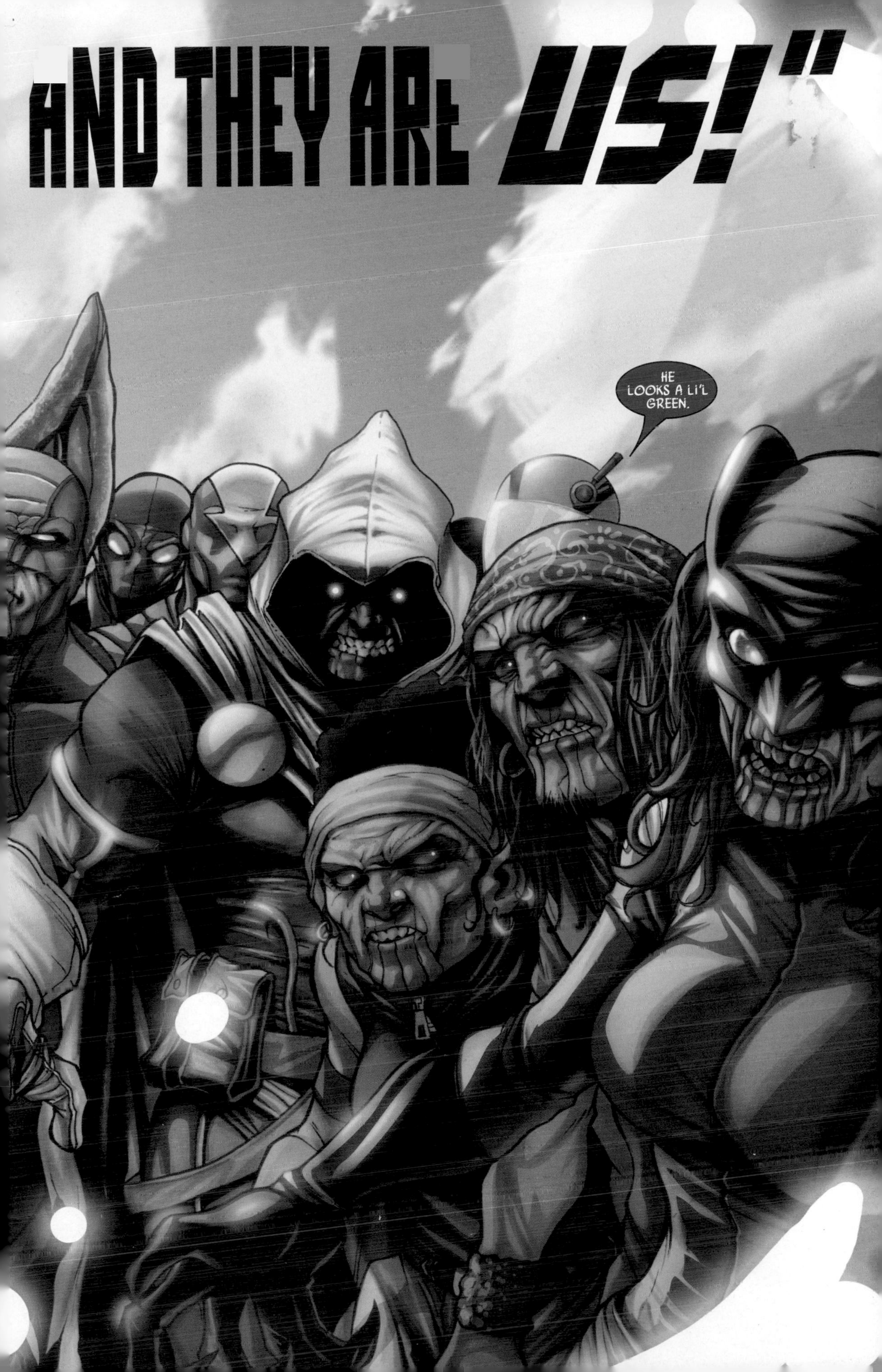
AND THEY ARE US!”
HE LOOKS A LI'L GREEN.

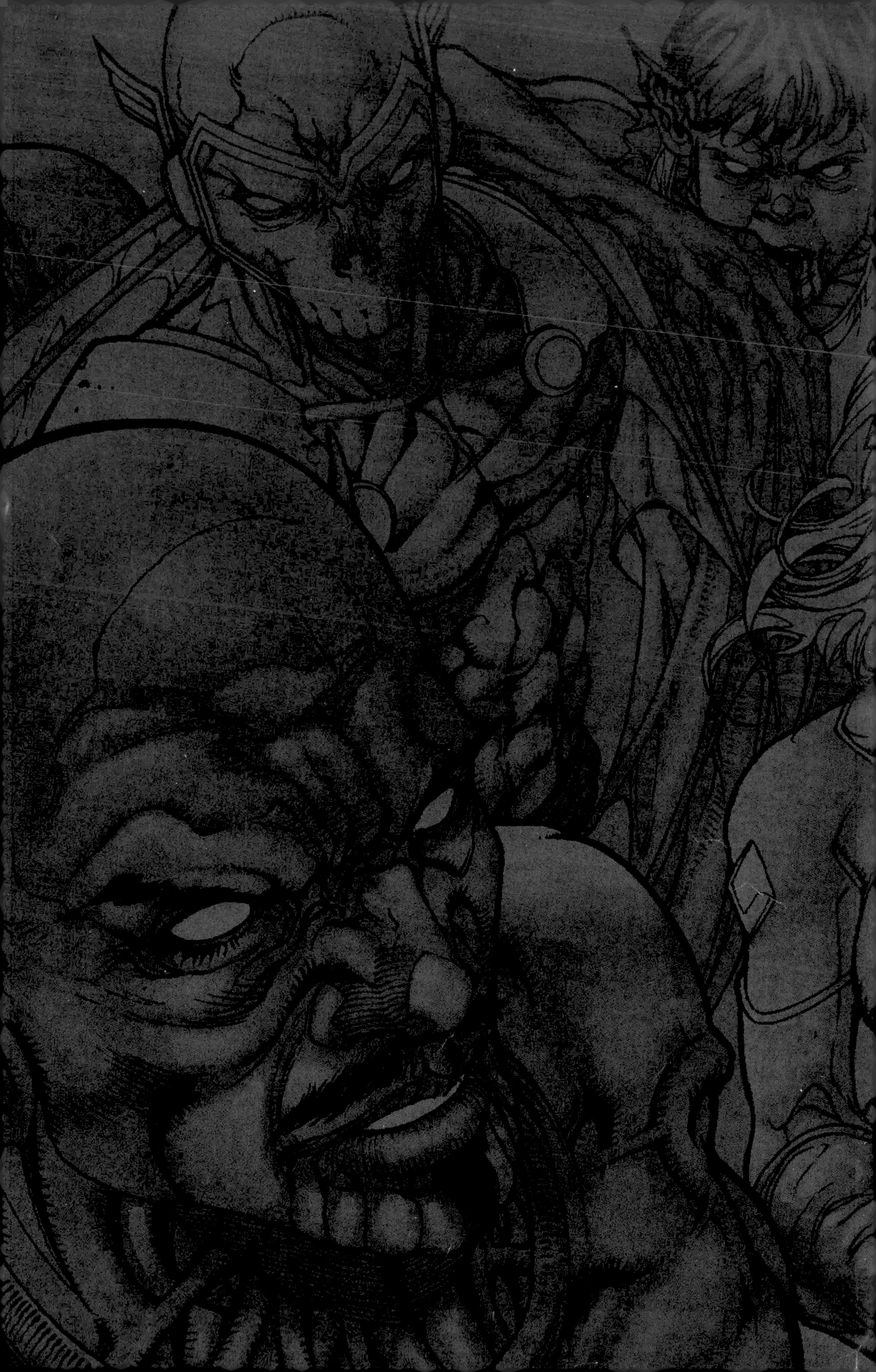

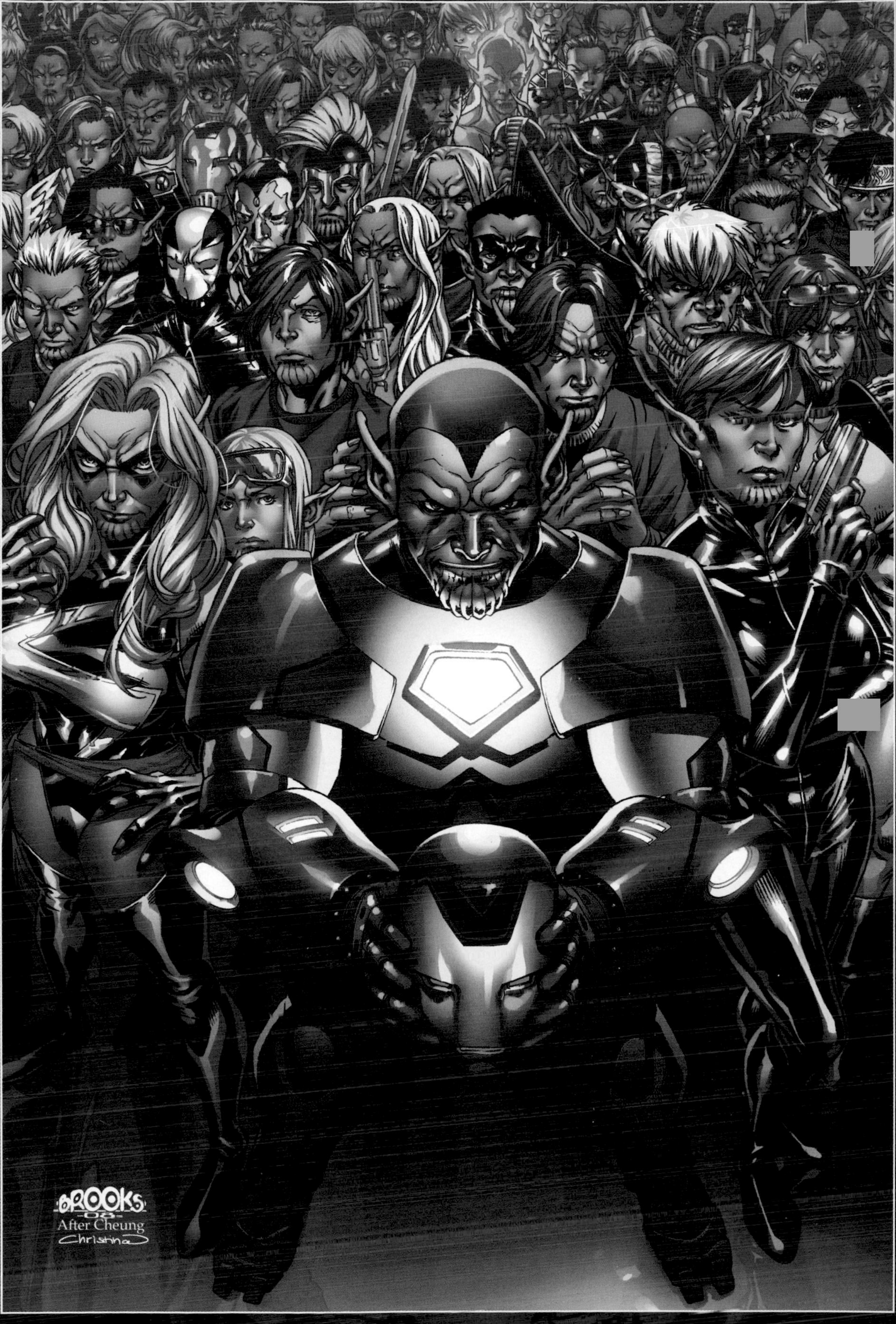
BROOKS
-08-
After Cheung
Christina

#15

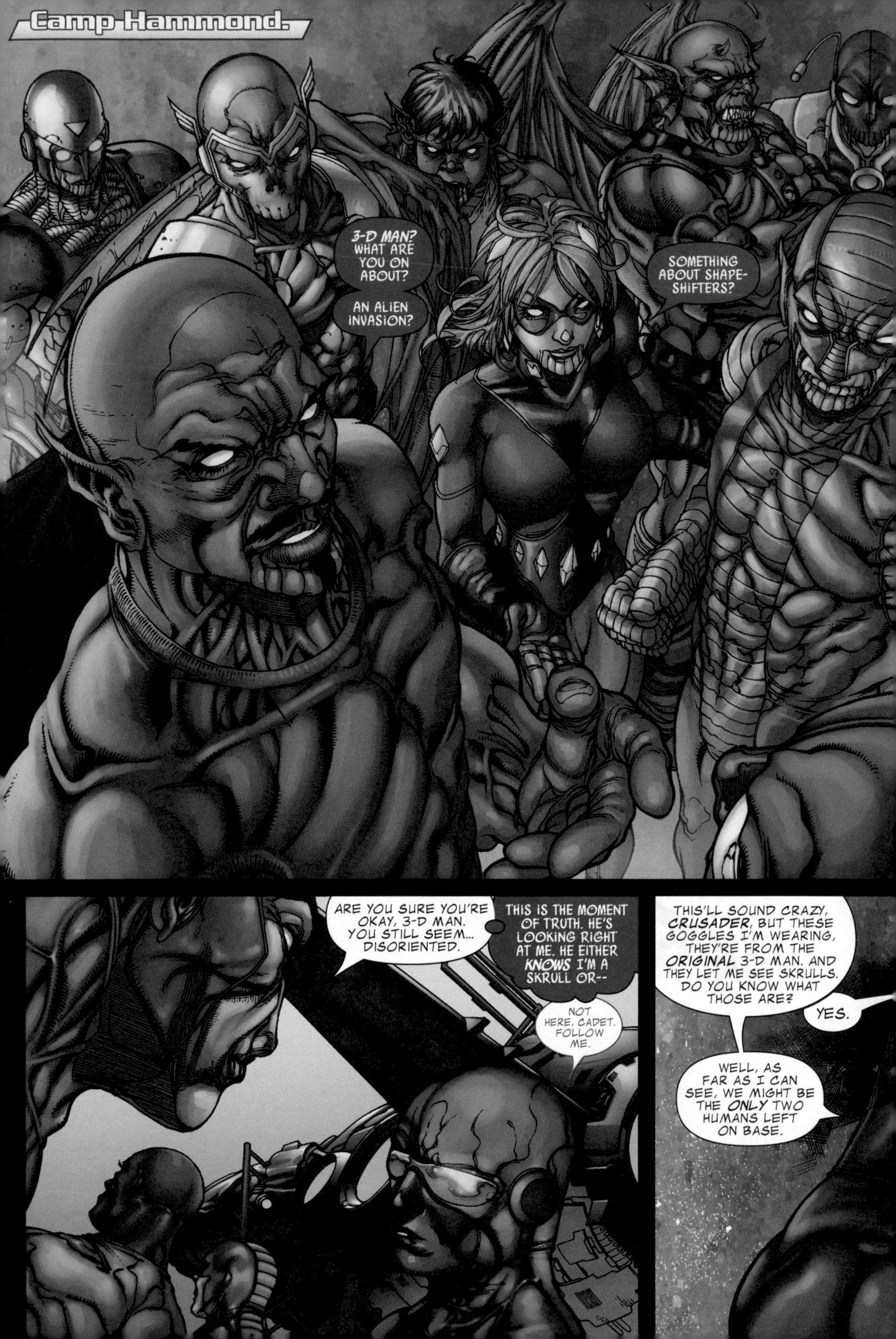
Camp Hammond.
3-D MAN? WHAT ARE YOU ON ABOUT?
AN ALIEN INVASION?
SOMETHING ABOUT SHAPE-SHIFTERS?
ARE YOU SURE YOU'RE OKAY, 3-D MAN. YOU STILL SEEM... DISORIENTED.
THIS IS THE MOMENT OF TRUTH. HE'S LOOKING RIGHT AT ME. HE EITHER KNOWS I'M A SKRULL OR--
NOT HERE, CADET. FOLLOW ME.
THIS'LL SOUND CRAZY, CRUSADER, BUT THESE GOGGLES I'M WEARING, THEY'RE FROM THE ORIGINAL 3-D MAN. AND THEY LET ME SEE SKRULLS. DO YOU KNOW WHAT THOSE ARE?
YES.
WELL, AS FAR AS I CAN SEE, WE MIGHT BE THE ONLY TWO HUMANS LEFT ON BASE.

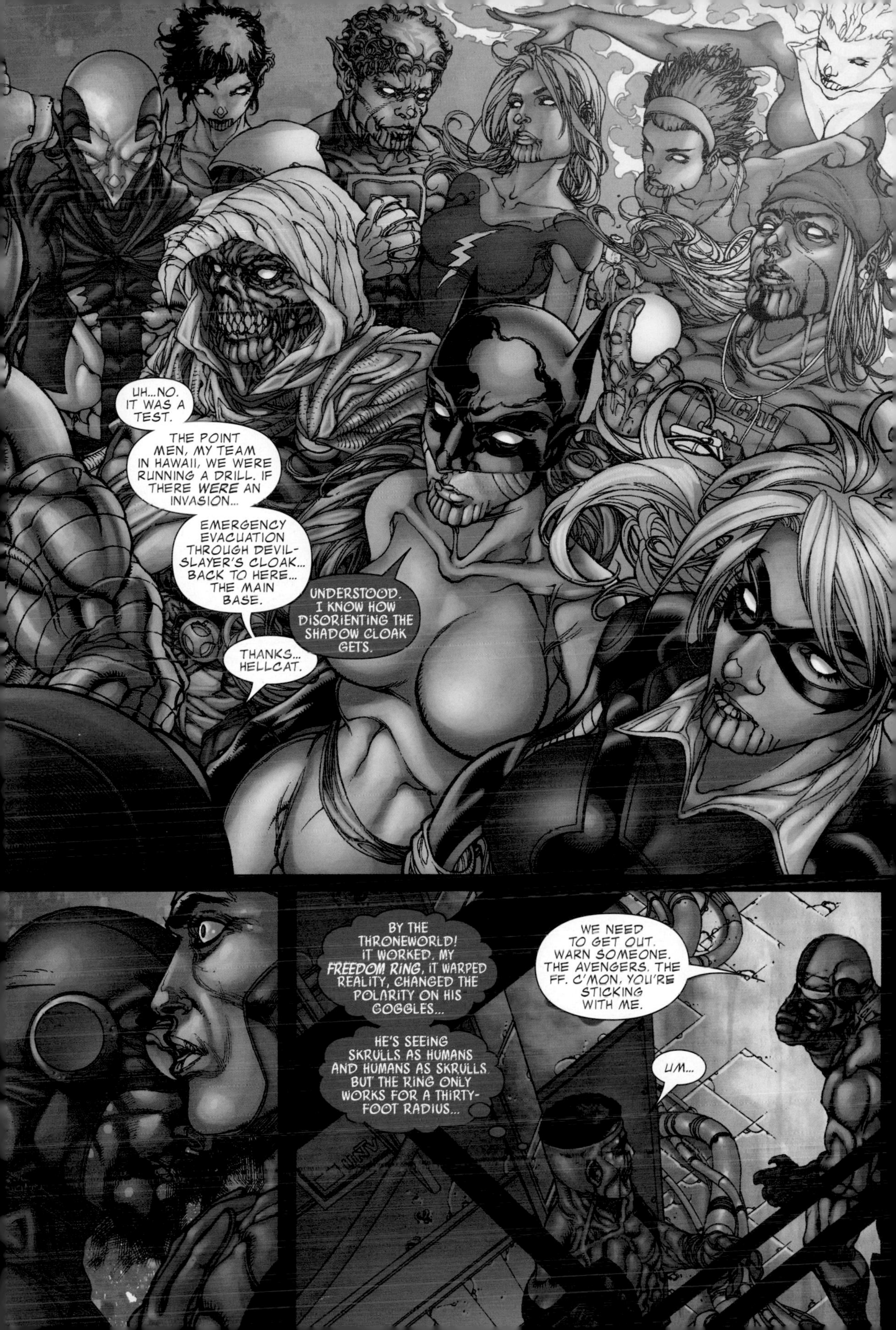
UH...NO. IT WAS A TEST.
THE POINT MEN, MY TEAM IN HAWAII, WE WERE RUNNING A DRILL. IF THERE WERE AN INVASION...
EMERGENCY EVACUATION THROUGH DEVIL-SLAYER'S CLOAK... BACK TO HERE... THE MAIN BASE.
UNDERSTOOD. I KNOW HOW DISORIENTING THE SHADOW CLOAK GETS.
THANKS... HELLCAT.
BY THE THRONEWORLD! IT WORKED. MY FREEDOM RING, IT WARPED REALITY, CHANGED THE POLARITY ON HIS GOGGLES...
HE'S SEEING SKRULLS AS HUMANS AND HUMANS AS SKRULLS. BUT THE RING ONLY WORKS FOR A THIRTY-FOOT RADIUS...
WE NEED TO GET OUT. WARN SOMEONE. THE AVENGERS. THE FF. C'MON, YOU'RE STICKING WITH ME.
UM...

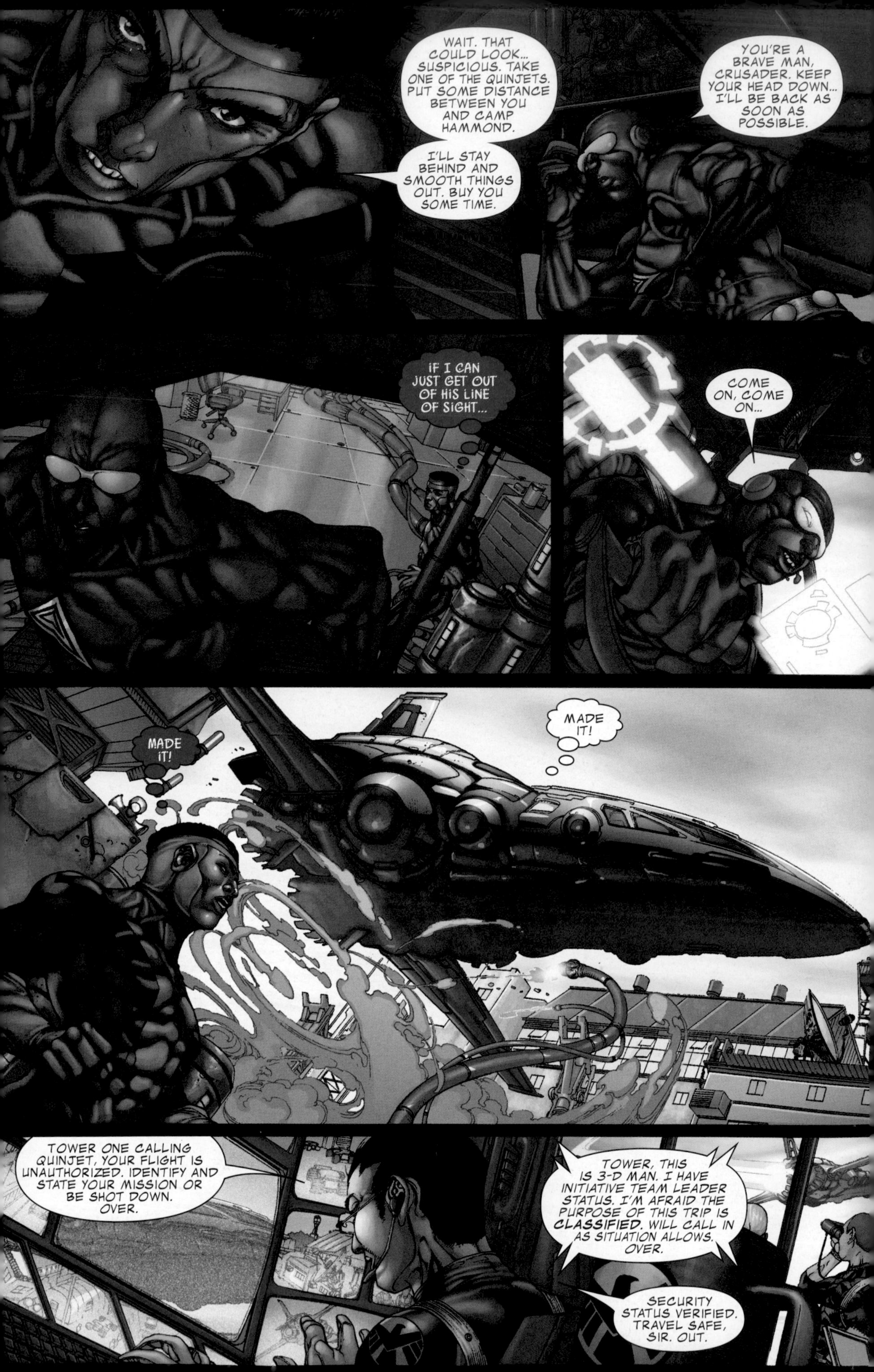
WAIT. THAT COULD LOOK... SUSPICIOUS. TAKE ONE OF THE QUINJETS. PUT SOME DISTANCE BETWEEN YOU AND CAMP HAMMOND.
I'LL STAY BEHIND AND SMOOTH THINGS OUT. BUY YOU SOME TIME.
YOU'RE A BRAVE MAN, CRUSADER. KEEP YOUR HEAD DOWN... I'LL BE BACK AS SOON AS POSSIBLE.
IF I CAN JUST GET OUT OF HIS LINE OF SIGHT...
COME ON, COME ON...
MADE IT!
MADE IT!
TOWER ONE CALLING QUINJET, YOUR FLIGHT IS UNAUTHORIZED. IDENTIFY AND STATE YOUR MISSION OR BE SHOT DOWN. OVER.
TOWER, THIS IS 3-D MAN. I HAVE INITIATIVE TEAM LEADER STATUS. I'M AFRAID THE PURPOSE OF THIS TRIP IS CLASSIFIED. WILL CALL IN AS SITUATION ALLOWS. OVER.
SECURITY STATUS VERIFIED. TRAVEL SAFE, SIR. OUT.

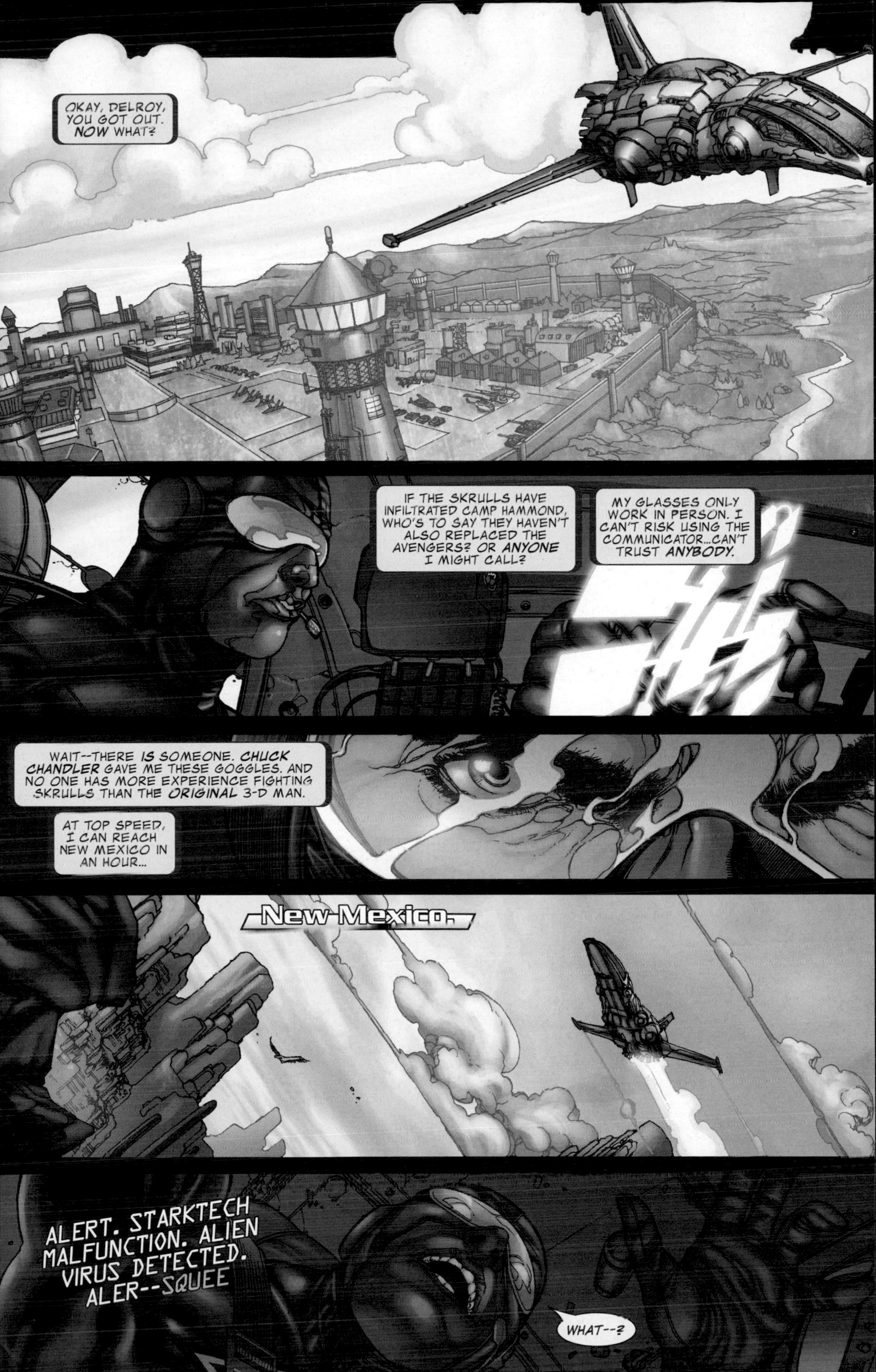
OKAY, DELROY, YOU GOT OUT. NOW WHAT?
IF THE SKRULLS HAVE INFILTRATED CAMP HAMMOND, WHO'S TO SAY THEY HAVEN'T ALSO REPLACED THE AVENGERS? OR ANYONE I MIGHT CALL?
MY GLASSES ONLY WORK IN PERSON. I CAN'T RISK USING THE COMMUNICATOR...CAN'T TRUST ANYBODY.
WAIT--THERE IS SOMEONE. CHUCK CHANDLER GAVE ME THESE GOGGLES. AND NO ONE HAS MORE EXPERIENCE FIGHTING SKRULLS THAN THE ORIGINAL 3-D MAN.
AT TOP SPEED, I CAN REACH NEW MEXICO IN AN HOUR...
New Mexico
ALERT. STARKTECH MALFUNCTION. ALIEN VIRUS DETECTED. ALER--SQUEE
WHAT--?

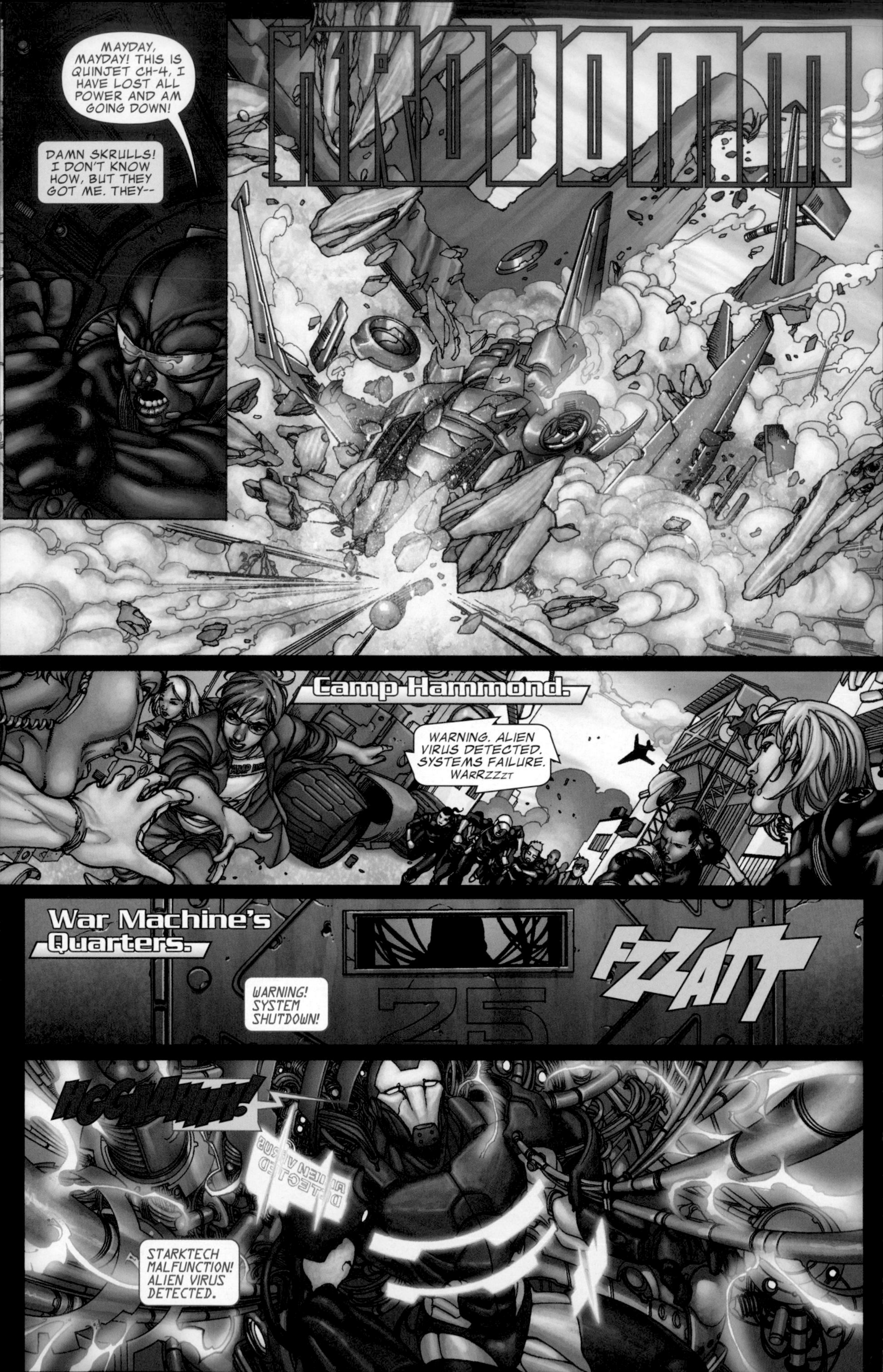
MAYDAY, MAYDAY! THIS IS QUINJET CH-4, I HAVE LOST ALL POWER AND AM GOING DOWN!
DAMN SKRULLS! I DON'T KNOW HOW, BUT THEY GOT ME. THEY--
KRADOOM
Camp Hammond.
WARNING. ALIEN VIRUS DETECTED. SYSTEMS FAILURE. WARRZZzt
War Machine's Quarters.
WARNING! SYSTEM SHUTDOWN!
FZZATT
NGGAHHH!
STARKTECH MALFUNCTION! ALIEN VIRUS DETECTED.

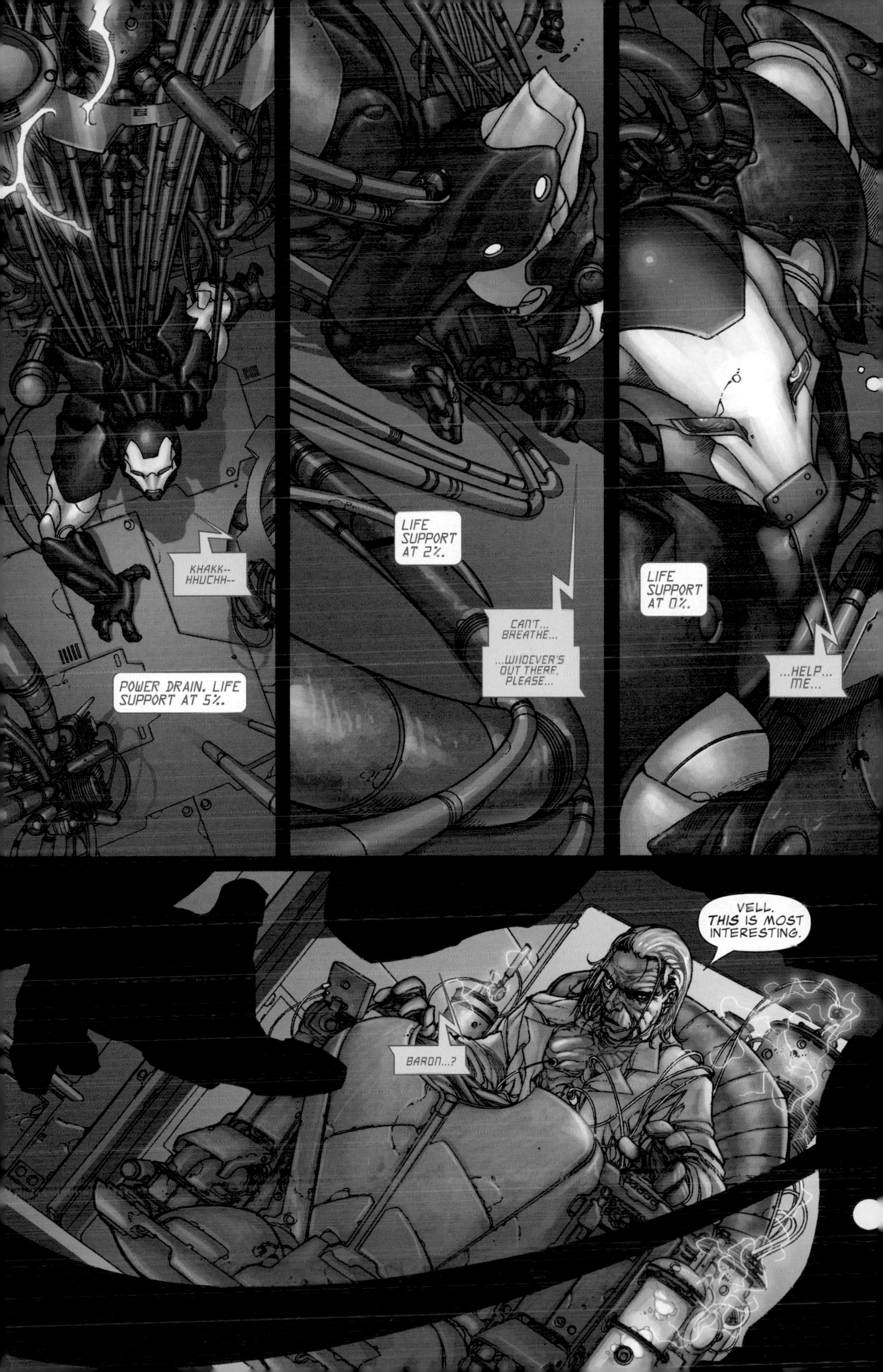
KHAKK--
HHUCHH--
POWER DRAIN. LIFE SUPPORT AT 5%.
LIFE SUPPORT AT 2%.
CAN'T... BREATHE...
...WHOEVER'S OUT THERE, PLEASE...
LIFE SUPPORT AT 0%.
...HELP... ME...
VELL. THIS IS MOST INTERESTING.
BARON...?

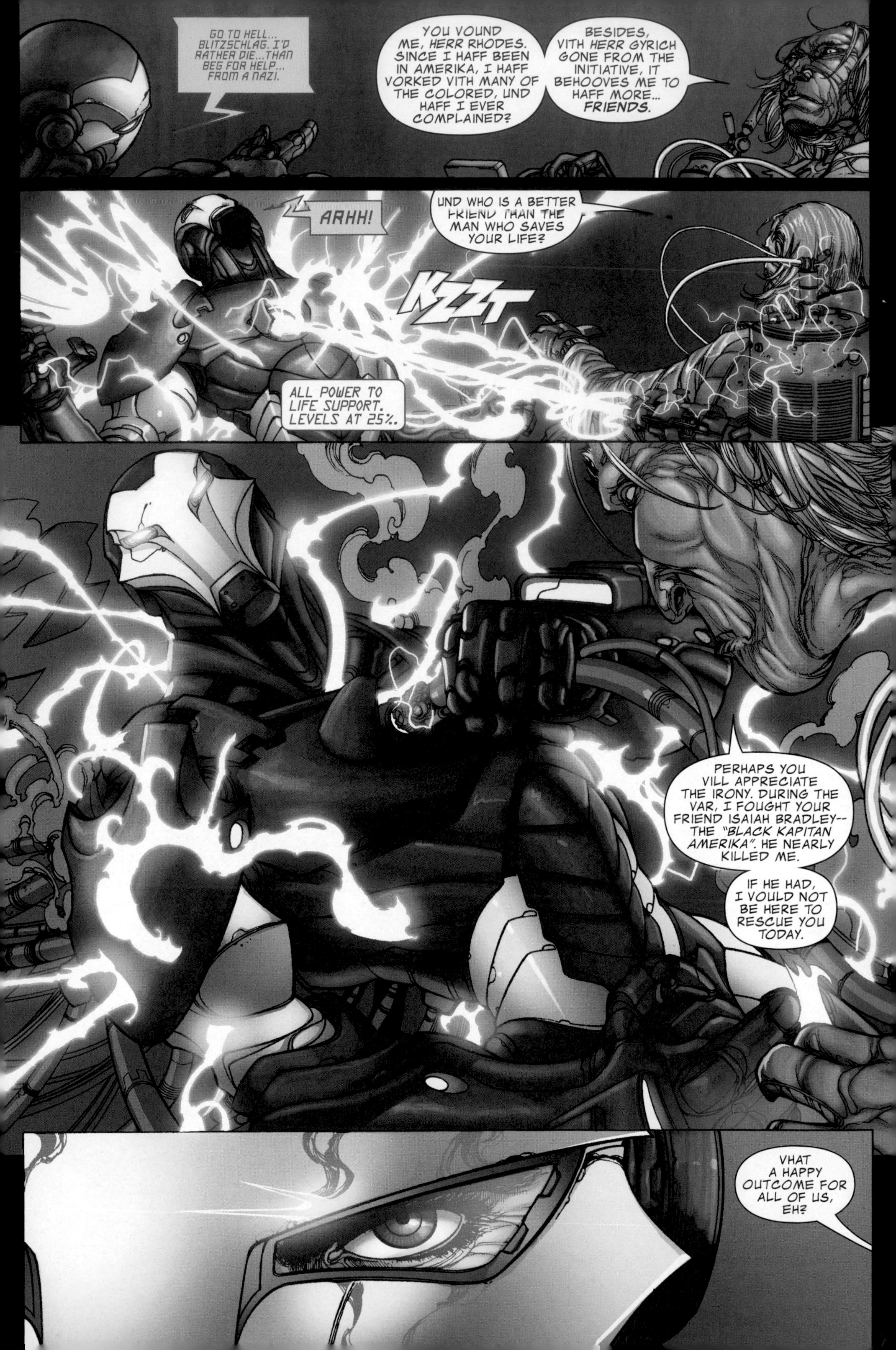
GO TO HELL... BLITZSCHLAG. I'D RATHER DIE...THAN BEG FOR HELP... FROM A NAZI.
YOU VOUND ME, HERR RHODES. SINCE I HAFF BEEN IN AMERIKA, I HAFF VORKED VITH MANY OF THE COLORED, UND HAFF I EVER COMPLAINED?
BESIDES, VITH HERR GYRICH GONE FROM THE INITIATIVE, IT BEHOOVES ME TO HAFF MORE... FRIENDS.
ARHH!
UND WHO IS A BETTER FRIEND THAN THE MAN WHO SAVES YOUR LIFE?
KZZT
ALL POWER TO LIFE SUPPORT. LEVELS AT 25%.
PERHAPS YOU VILL APPRECIATE THE IRONY. DURING THE VAR, I FOUGHT YOUR FRIEND ISAIAH BRADLEY-- THE "BLACK KAPITAN AMERIKA". HE NEARLY KILLED ME.
IF HE HAD, I VOULD NOT BE HERE TO RESCUE YOU TODAY.
VHAT A HAPPY OUTCOME FOR ALL OF US, EH?

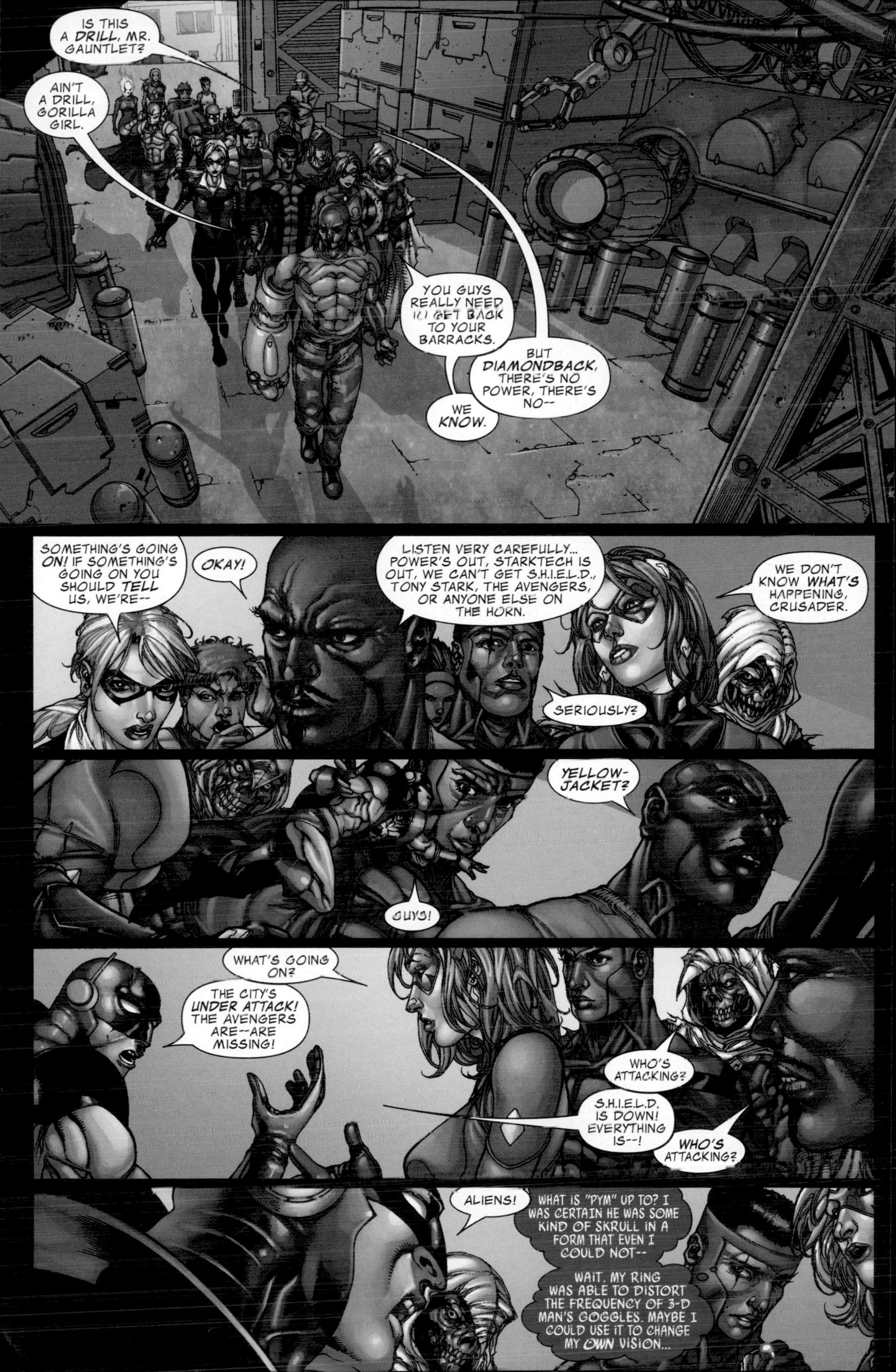

IS THIS A DRILL, MR. GAUNTLET?
AIN'T A DRILL, GORILLA GIRL.
YOU GUYS REALLY NEED TO GET BACK TO YOUR BARRACKS.
BUT DIAMONDBACK, THERE'S NO POWER, THERE'S NO--
WE KNOW.
SOMETHING'S GOING ON! IF SOMETHING'S GOING ON YOU SHOULD TELL US, WE'RE--
OKAY!
LISTEN VERY CAREFULLY... POWER'S OUT, STARKTECH IS OUT, WE CAN'T GET S.H.I.E.L.D., TONY STARK, THE AVENGERS, OR ANYONE ELSE ON THE HORN.
WE DON'T KNOW WHAT'S HAPPENING, CRUSADER.
SERIOUSLY?
YELLOW-JACKET?
GUYS!
WHAT'S GOING ON?
THE CITY'S UNDER ATTACK! THE AVENGERS ARE--ARE MISSING!
WHO'S ATTACKING?
S.H.I.E.L.D. IS DOWN! EVERYTHING IS--!
WHO'S ATTACKING?
ALIENS!
WHAT IS "PYM" UP TO? I WAS CERTAIN HE WAS SOME KIND OF SKRULL IN A FORM THAT EVEN I COULD NOT--
WAIT. MY RING WAS ABLE TO DISTORT THE FREQUENCY OF 3-D MAN'S GOGGLES. MAYBE I COULD USE IT TO CHANGE MY OWN VISION...

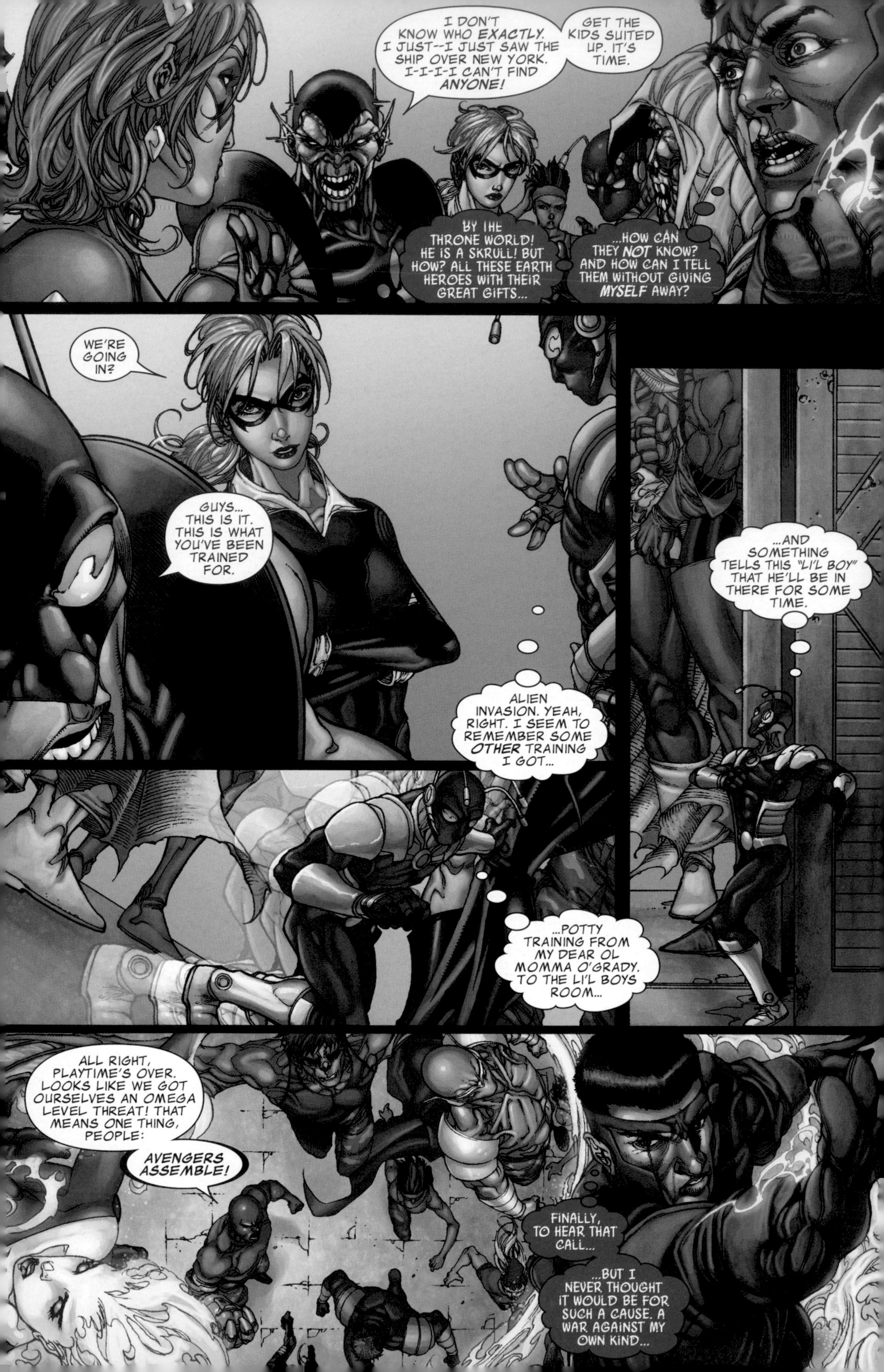
I DON'T KNOW WHO EXACTLY. I JUST--I JUST SAW THE SHIP OVER NEW YORK. I-I-I-I CAN'T FIND ANYONE!
GET THE KIDS SUITED UP. IT'S TIME.
BY THE THRONE WORLD! HE IS A SKRULL! BUT HOW? ALL THESE EARTH HEROES WITH THEIR GREAT GIFTS...
...HOW CAN THEY NOT KNOW? AND HOW CAN I TELL THEM WITHOUT GIVING MYSELF AWAY?
WE'RE GOING IN?
GUYS... THIS IS IT. THIS IS WHAT YOU'VE BEEN TRAINED FOR.
ALIEN INVASION. YEAH, RIGHT. I SEEM TO REMEMBER SOME OTHER TRAINING I GOT...
...POTTY TRAINING FROM MY DEAR OL MOMMA O'GRADY. TO THE LI'L BOYS ROOM...
...AND SOMETHING TELLS THIS "LI'L BOY" THAT HE'LL BE IN THERE FOR SOME TIME.
ALL RIGHT, PLAYTIME'S OVER. LOOKS LIKE WE GOT OURSELVES AN OMEGA LEVEL THREAT! THAT MEANS ONE THING, PEOPLE:
AVENGERS ASSEMBLE!
FINALLY, TO HEAR THAT CALL...
...BUT I NEVER THOUGHT IT WOULD BE FOR SUCH A CAUSE. A WAR AGAINST MY OWN KIND...

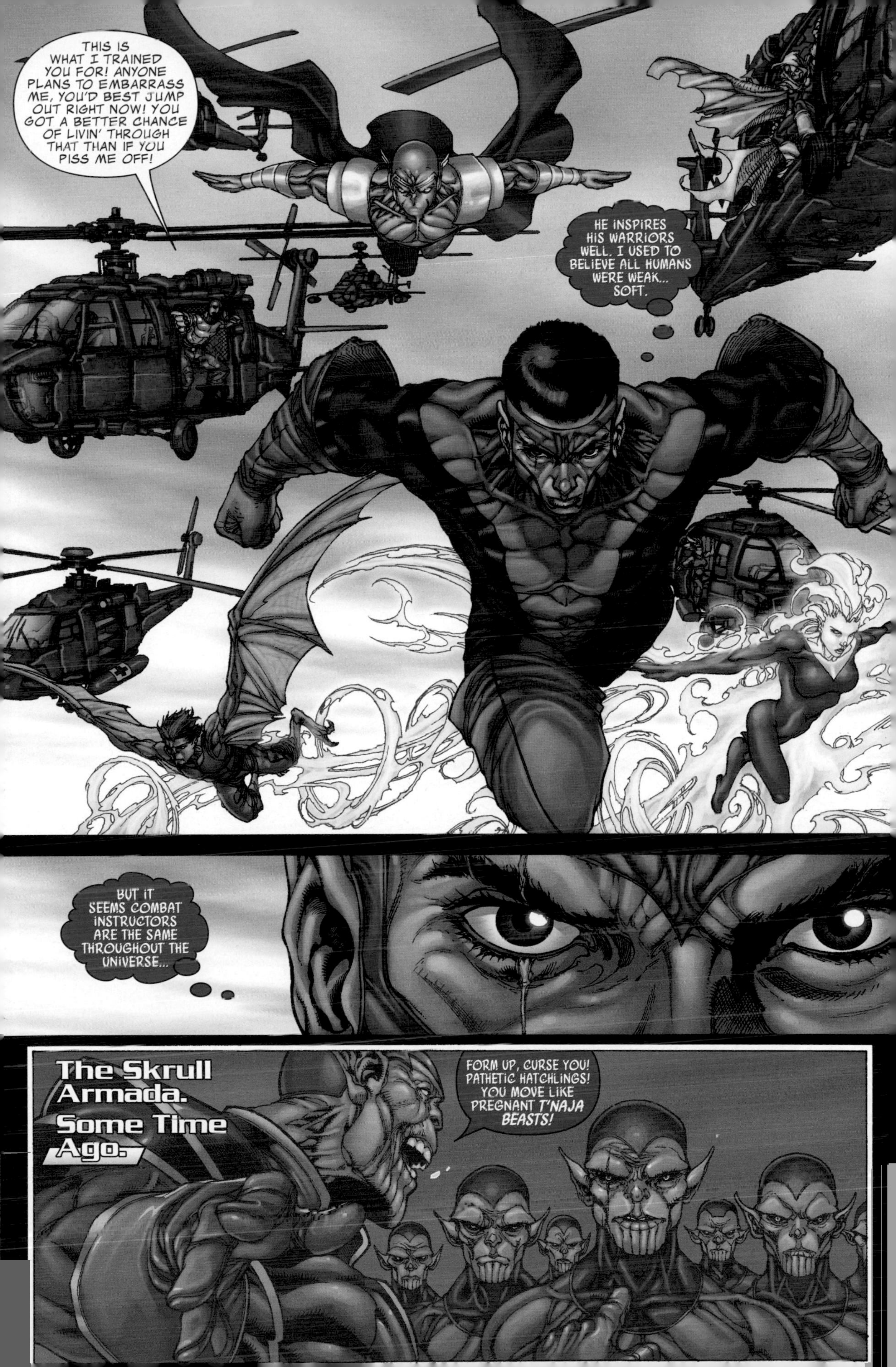
THIS IS WHAT I TRAINED YOU FOR! ANYONE PLANS TO EMBARRASS ME, YOU'D BEST JUMP OUT RIGHT NOW! YOU GOT A BETTER CHANCE OF LIVIN' THROUGH THAT THAN IF YOU PISS ME OFF!
HE INSPIRES HIS WARRIORS WELL. I USED TO BELIEVE ALL HUMANS WERE WEAK... SOFT.
BUT IT SEEMS COMBAT INSTRUCTORS ARE THE SAME THROUGHOUT THE UNIVERSE...
The Skrull Armada. Some Time Ago.
FORM UP, CURSE YOU! PATHETIC HATCHLINGS! YOU MOVE LIKE PREGNANT T'NAJA BEASTS!

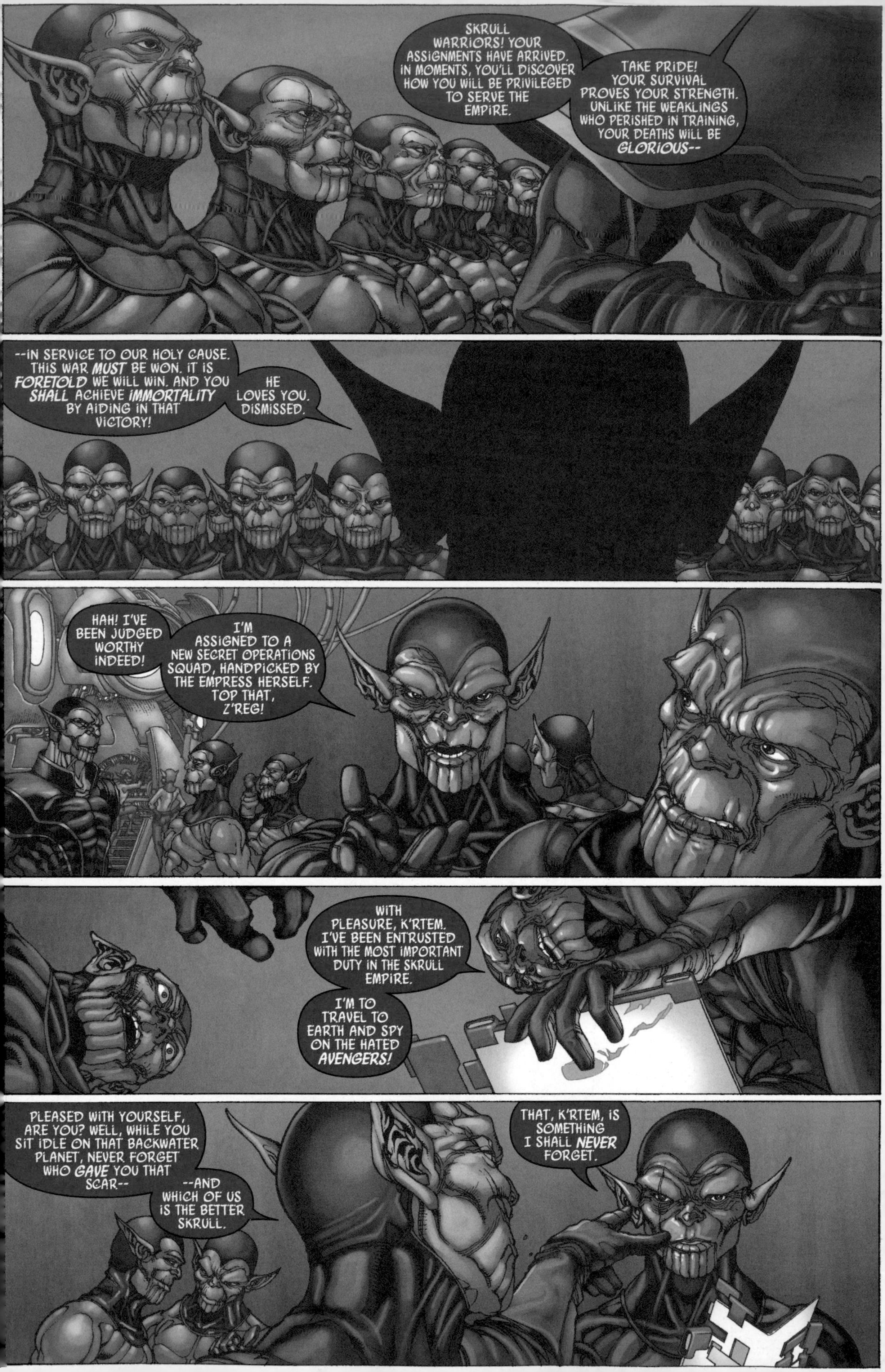
SKRULL WARRIORS! YOUR ASSIGNMENTS HAVE ARRIVED. IN MOMENTS, YOU'LL DISCOVER HOW YOU WILL BE PRIVILEGED TO SERVE THE EMPIRE.
TAKE PRIDE! YOUR SURVIVAL PROVES YOUR STRENGTH. UNLIKE THE WEAKLINGS WHO PERISHED IN TRAINING, YOUR DEATHS WILL BE GLORIOUS--
--IN SERVICE TO OUR HOLY CAUSE. THIS WAR MUST BE WON. IT IS FORETOLD WE WILL WIN. AND YOU SHALL ACHIEVE IMMORTALITY BY AIDING IN THAT VICTORY!
HE LOVES YOU. DISMISSED.
HAH! I'VE BEEN JUDGED WORTHY INDEED!
I'M ASSIGNED TO A NEW SECRET OPERATIONS SQUAD, HANDPICKED BY THE EMPRESS HERSELF. TOP THAT, Z'REG!
WITH PLEASURE, K'RTEM. I'VE BEEN ENTRUSTED WITH THE MOST IMPORTANT DUTY IN THE SKRULL EMPIRE.
I'M TO TRAVEL TO EARTH AND SPY ON THE HATED AVENGERS!
PLEASED WITH YOURSELF, ARE YOU? WELL, WHILE YOU SIT IDLE ON THAT BACKWATER PLANET, NEVER FORGET WHO GAVE YOU THAT SCAR--
--AND WHICH OF US IS THE BETTER SKRULL.
THAT, K'RTEM, IS SOMETHING I SHALL NEVER FORGET.

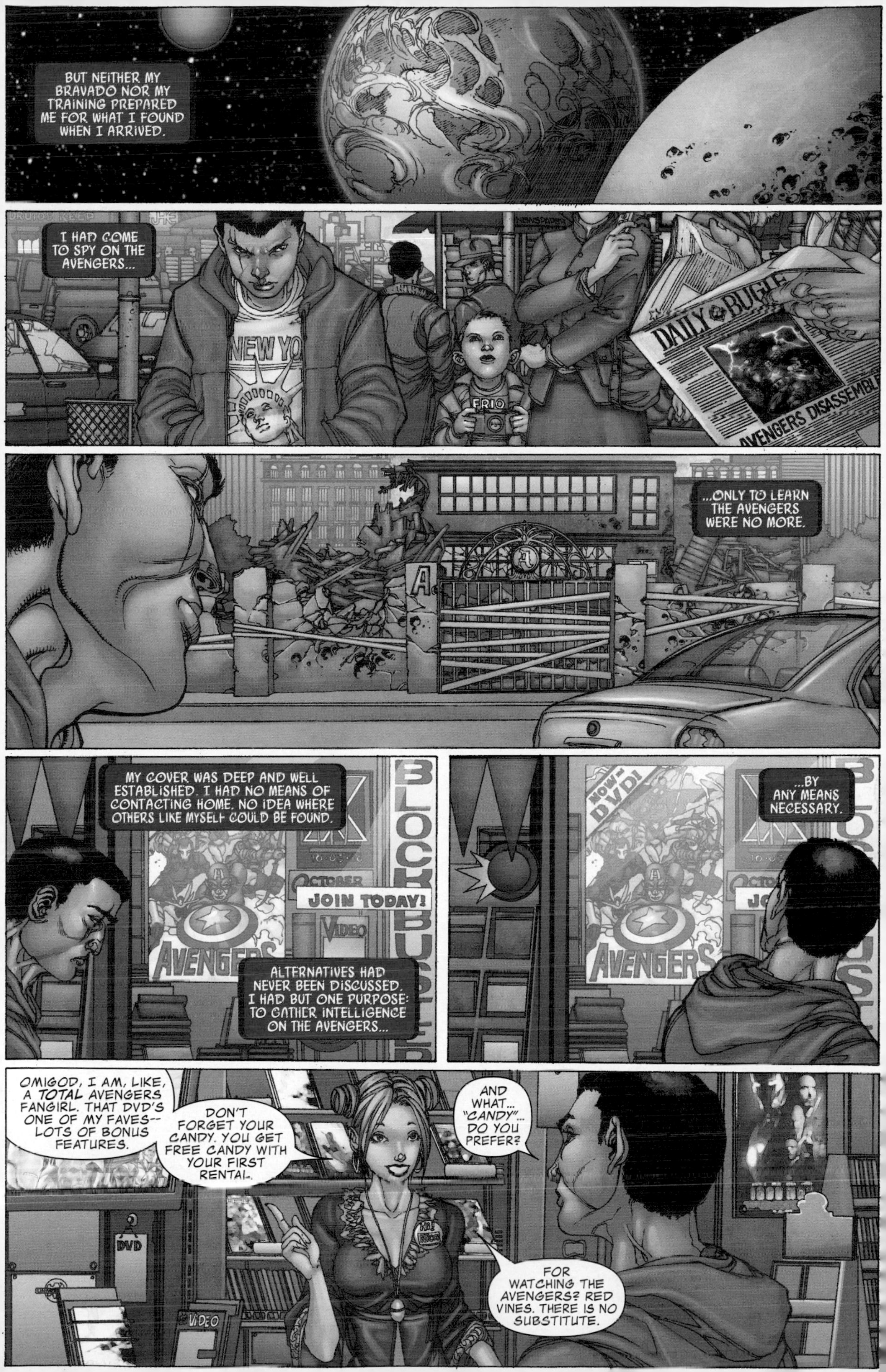
BUT NEITHER MY BRAVADO NOR MY TRAINING PREPARED ME FOR WHAT I FOUND WHEN I ARRIVED.
I HAD COME TO SPY ON THE AVENGERS...
NEW YO
FRIO
DAILY BUGLE
AVENGERS DISASSEMBLE
...ONLY TO LEARN THE AVENGERS WERE NO MORE.
MY COVER WAS DEEP AND WELL ESTABLISHED. I HAD NO MEANS OF CONTACTING HOME. NO IDEA WHERE OTHERS LIKE MYSELF COULD BE FOUND.
BLOCKBUSTER
OCTOBER
JOIN TODAY!
VIDEO
AVENGERS
ALTERNATIVES HAD NEVER BEEN DISCUSSED. I HAD BUT ONE PURPOSE: TO GATHER INTELLIGENCE ON THE AVENGERS...
NOW-DVD!
...BY ANY MEANS NECESSARY.
OMIGOD, I AM, LIKE, A *TOTAL* AVENGERS FANGIRL. THAT DVD'S ONE OF MY FAVES--LOTS OF BONUS FEATURES.
DON'T FORGET YOUR CANDY. YOU GET FREE CANDY WITH YOUR FIRST RENTAL.
AND WHAT... "CANDY"... DO YOU PREFER?
FOR WATCHING THE AVENGERS? RED VINES. THERE IS NO SUBSTITUTE.
DVD
VIDEO

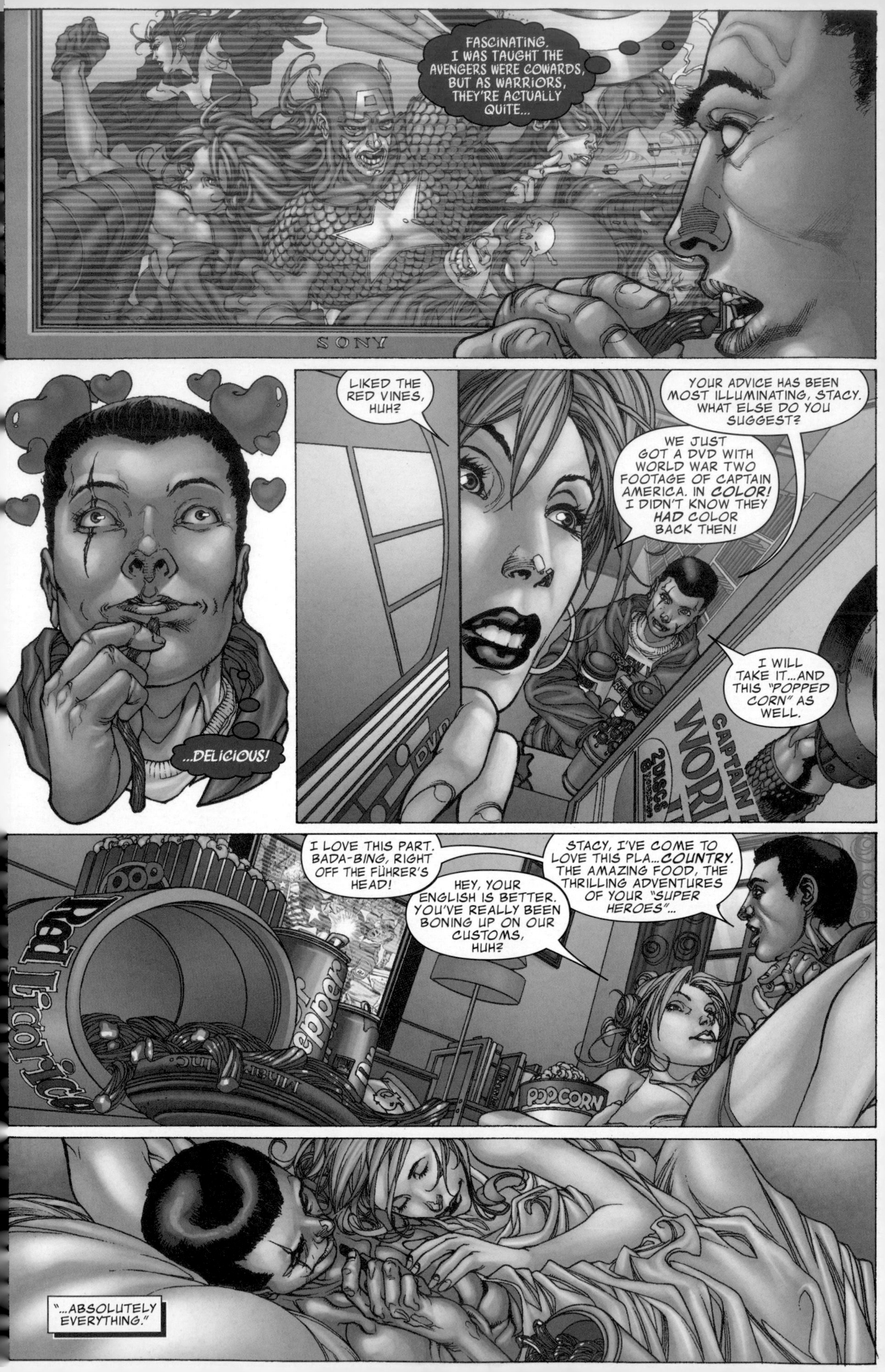

FASCINATING, I WAS TAUGHT THE AVENGERS WERE COWARDS, BUT AS WARRIORS, THEY'RE ACTUALLY QUITE...
SONY
...DELICIOUS!
LIKED THE RED VINES, HUH?
YOUR ADVICE HAS BEEN MOST ILLUMINATING, STACY. WHAT ELSE DO YOU SUGGEST?
WE JUST GOT A DVD WITH WORLD WAR TWO FOOTAGE OF CAPTAIN AMERICA. IN COLOR! I DIDN'T KNOW THEY HAD COLOR BACK THEN!
I WILL TAKE IT...AND THIS "POPPED CORN" AS WELL.
I LOVE THIS PART. BADA-BING, RIGHT OFF THE FÜHRER'S HEAD!
STACY, I'VE COME TO LOVE THIS PLA...COUNTRY. THE AMAZING FOOD, THE THRILLING ADVENTURES OF YOUR "SUPER HEROES"...
HEY, YOUR ENGLISH IS BETTER. YOU'VE REALLY BEEN BONING UP ON OUR CUSTOMS, HUH?
Red Licorice
POPCORN
"...ABSOLUTELY EVERYTHING."

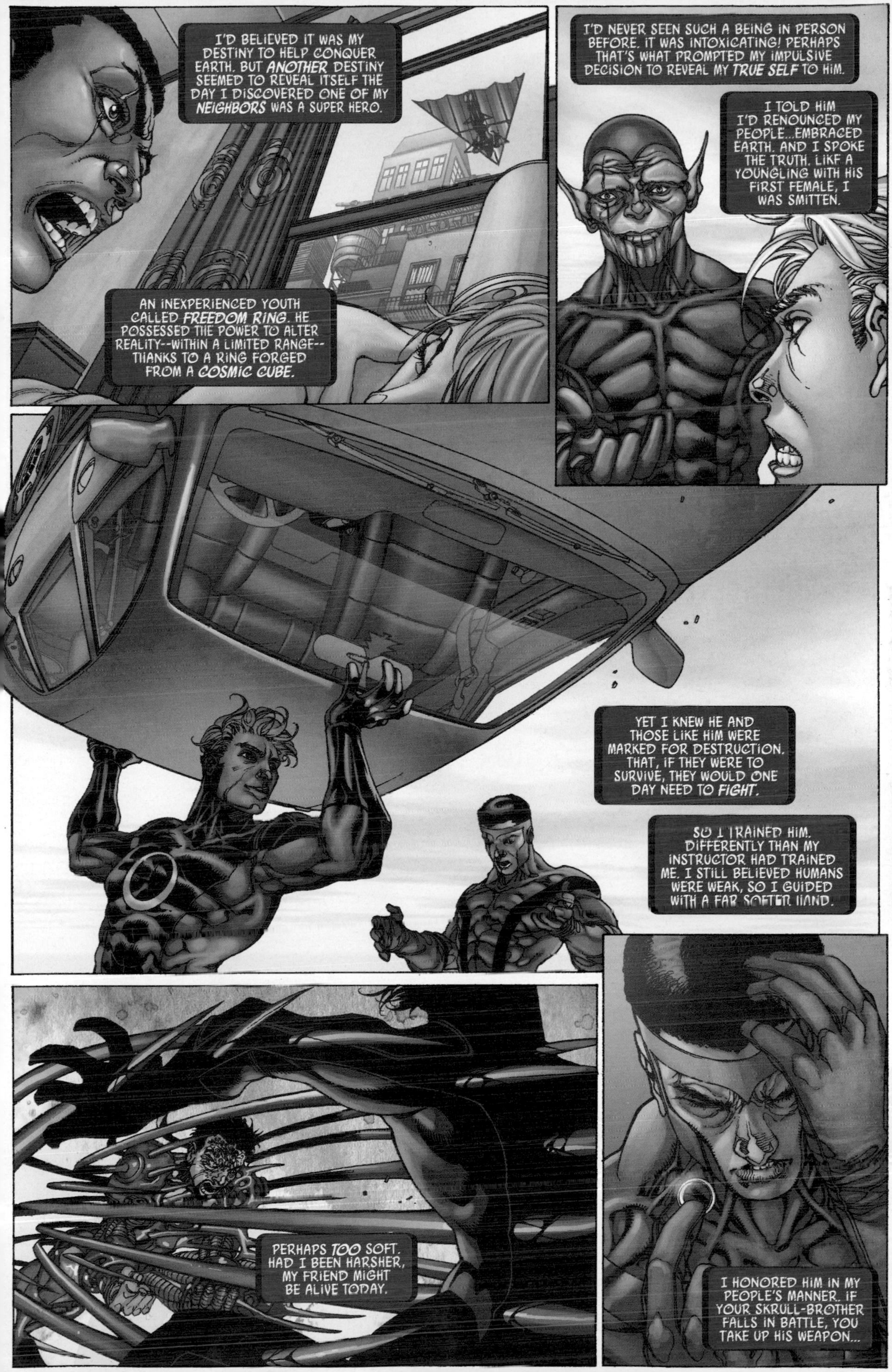
I'D BELIEVED IT WAS MY DESTINY TO HELP CONQUER EARTH. BUT ANOTHER DESTINY SEEMED TO REVEAL ITSELF THE DAY I DISCOVERED ONE OF MY NEIGHBORS WAS A SUPER HERO.
AN INEXPERIENCED YOUTH CALLED FREEDOM RING. HE POSSESSED THE POWER TO ALTER REALITY--WITHIN A LIMITED RANGE--THANKS TO A RING FORGED FROM A COSMIC CUBE.
I'D NEVER SEEN SUCH A BEING IN PERSON BEFORE. IT WAS INTOXICATING! PERHAPS THAT'S WHAT PROMPTED MY IMPULSIVE DECISION TO REVEAL MY TRUE SELF TO HIM.
I TOLD HIM I'D RENOUNCED MY PEOPLE...EMBRACED EARTH. AND I SPOKE THE TRUTH. LIKE A YOUNGLING WITH HIS FIRST FEMALE, I WAS SMITTEN.
YET I KNEW HE AND THOSE LIKE HIM WERE MARKED FOR DESTRUCTION. THAT, IF THEY WERE TO SURVIVE, THEY WOULD ONE DAY NEED TO FIGHT.
SO I TRAINED HIM. DIFFERENTLY THAN MY INSTRUCTOR HAD TRAINED ME. I STILL BELIEVED HUMANS WERE WEAK, SO I GUIDED WITH A FAR SOFTER HAND.
PERHAPS TOO SOFT. HAD I BEEN HARSHER, MY FRIEND MIGHT BE ALIVE TODAY.
I HONORED HIM IN MY PEOPLE'S MANNER. IF YOUR SKRULL-BROTHER FALLS IN BATTLE, YOU TAKE UP HIS WEAPON...

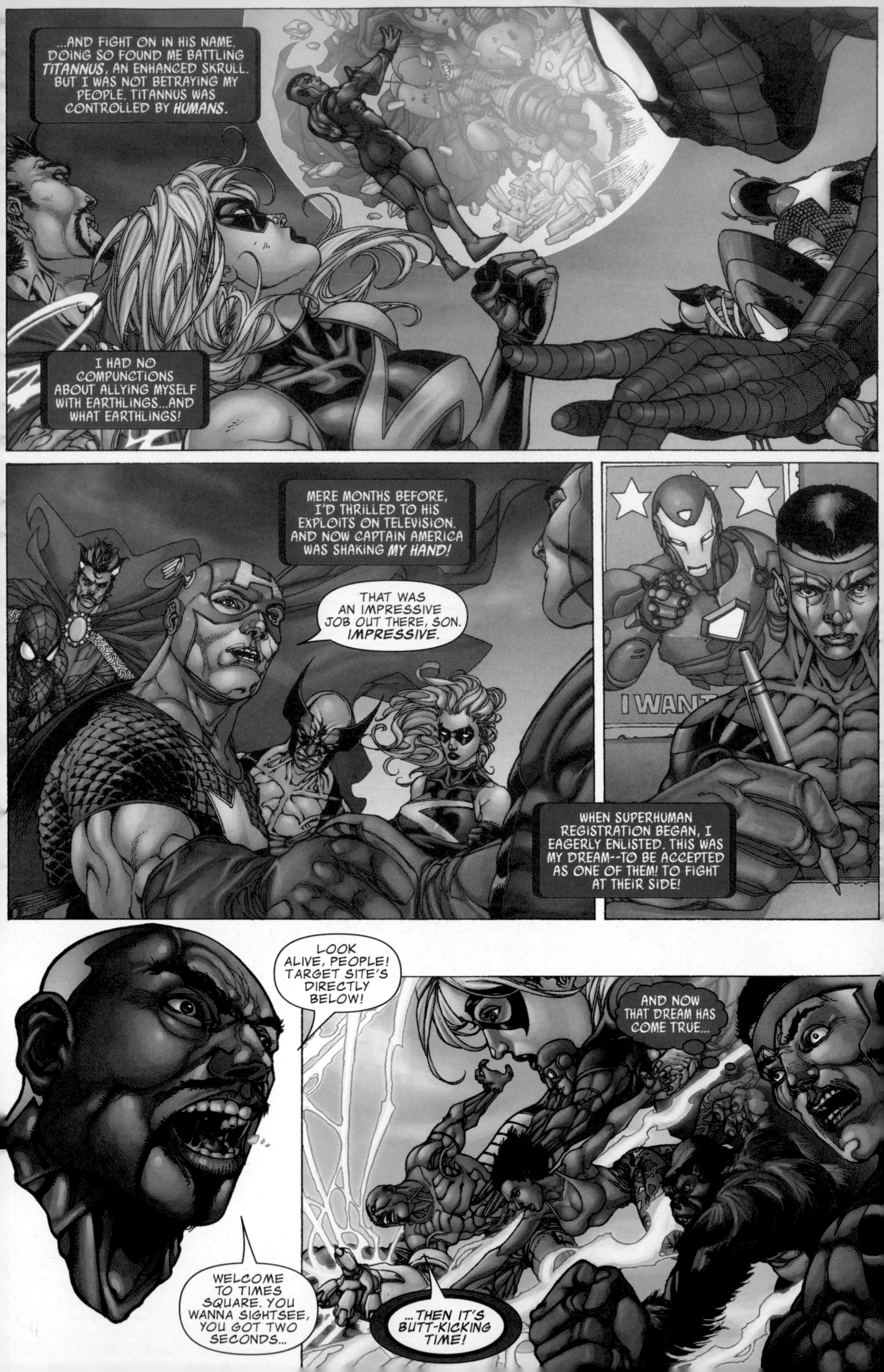
...AND FIGHT ON IN HIS NAME. DOING SO FOUND ME BATTLING TITANNUS, AN ENHANCED SKRULL. BUT I WAS NOT BETRAYING MY PEOPLE. TITANNUS WAS CONTROLLED BY HUMANS.
I HAD NO COMPUNCTIONS ABOUT ALLYING MYSELF WITH EARTHLINGS...AND WHAT EARTHLINGS!
MERE MONTHS BEFORE, I'D THRILLED TO HIS EXPLOITS ON TELEVISION, AND NOW CAPTAIN AMERICA WAS SHAKING MY HAND!
THAT WAS AN IMPRESSIVE JOB OUT THERE, SON. IMPRESSIVE.
I WANT
WHEN SUPERHUMAN REGISTRATION BEGAN, I EAGERLY ENLISTED. THIS WAS MY DREAM--TO BE ACCEPTED AS ONE OF THEM! TO FIGHT AT THEIR SIDE!
LOOK ALIVE, PEOPLE! TARGET SITE'S DIRECTLY BELOW!
WELCOME TO TIMES SQUARE. YOU WANNA SIGHTSEE, YOU GOT TWO SECONDS...
AND NOW THAT DREAM HAS COME TRUE...
...THEN IT'S BUTT-KICKING TIME!

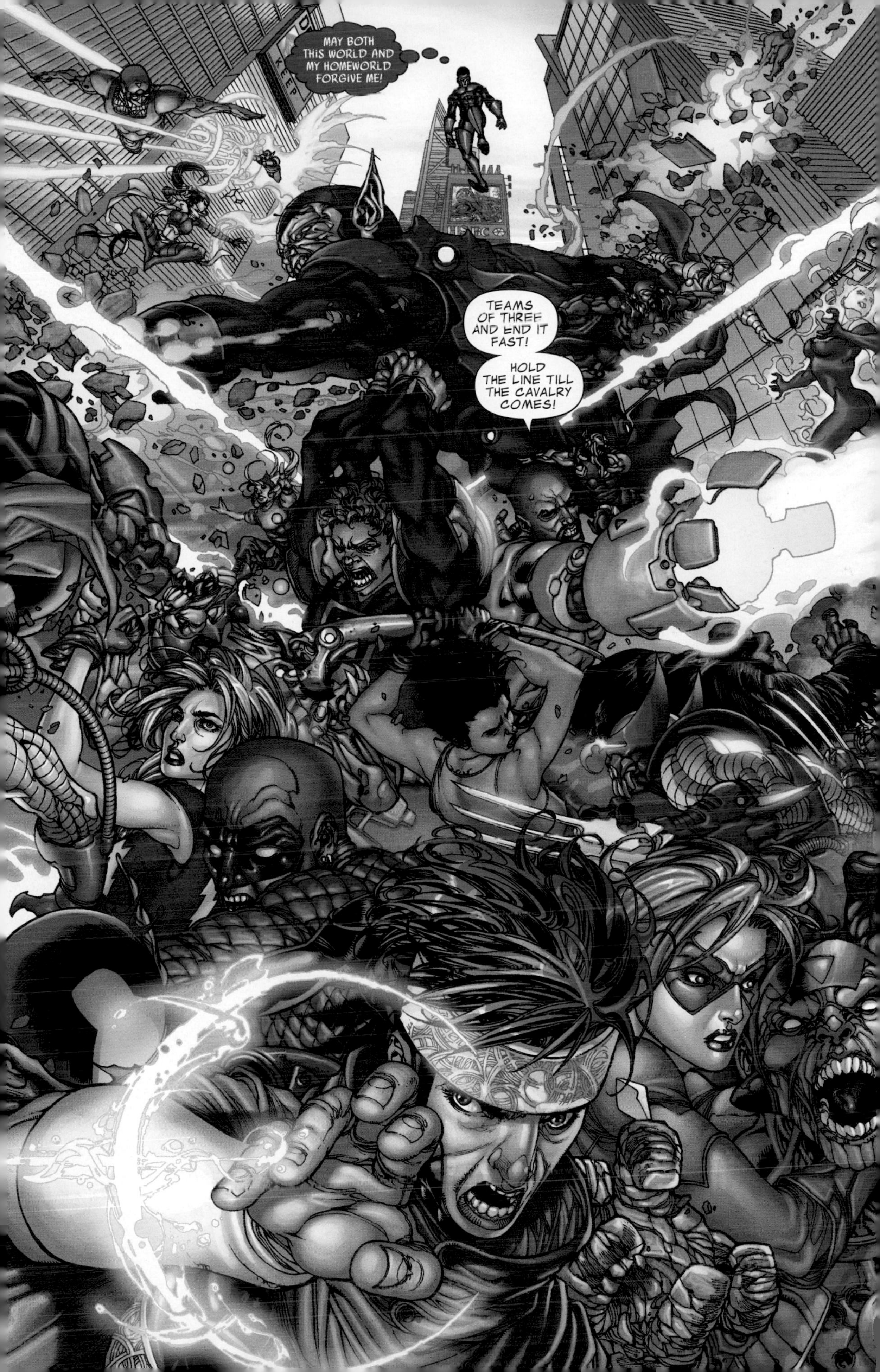
MAY BOTH THIS WORLD AND MY HOMEWORLD FORGIVE ME!
KEEP
HSBC
TEAMS OF THREE AND END IT FAST!
HOLD THE LINE TILL THE CAVALRY COMES!

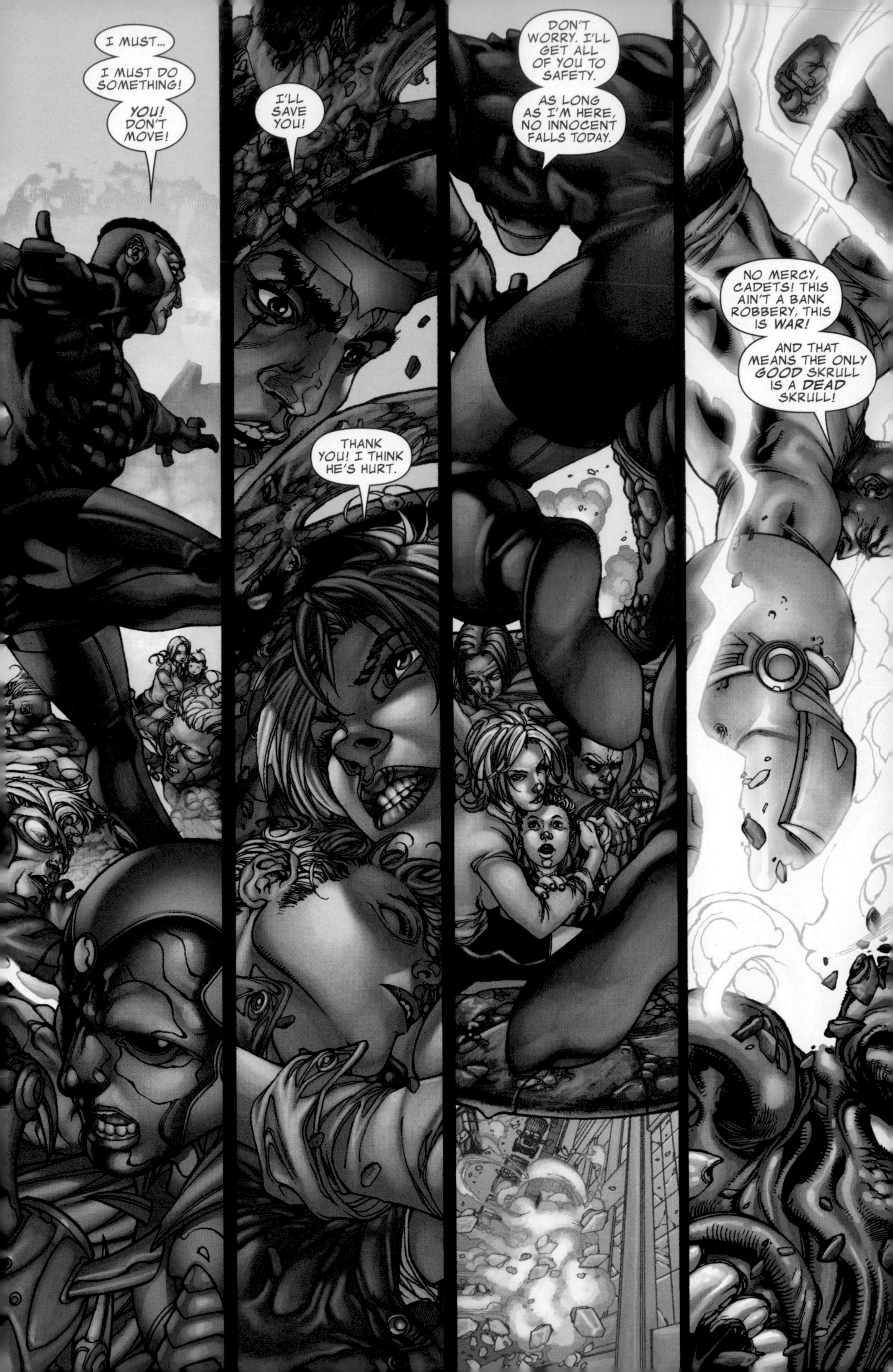
I MUST...
I MUST DO SOMETHING!
YOU! DON'T MOVE!
I'LL SAVE YOU!
THANK YOU! I THINK HE'S HURT.
DON'T WORRY. I'LL GET ALL OF YOU TO SAFETY.
AS LONG AS I'M HERE, NO INNOCENT FALLS TODAY.
NO MERCY, CADETS! THIS AIN'T A BANK ROBBERY, THIS IS *WAR!*
AND THAT MEANS THE ONLY *GOOD* SKRULL IS A *DEAD* SKRULL!

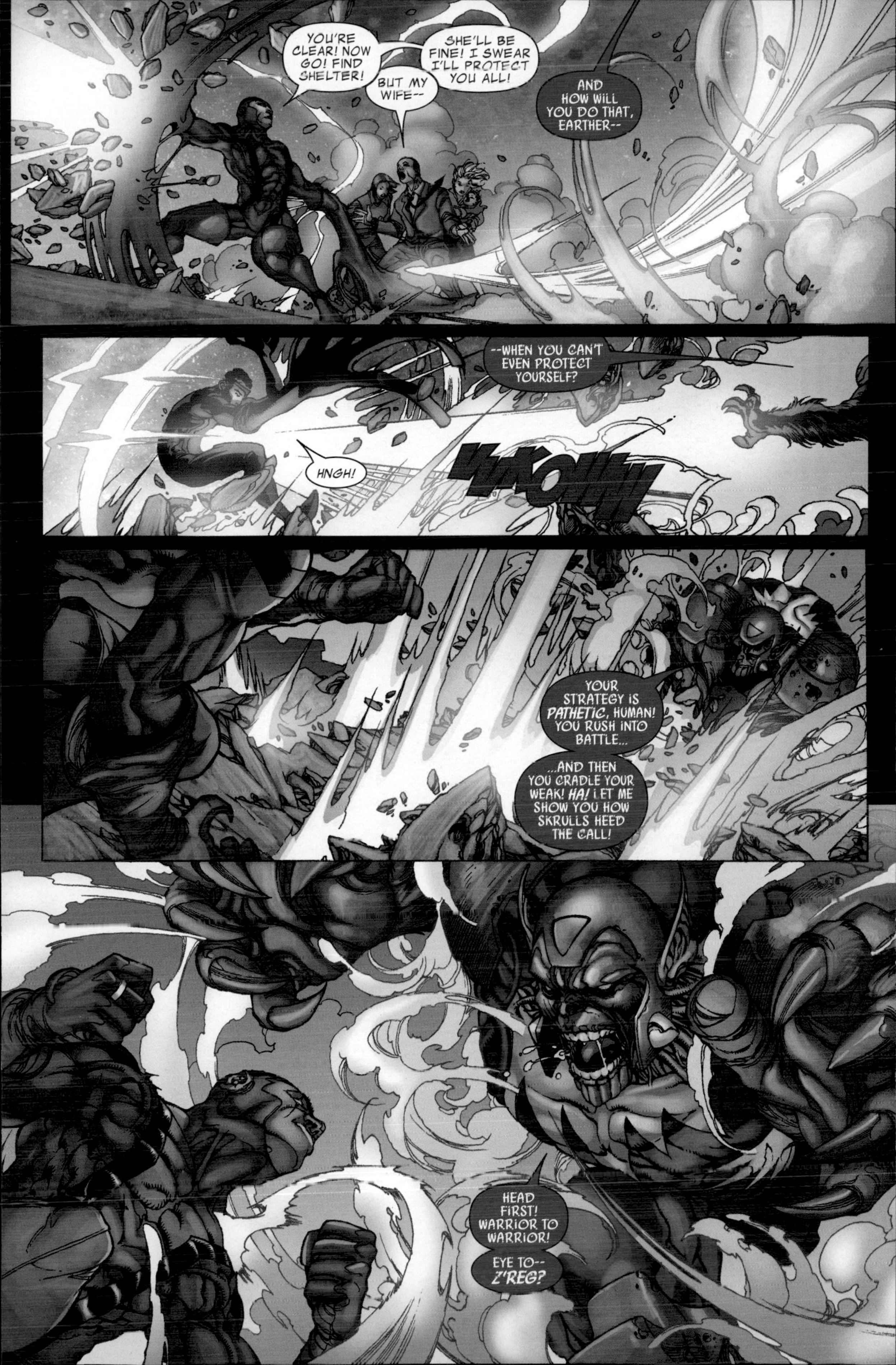
YOU'RE CLEAR! NOW GO! FIND SHELTER!
BUT MY WIFE--
SHE'LL BE FINE! I SWEAR I'LL PROTECT YOU ALL!
AND HOW WILL YOU DO THAT, EARTHER--
--WHEN YOU CAN'T EVEN PROTECT YOURSELF?
HNGH!
WHOOM
YOUR STRATEGY IS PATHETIC, HUMAN! YOU RUSH INTO BATTLE...
...AND THEN YOU CRADLE YOUR WEAK! HA! LET ME SHOW YOU HOW SKRULLS HEED THE CALL!
HEAD FIRST! WARRIOR TO WARRIOR!
EYE TO-- Z'REG?

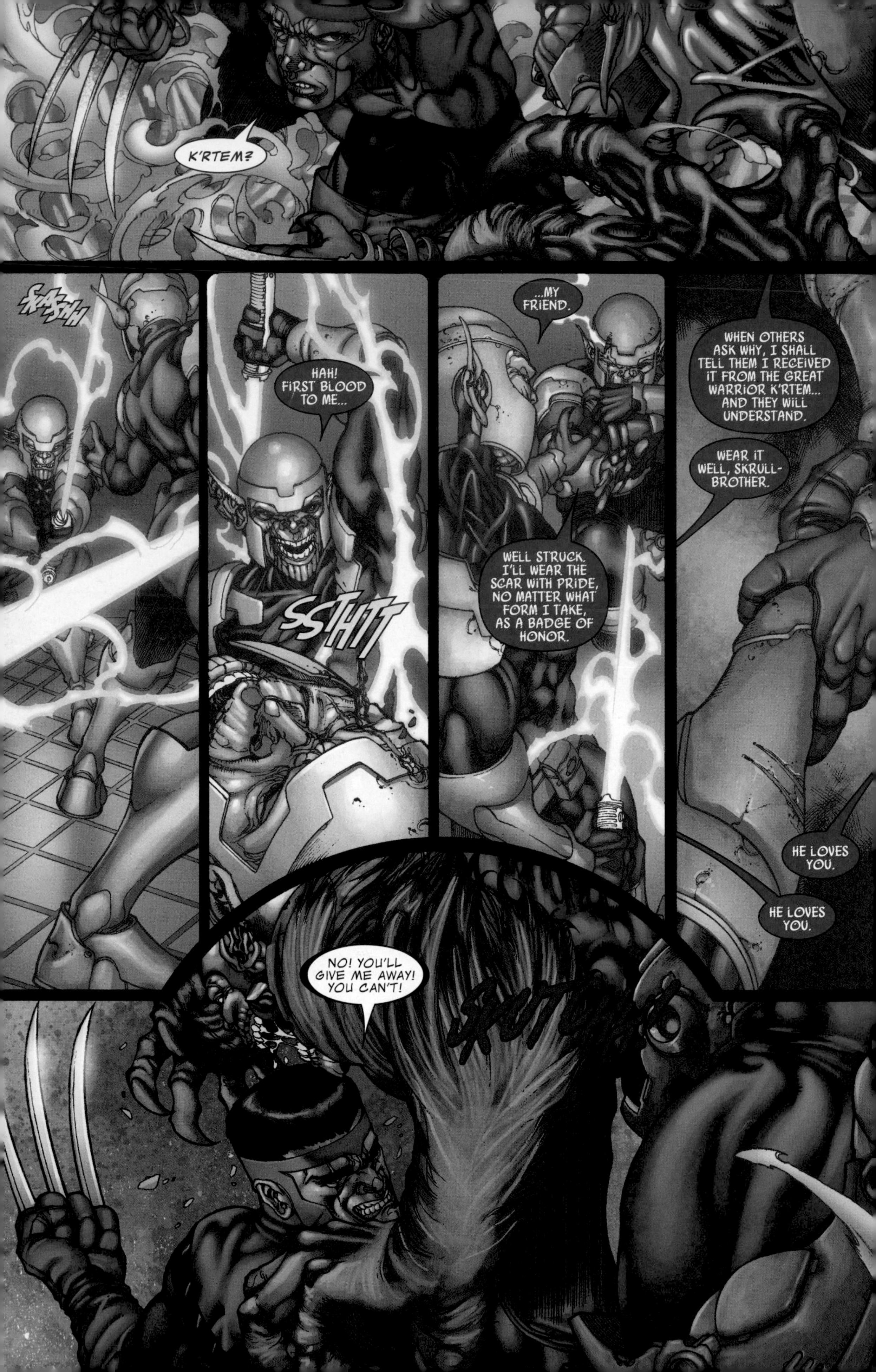
K'RTEM?
SKASHH
HAH! FIRST BLOOD TO ME...
SSHTT
...MY FRIEND.
WELL STRUCK. I'LL WEAR THE SCAR WITH PRIDE, NO MATTER WHAT FORM I TAKE, AS A BADGE OF HONOR.
WHEN OTHERS ASK WHY, I SHALL TELL THEM I RECEIVED IT FROM THE GREAT WARRIOR K'RTEM... AND THEY WILL UNDERSTAND.
WEAR IT WELL, SKRULL-BROTHER.
HE LOVES YOU.
HE LOVES YOU.
NO! YOU'LL GIVE ME AWAY! YOU CAN'T!

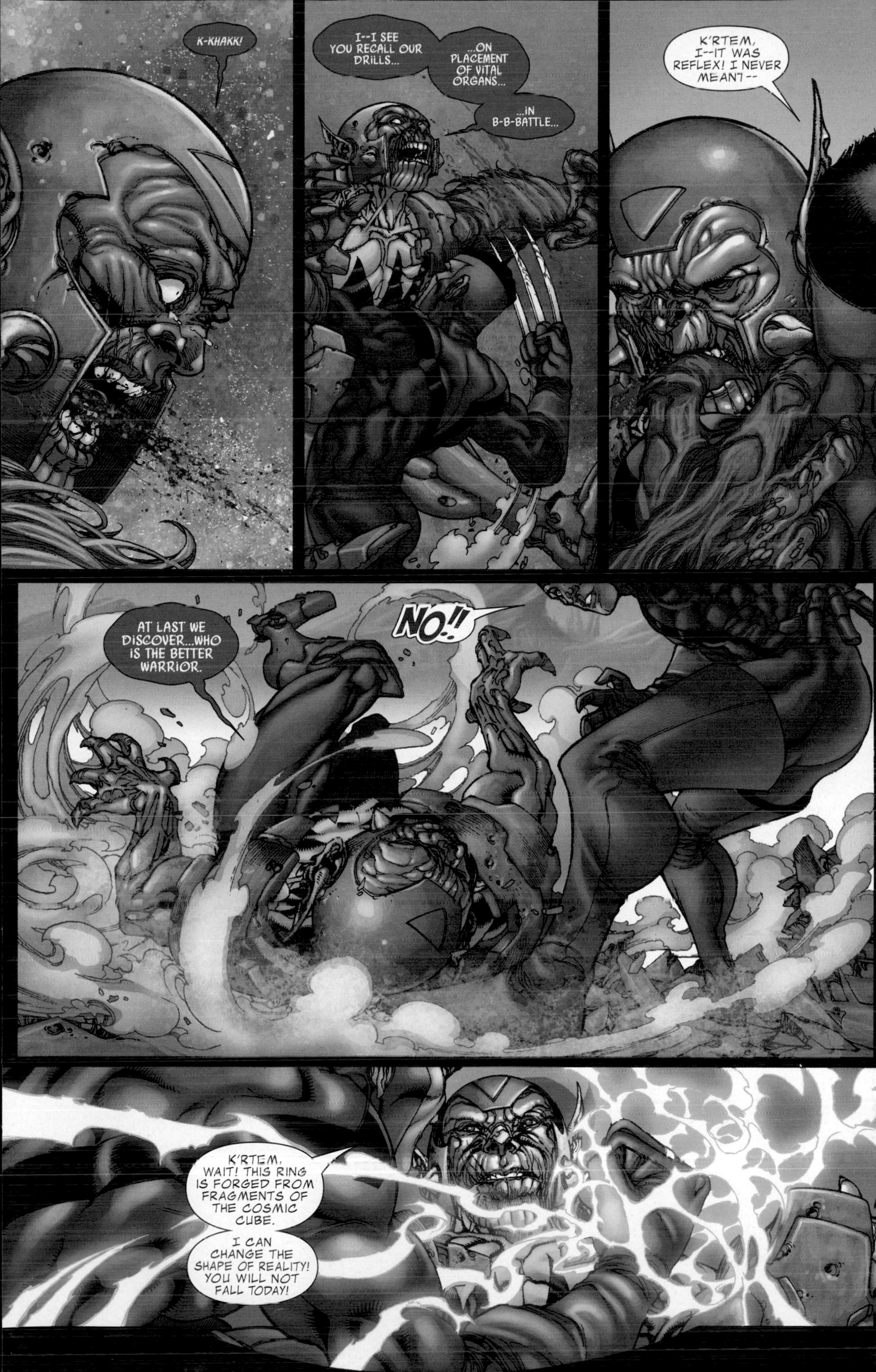
K-KHAKK!
I--I SEE YOU RECALL OUR DRILLS...
...ON PLACEMENT OF VITAL ORGANS...
...IN B-B-BATTLE...
K'RTEM, I--IT WAS REFLEX! I NEVER MEANT--
AT LAST WE DISCOVER...WHO IS THE BETTER WARRIOR.
NO!!
K'RTEM, WAIT! THIS RING IS FORGED FROM FRAGMENTS OF THE COSMIC CUBE.
I CAN CHANGE THE SHAPE OF REALITY! YOU WILL NOT FALL TODAY!

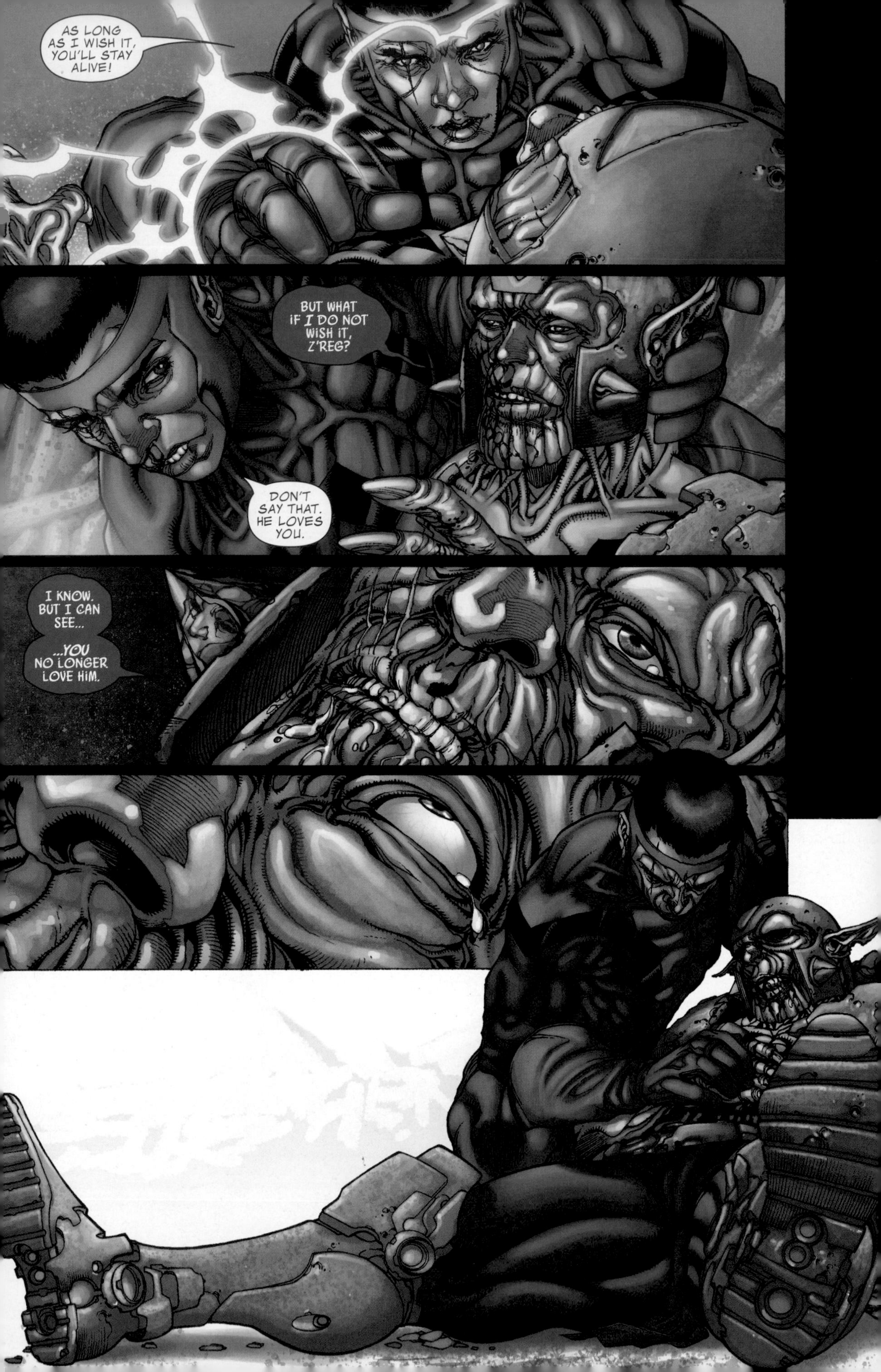
AS LONG AS I WISH IT, YOU'LL STAY ALIVE!
BUT WHAT IF I DO NOT WISH IT, Z'REG?
DON'T SAY THAT. HE LOVES YOU.
I KNOW. BUT I CAN SEE...
...YOU NO LONGER LOVE HIM.

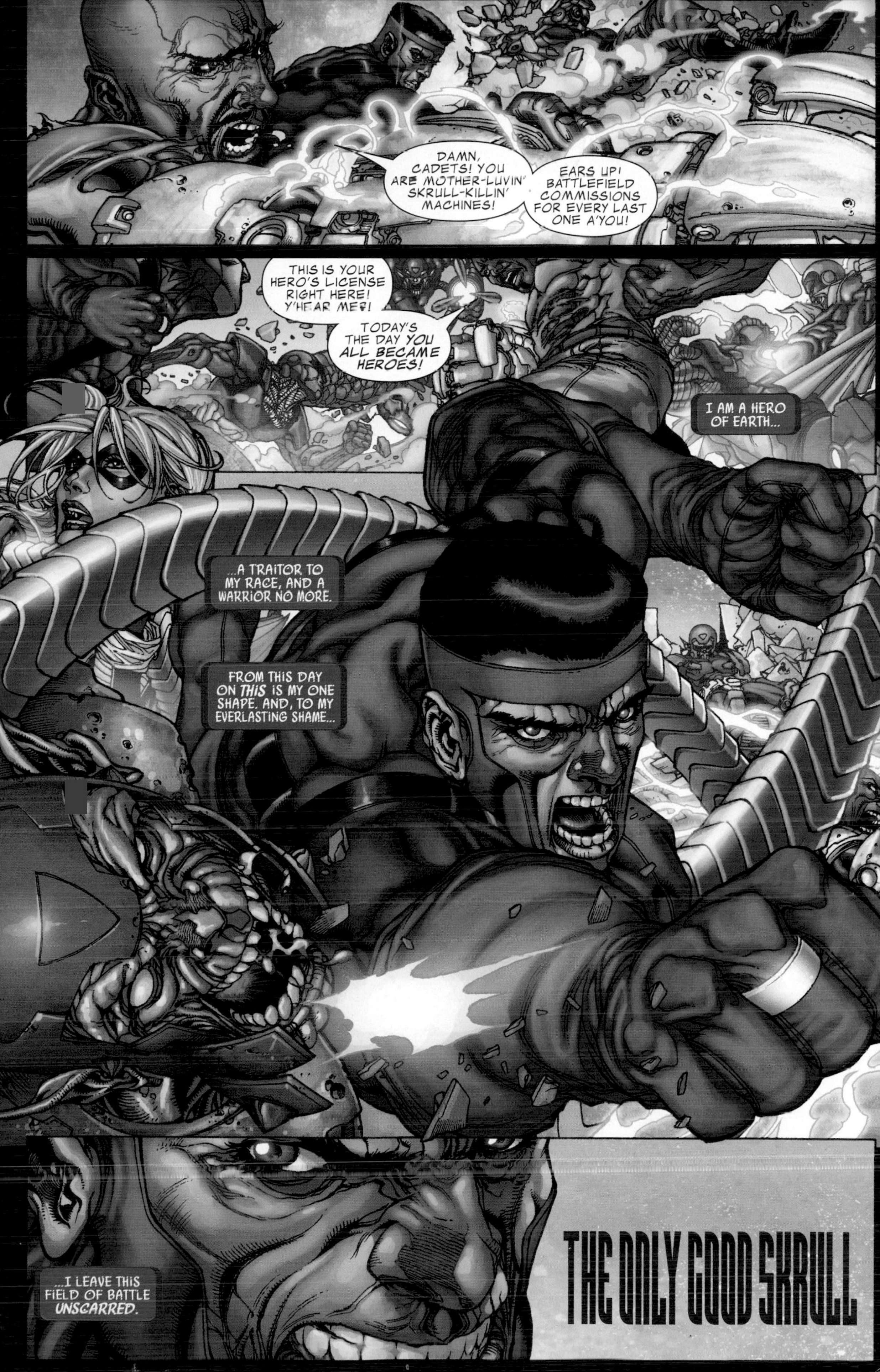
DAMN, CADETS! YOU ARE MOTHER-LUVIN' SKRULL-KILLIN' MACHINES!
EARS UP! BATTLEFIELD COMMISSIONS FOR EVERY LAST ONE A'YOU!
THIS IS YOUR HERO'S LICENSE RIGHT HERE! Y'HEAR ME?!
TODAY'S THE DAY YOU ALL BECAME HEROES!
I AM A HERO OF EARTH...
...A TRAITOR TO MY RACE, AND A WARRIOR NO MORE.
FROM THIS DAY ON THIS IS MY ONE SHAPE. AND, TO MY EVERLASTING SHAME...
...I LEAVE THIS FIELD OF BATTLE UNSCARRED.
THE ONLY GOOD SKRULL

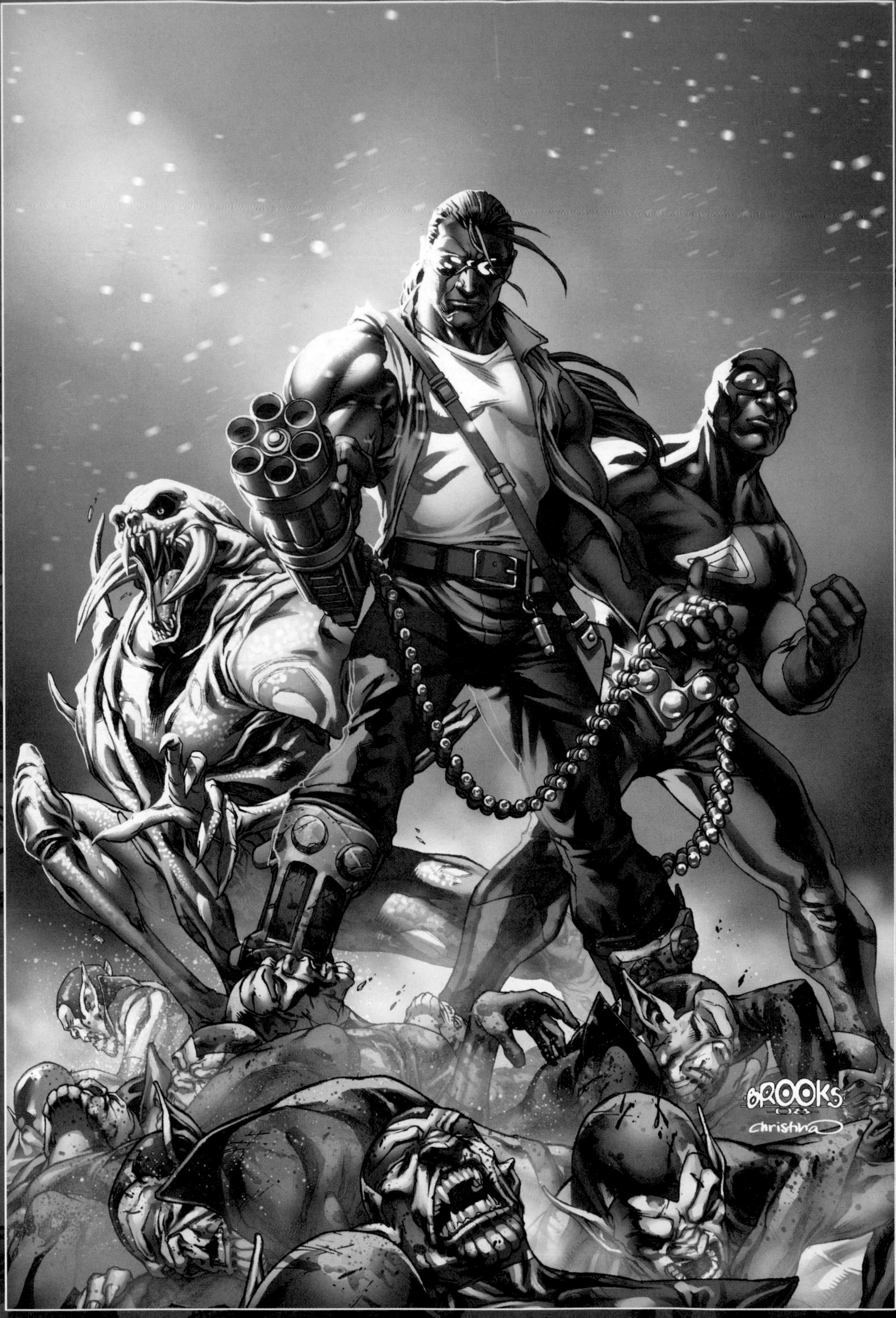
BROOKS
08
christina

#16

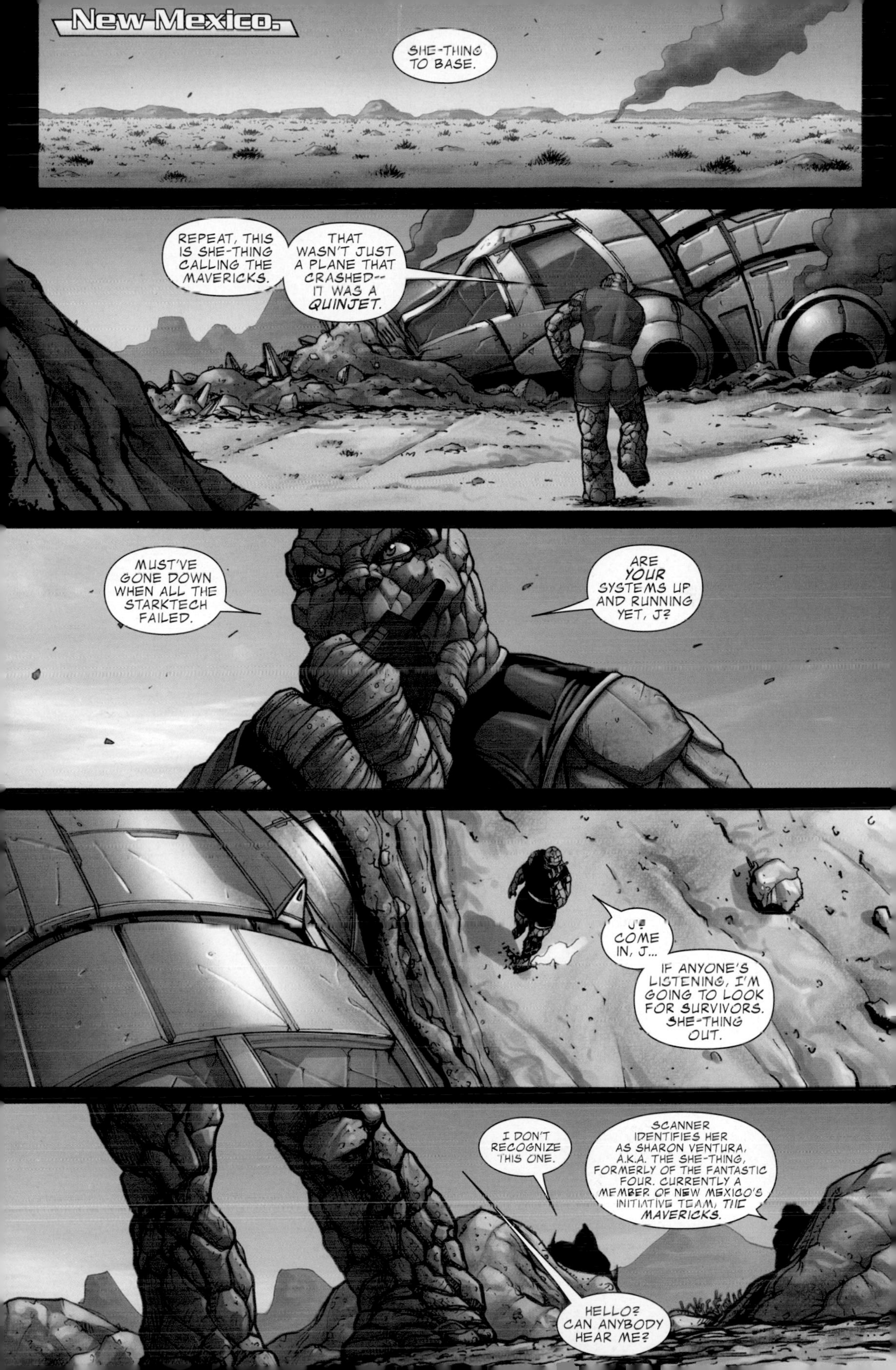
New Mexico.
SHE-THING TO BASE.
REPEAT, THIS IS SHE-THING CALLING THE MAVERICKS.
THAT WASN'T JUST A PLANE THAT CRASHED-- IT WAS A QUINJET.
MUST'VE GONE DOWN WHEN ALL THE STARKTECH FAILED.
ARE YOUR SYSTEMS UP AND RUNNING YET, J?
J? COME IN, J...
IF ANYONE'S LISTENING, I'M GOING TO LOOK FOR SURVIVORS. SHE-THING OUT.
I DON'T RECOGNIZE THIS ONE.
SCANNER IDENTIFIES HER AS SHARON VENTURA, A.K.A. THE SHE-THING, FORMERLY OF THE FANTASTIC FOUR. CURRENTLY A MEMBER OF NEW MEXICO'S INITIATIVE TEAM, THE MAVERICKS.
HELLO? CAN ANYBODY HEAR ME?

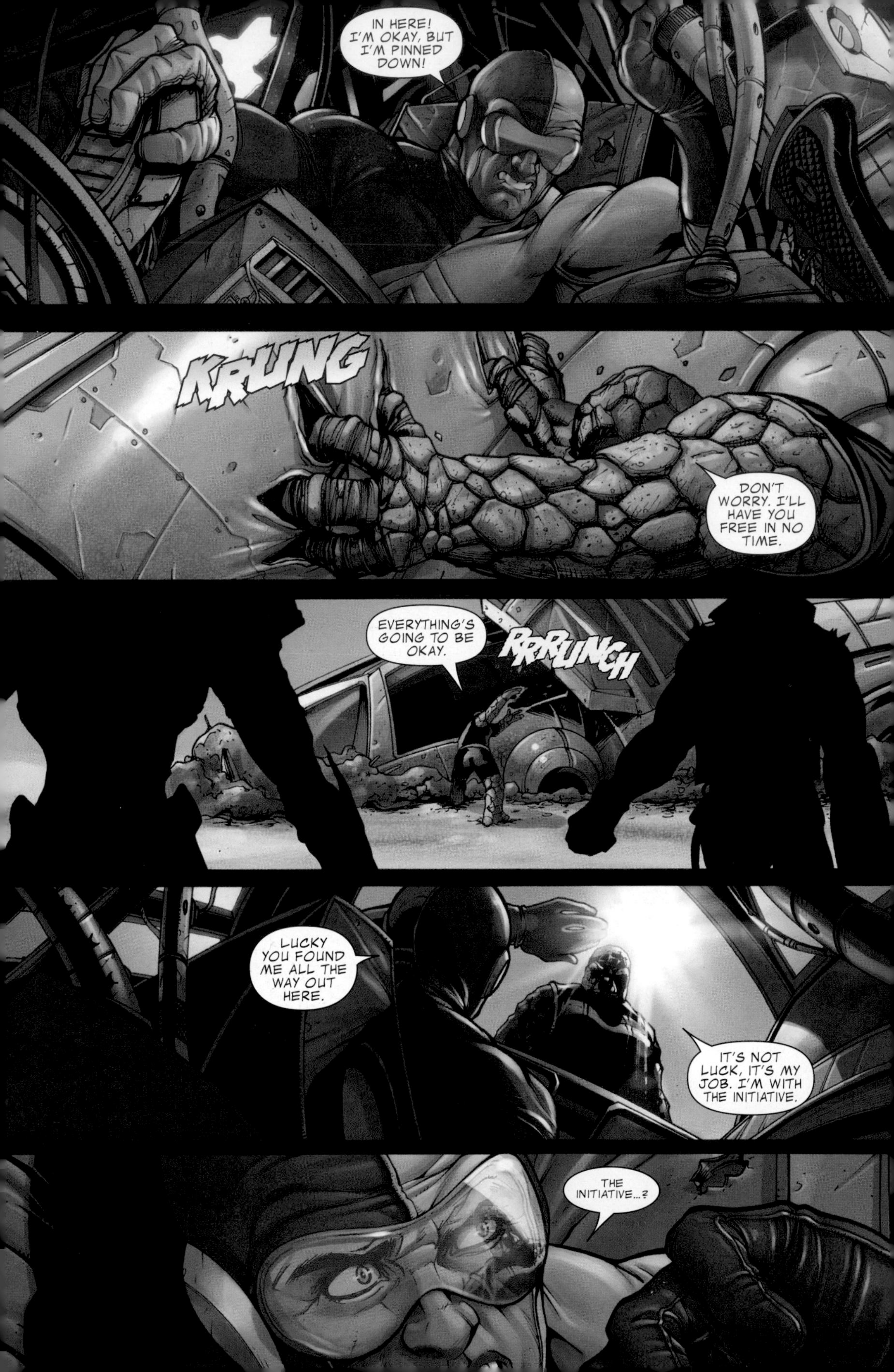
IN HERE! I'M OKAY, BUT I'M PINNED DOWN!
KRUNG
DON'T WORRY. I'LL HAVE YOU FREE IN NO TIME.
EVERYTHING'S GOING TO BE OKAY.
RRRRUNCH
LUCKY YOU FOUND ME ALL THE WAY OUT HERE.
IT'S NOT LUCK, IT'S MY JOB. I'M WITH THE INITIATIVE.
THE INITIATIVE...?

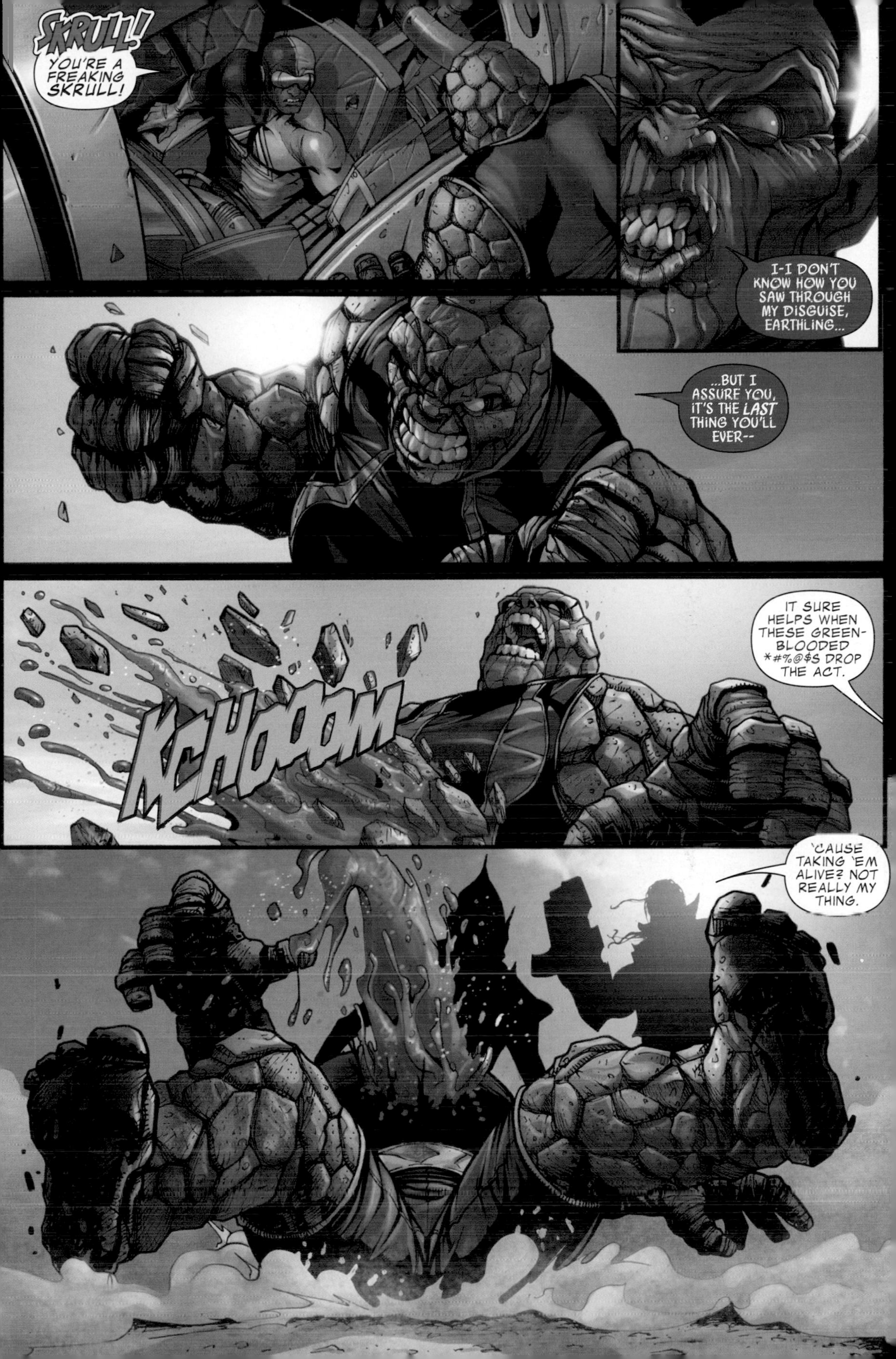
SKRULL!
YOU'RE A FREAKING SKRULL!
I-I DON'T KNOW HOW YOU SAW THROUGH MY DISGUISE, EARTHLING...
...BUT I ASSURE YOU, IT'S THE *LAST* THING YOU'LL EVER--
KCHOOOM
IT SURE HELPS WHEN THESE GREEN-BLOODED *#%@$S DROP THE ACT.
'CAUSE TAKING 'EM ALIVE? NOT REALLY MY THING.

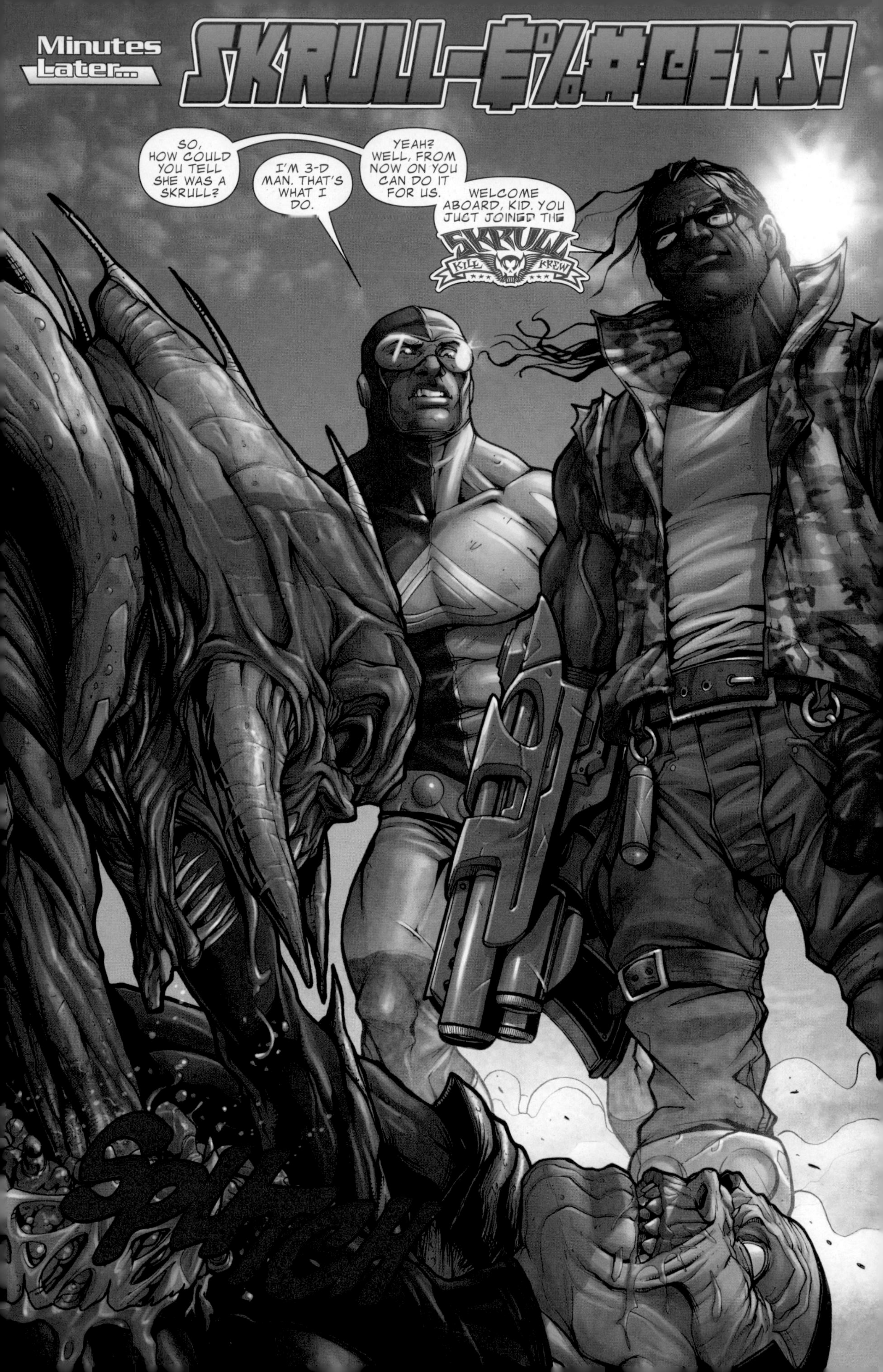
Minutes Later...
SKRULL-€%#@ERS!
SO, HOW COULD YOU TELL SHE WAS A SKRULL?
I'M 3-D MAN. THAT'S WHAT I DO.
YEAH? WELL, FROM NOW ON YOU CAN DO IT FOR US.
WELCOME ABOARD, KID. YOU JUST JOINED THE
SKRULL KILL KREW

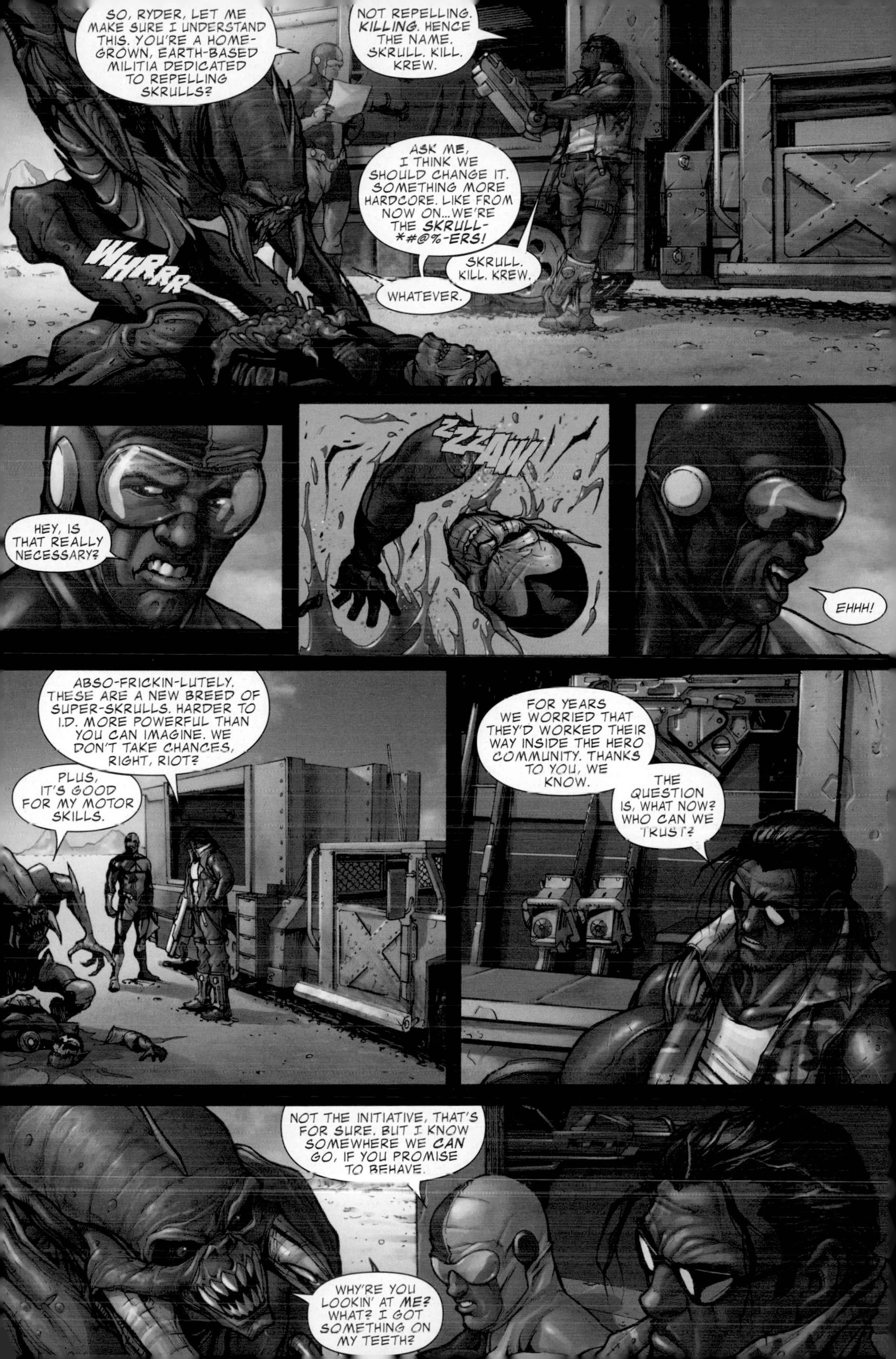
SO, RYDER, LET ME MAKE SURE I UNDERSTAND THIS. YOU'RE A HOME-GROWN, EARTH-BASED MILITIA DEDICATED TO REPELLING SKRULLS?
NOT REPELLING. KILLING. HENCE THE NAME. SKRULL. KILL. KREW.
ASK ME, I THINK WE SHOULD CHANGE IT. SOMETHING MORE HARDCORE. LIKE FROM NOW ON...WE'RE THE SKRULL-*#@%-ERS!
WHRRR
SKRULL. KILL. KREW.
WHATEVER.
HEY, IS THAT REALLY NECESSARY?
ZZZAW!
EHHH!
ABSO-FRICKIN-LUTELY. THESE ARE A NEW BREED OF SUPER-SKRULLS. HARDER TO I.D. MORE POWERFUL THAN YOU CAN IMAGINE. WE DON'T TAKE CHANCES, RIGHT, RIOT?
PLUS, IT'S GOOD FOR MY MOTOR SKILLS.
FOR YEARS WE WORRIED THAT THEY'D WORKED THEIR WAY INSIDE THE HERO COMMUNITY. THANKS TO YOU, WE KNOW.
THE QUESTION IS, WHAT NOW? WHO CAN WE TRUST?
NOT THE INITIATIVE, THAT'S FOR SURE. BUT I KNOW SOMEWHERE WE CAN GO, IF YOU PROMISE TO BEHAVE.
WHY'RE YOU LOOKIN' AT ME? WHAT? I GOT SOMETHING ON MY TEETH?

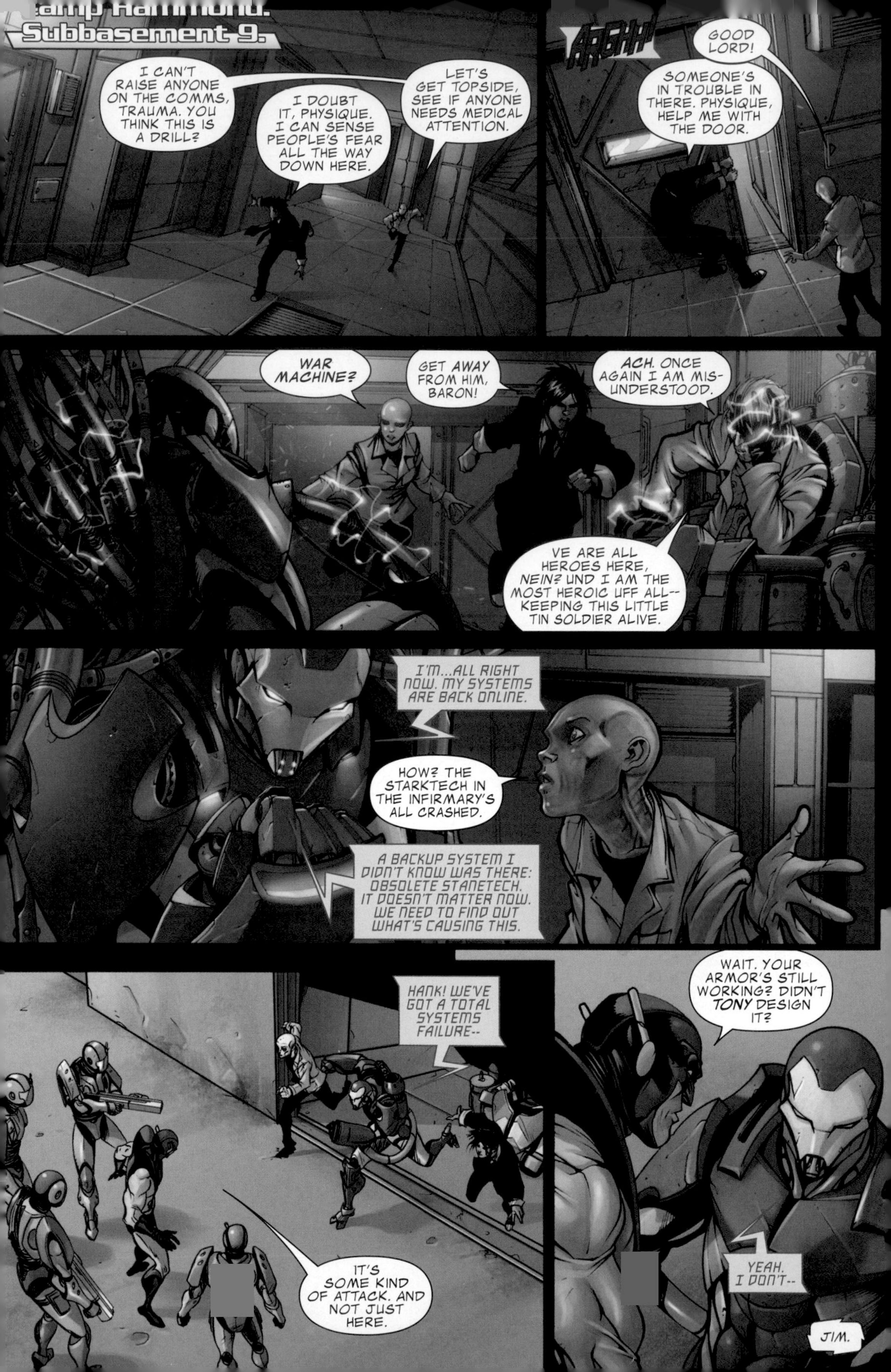
amp Hammond.
Subbasement 9.
I CAN'T RAISE ANYONE ON THE COMMS, TRAUMA. YOU THINK THIS IS A DRILL?
I DOUBT IT, PHYSIQUE. I CAN SENSE PEOPLE'S FEAR ALL THE WAY DOWN HERE.
LET'S GET TOPSIDE, SEE IF ANYONE NEEDS MEDICAL ATTENTION.
ARGHH!
GOOD LORD!
SOMEONE'S IN TROUBLE IN THERE. PHYSIQUE, HELP ME WITH THE DOOR.
WAR MACHINE?
GET AWAY FROM HIM, BARON!
ACH. ONCE AGAIN I AM MIS-UNDERSTOOD.
VE ARE ALL HEROES HERE, NEIN? UND I AM THE MOST HEROIC UFF ALL-- KEEPING THIS LITTLE TIN SOLDIER ALIVE.
I'M...ALL RIGHT NOW. MY SYSTEMS ARE BACK ONLINE.
HOW? THE STARKTECH IN THE INFIRMARY'S ALL CRASHED.
A BACKUP SYSTEM I DIDN'T KNOW WAS THERE: OBSOLETE STANETECH. IT DOESN'T MATTER NOW. WE NEED TO FIND OUT WHAT'S CAUSING THIS.
HANK! WE'VE GOT A TOTAL SYSTEMS FAILURE--
IT'S SOME KIND OF ATTACK. AND NOT JUST HERE.
WAIT. YOUR ARMOR'S STILL WORKING? DIDN'T TONY DESIGN IT?
YEAH. I DON'T--
JIM.

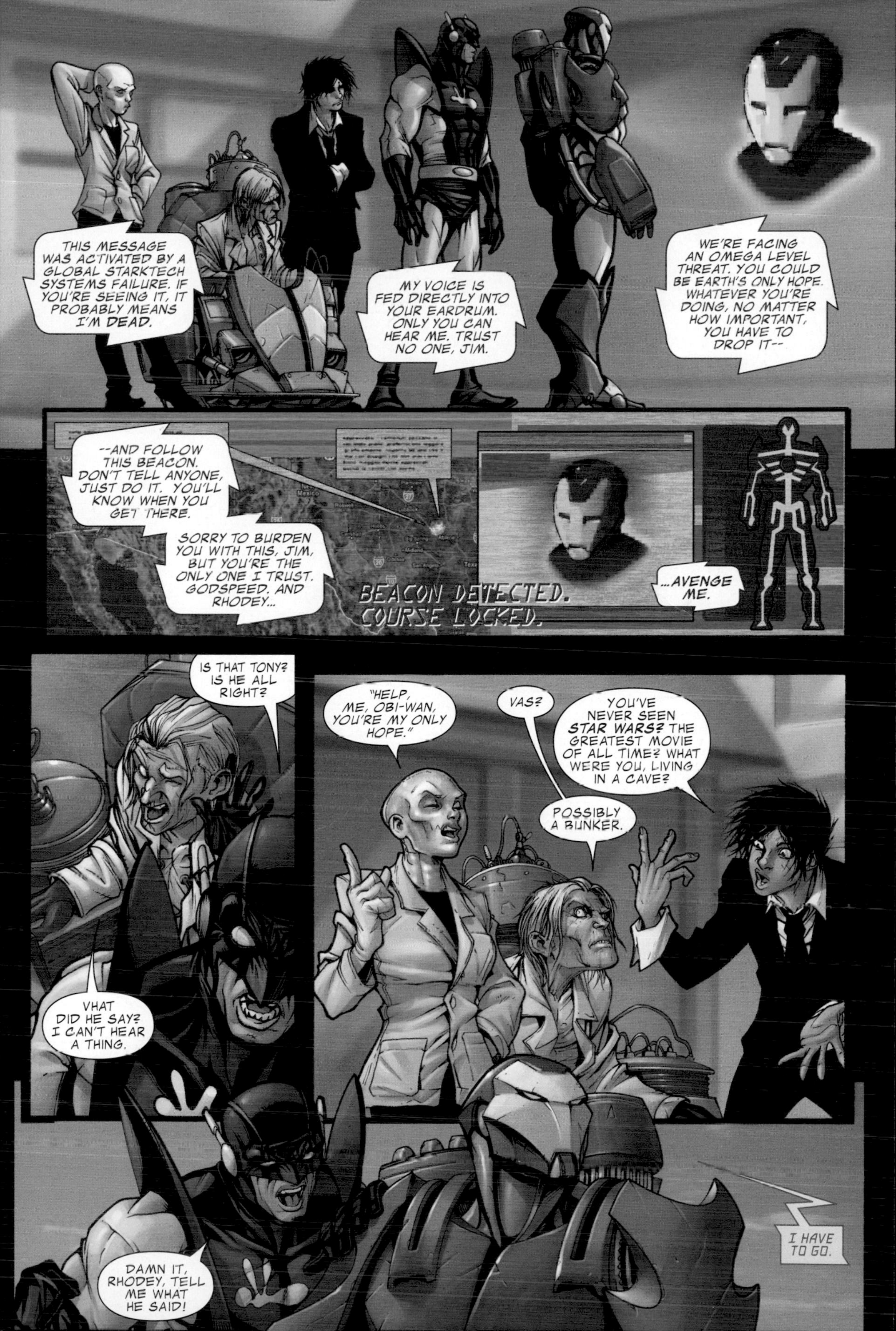
THIS MESSAGE WAS ACTIVATED BY A GLOBAL STARKTECH SYSTEMS FAILURE. IF YOU'RE SEEING IT, IT PROBABLY MEANS I'M **DEAD**.
MY VOICE IS FED DIRECTLY INTO YOUR EARDRUM. ONLY YOU CAN HEAR ME. TRUST NO ONE, JIM.
WE'RE FACING AN OMEGA LEVEL THREAT. YOU COULD BE EARTH'S ONLY HOPE. WHATEVER YOU'RE DOING, NO MATTER HOW IMPORTANT, YOU HAVE TO DROP IT--
--AND FOLLOW THIS BEACON. DON'T TELL ANYONE, JUST DO IT. YOU'LL KNOW WHEN YOU GET THERE.
SORRY TO BURDEN YOU WITH THIS, JIM, BUT YOU'RE THE ONLY ONE I TRUST. GODSPEED. AND RHODEY...
BEACON DETECTED. COURSE LOCKED.
...AVENGE ME.
IS THAT TONY? IS HE ALL RIGHT?
VHAT DID HE SAY? I CAN'T HEAR A THING.
"HELP, ME, OBI-WAN, YOU'RE MY ONLY HOPE."
VAS?
YOU'VE NEVER SEEN **STAR WARS?** THE GREATEST MOVIE OF ALL TIME? WHAT WERE YOU, LIVING IN A CAVE?
POSSIBLY A BUNKER.
DAMN IT, RHODEY, TELL ME WHAT HE SAID!
I HAVE TO GO.

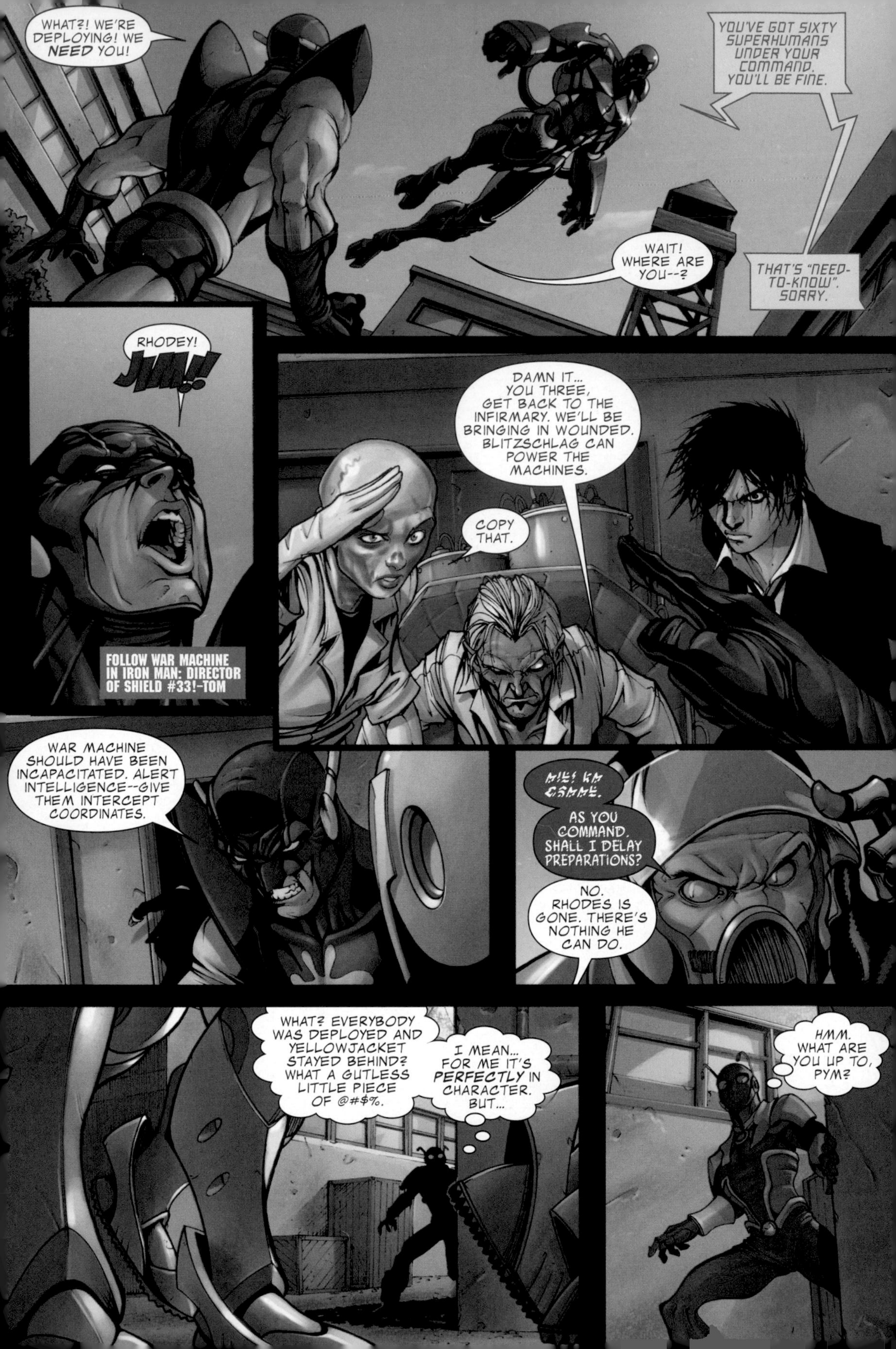

WHAT?! WE'RE DEPLOYING! WE NEED YOU!
YOU'VE GOT SIXTY SUPERHUMANS UNDER YOUR COMMAND. YOU'LL BE FINE.
WAIT! WHERE ARE YOU--?
THAT'S "NEED-TO-KNOW". SORRY.
RHODEY!
JIM!!
FOLLOW WAR MACHINE IN IRON MAN: DIRECTOR OF SHIELD #33!-TOM
DAMN IT... YOU THREE, GET BACK TO THE INFIRMARY. WE'LL BE BRINGING IN WOUNDED. BLITZSCHLAG CAN POWER THE MACHINES.
COPY THAT.
WAR MACHINE SHOULD HAVE BEEN INCAPACITATED. ALERT INTELLIGENCE--GIVE THEM INTERCEPT COORDINATES.
AS YOU COMMAND. SHALL I DELAY PREPARATIONS?
NO. RHODES IS GONE. THERE'S NOTHING HE CAN DO.
WHAT? EVERYBODY WAS DEPLOYED AND YELLOWJACKET STAYED BEHIND? WHAT A GUTLESS LITTLE PIECE OF @#$%.
I MEAN... FOR ME IT'S PERFECTLY IN CHARACTER. BUT...
HMM. WHAT ARE YOU UP TO, PYM?

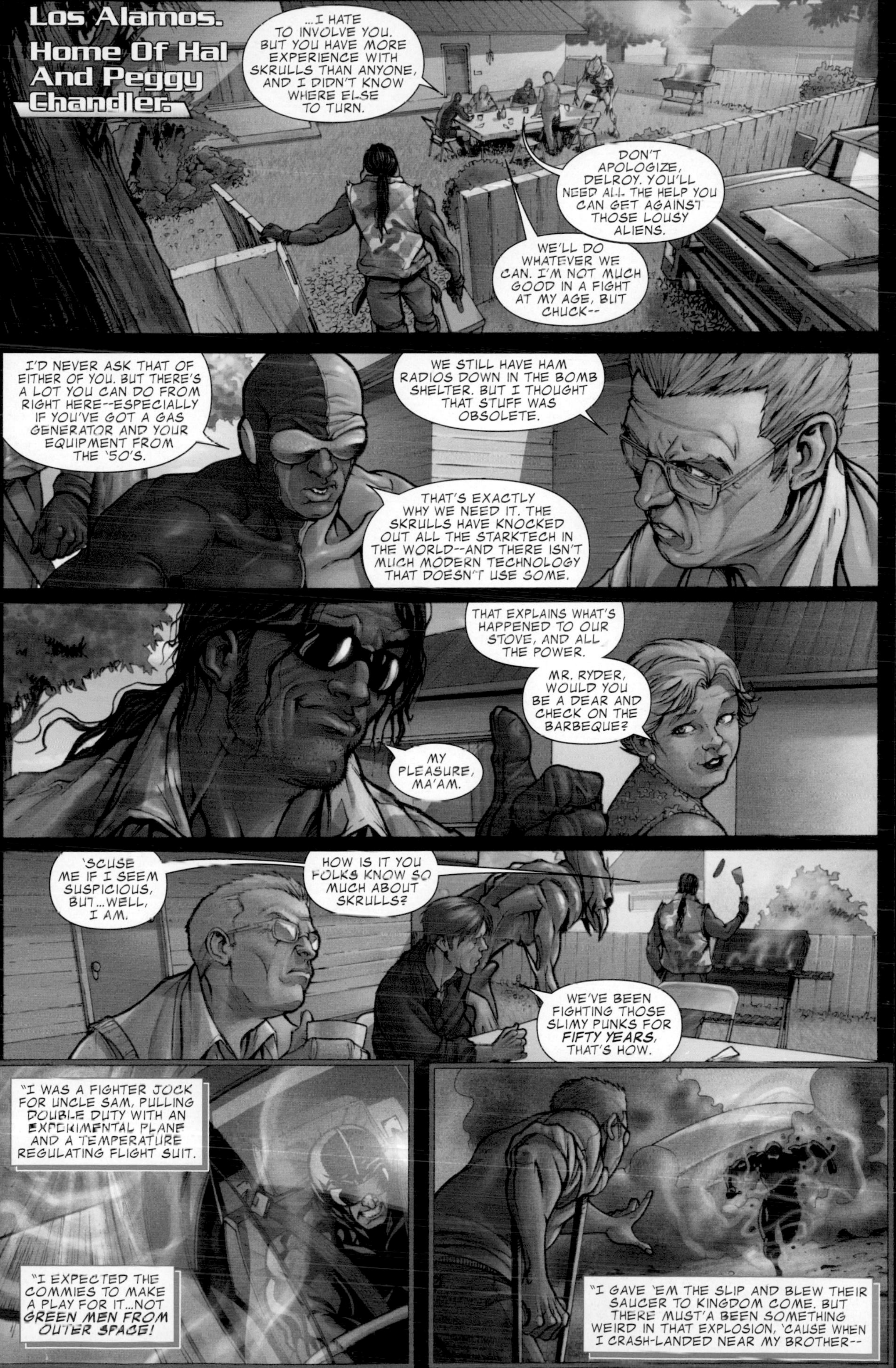
Los Alamos. Home Of Hal And Peggy Chandler.
...I HATE TO INVOLVE YOU. BUT YOU HAVE MORE EXPERIENCE WITH SKRULLS THAN ANYONE, AND I DIDN'T KNOW WHERE ELSE TO TURN.
DON'T APOLOGIZE, DELROY. YOU'LL NEED ALL THE HELP YOU CAN GET AGAINST THOSE LOUSY ALIENS.
WE'LL DO WHATEVER WE CAN. I'M NOT MUCH GOOD IN A FIGHT AT MY AGE, BUT CHUCK--
I'D NEVER ASK THAT OF EITHER OF YOU. BUT THERE'S A LOT YOU CAN DO FROM RIGHT HERE--ESPECIALLY IF YOU'VE GOT A GAS GENERATOR AND YOUR EQUIPMENT FROM THE '50'S.
WE STILL HAVE HAM RADIOS DOWN IN THE BOMB SHELTER. BUT I THOUGHT THAT STUFF WAS OBSOLETE.
THAT'S EXACTLY WHY WE NEED IT. THE SKRULLS HAVE KNOCKED OUT ALL THE STARKTECH IN THE WORLD--AND THERE ISN'T MUCH MODERN TECHNOLOGY THAT DOESN'T USE SOME.
THAT EXPLAINS WHAT'S HAPPENED TO OUR STOVE, AND ALL THE POWER.
MR. RYDER, WOULD YOU BE A DEAR AND CHECK ON THE BARBEQUE?
MY PLEASURE, MA'AM.
'SCUSE ME IF I SEEM SUSPICIOUS, BUT...WELL, I AM.
HOW IS IT YOU FOLKS KNOW SO MUCH ABOUT SKRULLS?
WE'VE BEEN FIGHTING THOSE SLIMY PUNKS FOR FIFTY YEARS, THAT'S HOW.
"I WAS A FIGHTER JOCK FOR UNCLE SAM, PULLING DOUBLE DUTY WITH AN EXPERIMENTAL PLANE AND A TEMPERATURE REGULATING FLIGHT SUIT.
"I EXPECTED THE COMMIES TO MAKE A PLAY FOR IT...NOT GREEN MEN FROM OUTER SPACE!
"I GAVE 'EM THE SLIP AND BLEW THEIR SAUCER TO KINGDOM COME. BUT THERE MUST'A BEEN SOMETHING WEIRD IN THAT EXPLOSION, 'CAUSE WHEN I CRASH-LANDED NEAR MY BROTHER--

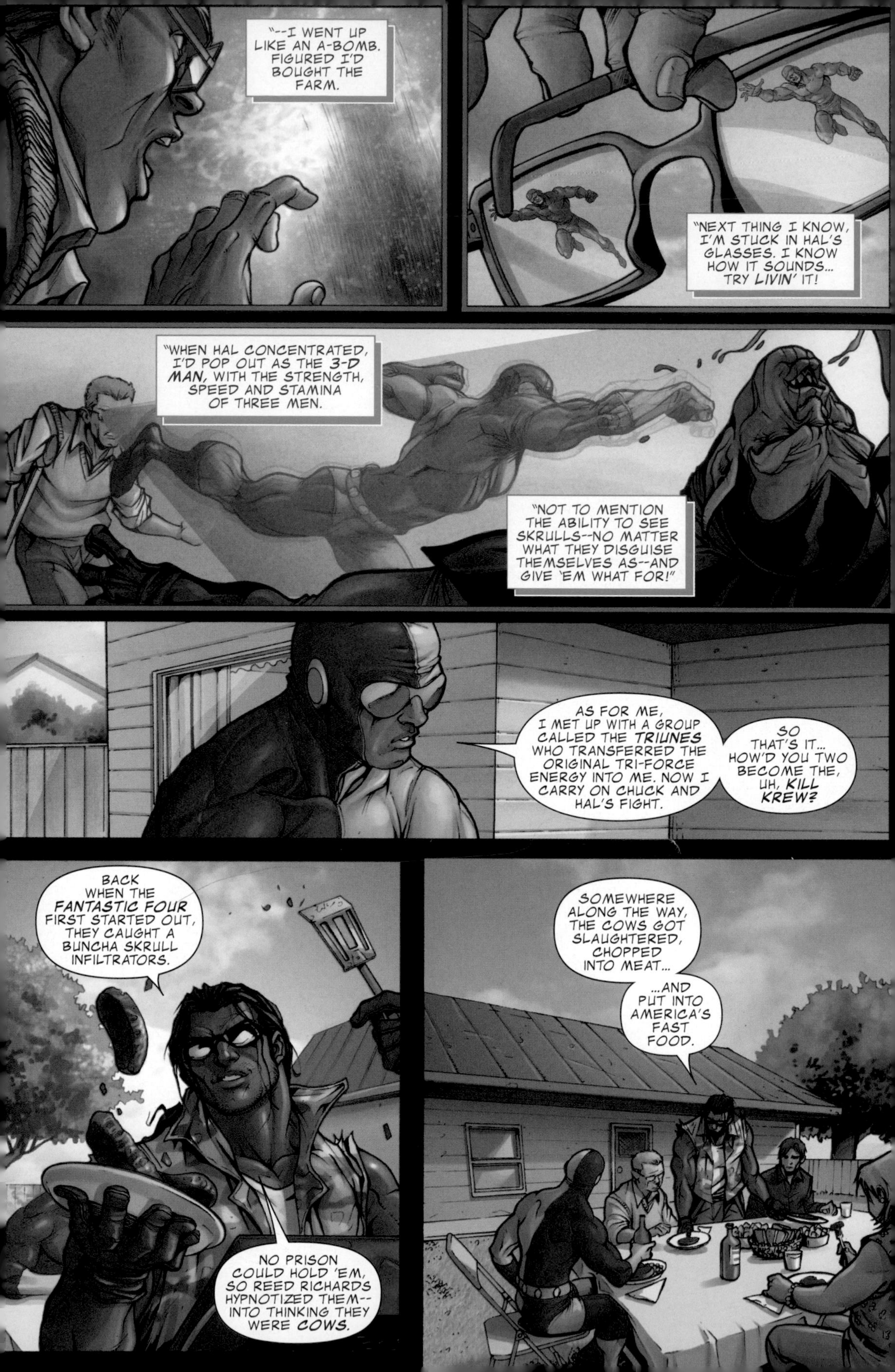
"--I WENT UP LIKE AN A-BOMB. FIGURED I'D BOUGHT THE FARM.
"NEXT THING I KNOW, I'M STUCK IN HAL'S GLASSES. I KNOW HOW IT SOUNDS... TRY LIVIN' IT!
"WHEN HAL CONCENTRATED, I'D POP OUT AS THE 3-D MAN, WITH THE STRENGTH, SPEED AND STAMINA OF THREE MEN.
"NOT TO MENTION THE ABILITY TO SEE SKRULLS--NO MATTER WHAT THEY DISGUISE THEMSELVES AS--AND GIVE 'EM WHAT FOR!"
AS FOR ME, I MET UP WITH A GROUP CALLED THE TRIUNES WHO TRANSFERRED THE ORIGINAL TRI-FORCE ENERGY INTO ME. NOW I CARRY ON CHUCK AND HAL'S FIGHT.
SO THAT'S IT... HOW'D YOU TWO BECOME THE, UH, KILL KREW?
BACK WHEN THE FANTASTIC FOUR FIRST STARTED OUT, THEY CAUGHT A BUNCHA SKRULL INFILTRATORS.
NO PRISON COULD HOLD 'EM, SO REED RICHARDS HYPNOTIZED THEM--INTO THINKING THEY WERE COWS.
SOMEWHERE ALONG THE WAY, THE COWS GOT SLAUGHTERED, CHOPPED INTO MEAT...
...AND PUT INTO AMERICA'S FAST FOOD.

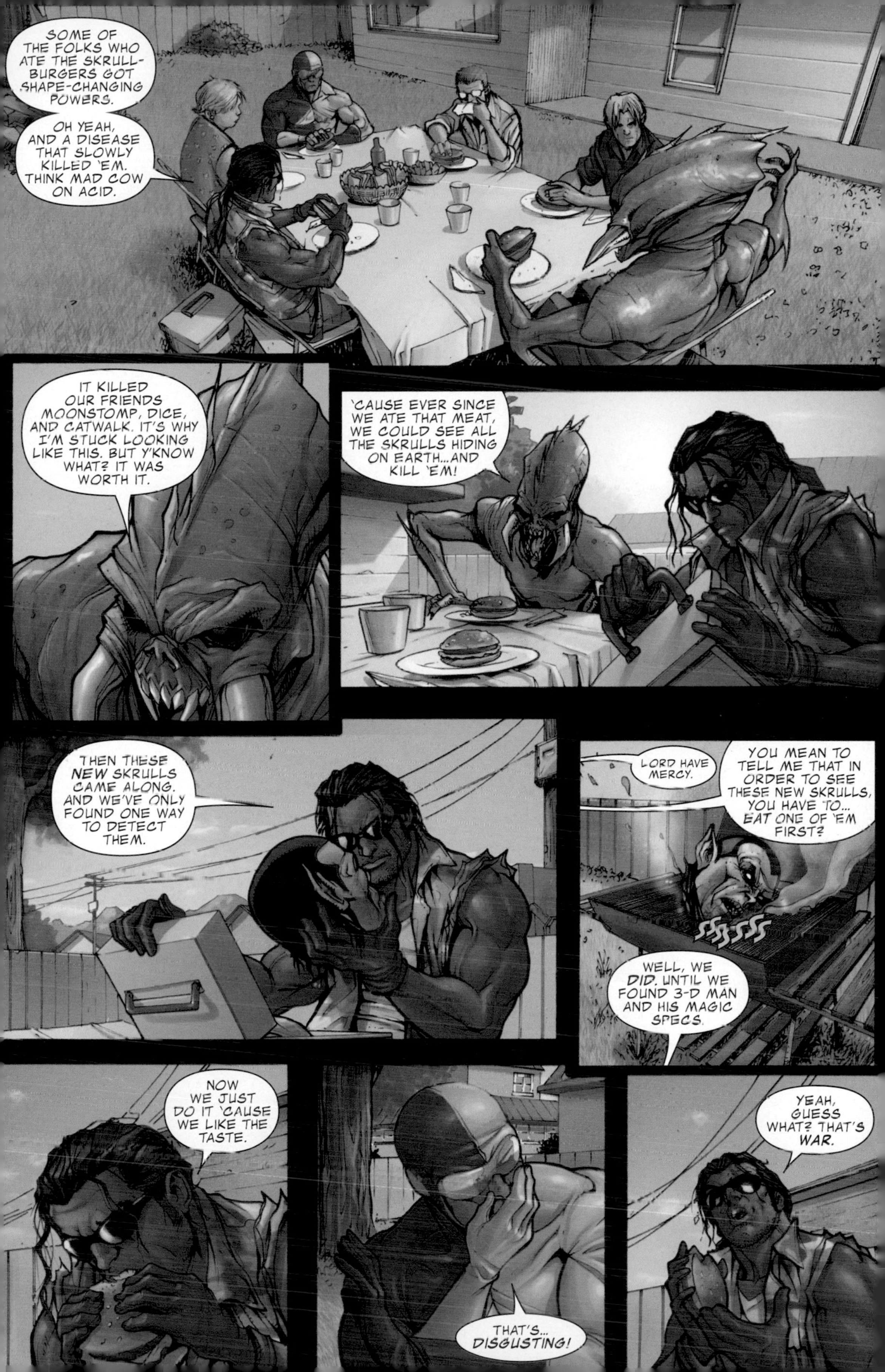
SOME OF THE FOLKS WHO ATE THE SKRULL-BURGERS GOT SHAPE-CHANGING POWERS.
OH YEAH, AND A DISEASE THAT SLOWLY KILLED 'EM. THINK MAD COW ON ACID.
IT KILLED OUR FRIENDS MOONSTOMP, DICE, AND CATWALK. IT'S WHY I'M STUCK LOOKING LIKE THIS. BUT Y'KNOW WHAT? IT WAS WORTH IT.
'CAUSE EVER SINCE WE ATE THAT MEAT, WE COULD SEE ALL THE SKRULLS HIDING ON EARTH...AND KILL 'EM!
THEN THESE NEW SKRULLS CAME ALONG. AND WE'VE ONLY FOUND ONE WAY TO DETECT THEM.
LORD HAVE MERCY.
YOU MEAN TO TELL ME THAT IN ORDER TO SEE THESE NEW SKRULLS, YOU HAVE TO... EAT ONE OF 'EM FIRST?
SSSSS
WELL, WE DID. UNTIL WE FOUND 3-D MAN AND HIS MAGIC SPECS.
NOW WE JUST DO IT 'CAUSE WE LIKE THE TASTE.
THAT'S... DISGUSTING!
YEAH, GUESS WHAT? THAT'S WAR.

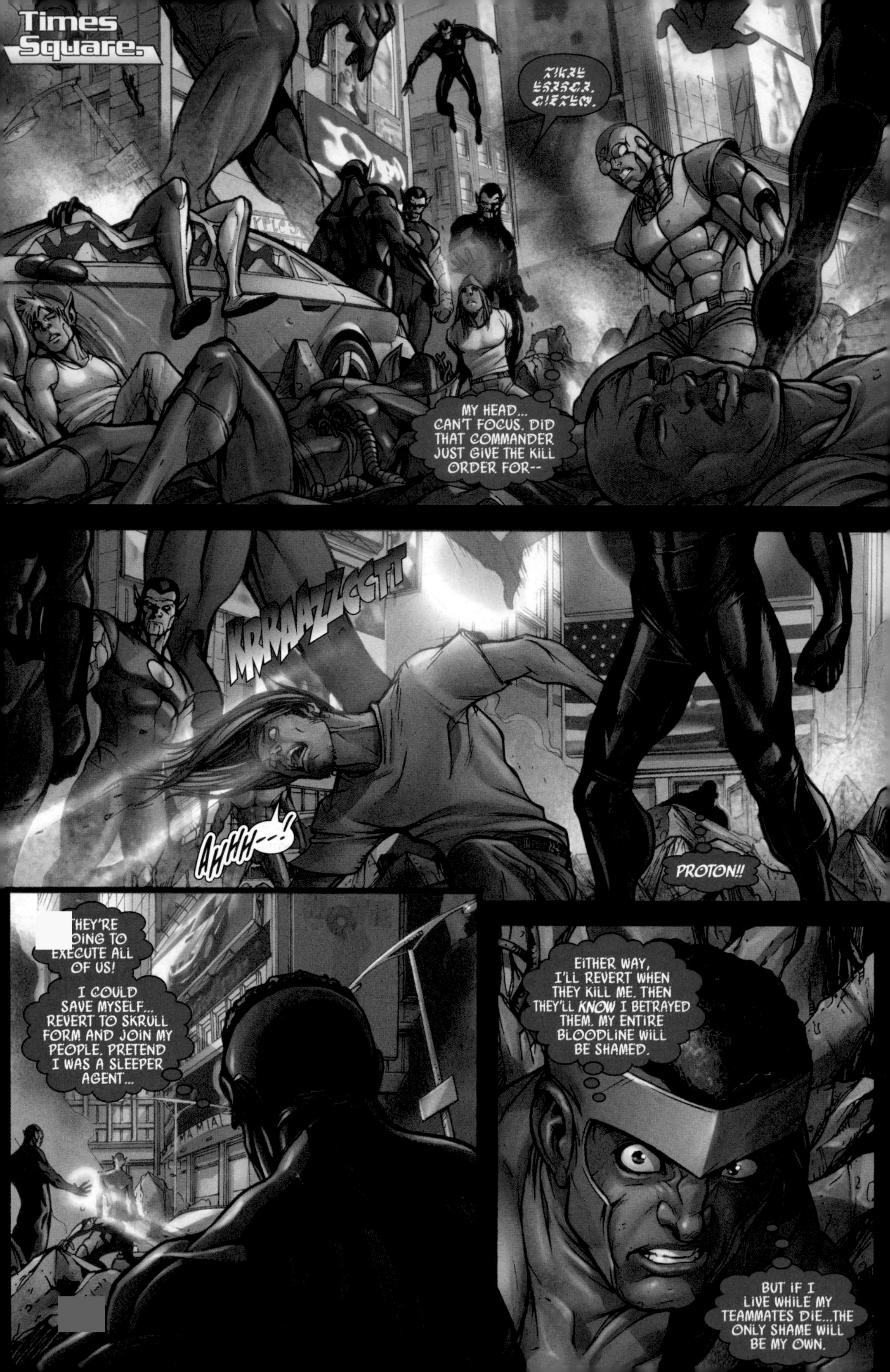
Times Square.
MY HEAD... CAN'T FOCUS. DID THAT COMMANDER JUST GIVE THE KILL ORDER FOR--
KRRAAZZCCTT
AHHH--!
PROTON!!
THEY'RE OING TO EXECUTE ALL OF US!
I COULD SAVE MYSELF... REVERT TO SKRULL FORM AND JOIN MY PEOPLE. PRETEND I WAS A SLEEPER AGENT...
EITHER WAY, I'LL REVERT WHEN THEY KILL ME. THEN THEY'LL KNOW I BETRAYED THEM. MY ENTIRE BLOODLINE WILL BE SHAMED.
BUT IF I LIVE WHILE MY TEAMMATES DIE...THE ONLY SHAME WILL BE MY OWN.

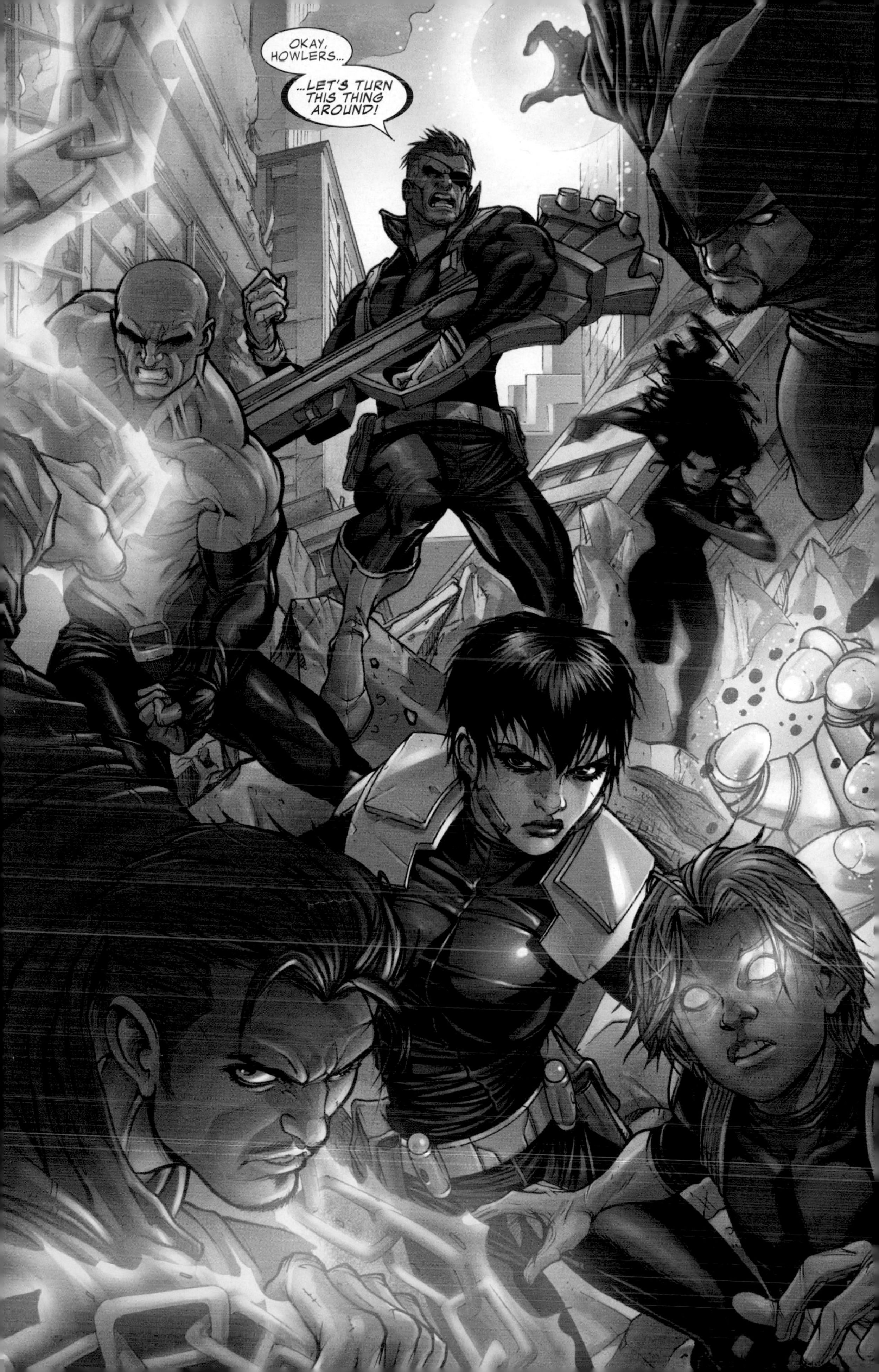
OKAY, HOWLERS...
...LET'S TURN THIS THING AROUND!

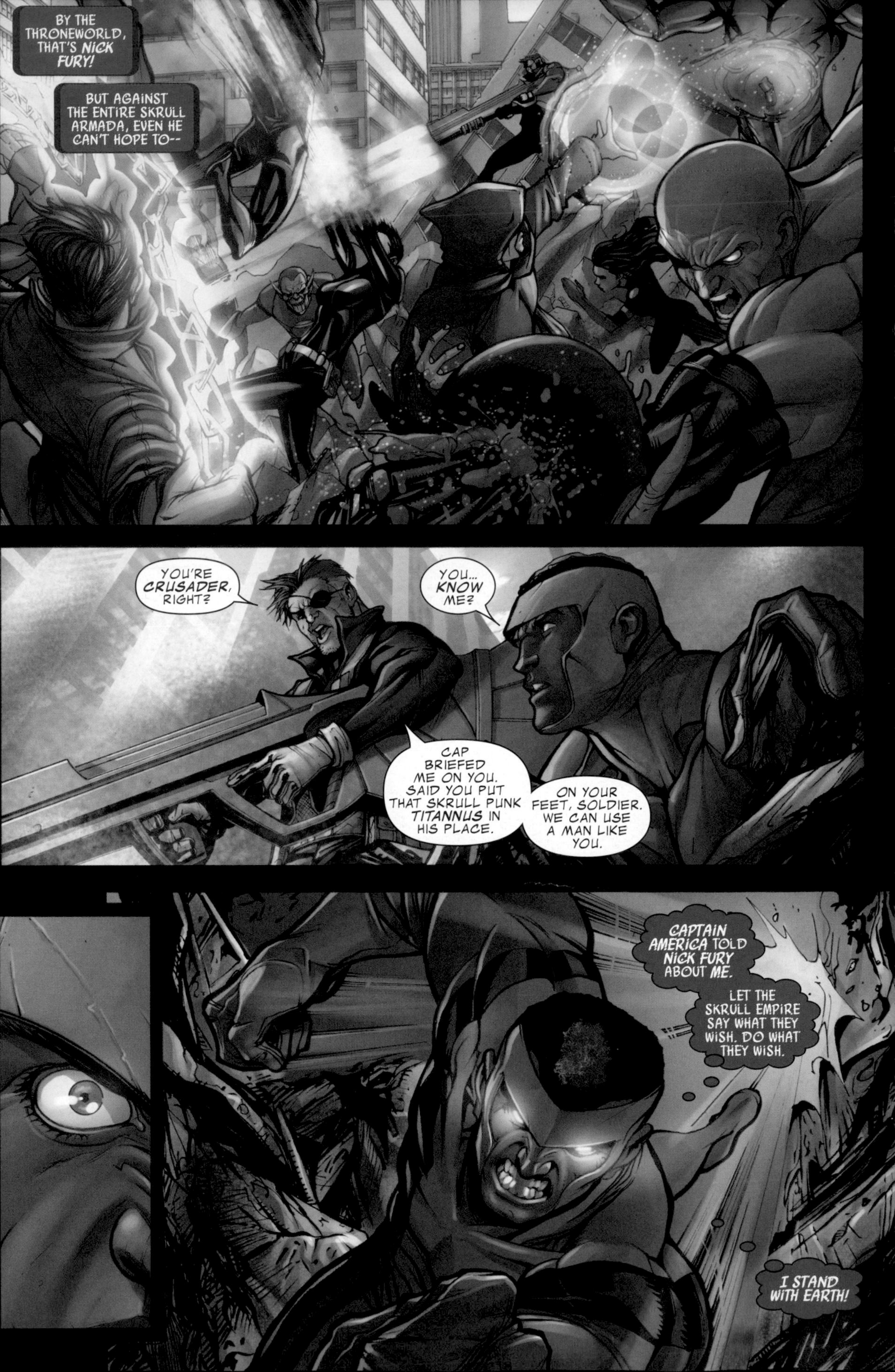
BY THE THRONEWORLD, THAT'S NICK FURY!
BUT AGAINST THE ENTIRE SKRULL ARMADA, EVEN HE CAN'T HOPE TO--
YOU'RE CRUSADER, RIGHT?
YOU... KNOW ME?
CAP BRIEFED ME ON YOU. SAID YOU PUT THAT SKRULL PUNK TITANNUS IN HIS PLACE.
ON YOUR FEET, SOLDIER. WE CAN USE A MAN LIKE YOU.
CAPTAIN AMERICA TOLD NICK FURY ABOUT ME.
LET THE SKRULL EMPIRE SAY WHAT THEY WISH. DO WHAT THEY WISH.
I STAND WITH EARTH!

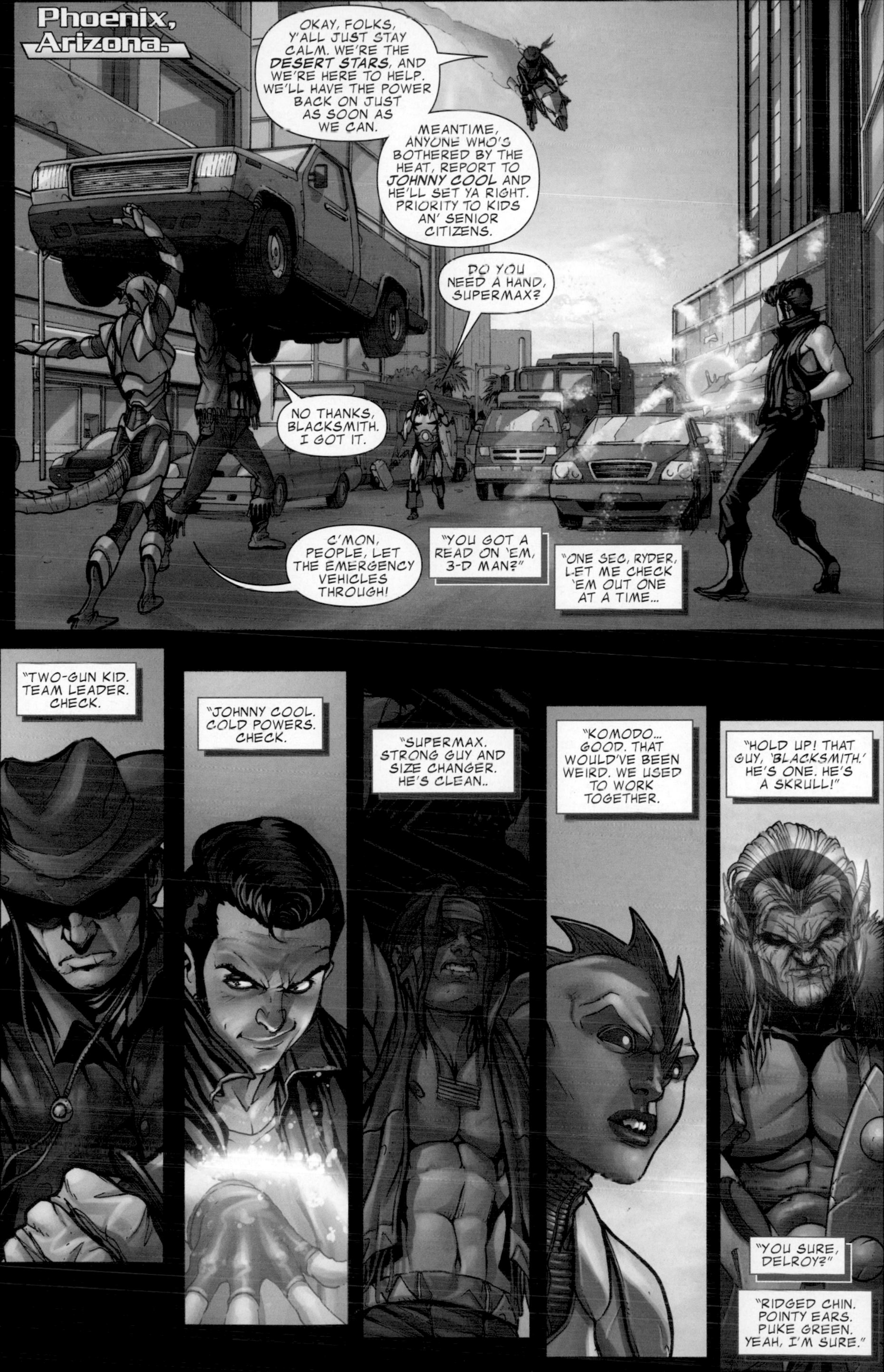
Phoenix, Arizona.
OKAY, FOLKS, Y'ALL JUST STAY CALM. WE'RE THE DESERT STARS, AND WE'RE HERE TO HELP. WE'LL HAVE THE POWER BACK ON JUST AS SOON AS WE CAN.
MEANTIME, ANYONE WHO'S BOTHERED BY THE HEAT, REPORT TO JOHNNY COOL AND HE'LL SET YA RIGHT. PRIORITY TO KIDS AN' SENIOR CITIZENS.
DO YOU NEED A HAND, SUPERMAX?
NO THANKS, BLACKSMITH. I GOT IT.
C'MON, PEOPLE, LET THE EMERGENCY VEHICLES THROUGH!
"YOU GOT A READ ON 'EM, 3-D MAN?"
"ONE SEC, RYDER, LET ME CHECK 'EM OUT ONE AT A TIME...
"TWO-GUN KID. TEAM LEADER. CHECK.
"JOHNNY COOL. COLD POWERS. CHECK.
"SUPERMAX. STRONG GUY AND SIZE CHANGER. HE'S CLEAN..
"KOMODO... GOOD. THAT WOULD'VE BEEN WEIRD. WE USED TO WORK TOGETHER.
"HOLD UP! THAT GUY, 'BLACKSMITH.' HE'S ONE. HE'S A SKRULL!"
"YOU SURE, DELROY?"
"RIDGED CHIN. POINTY EARS. PUKE GREEN. YEAH, I'M SURE."

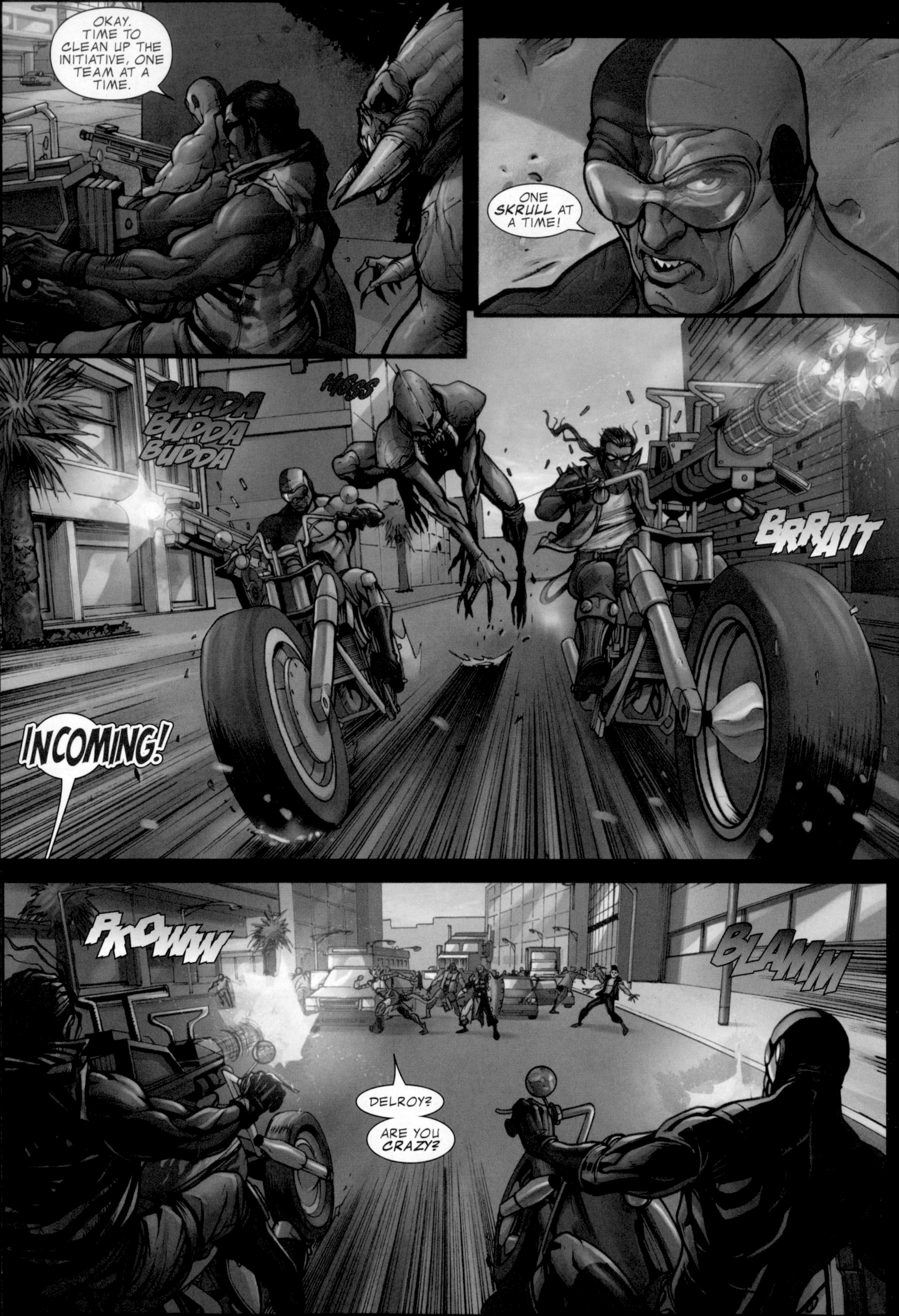
OKAY. TIME TO CLEAN UP THE INITIATIVE, ONE TEAM AT A TIME.
ONE SKRULL AT A TIME!
BUDDA BUDDA BUDDA
BRRATT
INCOMING!
PKOWW
BLAMM
DELROY?
ARE YOU CRAZY?

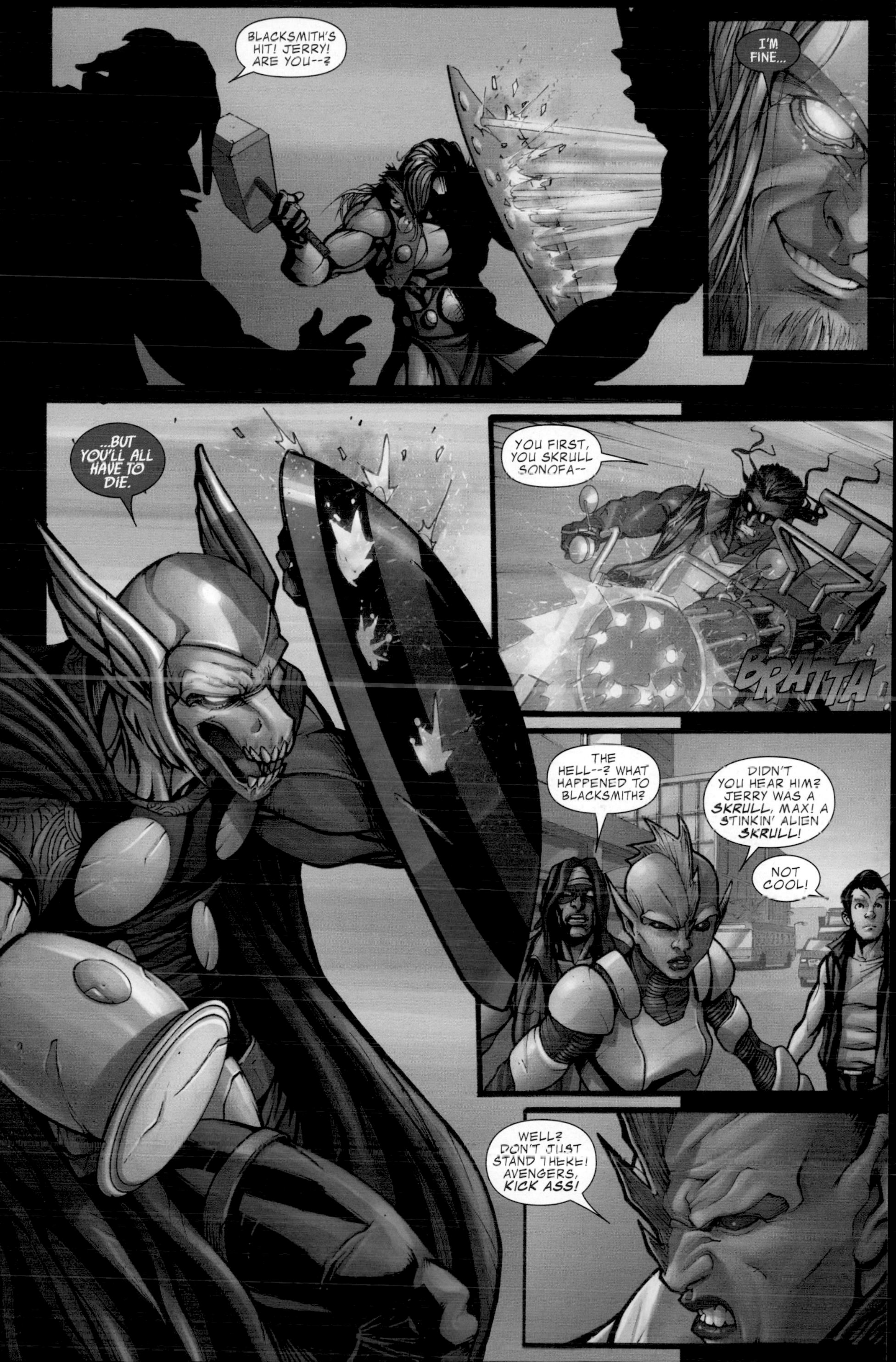

BLACKSMITH'S HIT! JERRY! ARE YOU--?
I'M FINE...
...BUT YOU'LL ALL HAVE TO DIE.
YOU FIRST, YOU SKRULL SONOFA--
BRATTA
THE HELL--? WHAT HAPPENED TO BLACKSMITH?
DIDN'T YOU HEAR HIM? JERRY WAS A SKRULL, MAX! A STINKIN' ALIEN SKRULL!
NOT COOL!
WELL? DON'T JUST STAND THERE! AVENGERS, KICK ASS!

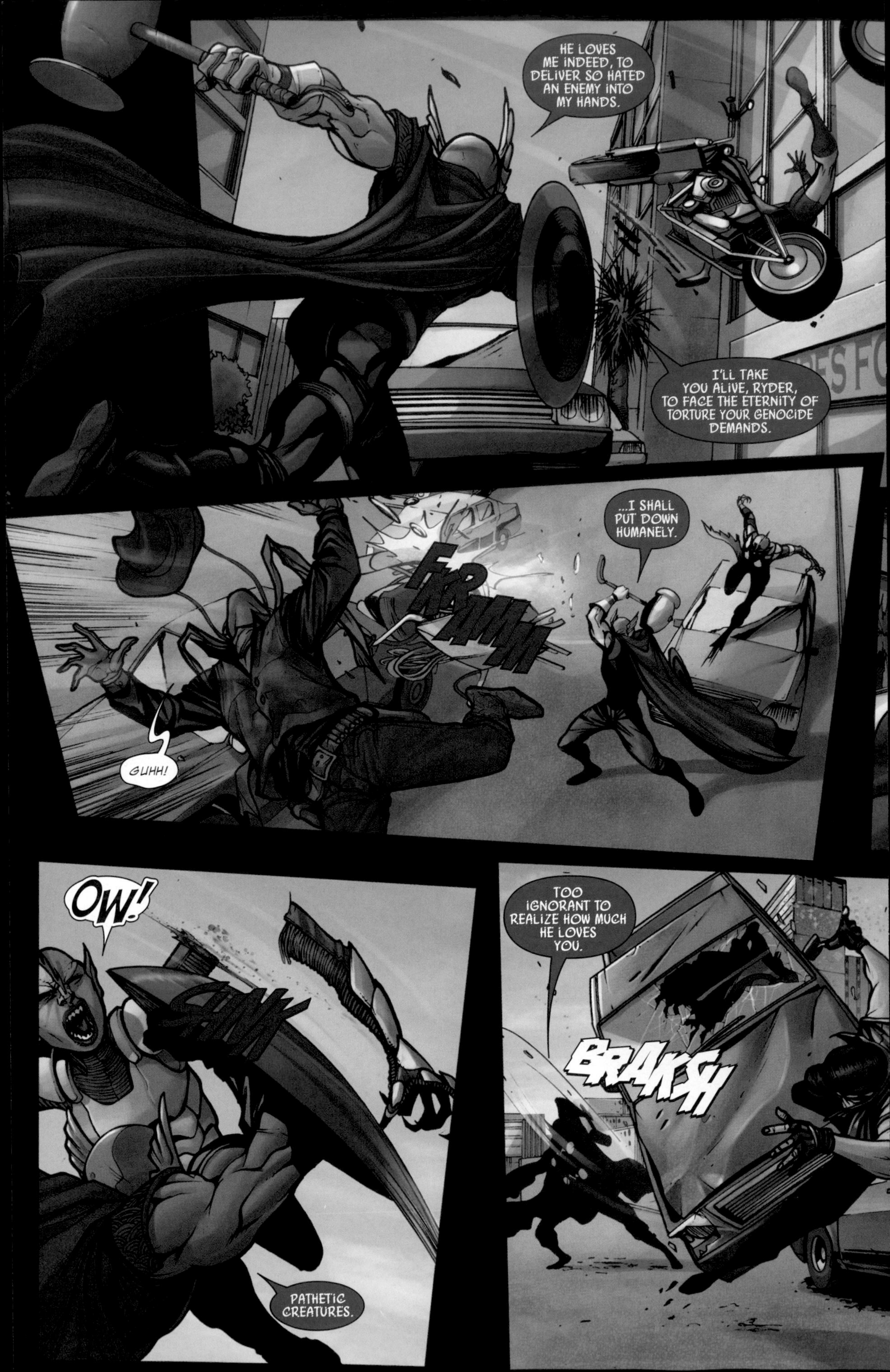
HE LOVES ME INDEED, TO DELIVER SO HATED AN ENEMY INTO MY HANDS.
I'LL TAKE YOU ALIVE, RYDER, TO FACE THE ETERNITY OF TORTURE YOUR GENOCIDE DEMANDS.
FRAMMM
...I SHALL PUT DOWN HUMANELY.
GUHH!
OW!
PATHETIC CREATURES.
TOO IGNORANT TO REALIZE HOW MUCH HE LOVES YOU.
BRAKSH

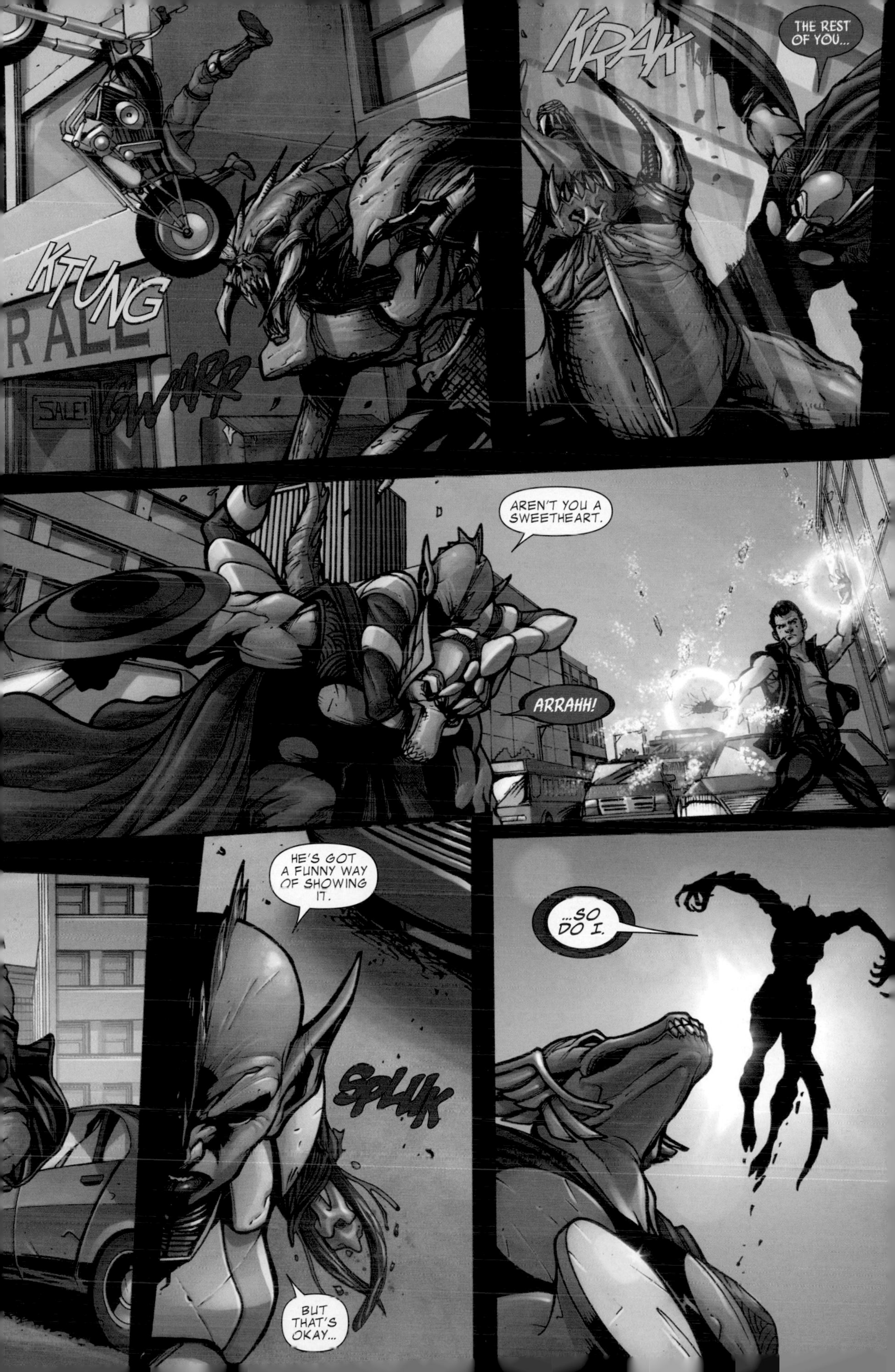
KTUNG
GWARR
SALE!
KRAK
THE REST OF YOU...
AREN'T YOU A SWEETHEART.
ARRAHH!
HE'S GOT A FUNNY WAY OF SHOWING IT.
SPLUK
BUT THAT'S OKAY...
...SO DO I.

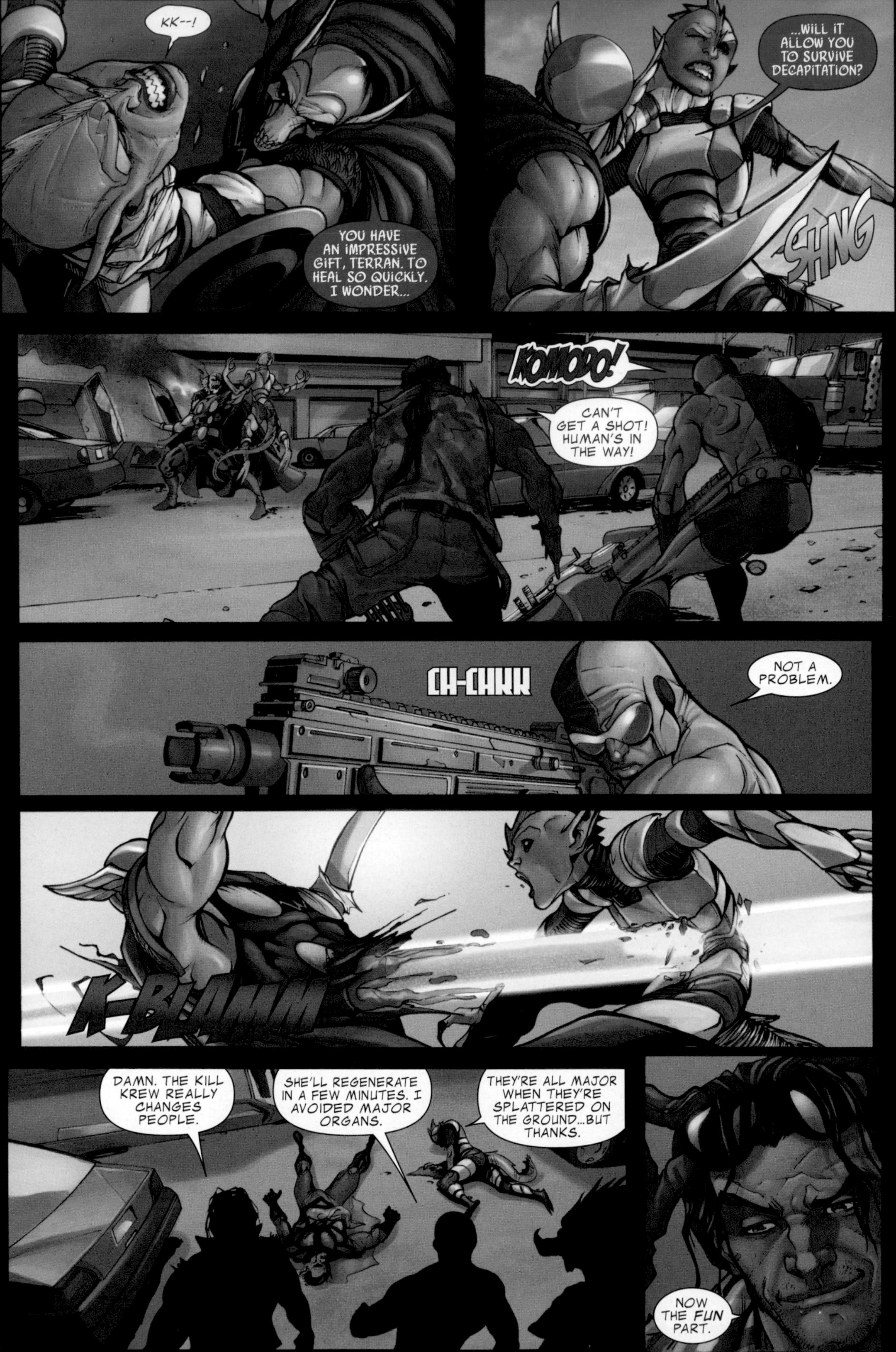
KK--!
YOU HAVE AN IMPRESSIVE GIFT, TERRAN. TO HEAL SO QUICKLY. I WONDER...
...WILL IT ALLOW YOU TO SURVIVE DECAPITATION?
SHNG
KOMODO!
CAN'T GET A SHOT! HUMAN'S IN THE WAY!
CH-CHKK
NOT A PROBLEM.
K-BLAMM
DAMN. THE KILL KREW REALLY CHANGES PEOPLE.
SHE'LL REGENERATE IN A FEW MINUTES. I AVOIDED MAJOR ORGANS.
THEY'RE ALL MAJOR WHEN THEY'RE SPLATTERED ON THE GROUND...BUT THANKS.
NOW THE FUN PART.

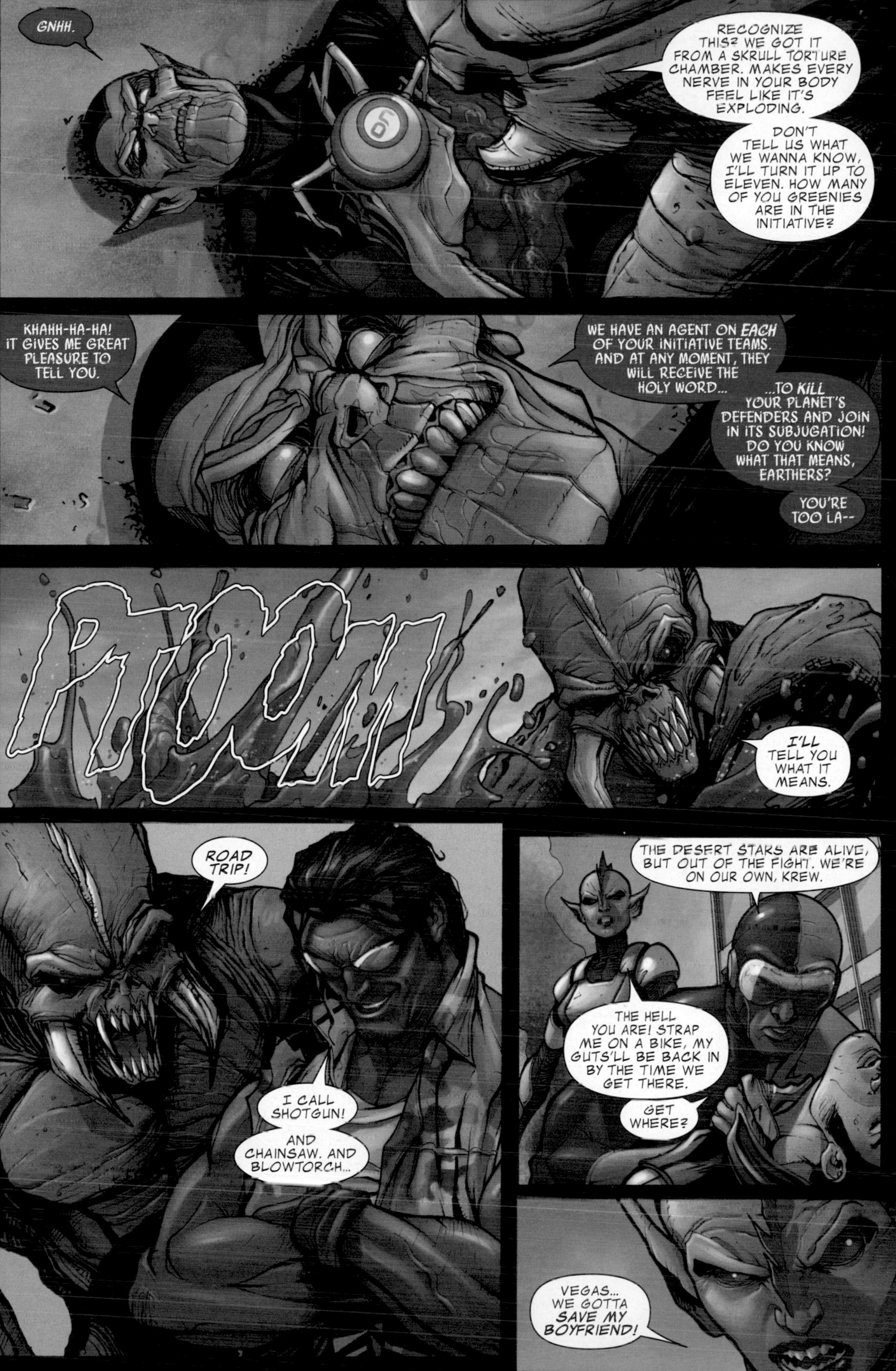
GNHH.
RECOGNIZE THIS? WE GOT IT FROM A SKRULL TORTURE CHAMBER. MAKES EVERY NERVE IN YOUR BODY FEEL LIKE IT'S EXPLODING.
DON'T TELL US WHAT WE WANNA KNOW, I'LL TURN IT UP TO ELEVEN. HOW MANY OF YOU GREENIES ARE IN THE INITIATIVE?
KHAHH-HA-HA! IT GIVES ME GREAT PLEASURE TO TELL YOU.
WE HAVE AN AGENT ON EACH OF YOUR INITIATIVE TEAMS. AND AT ANY MOMENT, THEY WILL RECEIVE THE HOLY WORD...
...TO KILL YOUR PLANET'S DEFENDERS AND JOIN IN ITS SUBJUGATION! DO YOU KNOW WHAT THAT MEANS, EARTHERS?
YOU'RE TOO LA--
BLOOM
I'LL TELL YOU WHAT IT MEANS.
ROAD TRIP!
I CALL SHOTGUN!
AND CHAINSAW. AND BLOWTORCH...
THE DESERT STARS ARE ALIVE, BUT OUT OF THE FIGHT. WE'RE ON OUR OWN, KREW.
THE HELL YOU ARE! STRAP ME ON A BIKE, MY GUTS'LL BE BACK IN BY THE TIME WE GET THERE.
GET WHERE?
VEGAS... WE GOTTA SAVE MY BOYFRIEND!

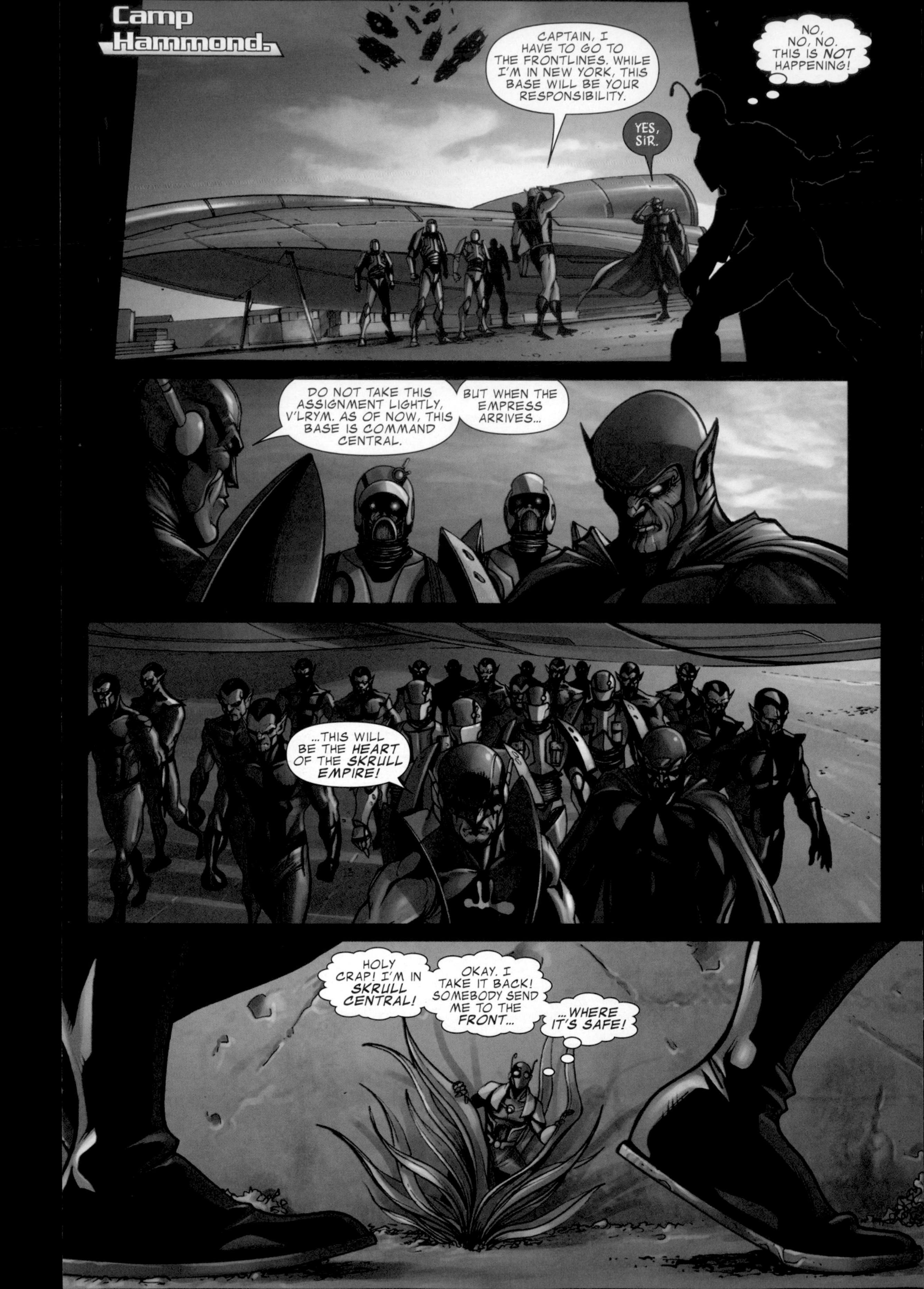
Camp Hammond.
CAPTAIN, I HAVE TO GO TO THE FRONTLINES. WHILE I'M IN NEW YORK, THIS BASE WILL BE YOUR RESPONSIBILITY.
YES, SIR.
NO, NO, NO. THIS IS NOT HAPPENING!
DO NOT TAKE THIS ASSIGNMENT LIGHTLY, V'LRYM. AS OF NOW, THIS BASE IS COMMAND CENTRAL.
BUT WHEN THE EMPRESS ARRIVES...
...THIS WILL BE THE HEART OF THE SKRULL EMPIRE!
HOLY CRAP! I'M IN SKRULL CENTRAL!
OKAY. I TAKE IT BACK! SOMEBODY SEND ME TO THE FRONT...
...WHERE IT'S SAFE!

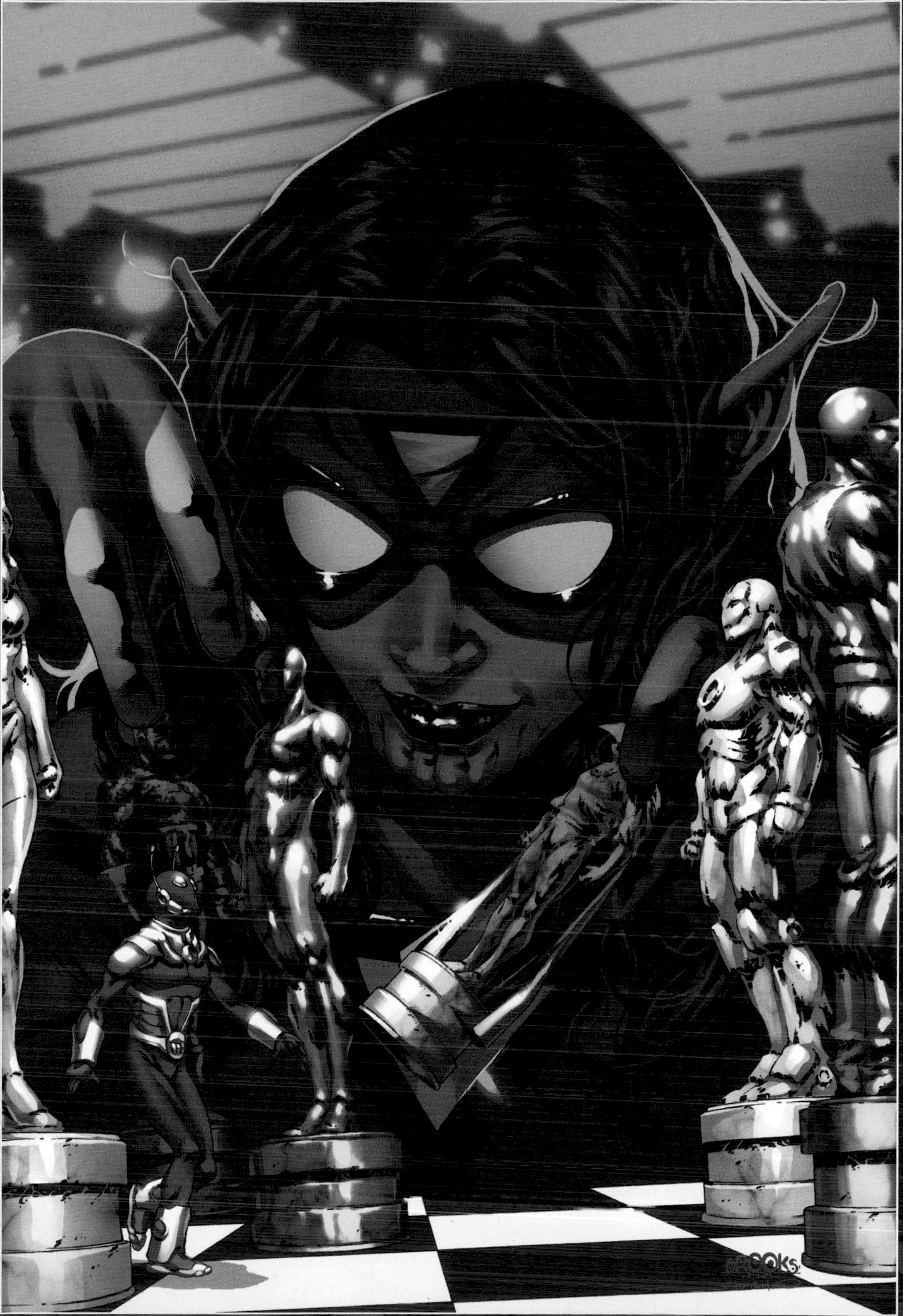

#17

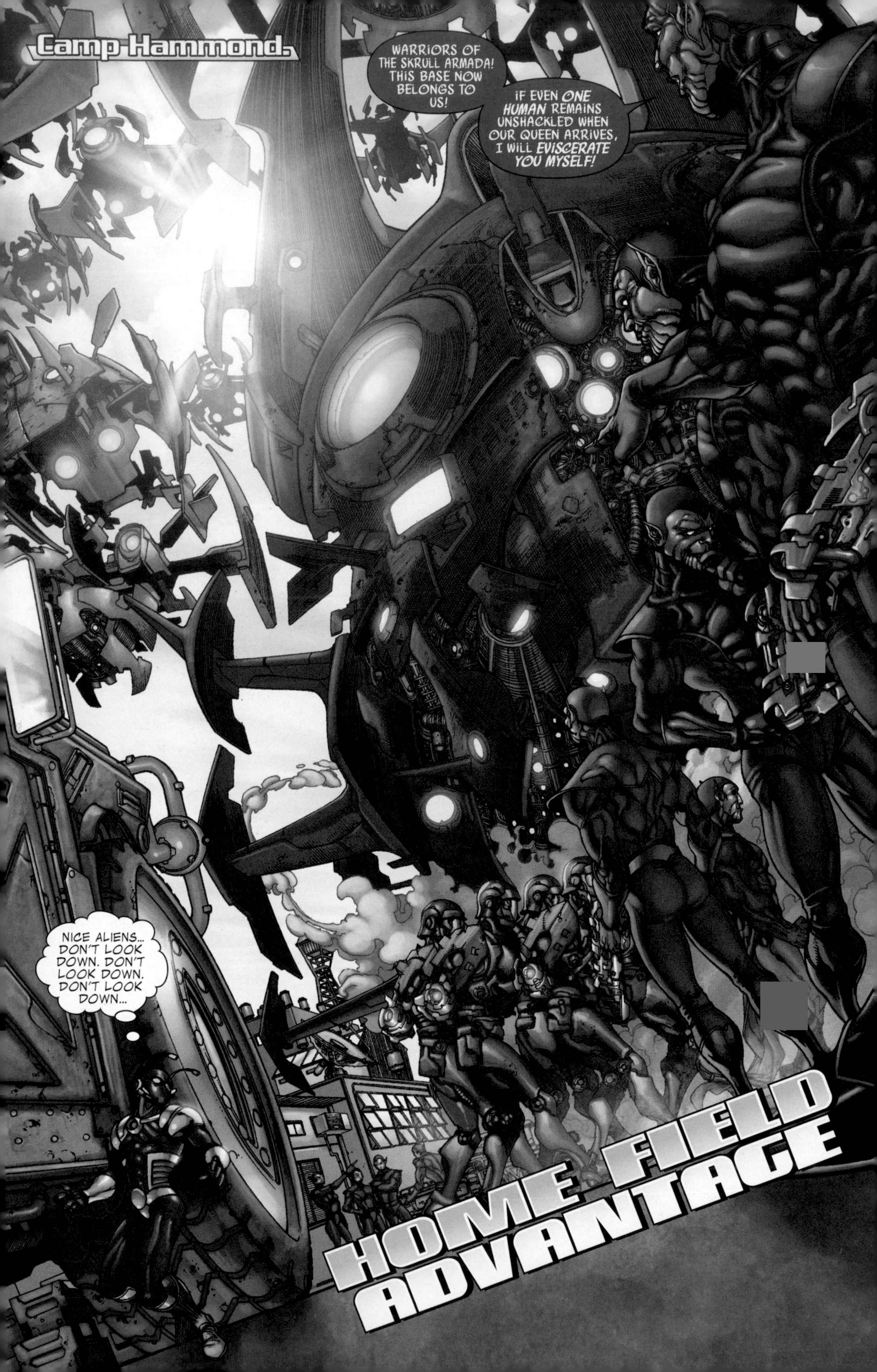
Camp Hammond.
WARRIORS OF THE SKRULL ARMADA! THIS BASE NOW BELONGS TO US!
IF EVEN ONE HUMAN REMAINS UNSHACKLED WHEN OUR QUEEN ARRIVES, I WILL EVISCERATE YOU MYSELF!
NICE ALIENS... DON'T LOOK DOWN. DON'T LOOK DOWN. DON'T LOOK DOWN...
HOME FIELD ADVANTAGE

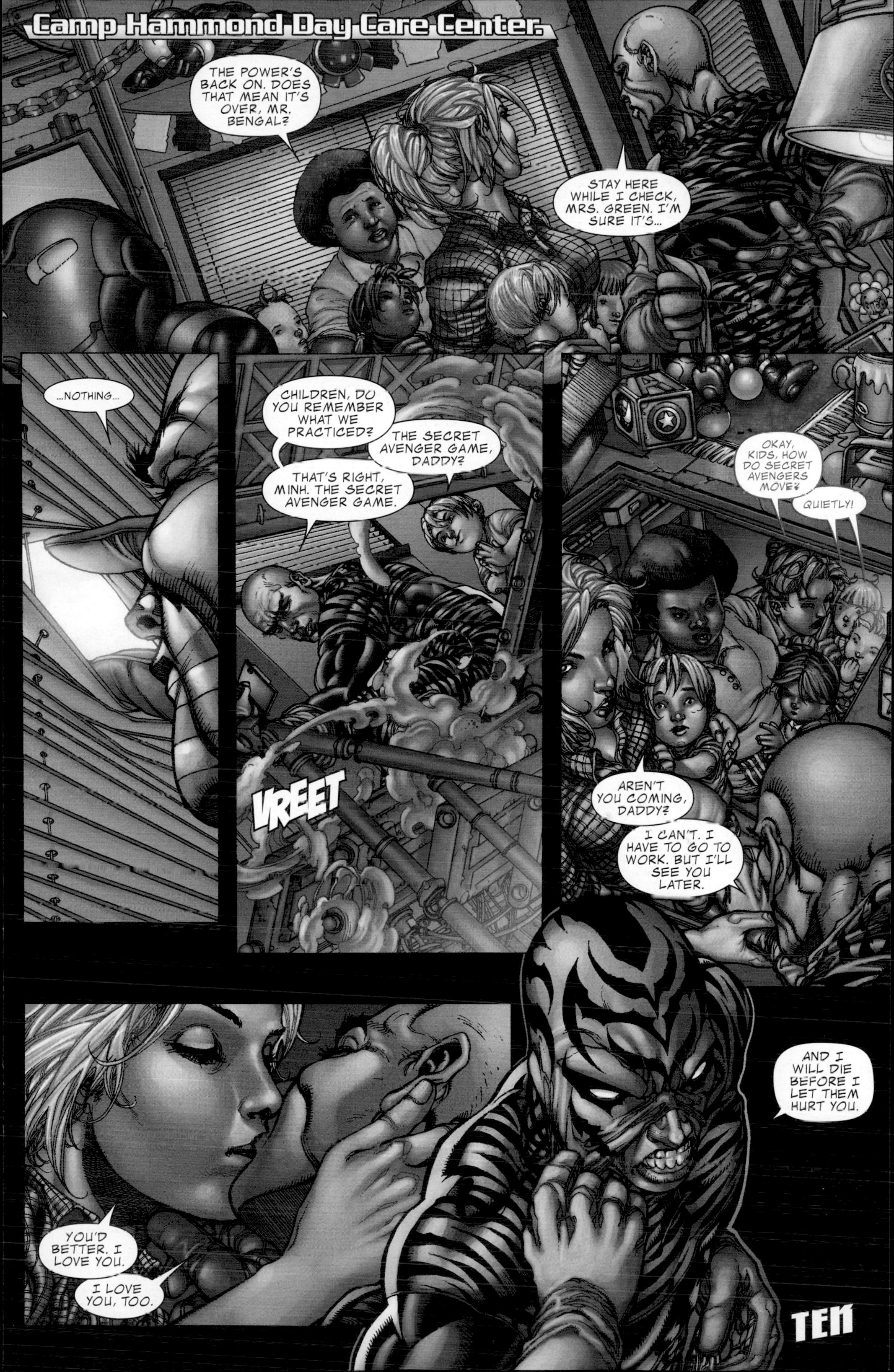
Camp Hammond Day Care Center.
THE POWER'S BACK ON. DOES THAT MEAN IT'S OVER, MR. BENGAL?
STAY HERE WHILE I CHECK, MRS. GREEN. I'M SURE IT'S...
...NOTHING...
CHILDREN, DO YOU REMEMBER WHAT WE PRACTICED?
THE SECRET AVENGER GAME, DADDY?
THAT'S RIGHT, MINH. THE SECRET AVENGER GAME.
VREET
OKAY, KIDS, HOW DO SECRET AVENGERS MOVE?
QUIETLY!
AREN'T YOU COMING, DADDY?
I CAN'T. I HAVE TO GO TO WORK. BUT I'LL SEE YOU LATER.
YOU'D BETTER. I LOVE YOU.
I LOVE YOU, TOO.
AND I WILL DIE BEFORE I LET THEM HURT YOU.
TEN

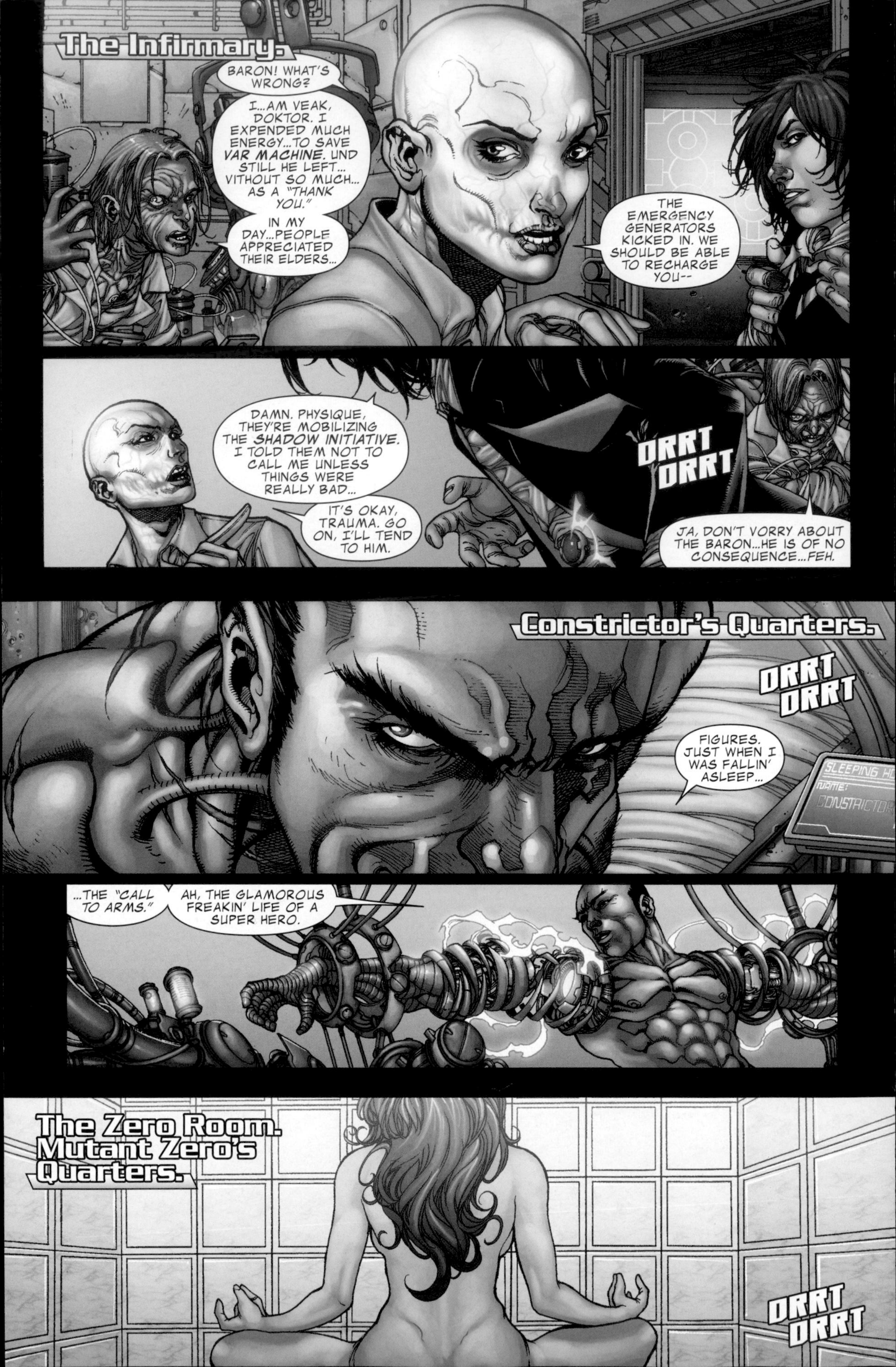
The Infirmary.
BARON! WHAT'S WRONG?
I...AM VEAK, DOKTOR. I EXPENDED MUCH ENERGY...TO SAVE VAR MACHINE. UND STILL HE LEFT... VITHOUT SO MUCH... AS A "THANK YOU."
IN MY DAY...PEOPLE APPRECIATED THEIR ELDERS...
THE EMERGENCY GENERATORS KICKED IN. WE SHOULD BE ABLE TO RECHARGE YOU--
DAMN. PHYSIQUE, THEY'RE MOBILIZING THE SHADOW INITIATIVE. I TOLD THEM NOT TO CALL ME UNLESS THINGS WERE REALLY BAD...
DRRT DRRT
IT'S OKAY, TRAUMA. GO ON, I'LL TEND TO HIM.
JA, DON'T VORRY ABOUT THE BARON...HE IS OF NO CONSEQUENCE...FEH.
Constrictor's Quarters.
DRRT DRRT
FIGURES. JUST WHEN I WAS FALLIN' ASLEEP...
SLEEPING H
NAME:
CONSTRICTOR
...THE "CALL TO ARMS."
AH, THE GLAMOROUS FREAKIN' LIFE OF A SUPER HERO.
The Zero Room. Mutant Zero's Quarters.
DRRT DRRT

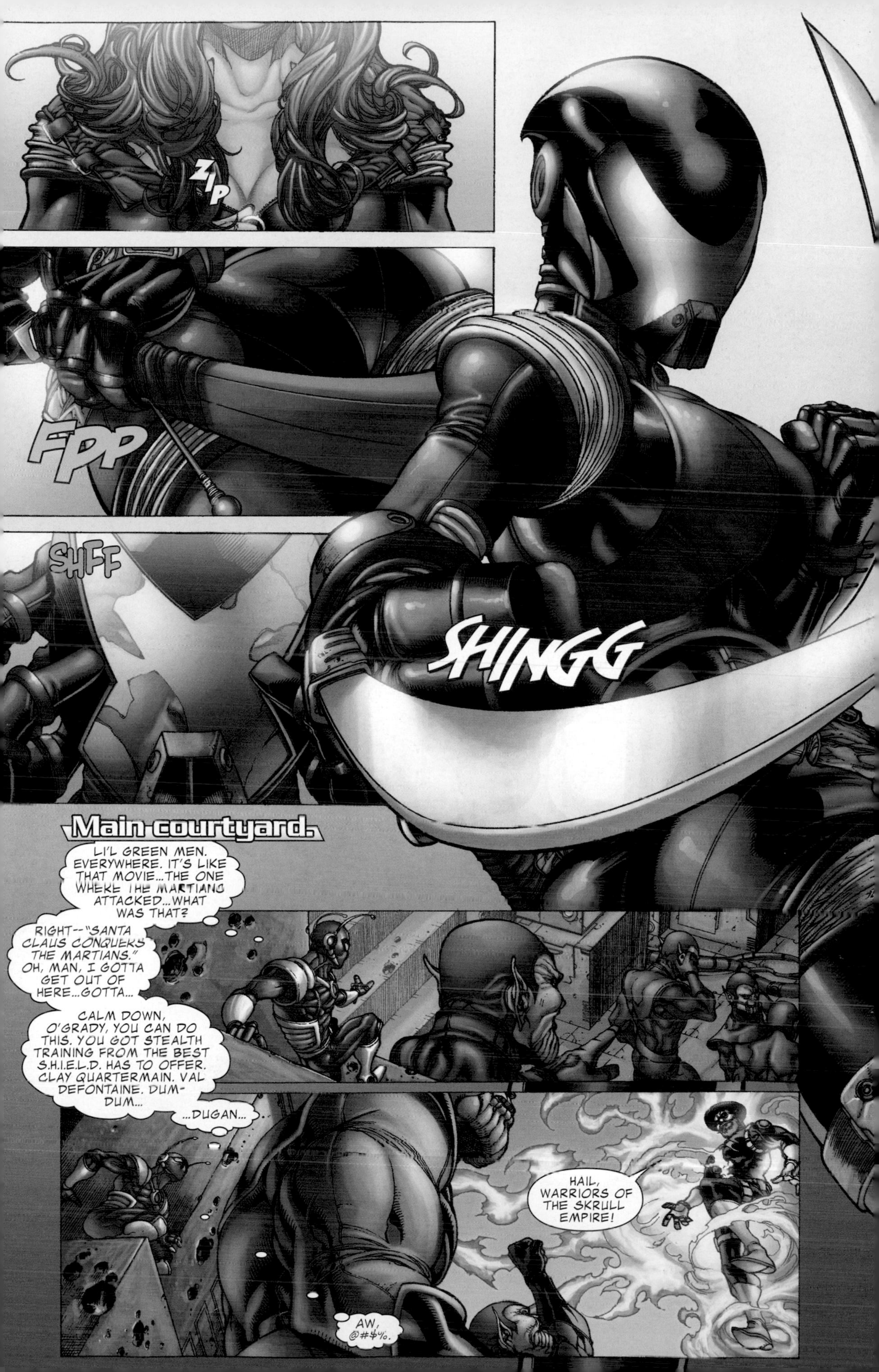
ZIP
FPP
SHFF
SHINGG
Main courtyard.
LI'L GREEN MEN. EVERYWHERE. IT'S LIKE THAT MOVIE...THE ONE WHERE THE MARTIANS ATTACKED...WHAT WAS THAT?
RIGHT--"SANTA CLAUS CONQUERS THE MARTIANS." OH, MAN, I GOTTA GET OUT OF HERE...GOTTA...
CALM DOWN, O'GRADY, YOU CAN DO THIS. YOU GOT STEALTH TRAINING FROM THE BEST S.H.I.E.L.D. HAS TO OFFER. CLAY QUARTERMAIN. VAL DEFONTAINE. DUM-DUM...
...DUGAN...
HAIL, WARRIORS OF THE SKRULL EMPIRE!
AW, @#$%.

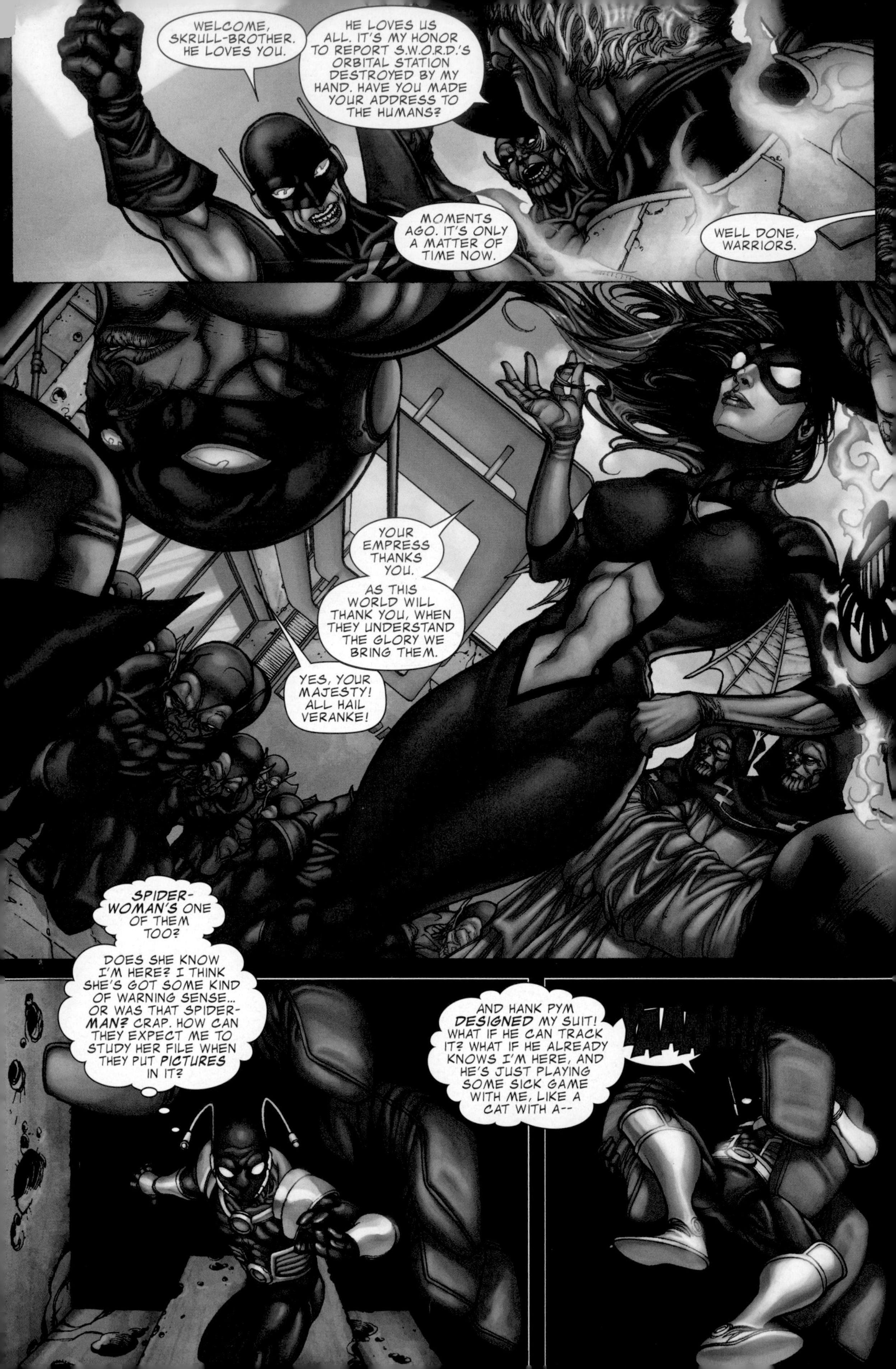
WELCOME, SKRULL-BROTHER. HE LOVES YOU.
HE LOVES US ALL. IT'S MY HONOR TO REPORT S.W.O.R.D.'S ORBITAL STATION DESTROYED BY MY HAND. HAVE YOU MADE YOUR ADDRESS TO THE HUMANS?
MOMENTS AGO. IT'S ONLY A MATTER OF TIME NOW.
WELL DONE, WARRIORS.
YOUR EMPRESS THANKS YOU.
AS THIS WORLD WILL THANK YOU, WHEN THEY UNDERSTAND THE GLORY WE BRING THEM.
YES, YOUR MAJESTY! ALL HAIL VERANKE!
SPIDER-WOMAN'S ONE OF THEM TOO?
DOES SHE KNOW I'M HERE? I THINK SHE'S GOT SOME KIND OF WARNING SENSE... OR WAS THAT SPIDER-MAN? CRAP. HOW CAN THEY EXPECT ME TO STUDY HER FILE WHEN THEY PUT PICTURES IN IT?
AND HANK PYM DESIGNED MY SUIT! WHAT IF HE CAN TRACK IT? WHAT IF HE ALREADY KNOWS I'M HERE, AND HE'S JUST PLAYING SOME SICK GAME WITH ME, LIKE A CAT WITH A--

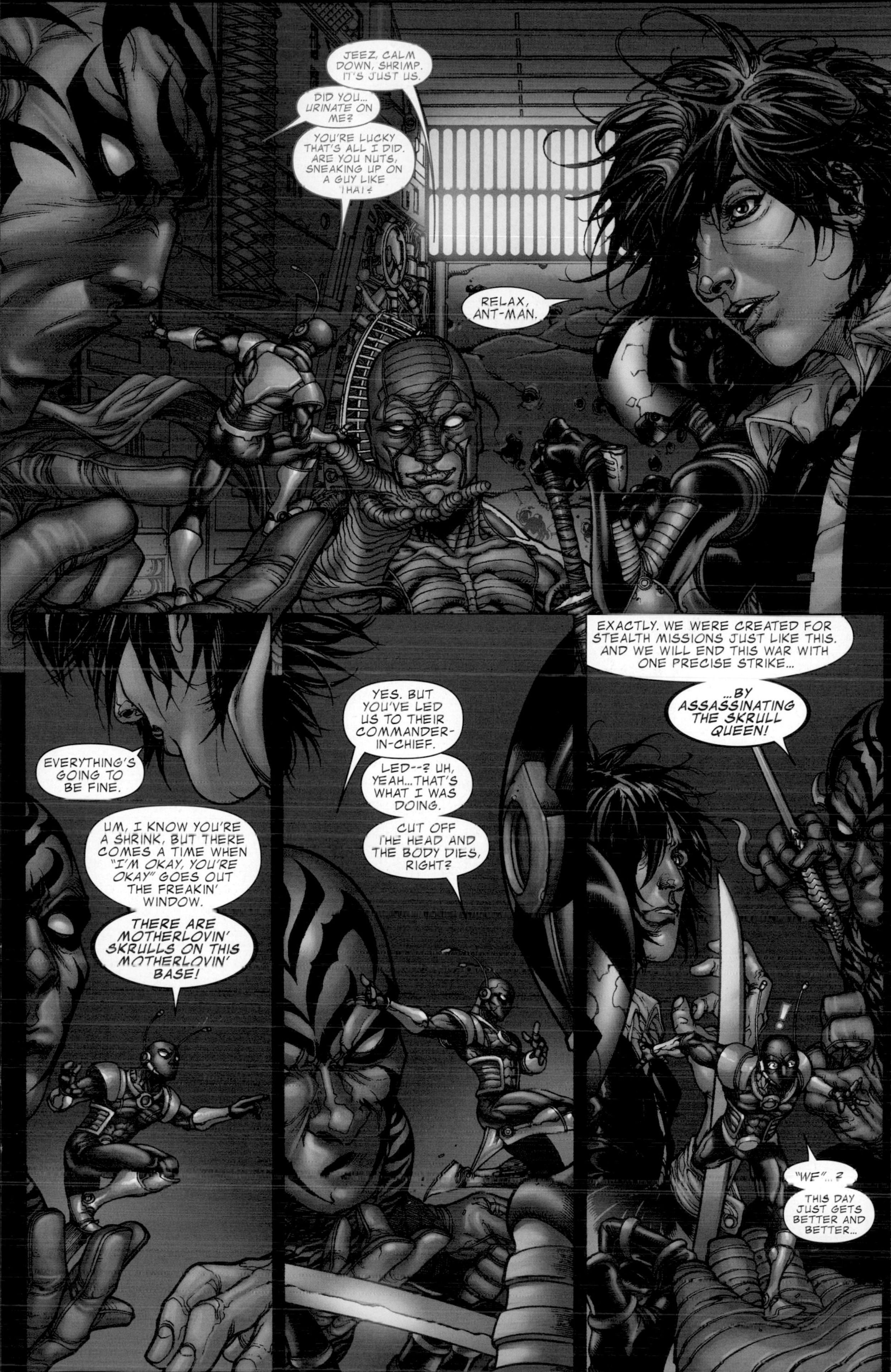

JEEZ, CALM DOWN, SHRIMP. IT'S JUST US.
DID YOU... URINATE ON ME?
YOU'RE LUCKY THAT'S ALL I DID. ARE YOU NUTS, SNEAKING UP ON A GUY LIKE THAT?!
RELAX, ANT-MAN.
EVERYTHING'S GOING TO BE FINE.
UM, I KNOW YOU'RE A SHRINK, BUT THERE COMES A TIME WHEN "I'M OKAY, YOU'RE OKAY" GOES OUT THE FREAKIN' WINDOW.
THERE ARE MOTHERLOVIN' SKRULLS ON THIS MOTHERLOVIN' BASE!
YES. BUT YOU'VE LED US TO THEIR COMMANDER-IN-CHIEF.
LED--? UH, YEAH...THAT'S WHAT I WAS DOING.
CUT OFF THE HEAD AND THE BODY DIES, RIGHT?
EXACTLY. WE WERE CREATED FOR STEALTH MISSIONS JUST LIKE THIS. AND WE WILL END THIS WAR WITH ONE PRECISE STRIKE...
...BY ASSASSINATING THE SKRULL QUEEN!
!
"WE"...?
THIS DAY JUST GETS BETTER AND BETTER...

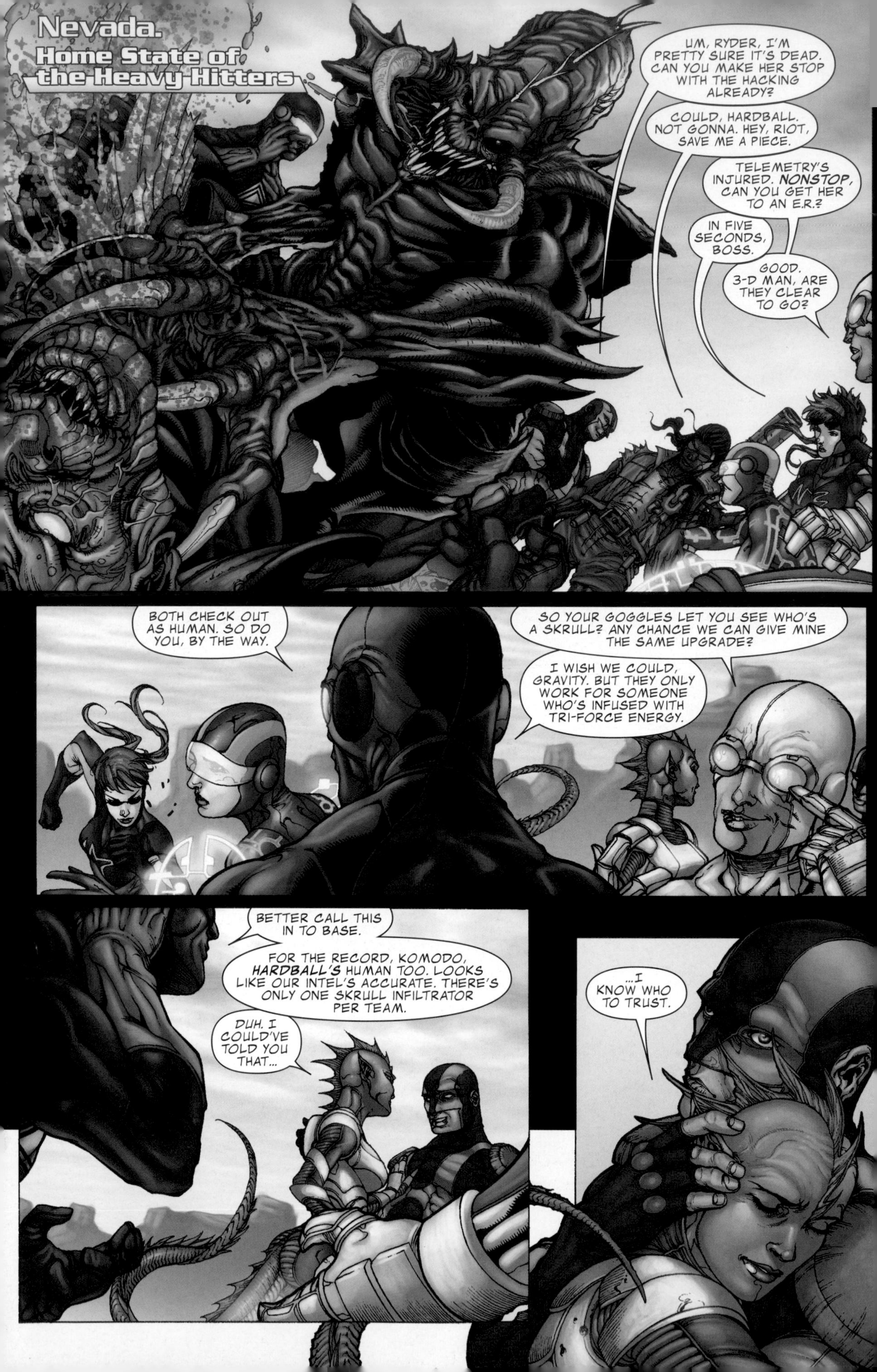
Nevada.
Home State of the Heavy Hitters
UM, RYDER, I'M PRETTY SURE IT'S DEAD. CAN YOU MAKE HER STOP WITH THE HACKING ALREADY?
COULD, HARDBALL. NOT GONNA. HEY, RIOT, SAVE ME A PIECE.
TELEMETRY'S INJURED. NONSTOP, CAN YOU GET HER TO AN E.R.?
IN FIVE SECONDS, BOSS.
GOOD. 3-D MAN, ARE THEY CLEAR TO GO?
BOTH CHECK OUT AS HUMAN. SO DO YOU, BY THE WAY.
SO YOUR GOGGLES LET YOU SEE WHO'S A SKRULL? ANY CHANCE WE CAN GIVE MINE THE SAME UPGRADE?
I WISH WE COULD, GRAVITY. BUT THEY ONLY WORK FOR SOMEONE WHO'S INFUSED WITH TRI-FORCE ENERGY.
BETTER CALL THIS IN TO BASE.
FOR THE RECORD, KOMODO, HARDBALL'S HUMAN TOO. LOOKS LIKE OUR INTEL'S ACCURATE. THERE'S ONLY ONE SKRULL INFILTRATOR PER TEAM.
DUH. I COULD'VE TOLD YOU THAT...
...I KNOW WHO TO TRUST.

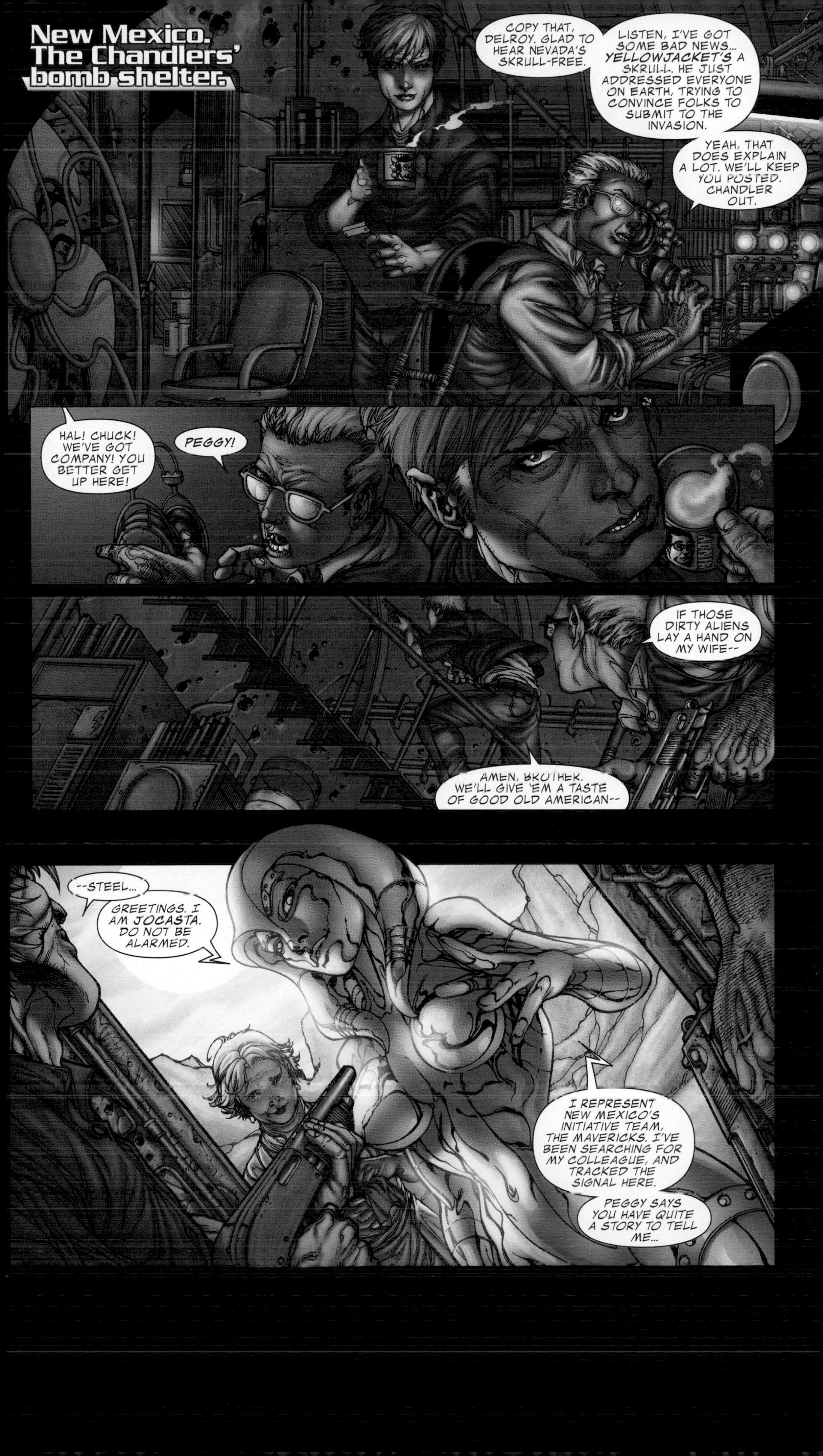
New Mexico. The Chandlers' bomb shelter.
COPY THAT, DELROY. GLAD TO HEAR NEVADA'S SKRULL-FREE.
LISTEN, I'VE GOT SOME BAD NEWS... YELLOWJACKET'S A SKRULL. HE JUST ADDRESSED EVERYONE ON EARTH, TRYING TO CONVINCE FOLKS TO SUBMIT TO THE INVASION.
YEAH, THAT DOES EXPLAIN A LOT. WE'LL KEEP YOU POSTED. CHANDLER OUT.
HAL! CHUCK! WE'VE GOT COMPANY! YOU BETTER GET UP HERE!
PEGGY!
IF THOSE DIRTY ALIENS LAY A HAND ON MY WIFE--
AMEN, BROTHER. WE'LL GIVE 'EM A TASTE OF GOOD OLD AMERICAN--
--STEEL...
GREETINGS. I AM JOCASTA. DO NOT BE ALARMED.
I REPRESENT NEW MEXICO'S INITIATIVE TEAM, THE MAVERICKS. I'VE BEEN SEARCHING FOR MY COLLEAGUE, AND TRACKED THE SIGNAL HERE.
PEGGY SAYS YOU HAVE QUITE A STORY TO TELL ME...

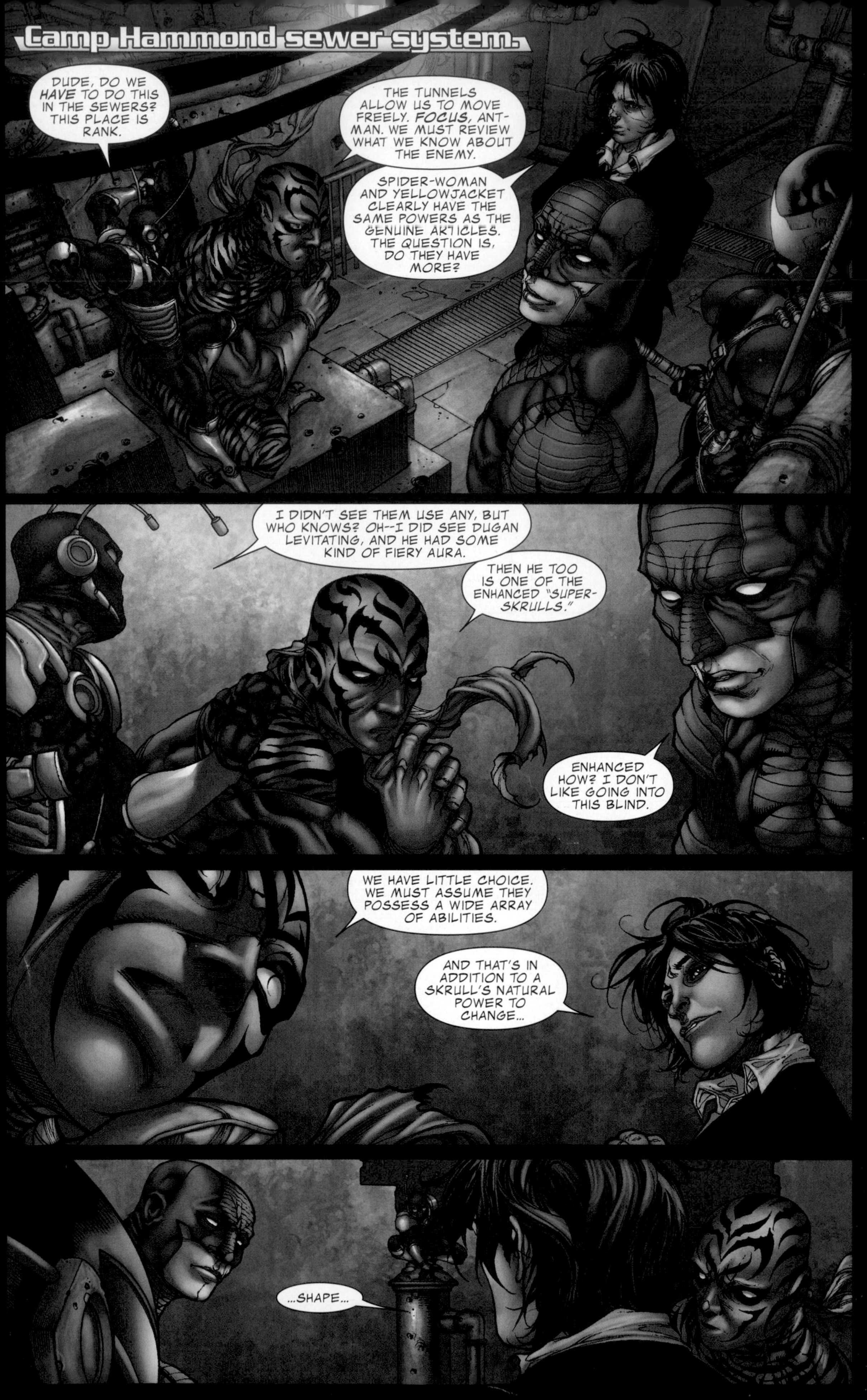
Camp Hammond sewer system.
DUDE, DO WE HAVE TO DO THIS IN THE SEWERS? THIS PLACE IS RANK.
THE TUNNELS ALLOW US TO MOVE FREELY. FOCUS, ANT-MAN. WE MUST REVIEW WHAT WE KNOW ABOUT THE ENEMY.
SPIDER-WOMAN AND YELLOWJACKET CLEARLY HAVE THE SAME POWERS AS THE GENUINE ARTICLES. THE QUESTION IS, DO THEY HAVE MORE?
I DIDN'T SEE THEM USE ANY, BUT WHO KNOWS? OH--I DID SEE DUGAN LEVITATING, AND HE HAD SOME KIND OF FIERY AURA.
THEN HE TOO IS ONE OF THE ENHANCED "SUPER-SKRULLS."
ENHANCED HOW? I DON'T LIKE GOING INTO THIS BLIND.
WE HAVE LITTLE CHOICE. WE MUST ASSUME THEY POSSESS A WIDE ARRAY OF ABILITIES.
AND THAT'S IN ADDITION TO A SKRULL'S NATURAL POWER TO CHANGE...
...SHAPE...

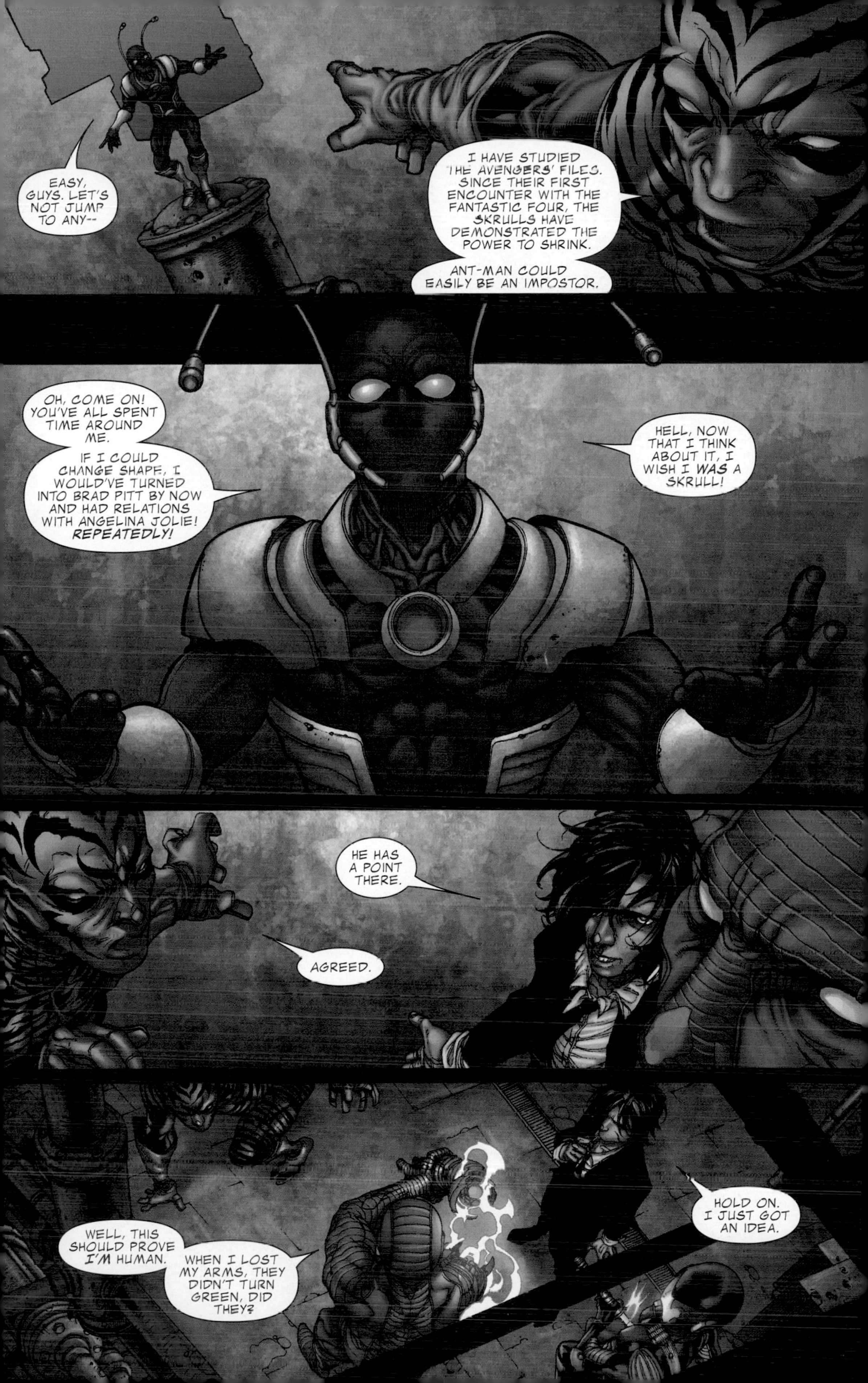
EASY, GUYS. LET'S NOT JUMP TO ANY--
I HAVE STUDIED THE AVENGERS' FILES. SINCE THEIR FIRST ENCOUNTER WITH THE FANTASTIC FOUR, THE SKRULLS HAVE DEMONSTRATED THE POWER TO SHRINK.
ANT-MAN COULD EASILY BE AN IMPOSTOR.
OH, COME ON! YOU'VE ALL SPENT TIME AROUND ME.
IF I COULD CHANGE SHAPE, I WOULD'VE TURNED INTO BRAD PITT BY NOW AND HAD RELATIONS WITH ANGELINA JOLIE! REPEATEDLY!
HELL, NOW THAT I THINK ABOUT IT, I WISH I WAS A SKRULL!
HE HAS A POINT THERE.
AGREED.
HOLD ON. I JUST GOT AN IDEA.
WELL, THIS SHOULD PROVE I'M HUMAN.
WHEN I LOST MY ARMS, THEY DIDN'T TURN GREEN, DID THEY?

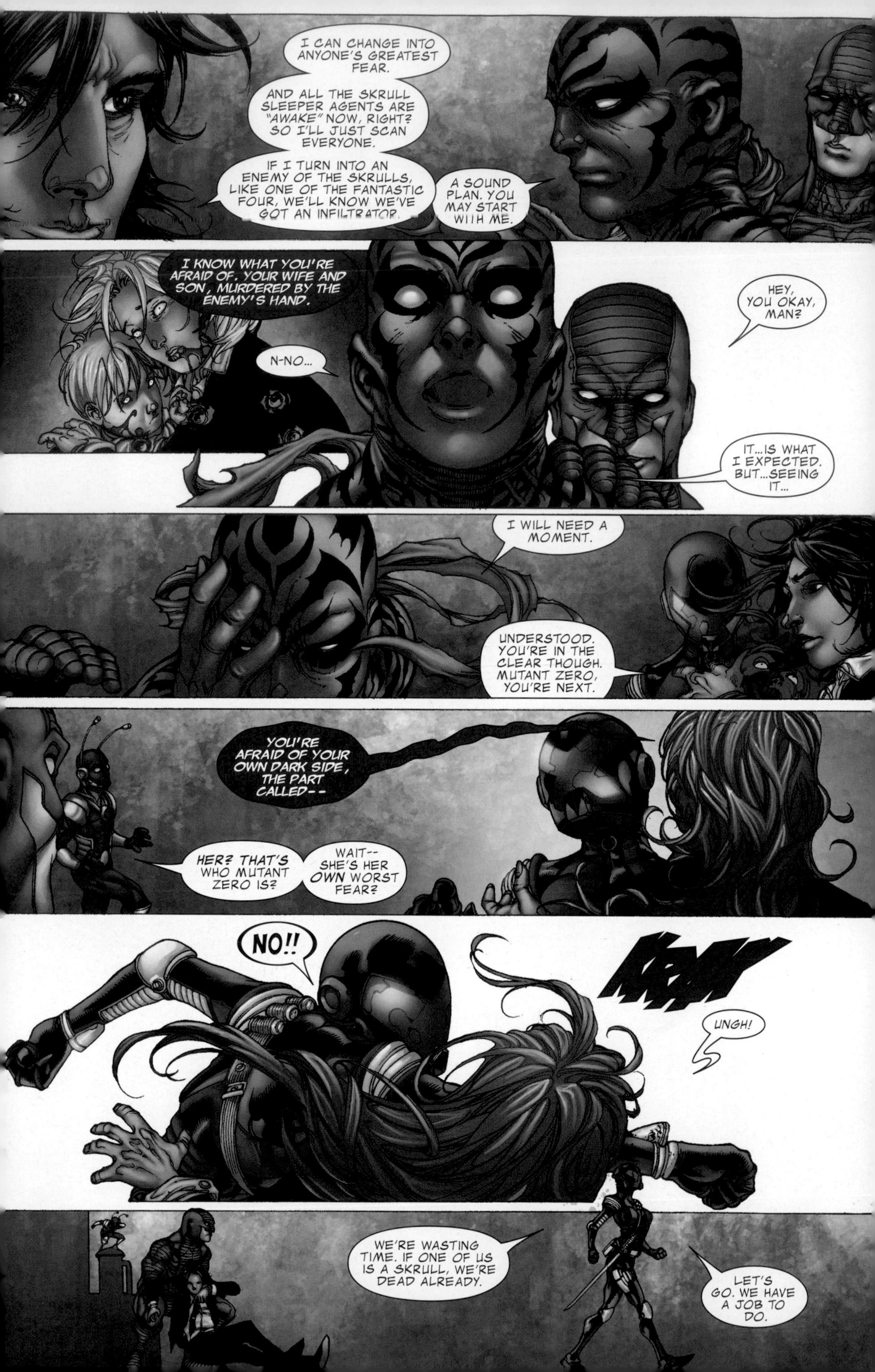
I CAN CHANGE INTO ANYONE'S GREATEST FEAR.
AND ALL THE SKRULL SLEEPER AGENTS ARE "AWAKE" NOW, RIGHT? SO I'LL JUST SCAN EVERYONE.
IF I TURN INTO AN ENEMY OF THE SKRULLS, LIKE ONE OF THE FANTASTIC FOUR, WE'LL KNOW WE'VE GOT AN INFILTRATOR.
A SOUND PLAN. YOU MAY START WITH ME.
I KNOW WHAT YOU'RE AFRAID OF. YOUR WIFE AND SON, MURDERED BY THE ENEMY'S HAND.
N-NO...
HEY, YOU OKAY, MAN?
IT...IS WHAT I EXPECTED. BUT...SEEING IT...
I WILL NEED A MOMENT.
UNDERSTOOD. YOU'RE IN THE CLEAR THOUGH. MUTANT ZERO, YOU'RE NEXT.
YOU'RE AFRAID OF YOUR OWN DARK SIDE, THE PART CALLED--
HER? THAT'S WHO MUTANT ZERO IS?
WAIT-- SHE'S HER OWN WORST FEAR?
NO!!
KRAK
UNGH!
WE'RE WASTING TIME. IF ONE OF US IS A SKRULL, WE'RE DEAD ALREADY.
LET'S GO. WE HAVE A JOB TO DO.

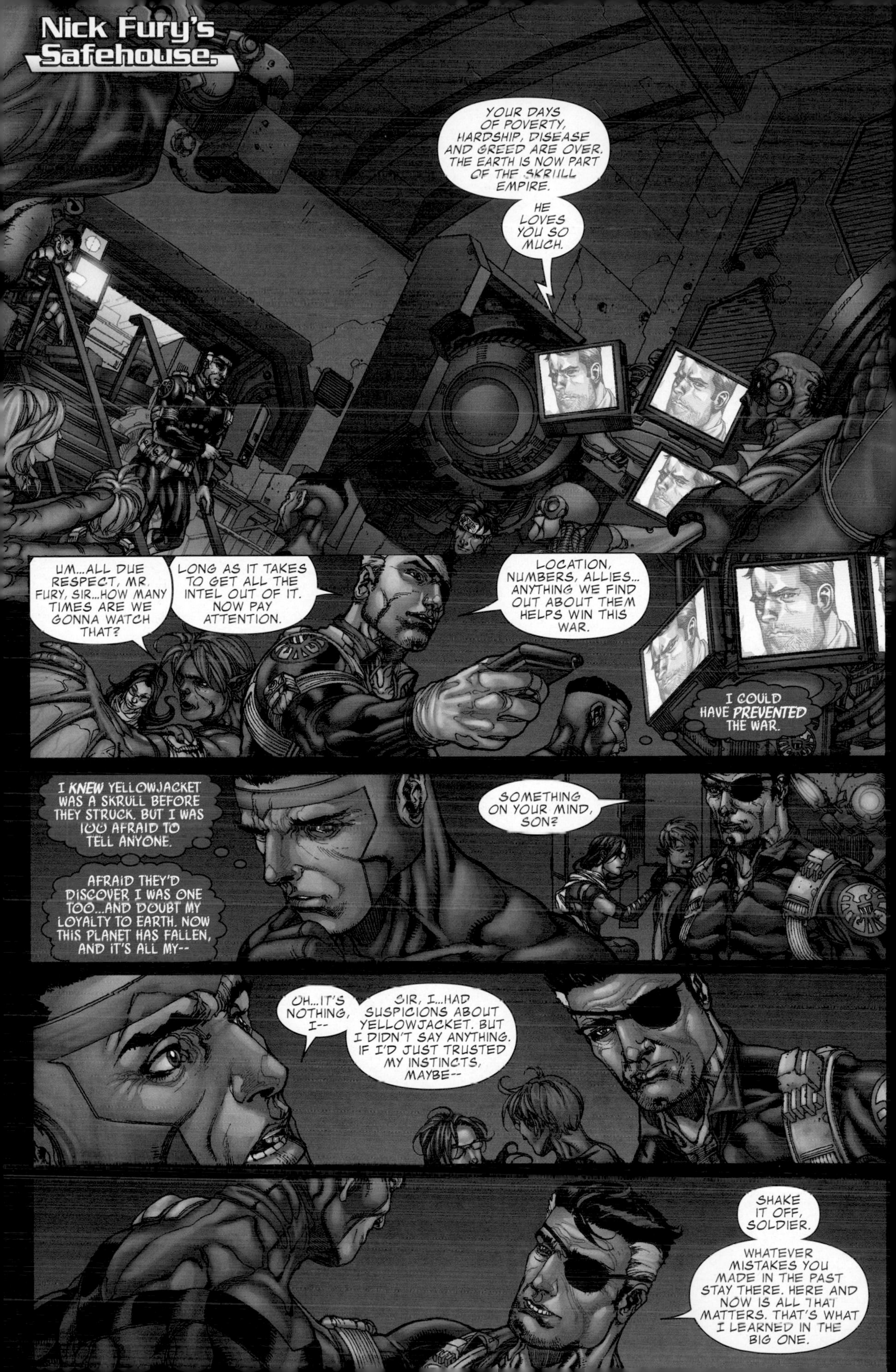
Nick Fury's Safehouse.
YOUR DAYS OF POVERTY, HARDSHIP, DISEASE AND GREED ARE OVER. THE EARTH IS NOW PART OF THE SKRULL EMPIRE.
HE LOVES YOU SO MUCH.
UM...ALL DUE RESPECT, MR. FURY, SIR...HOW MANY TIMES ARE WE GONNA WATCH THAT?
LONG AS IT TAKES TO GET ALL THE INTEL OUT OF IT. NOW PAY ATTENTION.
LOCATION, NUMBERS, ALLIES... ANYTHING WE FIND OUT ABOUT THEM HELPS WIN THIS WAR.
I COULD HAVE PREVENTED THE WAR.
I KNEW YELLOWJACKET WAS A SKRULL BEFORE THEY STRUCK. BUT I WAS TOO AFRAID TO TELL ANYONE.
AFRAID THEY'D DISCOVER I WAS ONE TOO...AND DOUBT MY LOYALTY TO EARTH. NOW THIS PLANET HAS FALLEN, AND IT'S ALL MY--
SOMETHING ON YOUR MIND, SON?
OH...IT'S NOTHING, I--
SIR, I...HAD SUSPICIONS ABOUT YELLOWJACKET. BUT I DIDN'T SAY ANYTHING. IF I'D JUST TRUSTED MY INSTINCTS, MAYBE--
SHAKE IT OFF, SOLDIER.
WHATEVER MISTAKES YOU MADE IN THE PAST STAY THERE. HERE AND NOW IS ALL THAT MATTERS. THAT'S WHAT I LEARNED IN THE BIG ONE.

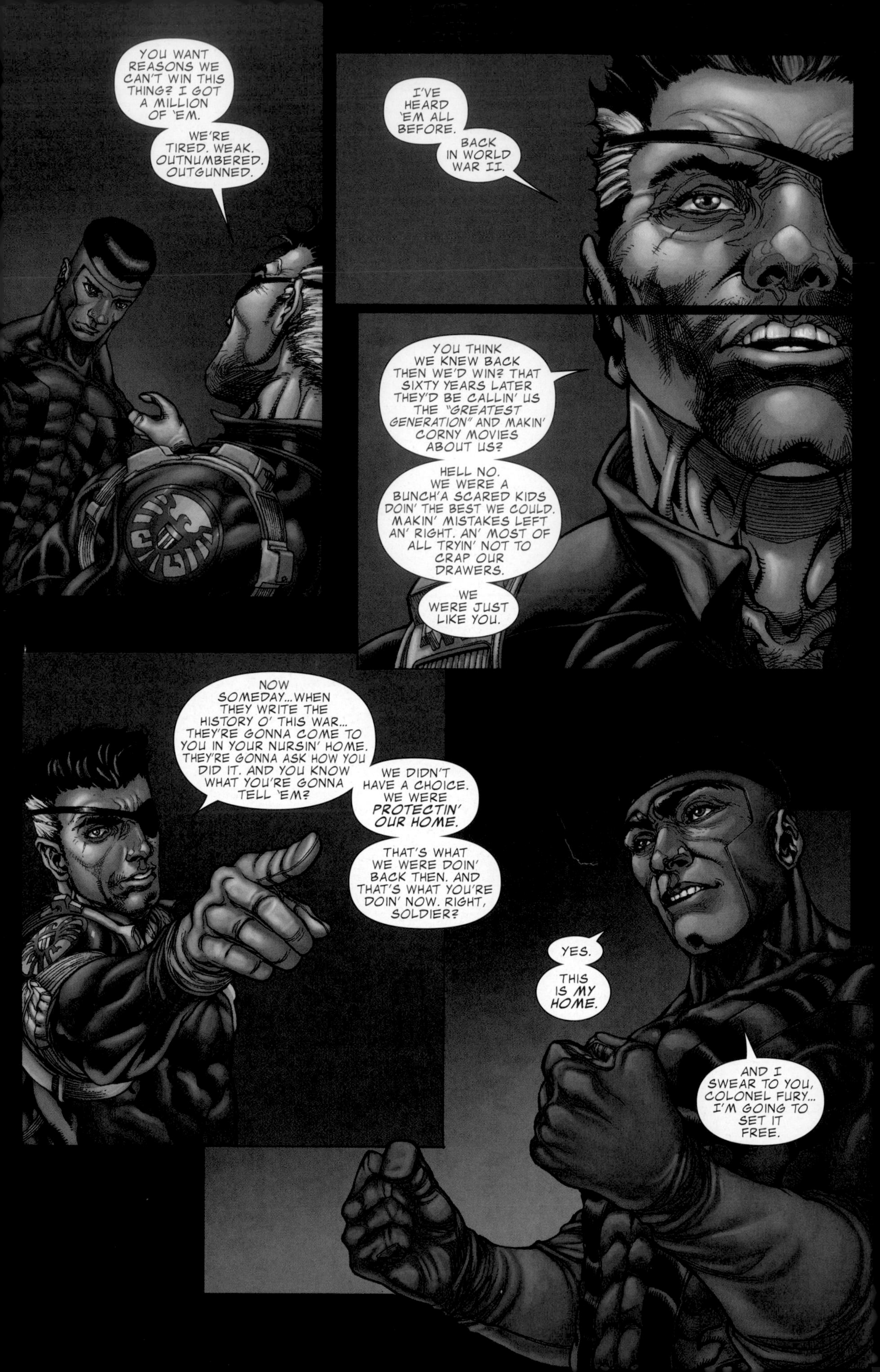
YOU WANT REASONS WE CAN'T WIN THIS THING? I GOT A MILLION OF 'EM.
WE'RE TIRED. WEAK. OUTNUMBERED. OUTGUNNED.
I'VE HEARD 'EM ALL BEFORE.
BACK IN WORLD WAR II.
YOU THINK THEN WE KNEW BACK THEN WE'D WIN? THAT SIXTY YEARS LATER THEY'D BE CALLIN' US THE "GREATEST GENERATION" AND MAKIN' CORNY MOVIES ABOUT US?
HELL NO. WE WERE A BUNCH'A SCARED KIDS DOIN' THE BEST WE COULD. MAKIN' MISTAKES LEFT AN' RIGHT. AN' MOST OF ALL TRYIN' NOT TO CRAP OUR DRAWERS.
WE WERE JUST LIKE YOU.
NOW SOMEDAY...WHEN THEY WRITE THE HISTORY O' THIS WAR... THEY'RE GONNA COME TO YOU IN YOUR NURSIN' HOME. THEY'RE GONNA ASK HOW YOU DID IT. AND YOU KNOW WHAT YOU'RE GONNA TELL 'EM?
WE DIDN'T HAVE A CHOICE. WE WERE *PROTECTIN' OUR HOME.*
THAT'S WHAT WE WERE DOIN' BACK THEN. AND THAT'S WHAT YOU'RE DOIN' NOW. RIGHT, SOLDIER?
YES.
THIS IS *MY HOME.*
AND I SWEAR TO YOU, COLONEL FURY... I'M GOING TO SET IT FREE.

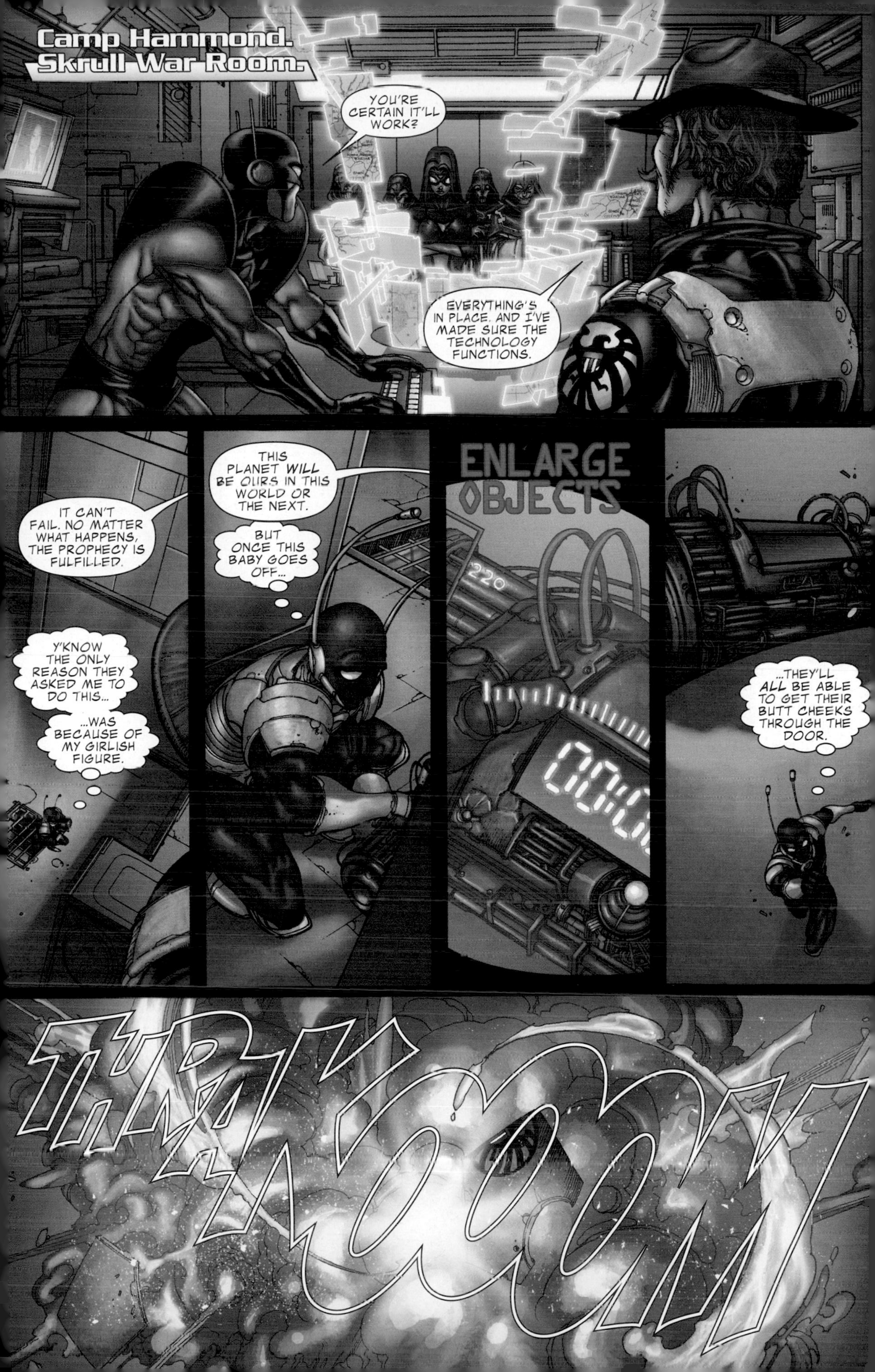
Camp Hammond. Skrull War Room.
YOU'RE CERTAIN IT'LL WORK?
EVERYTHING'S IN PLACE. AND I'VE MADE SURE THE TECHNOLOGY FUNCTIONS.
IT CAN'T FAIL. NO MATTER WHAT HAPPENS, THE PROPHECY IS FULFILLED.
Y'KNOW THE ONLY REASON THEY ASKED ME TO DO THIS...
...WAS BECAUSE OF MY GIRLISH FIGURE.
THIS PLANET WILL BE OURS IN THIS WORLD OR THE NEXT.
BUT ONCE THIS BABY GOES OFF...
ENLARGE OBJECTS
...THEY'LL ALL BE ABLE TO GET THEIR BUTT CHEEKS THROUGH THE DOOR.
THRKOOOM

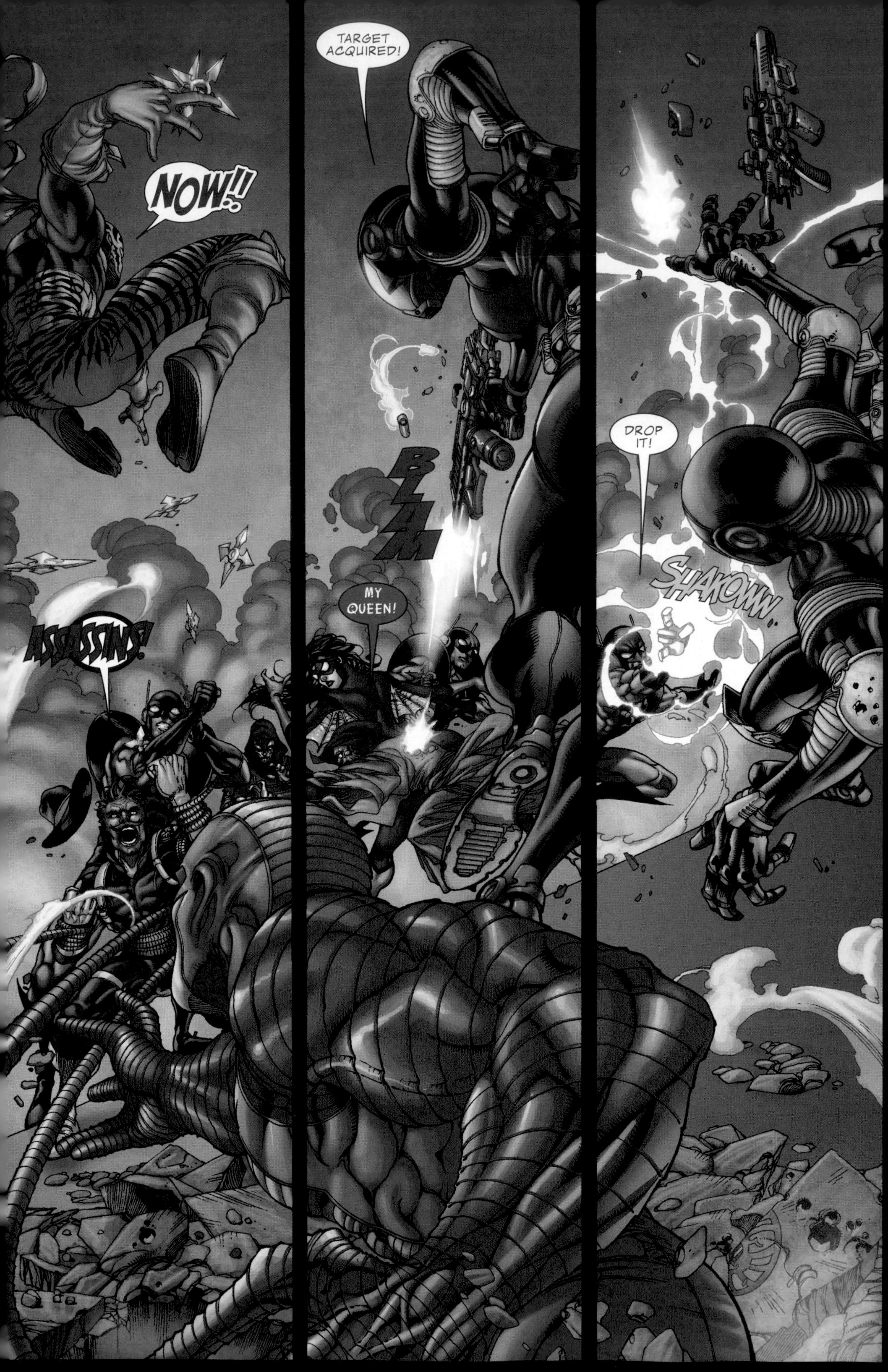
NOW!!
ASSASSINS!
TARGET ACQUIRED!
BLAM
MY QUEEN!
DROP IT!
SHAKOWW

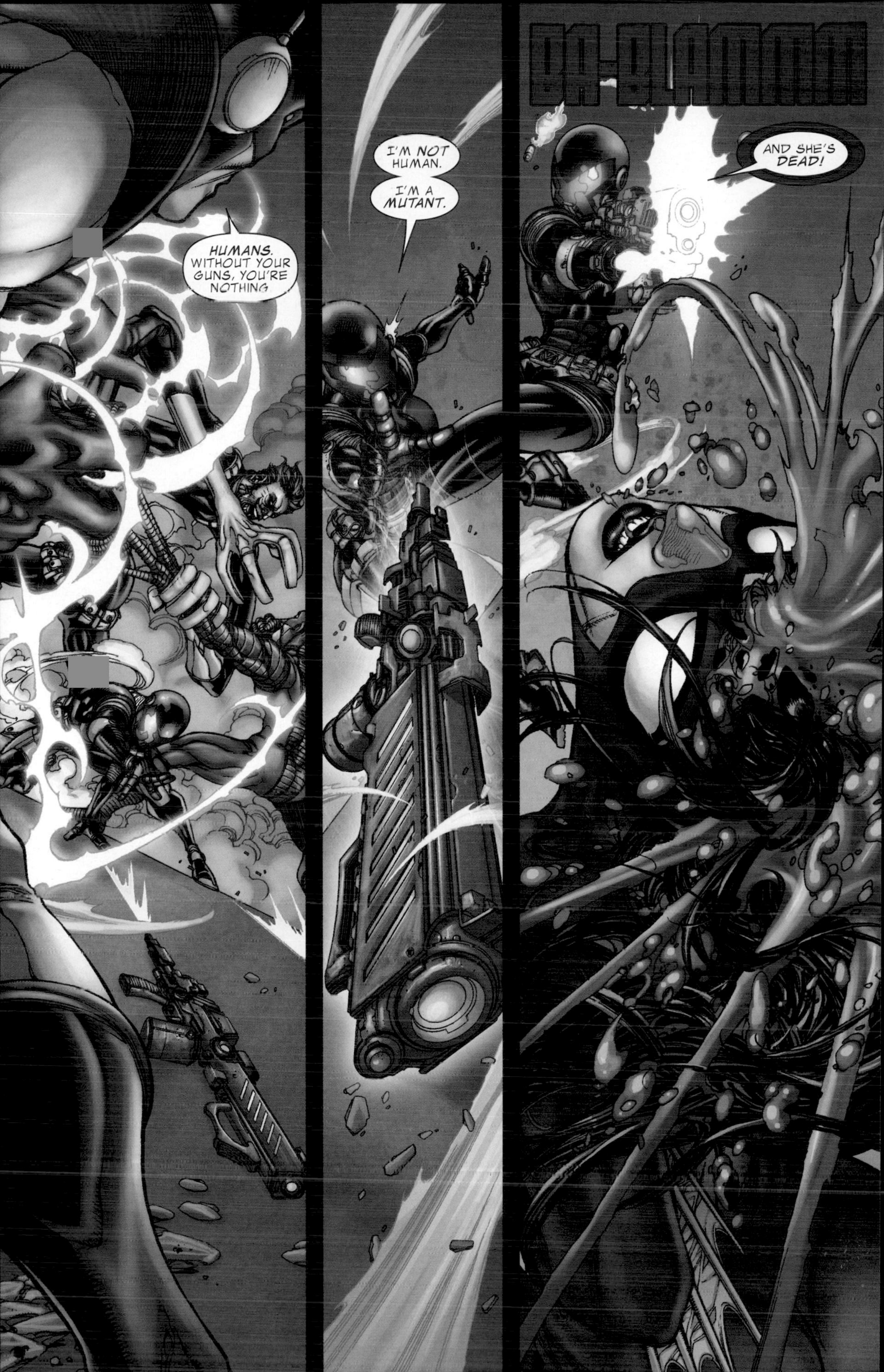
HUMANS. WITHOUT YOUR GUNS, YOU'RE NOTHING.
I'M NOT HUMAN.
I'M A MUTANT.
BA-BLAMMM
AND SHE'S DEAD!

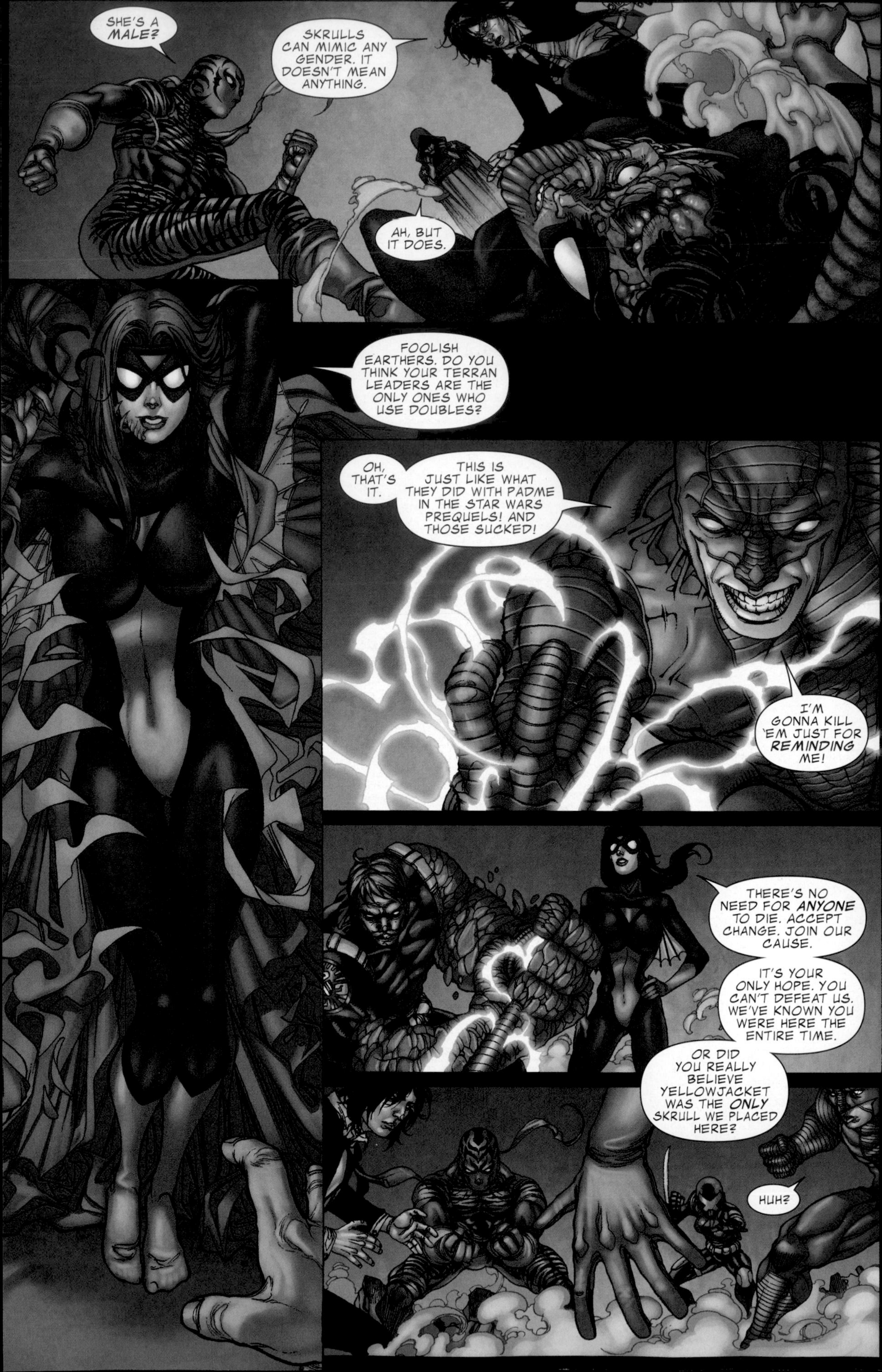
SHE'S A MALE?
SKRULLS CAN MIMIC ANY GENDER. IT DOESN'T MEAN ANYTHING.
AH, BUT IT DOES.
FOOLISH EARTHERS. DO YOU THINK YOUR TERRAN LEADERS ARE THE ONLY ONES WHO USE DOUBLES?
OH, THAT'S IT.
THIS IS JUST LIKE WHAT THEY DID WITH PADME IN THE STAR WARS PREQUELS! AND THOSE SUCKED!
I'M GONNA KILL 'EM JUST FOR REMINDING ME!
THERE'S NO NEED FOR ANYONE TO DIE. ACCEPT CHANGE. JOIN OUR CAUSE.
IT'S YOUR ONLY HOPE. YOU CAN'T DEFEAT US. WE'VE KNOWN YOU WERE HERE THE ENTIRE TIME.
OR DID YOU REALLY BELIEVE YELLOWJACKET WAS THE ONLY SKRULL WE PLACED HERE?
HUH?

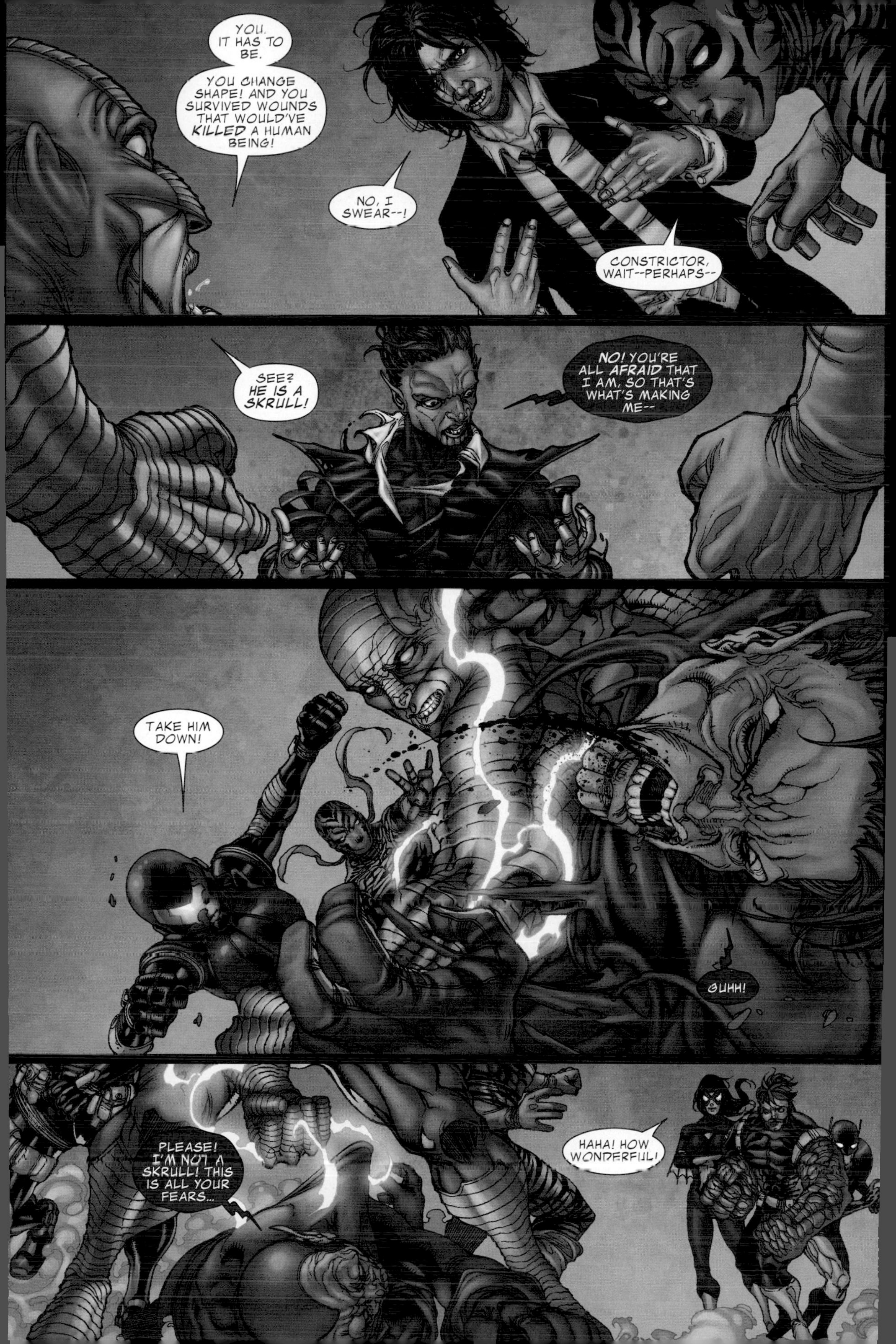
YOU. IT HAS TO BE.
YOU CHANGE SHAPE! AND YOU SURVIVED WOUNDS THAT WOULD'VE KILLED A HUMAN BEING!
NO, I SWEAR--!
CONSTRICTOR, WAIT--PERHAPS--
SEE? HE IS A SKRULL!
NO! YOU'RE ALL AFRAID THAT I AM, SO THAT'S WHAT'S MAKING ME--
TAKE HIM DOWN!
GUHH!
PLEASE! I'M NOT A SKRULL! THIS IS ALL YOUR FEARS...
HAHA! HOW WONDERFUL!

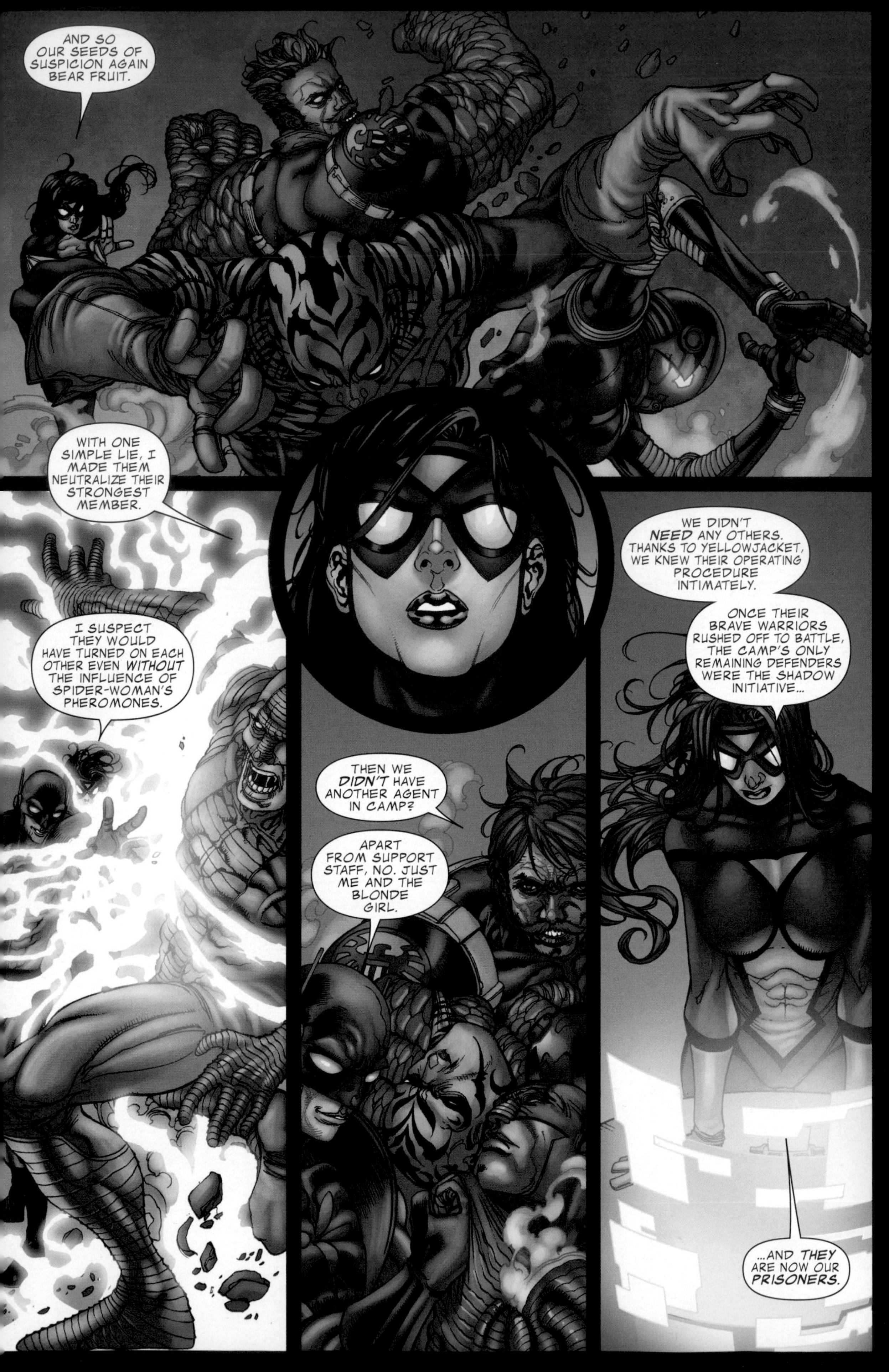
AND SO OUR SEEDS OF SUSPICION AGAIN BEAR FRUIT.
WITH ONE SIMPLE LIE, I MADE THEM NEUTRALIZE THEIR STRONGEST MEMBER.
I SUSPECT THEY WOULD HAVE TURNED ON EACH OTHER EVEN WITHOUT THE INFLUENCE OF SPIDER-WOMAN'S PHEROMONES.
THEN WE DIDN'T HAVE ANOTHER AGENT IN CAMP?
APART FROM SUPPORT STAFF, NO. JUST ME AND THE BLONDE GIRL.
WE DIDN'T NEED ANY OTHERS. THANKS TO YELLOWJACKET, WE KNEW THEIR OPERATING PROCEDURE INTIMATELY.
ONCE THEIR BRAVE WARRIORS RUSHED OFF TO BATTLE, THE CAMP'S ONLY REMAINING DEFENDERS WERE THE SHADOW INITIATIVE...
...AND THEY ARE NOW OUR PRISONERS.

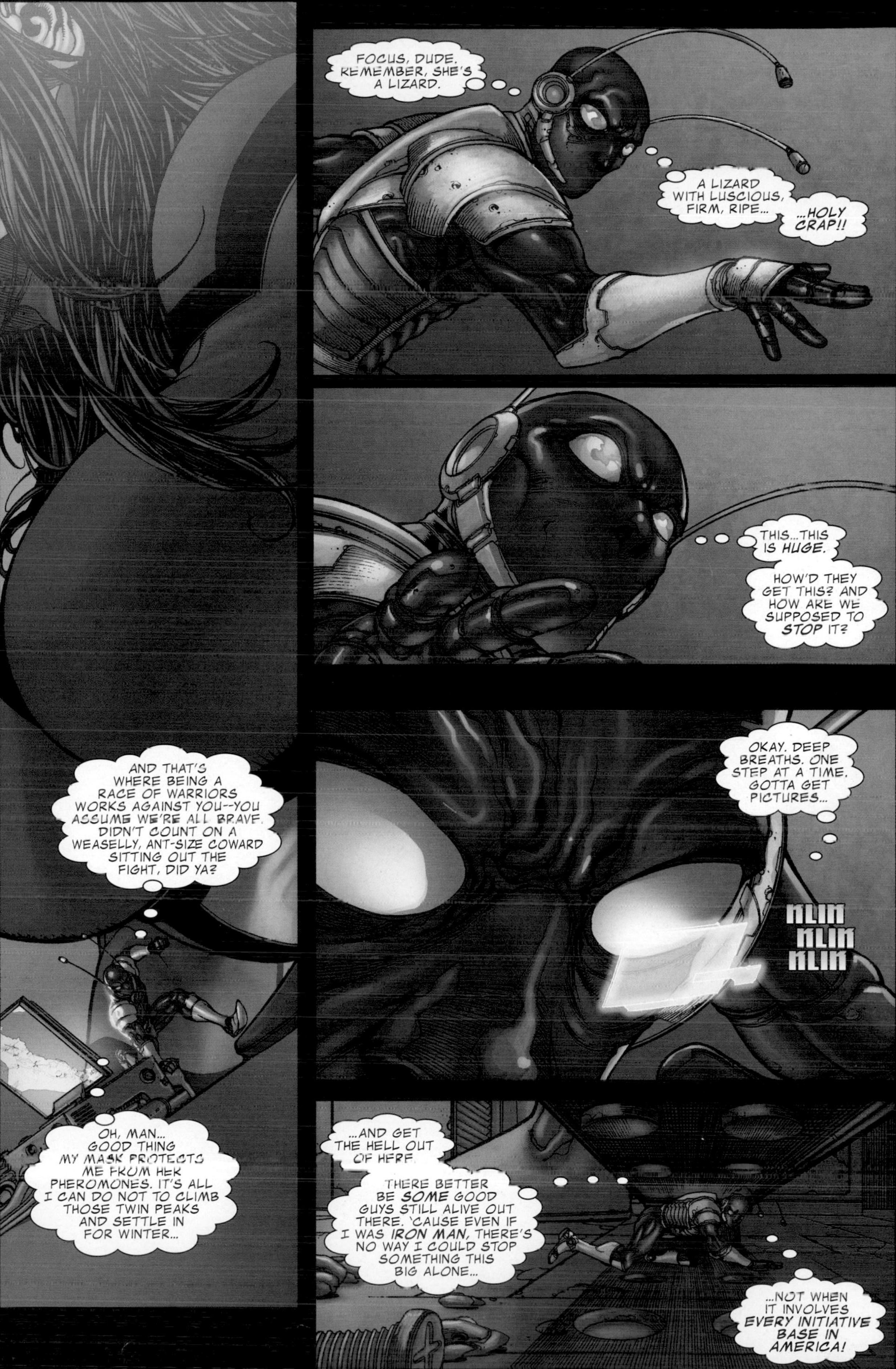
FOCUS, DUDE. REMEMBER, SHE'S A LIZARD.
A LIZARD WITH LUSCIOUS, FIRM, RIPE...
...HOLY CRAP!!
THIS...THIS IS HUGE.
HOW'D THEY GET THIS? AND HOW ARE WE SUPPOSED TO STOP IT?
AND THAT'S WHERE BEING A RACE OF WARRIORS WORKS AGAINST YOU--YOU ASSUME WE'RE ALL BRAVE. DIDN'T COUNT ON A WEASELLY, ANT-SIZE COWARD SITTING OUT THE FIGHT, DID YA?
OH, MAN... GOOD THING MY MASK PROTECTS ME FROM HER PHEROMONES. IT'S ALL I CAN DO NOT TO CLIMB THOSE TWIN PEAKS AND SETTLE IN FOR WINTER...
OKAY. DEEP BREATHS. ONE STEP AT A TIME. GOTTA GET PICTURES...
KLIK KLIK KLIK
...AND GET THE HELL OUT OF HERE.
THERE BETTER BE SOME GOOD GUYS STILL ALIVE OUT THERE. 'CAUSE EVEN IF I WAS IRON MAN, THERE'S NO WAY I COULD STOP SOMETHING THIS BIG ALONE...
...NOT WHEN IT INVOLVES EVERY INITIATIVE BASE IN AMERICA!

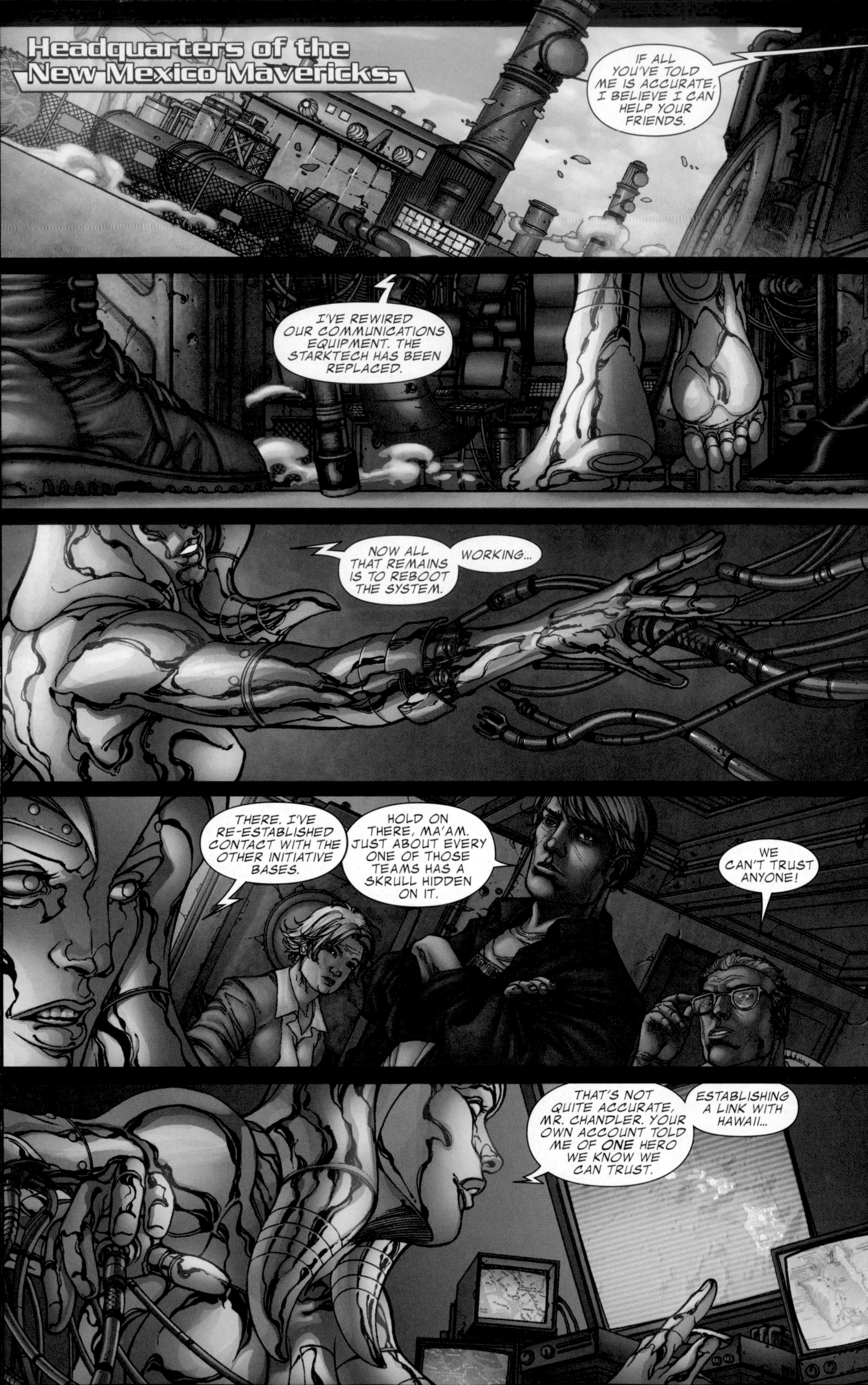
Headquarters of the New Mexico Mavericks.
IF ALL YOU'VE TOLD ME IS ACCURATE, I BELIEVE I CAN HELP YOUR FRIENDS.
I'VE REWIRED OUR COMMUNICATIONS EQUIPMENT. THE STARKTECH HAS BEEN REPLACED.
NOW ALL THAT REMAINS IS TO REBOOT THE SYSTEM.
WORKING...
THERE. I'VE RE-ESTABLISHED CONTACT WITH THE OTHER INITIATIVE BASES.
HOLD ON THERE, MA'AM. JUST ABOUT EVERY ONE OF THOSE TEAMS HAS A SKRULL HIDDEN ON IT.
WE CAN'T TRUST ANYONE!
THAT'S NOT QUITE ACCURATE, MR. CHANDLER. YOUR OWN ACCOUNT TOLD ME OF ONE HERO WE KNOW WE CAN TRUST.
ESTABLISHING A LINK WITH HAWAII...

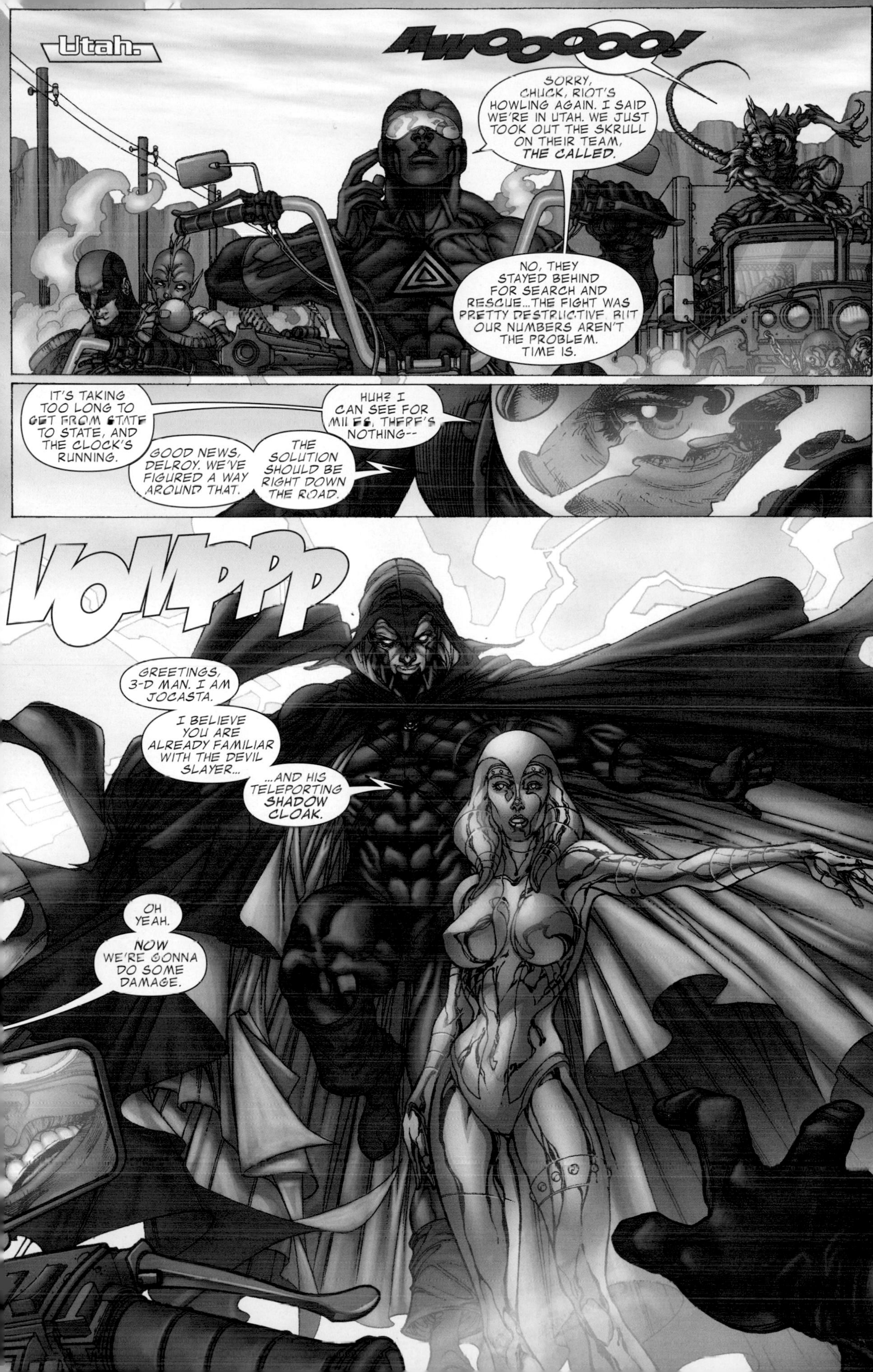

Utah.
AWOOOOOO!
SORRY, CHUCK, RIOT'S HOWLING AGAIN. I SAID WE'RE IN UTAH. WE JUST TOOK OUT THE SKRULL ON THEIR TEAM, THE CALLED.
NO, THEY STAYED BEHIND FOR SEARCH AND RESCUE...THE FIGHT WAS PRETTY DESTRUCTIVE, BUT OUR NUMBERS AREN'T THE PROBLEM. TIME IS.
IT'S TAKING TOO LONG TO GET FROM STATE TO STATE, AND THE CLOCK'S RUNNING.
GOOD NEWS, DELROY. WE'VE FIGURED A WAY AROUND THAT.
THE SOLUTION SHOULD BE RIGHT DOWN THE ROAD.
HUH? I CAN SEE FOR MILES. THERE'S NOTHING--
VOMPP
GREETINGS, 3-D MAN. I AM JOCASTA.
I BELIEVE YOU ARE ALREADY FAMILIAR WITH THE DEVIL SLAYER...
...AND HIS TELEPORTING SHADOW CLOAK.
OH YEAH.
NOW WE'RE GONNA DO SOME DAMAGE.

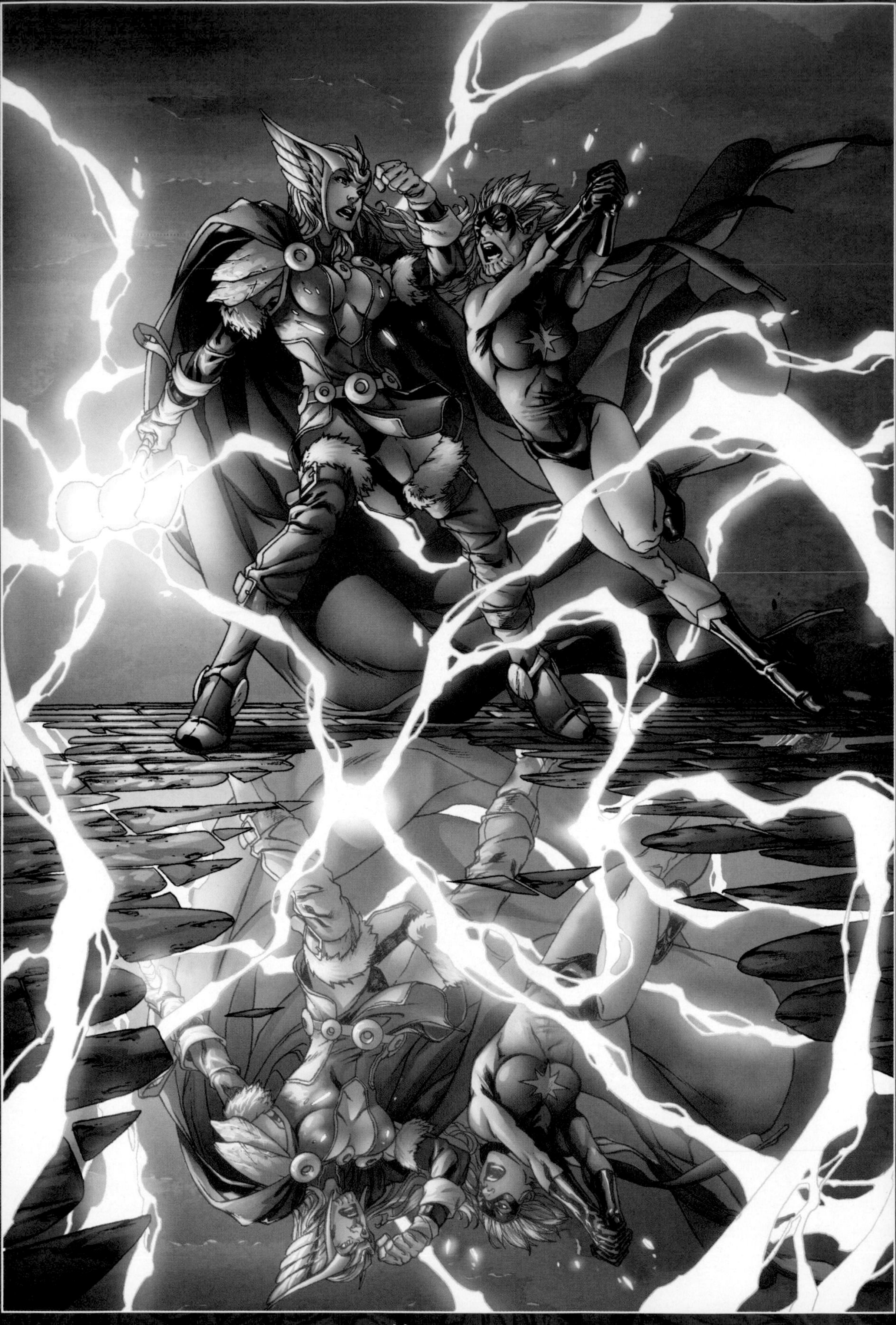

#18

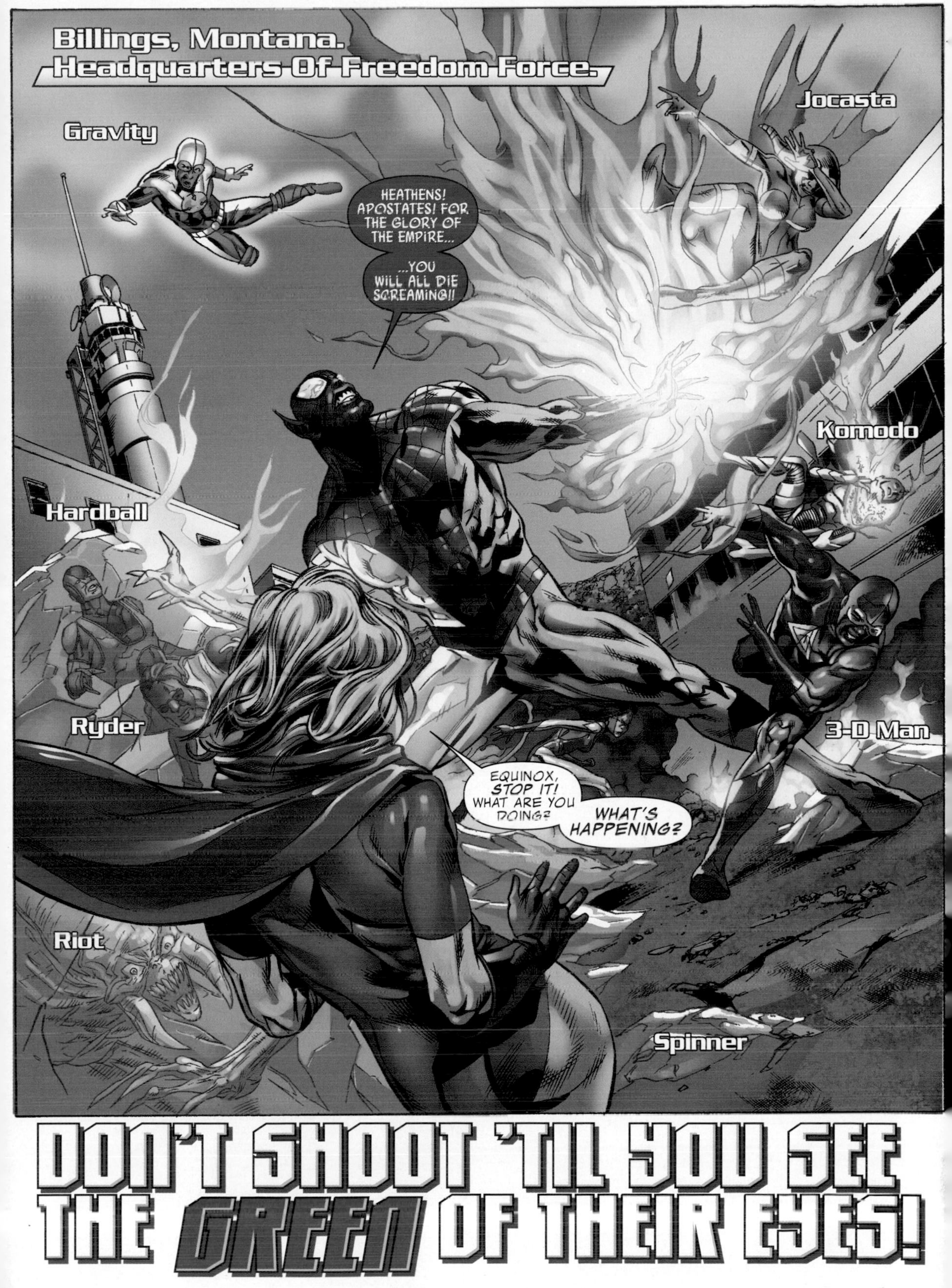
Billings, Montana. Headquarters Of Freedom Force.
Gravity
Jocasta
HEATHENS! APOSTATES! FOR THE GLORY OF THE EMPIRE...
...YOU WILL ALL DIE SCREAMING!!
Komodo
Hardball
Ryder
3-D Man
EQUINOX, STOP IT! WHAT ARE YOU DOING?
WHAT'S HAPPENING?
Riot
Spinner

DON'T SHOOT 'TIL YOU SEE THE *GREEN* OF THEIR EYES!

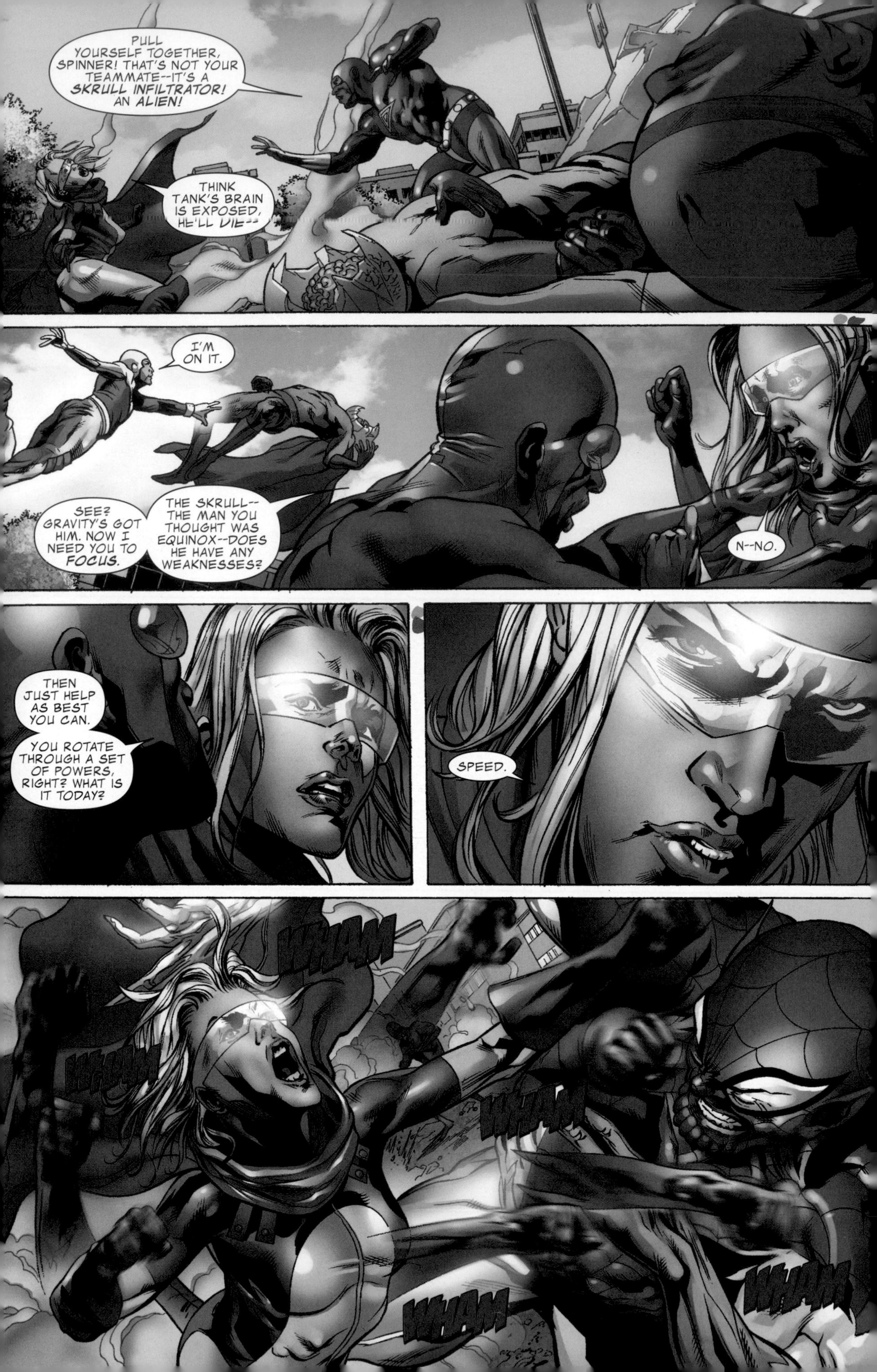
PULL YOURSELF TOGETHER, SPINNER! THAT'S NOT YOUR TEAMMATE--IT'S A SKRULL INFILTRATOR! AN ALIEN!
THINK TANK'S BRAIN IS EXPOSED, HE'LL DIE--
I'M ON IT.
SEE? GRAVITY'S GOT HIM. NOW I NEED YOU TO FOCUS.
THE SKRULL-- THE MAN YOU THOUGHT WAS EQUINOX--DOES HE HAVE ANY WEAKNESSES?
N--NO.
THEN JUST HELP AS BEST YOU CAN.
YOU ROTATE THROUGH A SET OF POWERS, RIGHT? WHAT IS IT TODAY?
SPEED.
WHAM
WHAM
WHAM
WHAM
WHAM

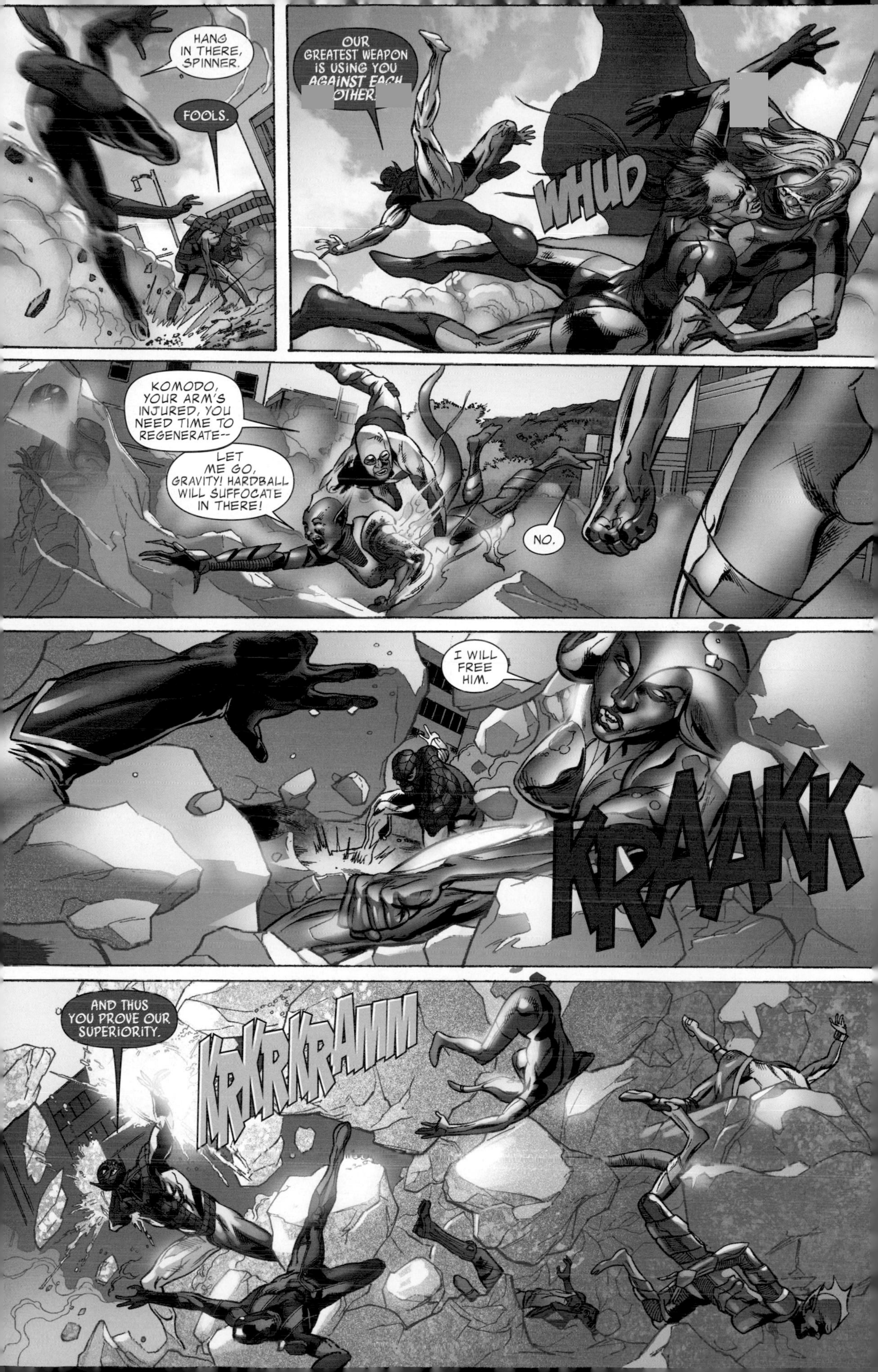
HANG IN THERE, SPINNER.
FOOLS.
OUR GREATEST WEAPON IS USING YOU AGAINST EACH OTHER.
WHUD
KOMODO, YOUR ARM'S INJURED, YOU NEED TIME TO REGENERATE--
LET ME GO, GRAVITY! HARDBALL WILL SUFFOCATE IN THERE!
NO.
I WILL FREE HIM.
KRAAKK
AND THUS YOU PROVE OUR SUPERIORITY.
KRKRKRAMM

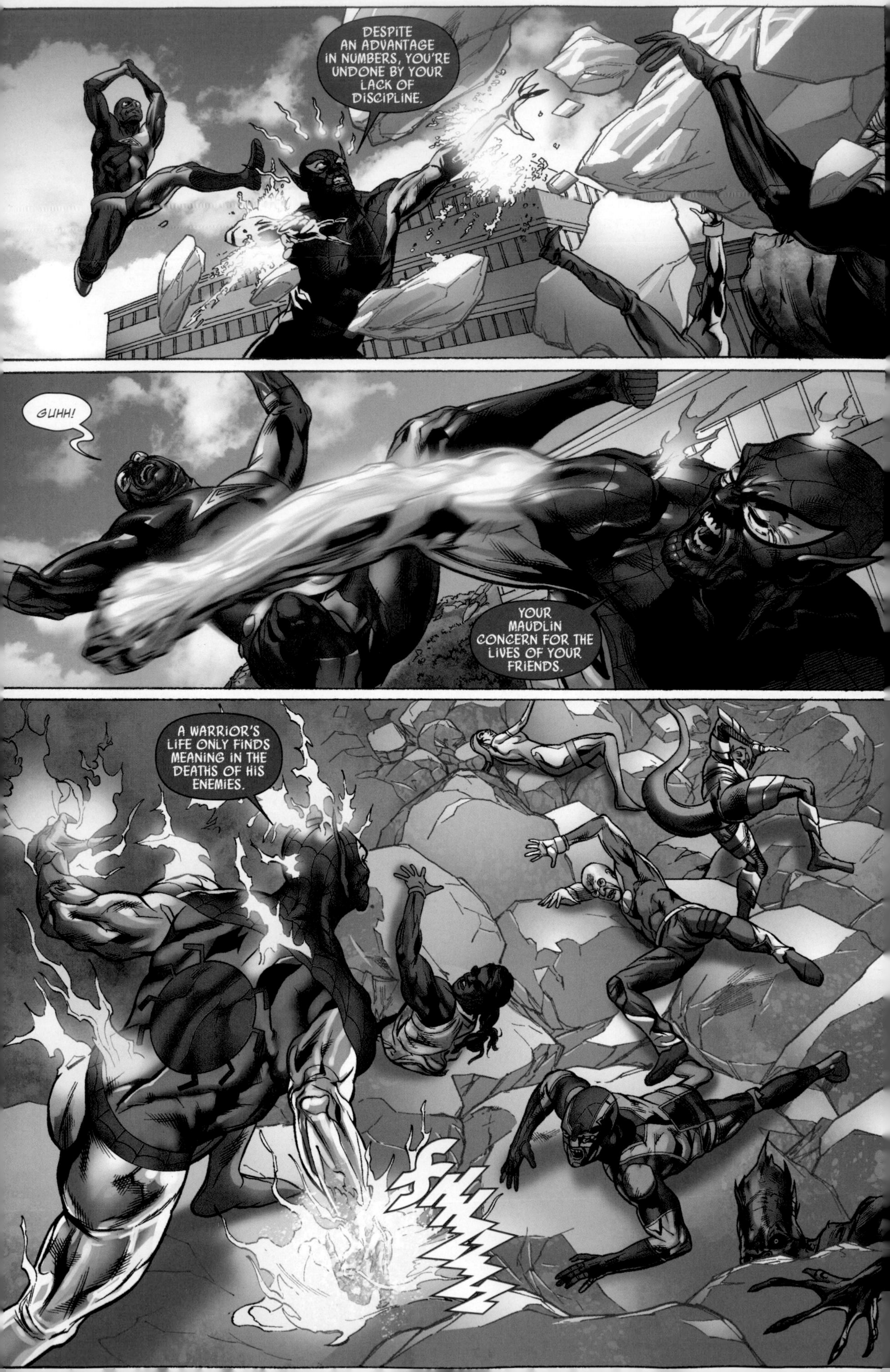
DESPITE AN ADVANTAGE IN NUMBERS, YOU'RE UNDONE BY YOUR LACK OF DISCIPLINE.
GUHH!
YOUR MAUDLIN CONCERN FOR THE LIVES OF YOUR FRIENDS.
A WARRIOR'S LIFE ONLY FINDS MEANING IN THE DEATHS OF HIS ENEMIES.

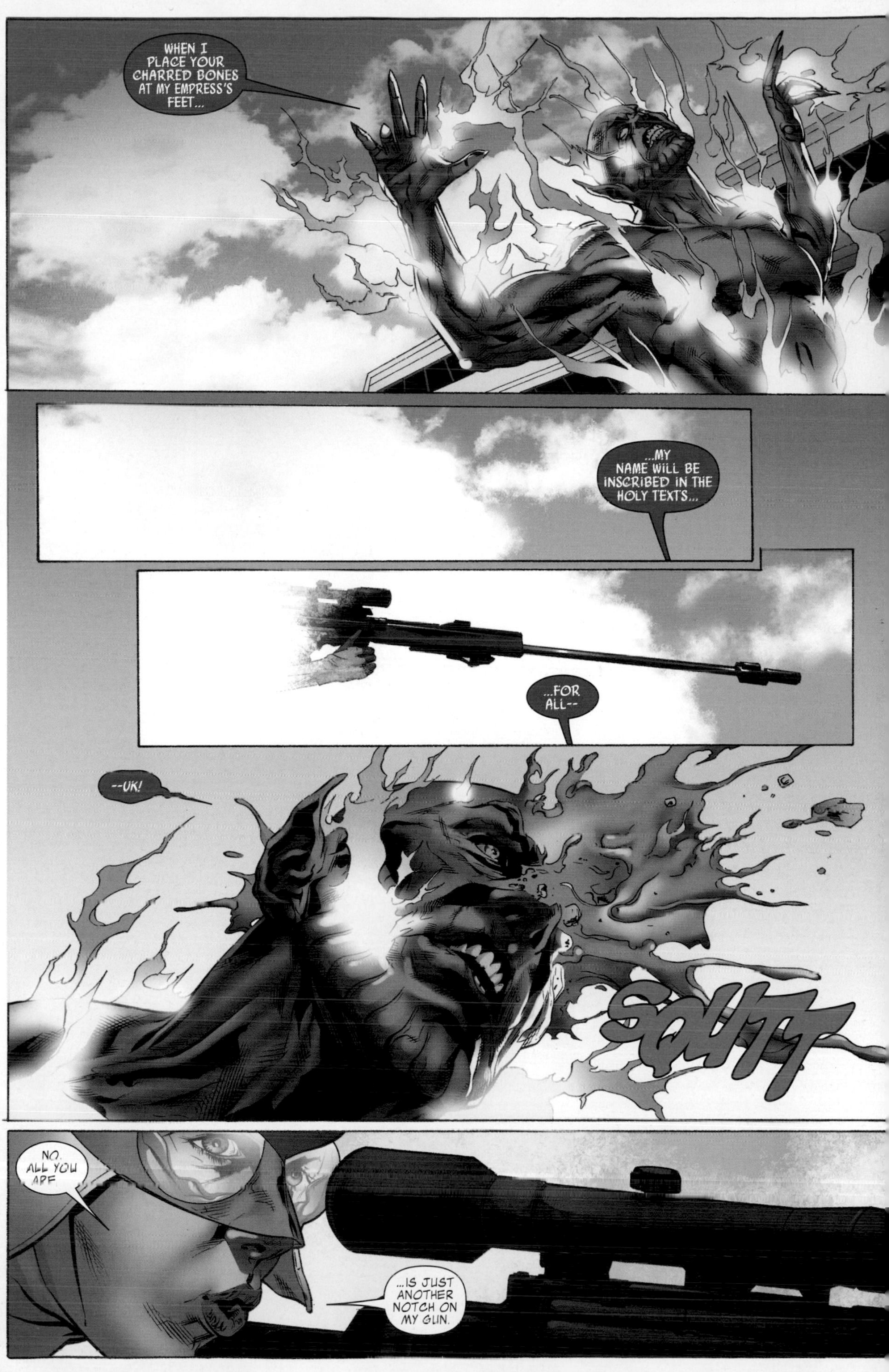
WHEN I PLACE YOUR CHARRED BONES AT MY EMPRESS'S FEET...
...MY NAME WILL BE INSCRIBED IN THE HOLY TEXTS...
...FOR ALL--
--UK!
SQUTT
NO. ALL YOU ARE
...IS JUST ANOTHER NOTCH ON MY GUN.

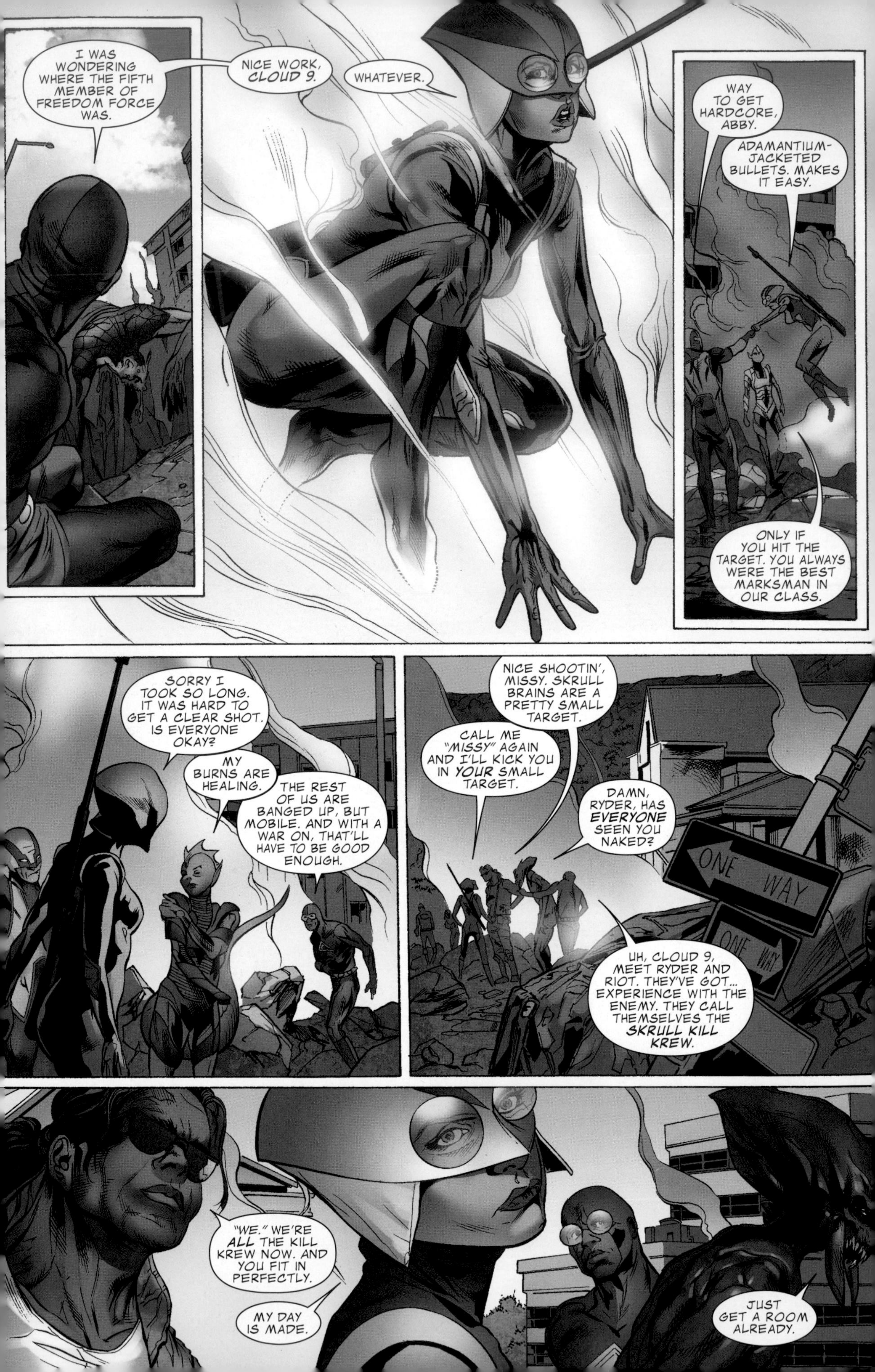
I WAS WONDERING WHERE THE FIFTH MEMBER OF FREEDOM FORCE WAS.
NICE WORK, CLOUD 9.
WHATEVER.
WAY TO GET HARDCORE, ABBY.
ADAMANTIUM-JACKETED BULLETS. MAKES IT EASY.
ONLY IF YOU HIT THE TARGET. YOU ALWAYS WERE THE BEST MARKSMAN IN OUR CLASS.
SORRY I TOOK SO LONG. IT WAS HARD TO GET A CLEAR SHOT. IS EVERYONE OKAY?
MY BURNS ARE HEALING.
THE REST OF US ARE BANGED UP, BUT MOBILE. AND WITH A WAR ON, THAT'LL HAVE TO BE GOOD ENOUGH.
NICE SHOOTIN', MISSY. SKRULL BRAINS ARE A PRETTY SMALL TARGET.
CALL ME "MISSY" AGAIN AND I'LL KICK YOU IN YOUR SMALL TARGET.
DAMN, RYDER, HAS EVERYONE SEEN YOU NAKED?
ONE WAY
ONE WAY
UH, CLOUD 9, MEET RYDER AND RIOT. THEY'VE GOT... EXPERIENCE WITH THE ENEMY. THEY CALL THEMSELVES THE SKRULL KILL KREW.
"WE." WE'RE ALL THE KILL KREW NOW. AND YOU FIT IN PERFECTLY.
MY DAY IS MADE.
JUST GET A ROOM ALREADY.

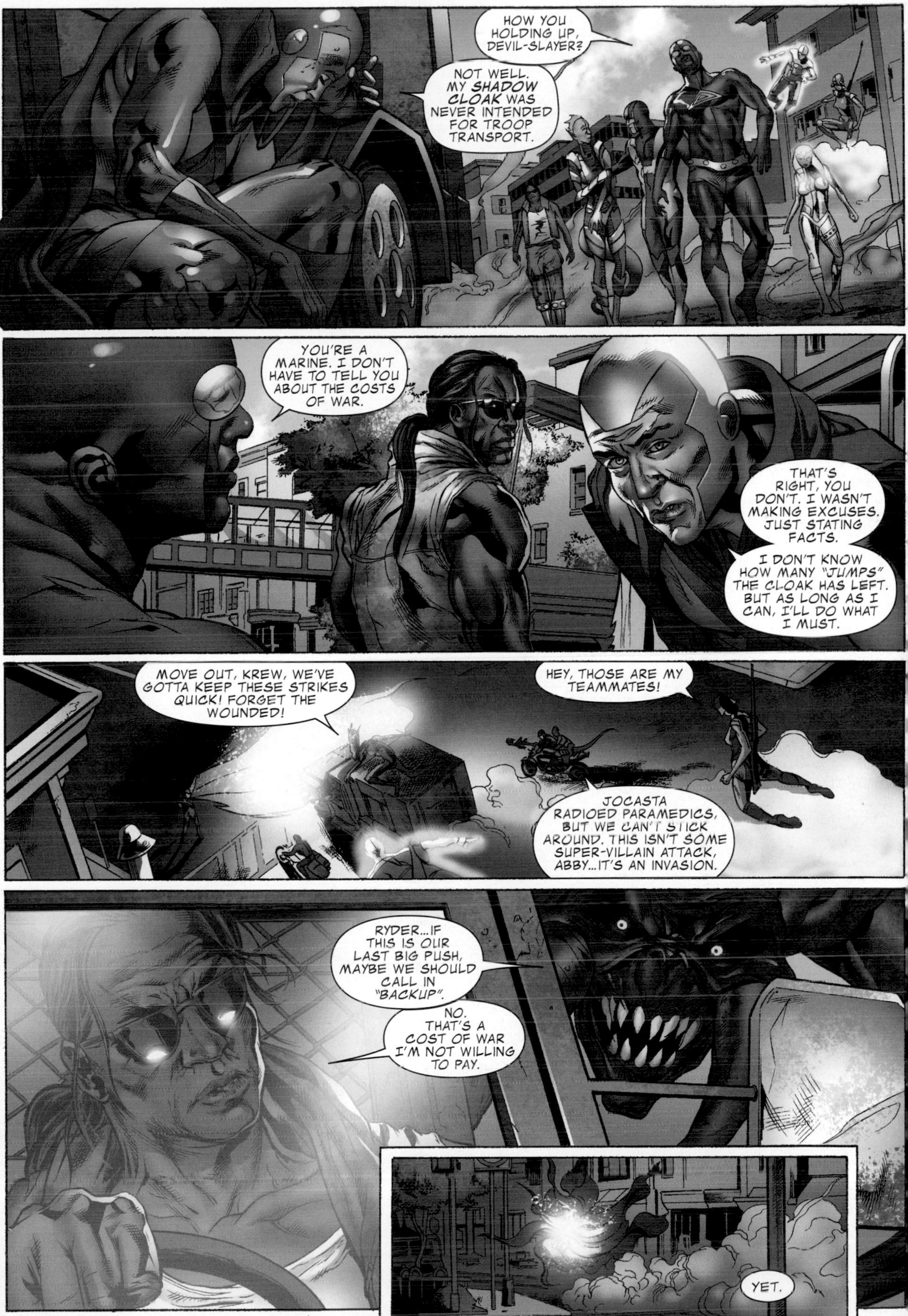
HOW YOU HOLDING UP, DEVIL-SLAYER?
NOT WELL. MY *SHADOW CLOAK* WAS NEVER INTENDED FOR TROOP TRANSPORT.
YOU'RE A MARINE. I DON'T HAVE TO TELL YOU ABOUT THE COSTS OF WAR.
THAT'S RIGHT, YOU DON'T. I WASN'T MAKING EXCUSES. JUST STATING FACTS.
I DON'T KNOW HOW MANY "*JUMPS*" THE CLOAK HAS LEFT. BUT AS LONG AS I CAN, I'LL DO WHAT I MUST.
MOVE OUT, KREW, WE'VE GOTTA KEEP THESE STRIKES QUICK! FORGET THE WOUNDED!
HEY, THOSE ARE MY TEAMMATES!
JOCASTA RADIOED PARAMEDICS, BUT WE CAN'T STICK AROUND. THIS ISN'T SOME SUPER-VILLAIN ATTACK, ABBY...IT'S AN INVASION.
RYDER...IF THIS IS OUR LAST BIG PUSH, MAYBE WE SHOULD CALL IN "*BACKUP*".
NO. THAT'S A COST OF WAR I'M NOT WILLING TO PAY.
YET.

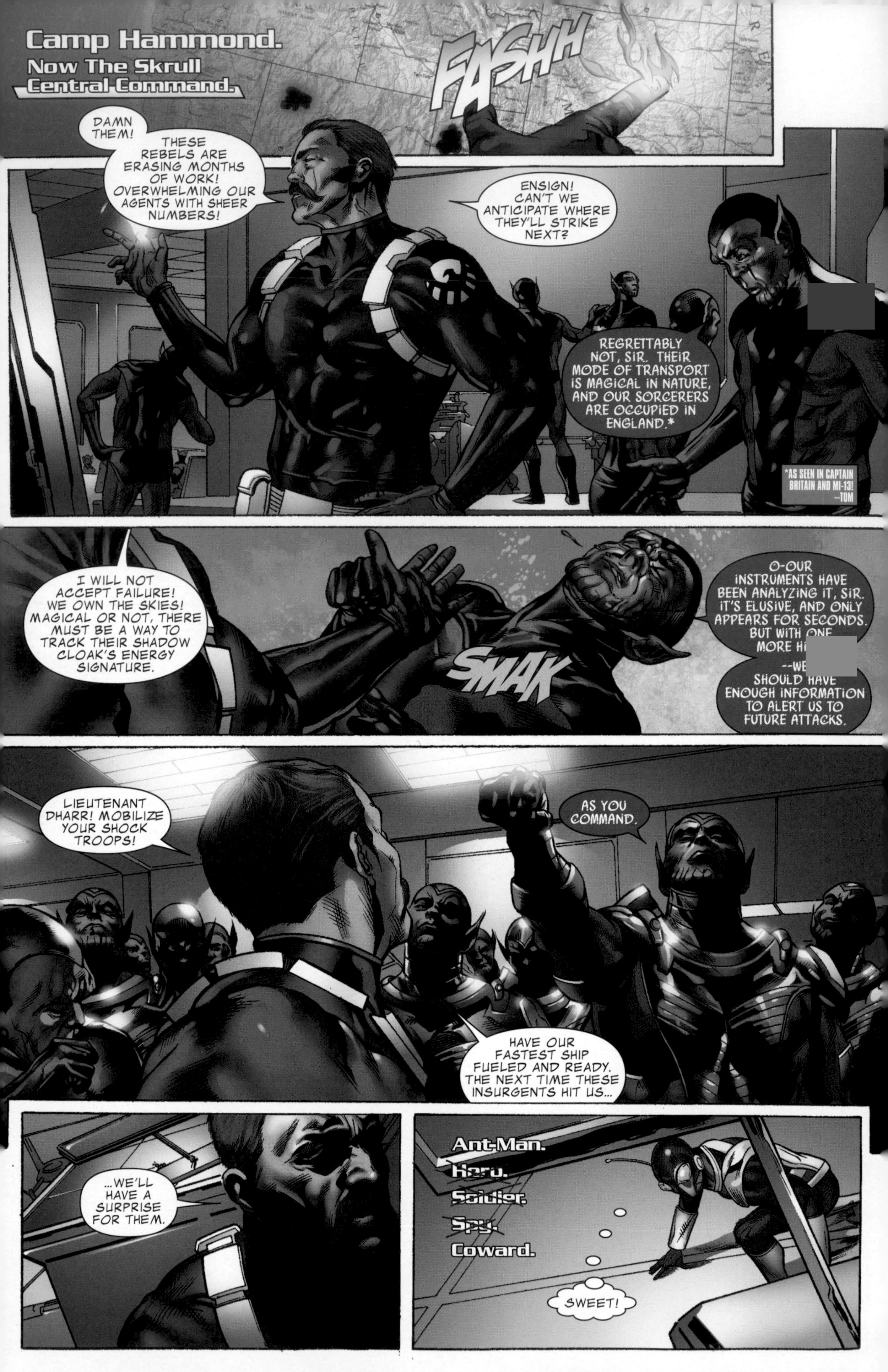
Camp Hammond.
Now The Skrull Central Command.
FASHH
DAMN THEM!
THESE REBELS ARE ERASING MONTHS OF WORK! OVERWHELMING OUR AGENTS WITH SHEER NUMBERS!
ENSIGN! CAN'T WE ANTICIPATE WHERE THEY'LL STRIKE NEXT?
REGRETTABLY NOT, SIR. THEIR MODE OF TRANSPORT IS MAGICAL IN NATURE, AND OUR SORCERERS ARE OCCUPIED IN ENGLAND.*
*AS SEEN IN CAPTAIN BRITAIN AND MI-13! --TOM
I WILL NOT ACCEPT FAILURE! WE OWN THE SKIES! MAGICAL OR NOT, THERE MUST BE A WAY TO TRACK THEIR SHADOW CLOAK'S ENERGY SIGNATURE.
SMAK
O-OUR INSTRUMENTS HAVE BEEN ANALYZING IT, SIR. IT'S ELUSIVE, AND ONLY APPEARS FOR SECONDS. BUT WITH ONE MORE HI
--WE SHOULD HAVE ENOUGH INFORMATION TO ALERT US TO FUTURE ATTACKS.
LIEUTENANT DHARR! MOBILIZE YOUR SHOCK TROOPS!
AS YOU COMMAND.
HAVE OUR FASTEST SHIP FUELED AND READY. THE NEXT TIME THESE INSURGENTS HIT US...
...WE'LL HAVE A SURPRISE FOR THEM.
Ant-Man.
~~Hero.~~
~~Soldier.~~
~~Spy.~~
Coward.
SWEET!

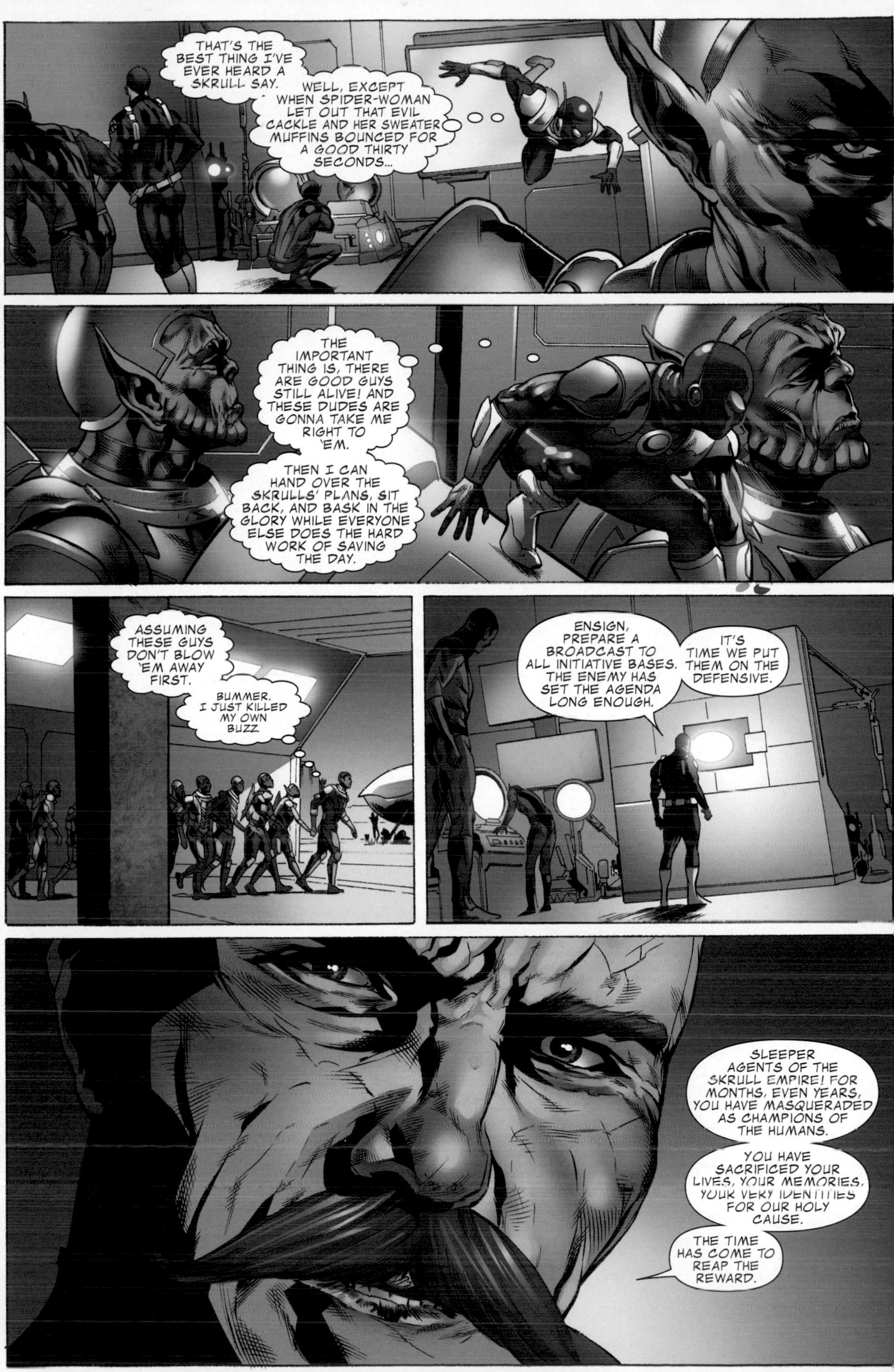
THAT'S THE BEST THING I'VE EVER HEARD A SKRULL SAY.
WELL, EXCEPT WHEN SPIDER-WOMAN LET OUT THAT EVIL CACKLE AND HER SWEATER MUFFINS BOUNCED FOR A GOOD THIRTY SECONDS...
THE IMPORTANT THING IS, THERE ARE GOOD GUYS STILL ALIVE! AND THESE DUDES ARE GONNA TAKE ME RIGHT TO 'EM.
THEN I CAN HAND OVER THE SKRULLS' PLANS, SIT BACK, AND BASK IN THE GLORY WHILE EVERYONE ELSE DOES THE HARD WORK OF SAVING THE DAY.
ASSUMING THESE GUYS DON'T BLOW 'EM AWAY FIRST.
BUMMER. I JUST KILLED MY OWN BUZZ.
ENSIGN, PREPARE A BROADCAST TO ALL INITIATIVE BASES. THE ENEMY HAS SET THE AGENDA LONG ENOUGH.
IT'S TIME WE PUT THEM ON THE DEFENSIVE.
SLEEPER AGENTS OF THE SKRULL EMPIRE! FOR MONTHS, EVEN YEARS, YOU HAVE MASQUERADED AS CHAMPIONS OF THE HUMANS.
YOU HAVE SACRIFICED YOUR LIVES, YOUR MEMORIES, YOUR VERY IDENTITIES FOR OUR HOLY CAUSE.
THE TIME HAS COME TO REAP THE REWARD.

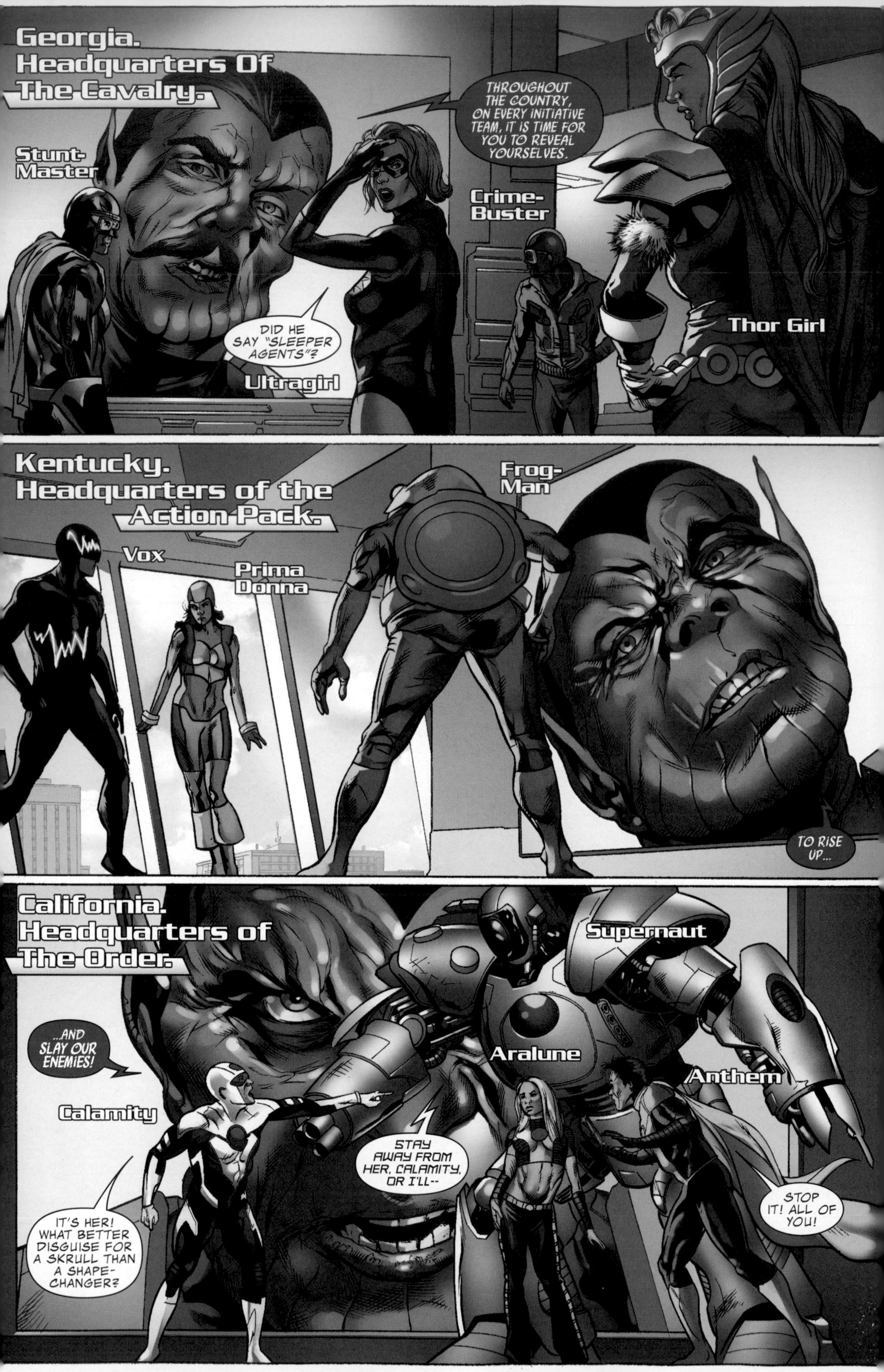
Georgia. Headquarters Of The Cavalry.
Stunt-Master
THROUGHOUT THE COUNTRY, ON EVERY INITIATIVE TEAM, IT IS TIME FOR YOU TO REVEAL YOURSELVES.
Crime-Buster
DID HE SAY "SLEEPER AGENTS"?
Ultragirl
Thor Girl
Kentucky. Headquarters of the Action Pack.
Frog-Man
Vox
Prima Donna
TO RISE UP...
California. Headquarters of The Order.
Supernaut
...AND SLAY OUR ENEMIES!
Aralune
Anthem
Calamity
STAY AWAY FROM HER, CALAMITY, OR I'LL--
IT'S HER! WHAT BETTER DISGUISE FOR A SKRULL THAN A SHAPE-CHANGER?
STOP IT! ALL OF YOU!

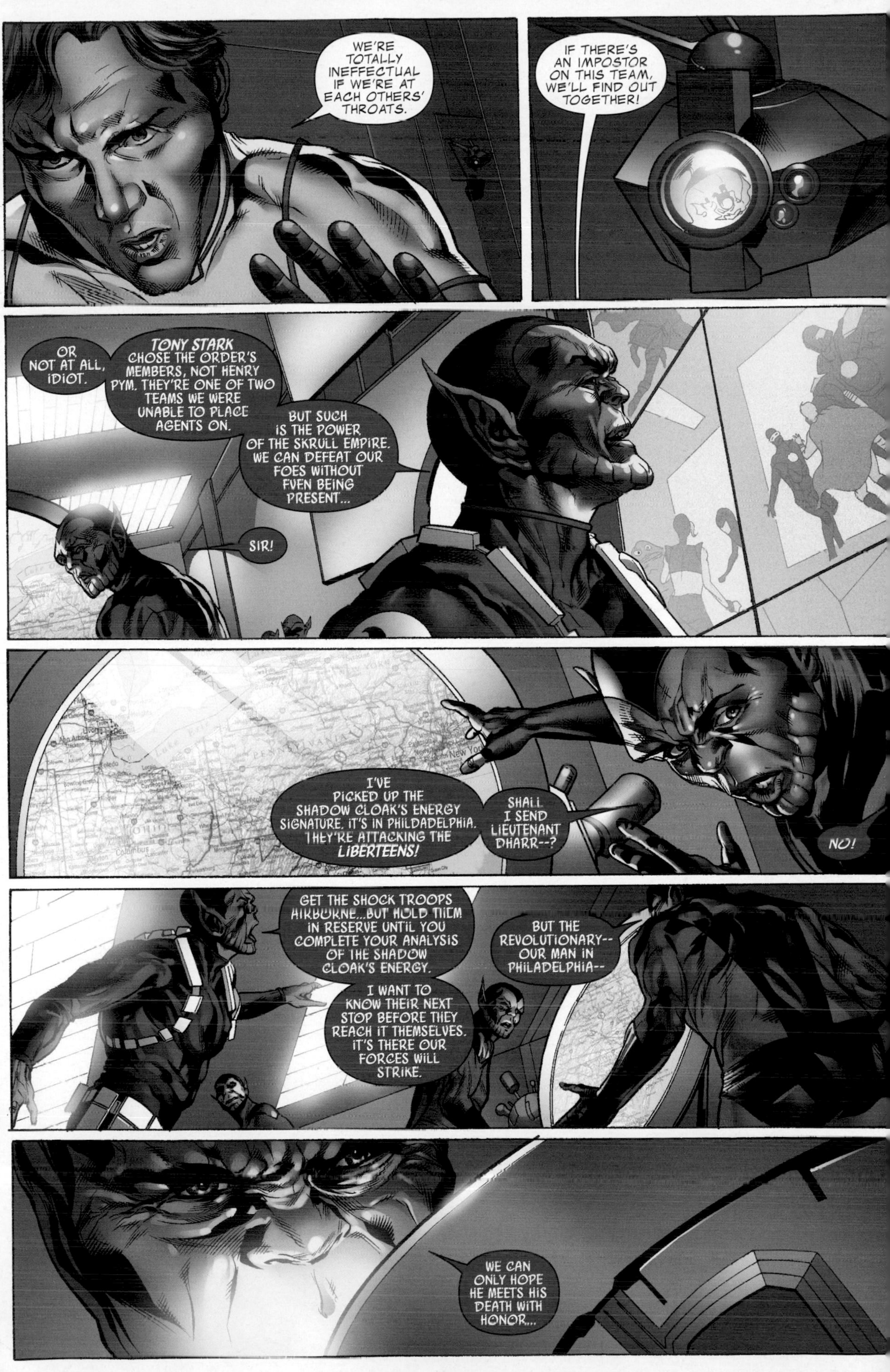
WE'RE TOTALLY INEFFECTUAL IF WE'RE AT EACH OTHERS' THROATS.
IF THERE'S AN IMPOSTOR ON THIS TEAM, WE'LL FIND OUT TOGETHER!
OR NOT AT ALL, IDIOT.
TONY STARK CHOSE THE ORDER'S MEMBERS, NOT HENRY PYM. THEY'RE ONE OF TWO TEAMS WE WERE UNABLE TO PLACE AGENTS ON.
BUT SUCH IS THE POWER OF THE SKRULL EMPIRE. WE CAN DEFEAT OUR FOES WITHOUT EVEN BEING PRESENT...
SIR!
I'VE PICKED UP THE SHADOW CLOAK'S ENERGY SIGNATURE. IT'S IN PHILADELPHIA. THEY'RE ATTACKING THE LIBERTEENS!
SHALL I SEND LIEUTENANT DHARR--?
NO!
GET THE SHOCK TROOPS AIRBORNE...BUT HOLD THEM IN RESERVE UNTIL YOU COMPLETE YOUR ANALYSIS OF THE SHADOW CLOAK'S ENERGY.
I WANT TO KNOW THEIR NEXT STOP BEFORE THEY REACH IT THEMSELVES. IT'S THERE OUR FORCES WILL STRIKE.
BUT THE REVOLUTIONARY-- OUR MAN IN PHILADELPHIA--
WE CAN ONLY HOPE HE MEETS HIS DEATH WITH HONOR...

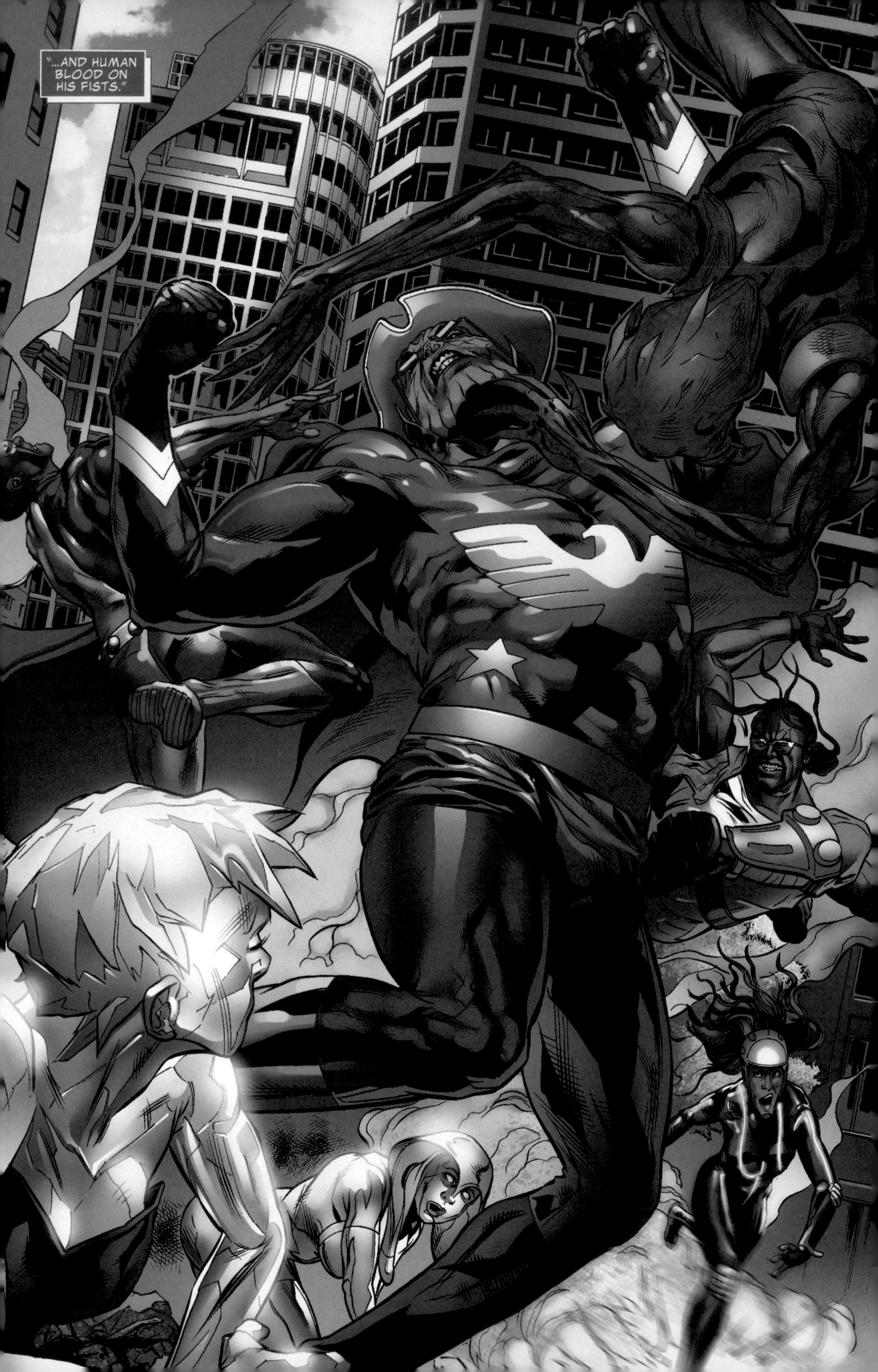
"...AND HUMAN BLOOD ON HIS FISTS."

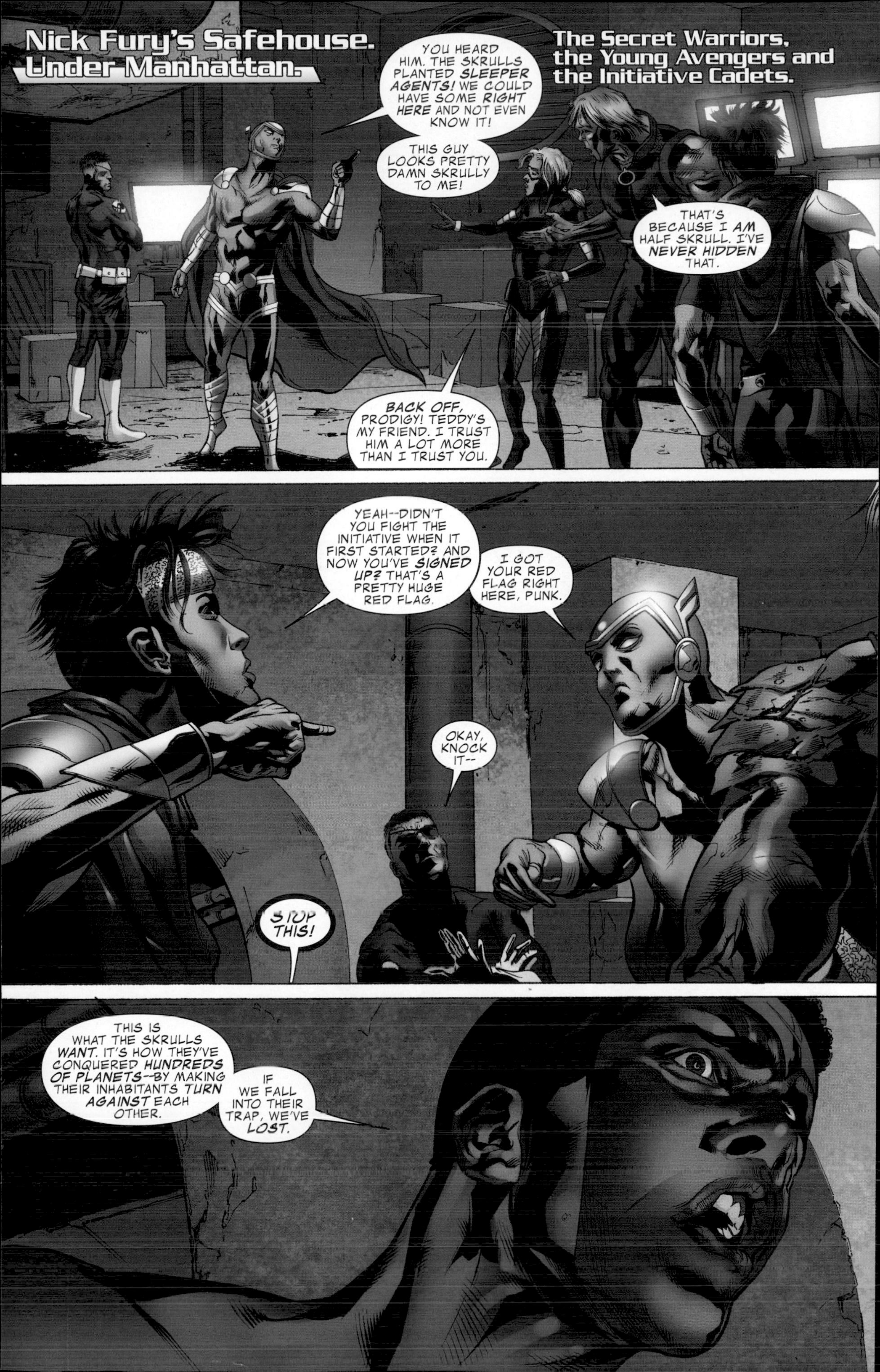
Nick Fury's Safehouse. Under Manhattan.
The Secret Warriors, the Young Avengers and the Initiative Cadets.
YOU HEARD HIM. THE SKRULLS PLANTED SLEEPER AGENTS! WE COULD HAVE SOME RIGHT HERE AND NOT EVEN KNOW IT!
THIS GUY LOOKS PRETTY DAMN SKRULLY TO ME!
THAT'S BECAUSE I AM HALF SKRULL. I'VE NEVER HIDDEN THAT.
BACK OFF, PRODIGY! TEDDY'S MY FRIEND. I TRUST HIM A LOT MORE THAN I TRUST YOU.
YEAH--DIDN'T YOU FIGHT THE INITIATIVE WHEN IT FIRST STARTED? AND NOW YOU'VE SIGNED UP? THAT'S A PRETTY HUGE RED FLAG.
I GOT YOUR RED FLAG RIGHT HERE, PUNK.
OKAY, KNOCK IT--
STOP THIS!
THIS IS WHAT THE SKRULLS WANT. IT'S HOW THEY'VE CONQUERED HUNDREDS OF PLANETS--BY MAKING THEIR INHABITANTS TURN AGAINST EACH OTHER.
IF WE FALL INTO THEIR TRAP, WE'VE LOST.

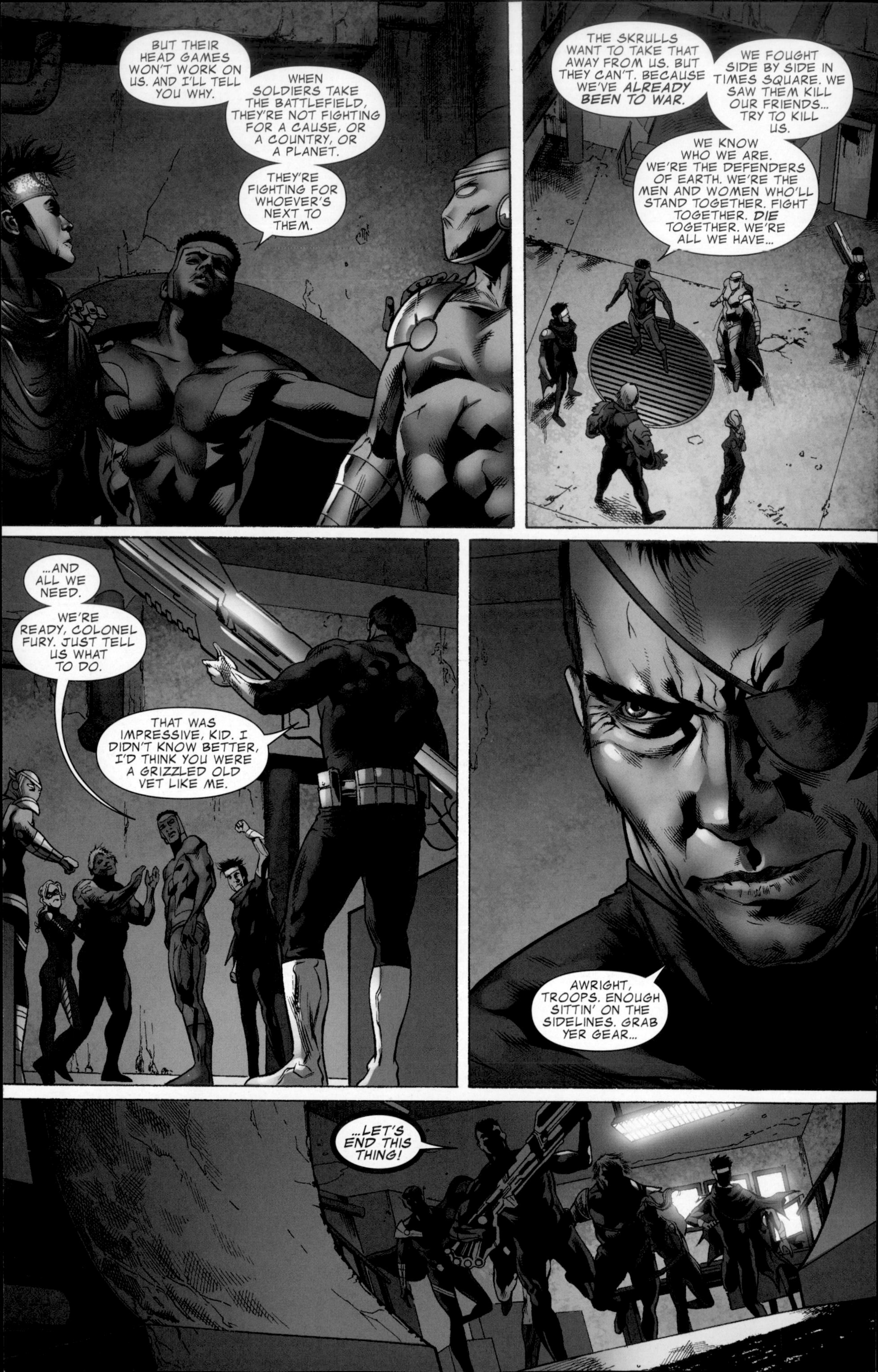
BUT THEIR HEAD GAMES WON'T WORK ON US. AND I'LL TELL YOU WHY.
WHEN SOLDIERS TAKE THE BATTLEFIELD, THEY'RE NOT FIGHTING FOR A CAUSE, OR A COUNTRY, OR A PLANET.
THEY'RE FIGHTING FOR WHOEVER'S NEXT TO THEM.
THE SKRULLS WANT TO TAKE THAT AWAY FROM US. BUT THEY CAN'T. BECAUSE WE'VE *ALREADY BEEN TO WAR.*
WE FOUGHT SIDE BY SIDE IN TIMES SQUARE. WE SAW THEM KILL OUR FRIENDS... TRY TO KILL US.
WE KNOW WHO WE ARE. WE'RE THE DEFENDERS OF EARTH. WE'RE THE MEN AND WOMEN WHO'LL STAND TOGETHER. FIGHT TOGETHER. *DIE* TOGETHER. WE'RE ALL WE HAVE...
...AND ALL WE NEED.
WE'RE READY, COLONEL FURY. JUST TELL US WHAT TO DO.
THAT WAS IMPRESSIVE, KID. I DIDN'T KNOW BETTER, I'D THINK YOU WERE A GRIZZLED OLD VET LIKE ME.
AWRIGHT, TROOPS. ENOUGH SITTIN' ON THE SIDELINES. GRAB YER GEAR...
...LET'S END THIS THING!

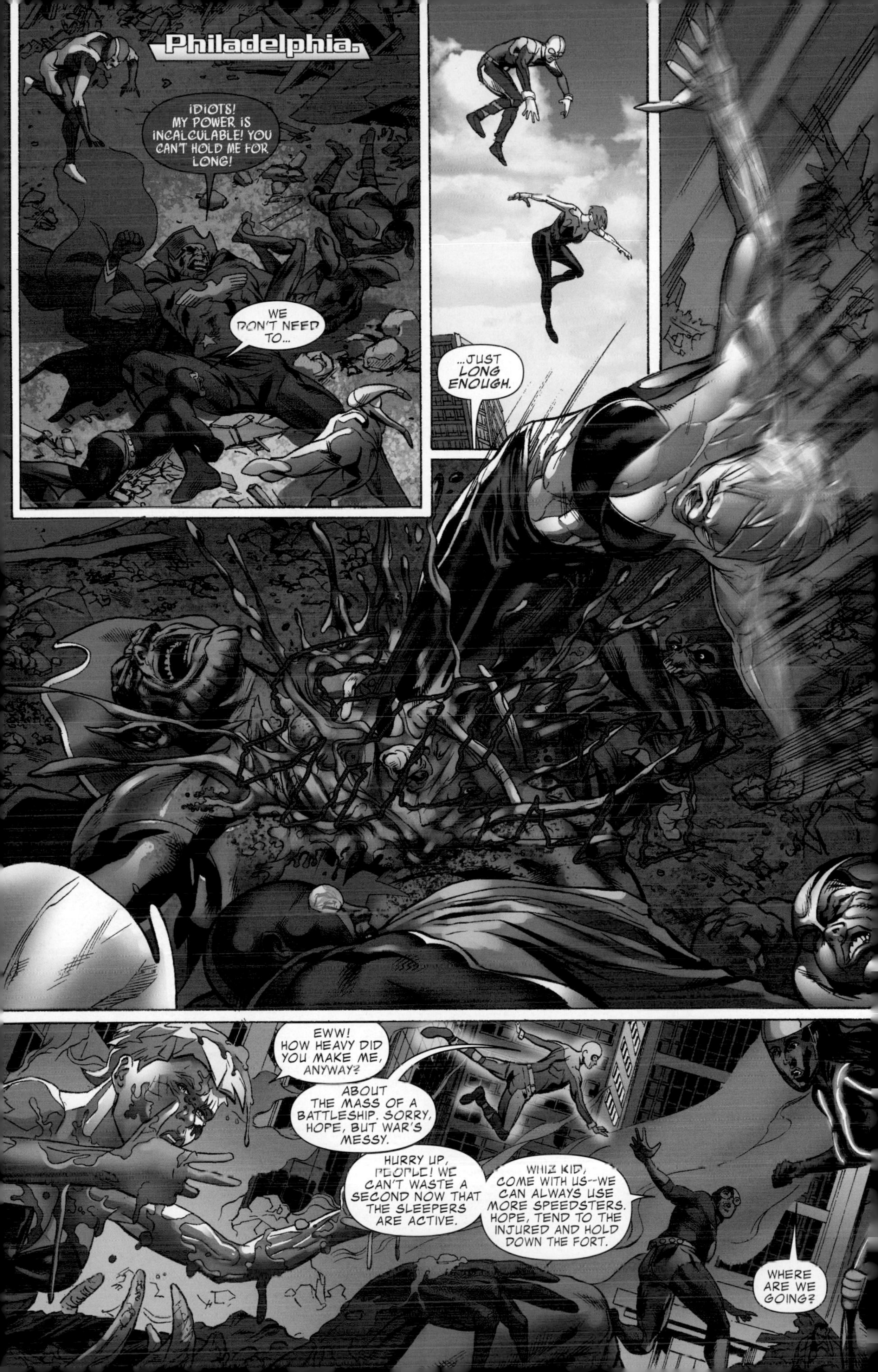
Philadelphia.
IDIOTS! MY POWER IS INCALCULABLE! YOU CAN'T HOLD ME FOR LONG!
WE DON'T NEED TO...
...JUST LONG ENOUGH.
EWW! HOW HEAVY DID YOU MAKE ME, ANYWAY?
ABOUT THE MASS OF A BATTLESHIP. SORRY, HOPE, BUT WAR'S MESSY.
HURRY UP, PEOPLE! WE CAN'T WASTE A SECOND NOW THAT THE SLEEPERS ARE ACTIVE.
WHIZ KID, COME WITH US--WE CAN ALWAYS USE MORE SPEEDSTERS. HOPE, TEND TO THE INJURED AND HOLD DOWN THE FORT.
WHERE ARE WE GOING?

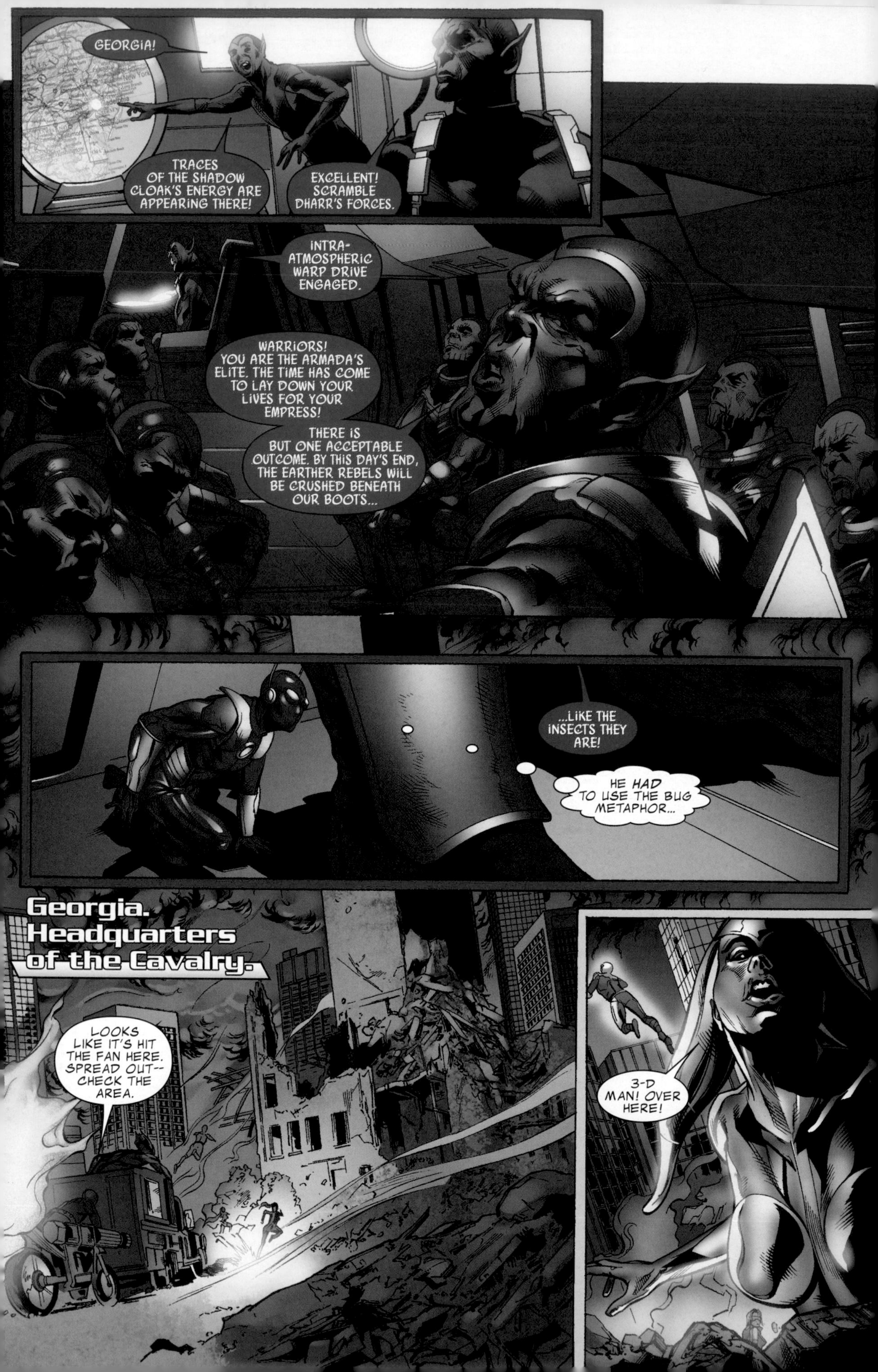
GEORGIA!
TRACES OF THE SHADOW CLOAK'S ENERGY ARE APPEARING THERE!
EXCELLENT! SCRAMBLE DHARR'S FORCES.
INTRA-ATMOSPHERIC WARP DRIVE ENGAGED.
WARRIORS! YOU ARE THE ARMADA'S ELITE. THE TIME HAS COME TO LAY DOWN YOUR LIVES FOR YOUR EMPRESS!
THERE IS BUT ONE ACCEPTABLE OUTCOME. BY THIS DAY'S END, THE EARTHER REBELS WILL BE CRUSHED BENEATH OUR BOOTS...
...LIKE THE INSECTS THEY ARE!
HE HAD TO USE THE BUG METAPHOR...
Georgia. Headquarters of the Cavalry.
LOOKS LIKE IT'S HIT THE FAN HERE. SPREAD OUT-- CHECK THE AREA.
3-D MAN! OVER HERE!

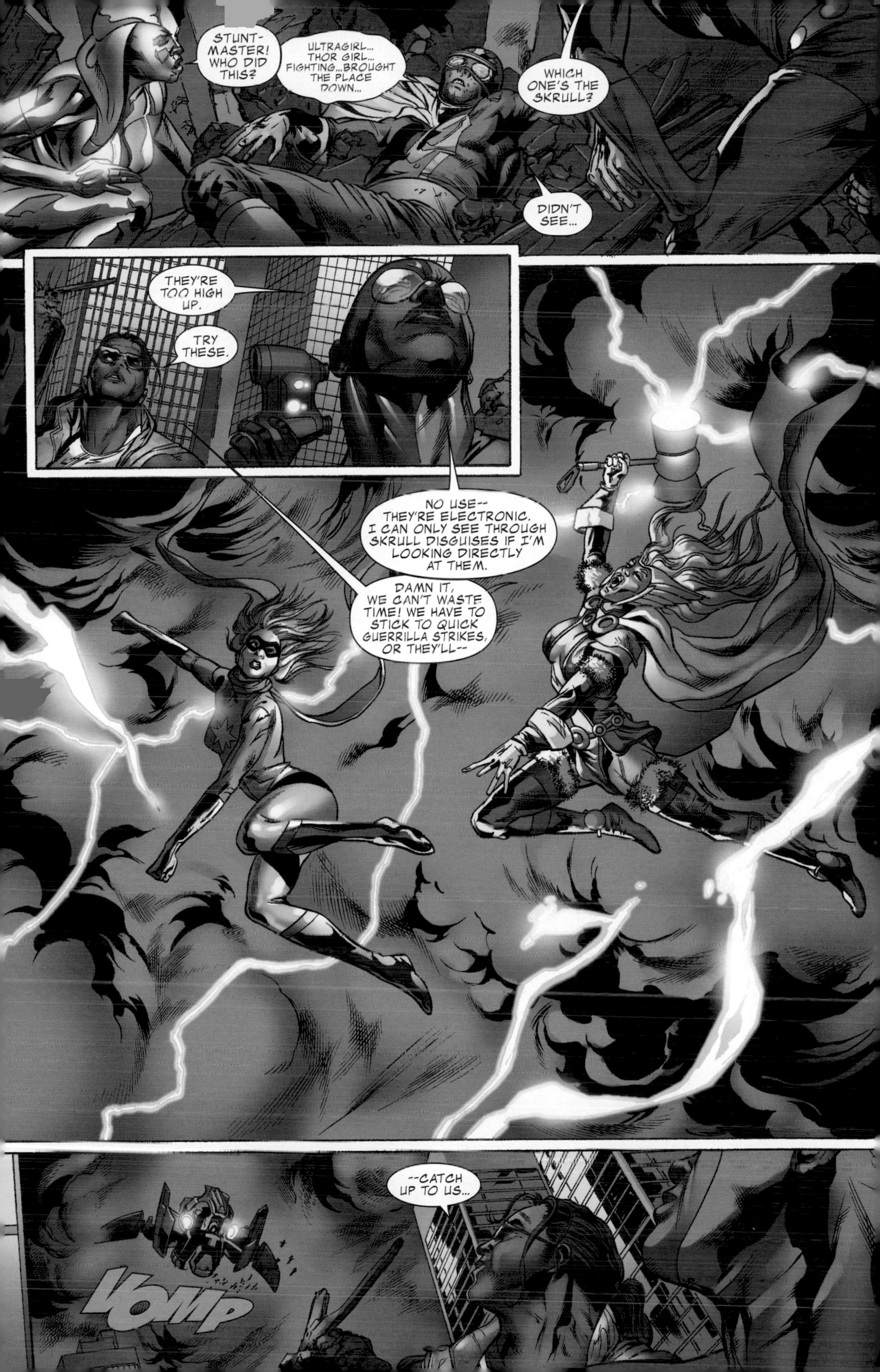
STUNT-MASTER! WHO DID THIS?
ULTRAGIRL... THOR GIRL... FIGHTING...BROUGHT THE PLACE DOWN...
WHICH ONE'S THE SKRULL?
DIDN'T SEE...
THEY'RE TOO HIGH UP.
TRY THESE.
NO USE-- THEY'RE ELECTRONIC. I CAN ONLY SEE THROUGH SKRULL DISGUISES IF I'M LOOKING DIRECTLY AT THEM.
DAMN IT, WE CAN'T WASTE TIME! WE HAVE TO STICK TO QUICK GUERRILLA STRIKES, OR THEY'LL--
--CATCH UP TO US...
VOMP

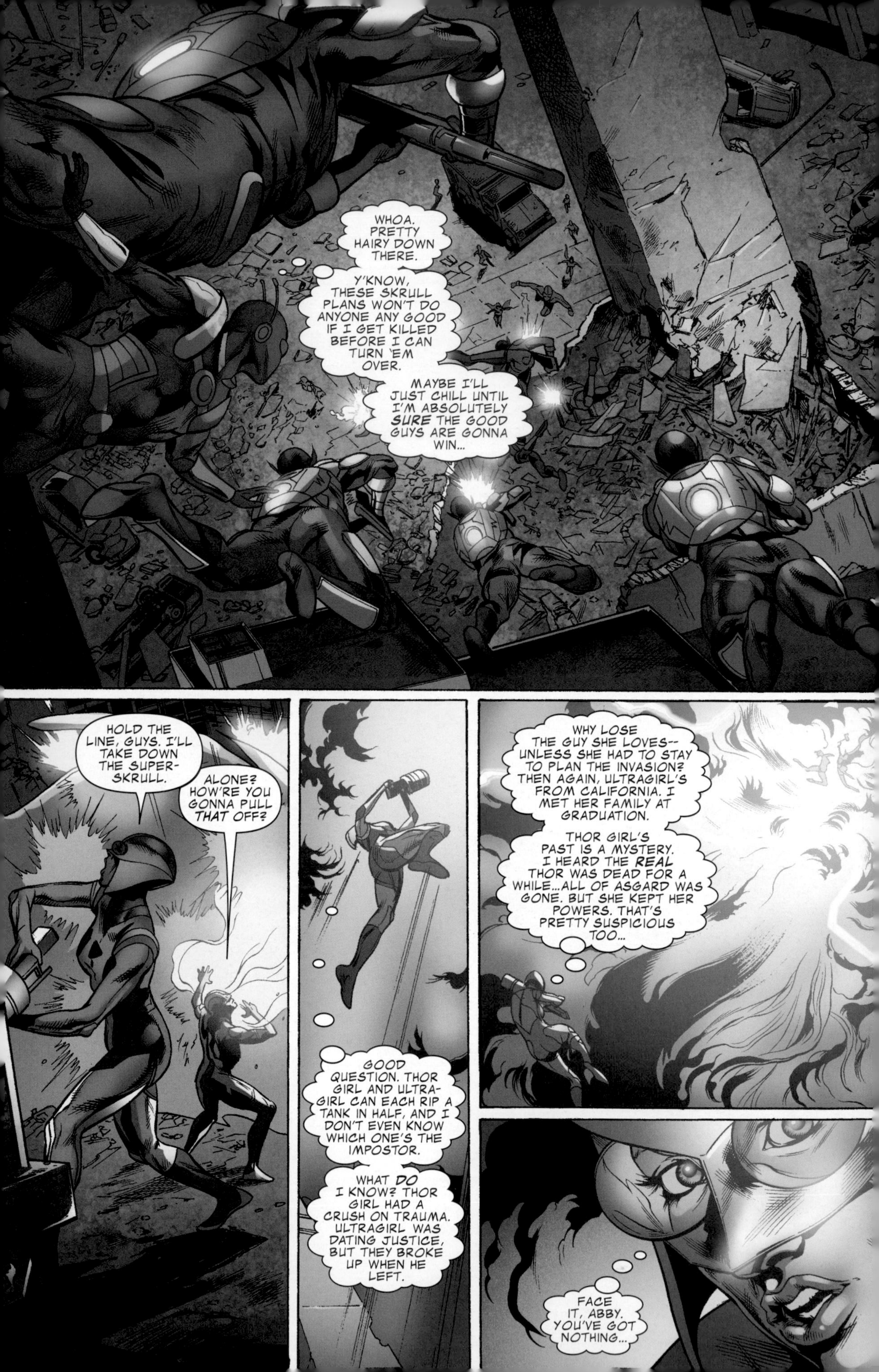

WHOA. PRETTY HAIRY DOWN THERE.
Y'KNOW, THESE SKRULL PLANS WON'T DO ANYONE ANY GOOD IF I GET KILLED BEFORE I CAN TURN 'EM OVER.
MAYBE I'LL JUST CHILL UNTIL I'M ABSOLUTELY SURE THE GOOD GUYS ARE GONNA WIN...
HOLD THE LINE, GUYS. I'LL TAKE DOWN THE SUPER-SKRULL.
ALONE? HOW'RE YOU GONNA PULL THAT OFF?
GOOD QUESTION. THOR GIRL AND ULTRA-GIRL CAN EACH RIP A TANK IN HALF, AND I DON'T EVEN KNOW WHICH ONE'S THE IMPOSTOR.
WHAT DO I KNOW? THOR GIRL HAD A CRUSH ON TRAUMA. ULTRAGIRL WAS DATING JUSTICE, BUT THEY BROKE UP WHEN HE LEFT.
WHY LOSE THE GUY SHE LOVES-- UNLESS SHE HAD TO STAY TO PLAN THE INVASION? THEN AGAIN, ULTRAGIRL'S FROM CALIFORNIA. I MET HER FAMILY AT GRADUATION.
THOR GIRL'S PAST IS A MYSTERY. I HEARD THE REAL THOR WAS DEAD FOR A WHILE...ALL OF ASGARD WAS GONE. BUT SHE KEPT HER POWERS. THAT'S PRETTY SUSPICIOUS TOO...
FACE IT, ABBY. YOU'VE GOT NOTHING...

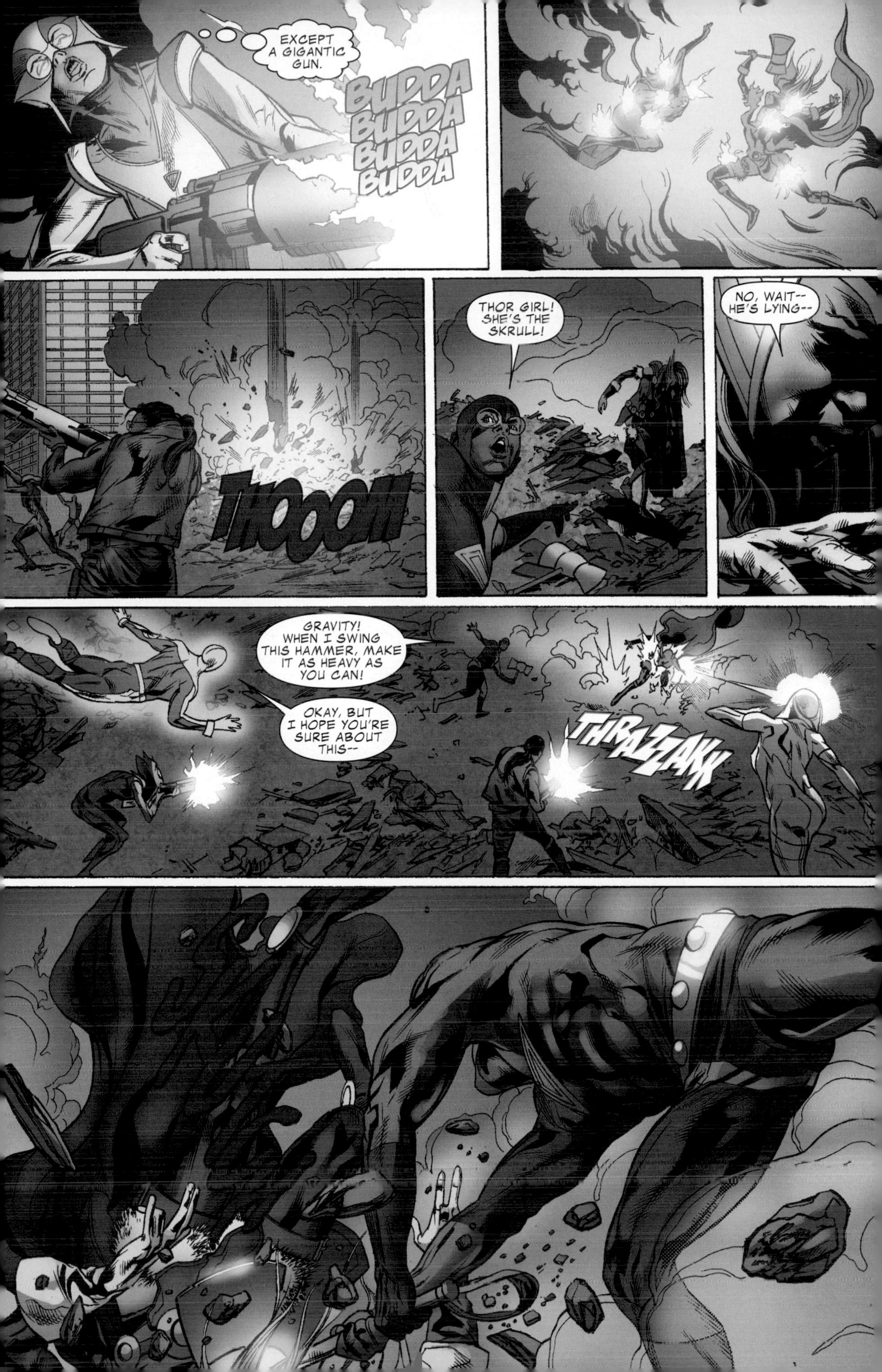
EXCEPT A GIGANTIC GUN.
BUDDA BUDDA BUDDA BUDDA
THOOOM
THOR GIRL! SHE'S THE SKRULL!
NO, WAIT-- HE'S LYING--
GRAVITY! WHEN I SWING THIS HAMMER, MAKE IT AS HEAVY AS YOU CAN!
OKAY, BUT I HOPE YOU'RE SURE ABOUT THIS--
THRAZZAKK

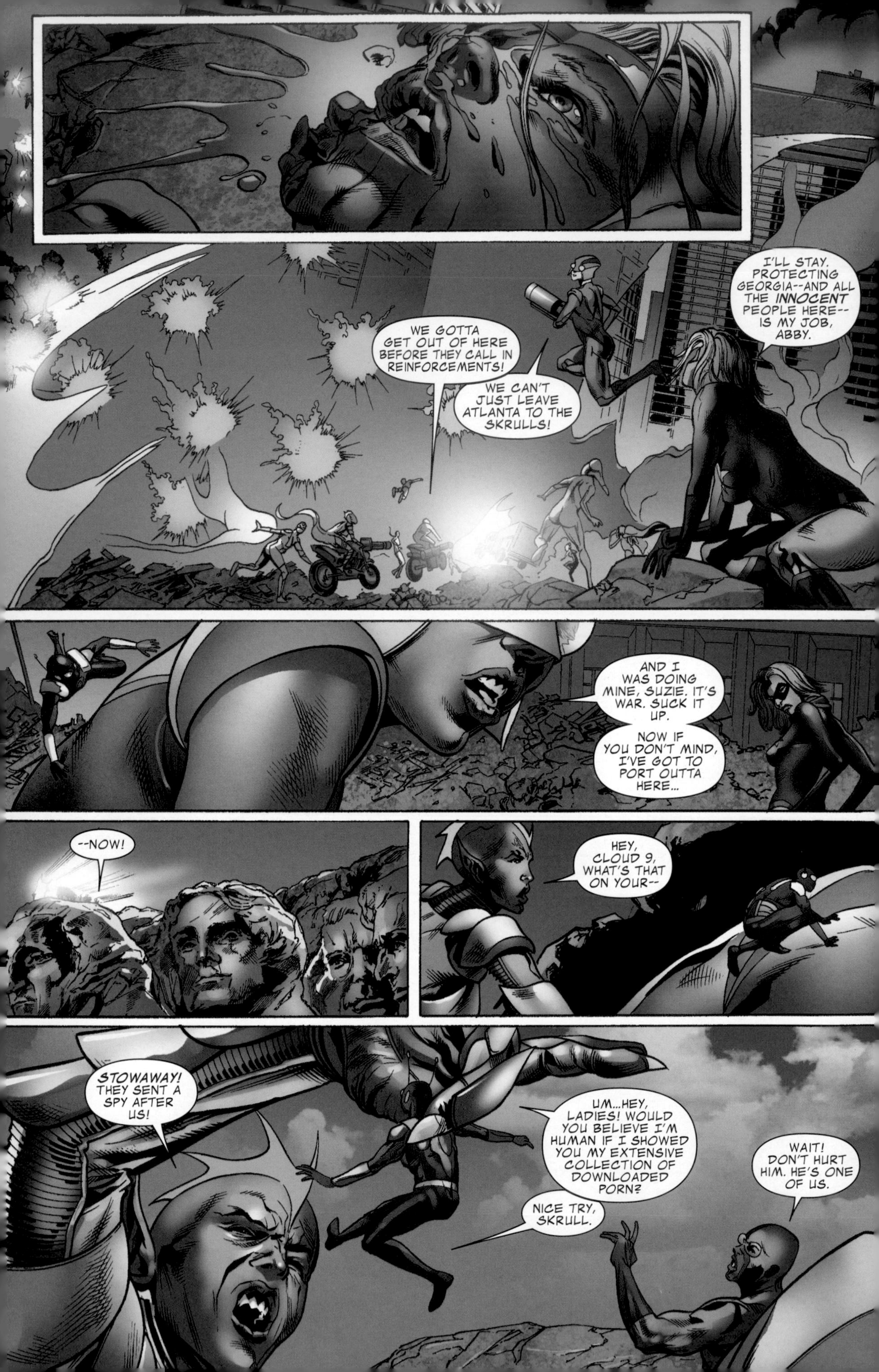

WE GOTTA GET OUT OF HERE BEFORE THEY CALL IN REINFORCEMENTS!
WE CAN'T JUST LEAVE ATLANTA TO THE SKRULLS!
I'LL STAY. PROTECTING GEORGIA--AND ALL THE INNOCENT PEOPLE HERE--IS MY JOB, ABBY.
AND I WAS DOING MINE, SUZIE. IT'S WAR. SUCK IT UP.
NOW IF YOU DON'T MIND, I'VE GOT TO PORT OUTTA HERE...
--NOW!
HEY, CLOUD 9, WHAT'S THAT ON YOUR--
STOWAWAY! THEY SENT A SPY AFTER US!
UM...HEY, LADIES! WOULD YOU BELIEVE I'M HUMAN IF I SHOWED YOU MY EXTENSIVE COLLECTION OF DOWNLOADED PORN?
NICE TRY, SKRULL.
WAIT! DON'T HURT HIM. HE'S ONE OF US.

GLAD WE CLEARED THAT UP. 'CAUSE, UH, I WAS JUST KIDDING ABOUT THE PORN.

WHAT ARE YOU DOING HERE, ANT-MAN?

SAVING THE WORLD, OF COURSE. AT GREAT RISK TO MYSELF, I INFILTRATED THE SKRULLS' COMMAND CENTER AND GOT PICTURES OF THEIR MASTER PLAN.

OR AS I LIKE TO CALL IT, THE "IF WE CAN'T HAVE IT, YOU CAN'T HAVE IT" PLAN. IT GOES SOMETHING LIKE THIS...

BUILD INITIATIVE BASES ALL ACROSS THE U.S., PUT A BI-I-I-G TOWER, BASE OR ANTENNA IN EACH ONE...

...LINK 'EM UP TO OUR NEGATIVE ZONE JUMP GATES AND...

IT WOULD CREATE A NATIONWIDE PORTAL TO THE NEGATIVE ZONE! ALL IT WOULD REQUIRE ARE THREE WORKING PYLONS...

...AND A SIGNIFICANT PORTION OF THE PLANET WOULD BE SHUNTED INTO ANOTHER DIMENSION.

MY GOD! COULD WE REVERSE IT?

NOT BEFORE THE RESULTING LOSS OF MASS WOULD ALTER EARTH'S ORBIT. THIS IS A DOOMSDAY SCENARIO.

WHAT CAN WE DO? THERE ARE STILL SIX BASES LEFT AND ONLY THREE OF US CAN DETECT SKRULLS.

NOT TRUE.

A BLENDER? REALLY?

I'VE GOTTEN USED TO YOU KILL KREW GUYS EATING SKRULL MEAT...BUT "SKRULL SMOOTHIES"? THAT'S DISGUSTING!

WHRRR

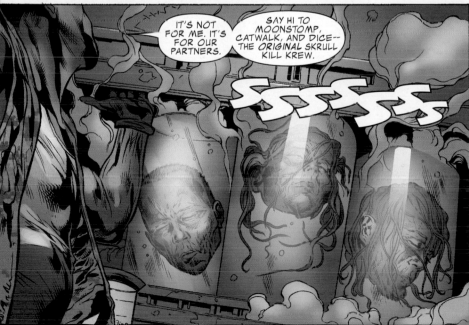

IT'S NOT FOR ME. IT'S FOR OUR PARTNERS.

SAY HI TO MOONSTOMP, CATWALK, AND DICE-- THE ORIGINAL SKRULL KILL KREW.

SSSSS

HOLD ON. YOU SAID YOUR PARTNERS WERE DEAD!

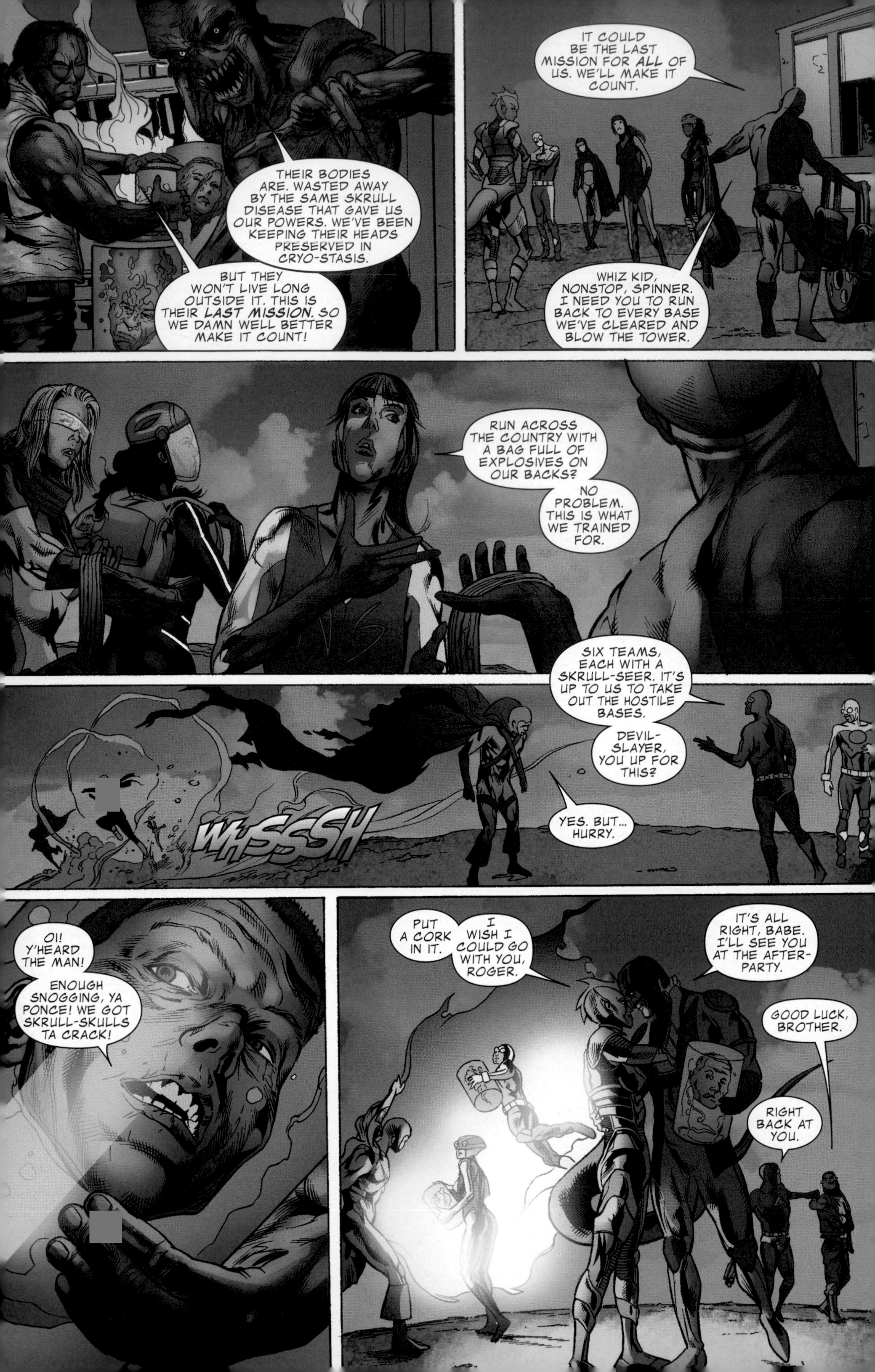
THEIR BODIES ARE. WASTED AWAY BY THE SAME SKRULL DISEASE THAT GAVE US OUR POWERS. WE'VE BEEN KEEPING THEIR HEADS PRESERVED IN CRYO-STASIS.
BUT THEY WON'T LIVE LONG OUTSIDE IT. THIS IS THEIR LAST MISSION. SO WE DAMN WELL BETTER MAKE IT COUNT!
IT COULD BE THE LAST MISSION FOR ALL OF US. WE'LL MAKE IT COUNT.
WHIZ KID, NONSTOP, SPINNER. I NEED YOU TO RUN BACK TO EVERY BASE WE'VE CLEARED AND BLOW THE TOWER.
RUN ACROSS THE COUNTRY WITH A BAG FULL OF EXPLOSIVES ON OUR BACKS?
NO PROBLEM. THIS IS WHAT WE TRAINED FOR.
SIX TEAMS, EACH WITH A SKRULL-SEER. IT'S UP TO US TO TAKE OUT THE HOSTILE BASES.
DEVIL-SLAYER, YOU UP FOR THIS?
YES. BUT... HURRY.
WHSSSH
OI! Y'HEARD THE MAN!
ENOUGH SNOGGING, YA PONCE! WE GOT SKRULL-SKULLS TA CRACK!
PUT A CORK IN IT.
I WISH I COULD GO WITH YOU, ROGER.
IT'S ALL RIGHT, BABE. I'LL SEE YOU AT THE AFTER-PARTY.
GOOD LUCK, BROTHER.
RIGHT BACK AT YOU.

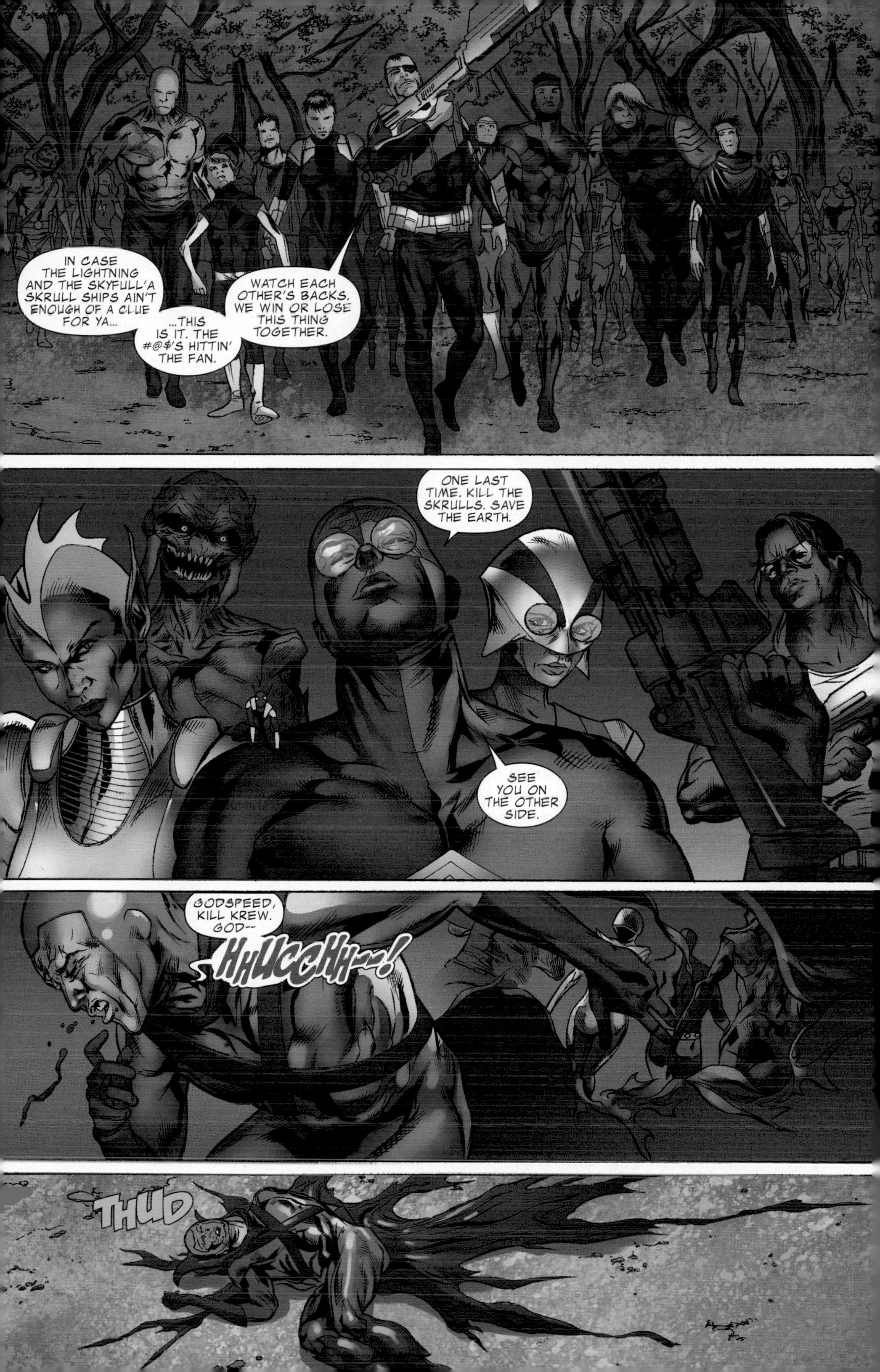
IN CASE THE LIGHTNING AND THE SKYFULL'A SKRULL SHIPS AIN'T ENOUGH OF A CLUE FOR YA...
...THIS IS IT. THE #@$'S HITTIN' THE FAN.
WATCH EACH OTHER'S BACKS. WE WIN OR LOSE THIS THING TOGETHER.
ONE LAST TIME. KILL THE SKRULLS. SAVE THE EARTH.
SEE YOU ON THE OTHER SIDE.
GODSPEED, KILL KREW. GOD--
HHUCCHH--!
THUD

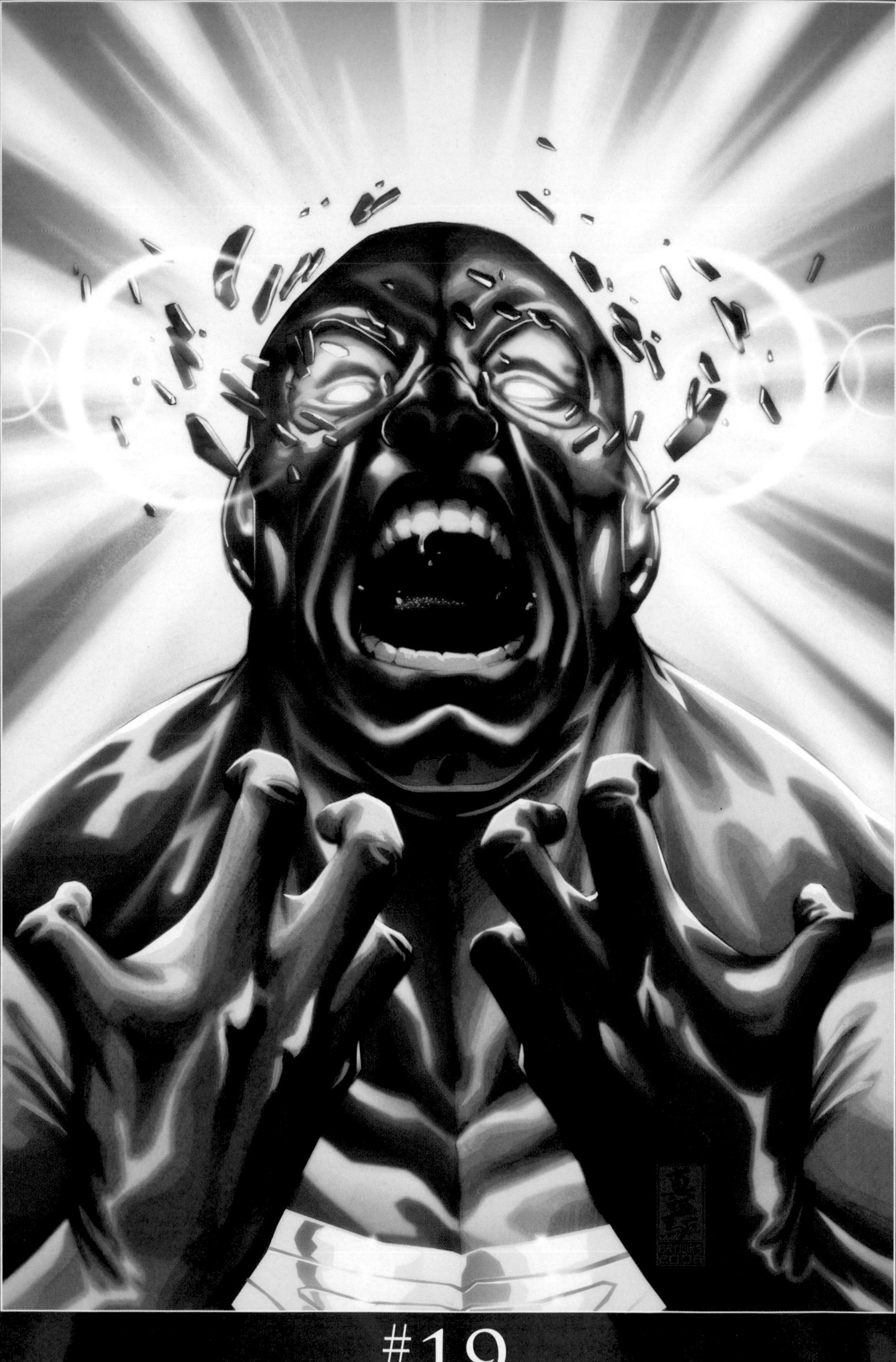

#19

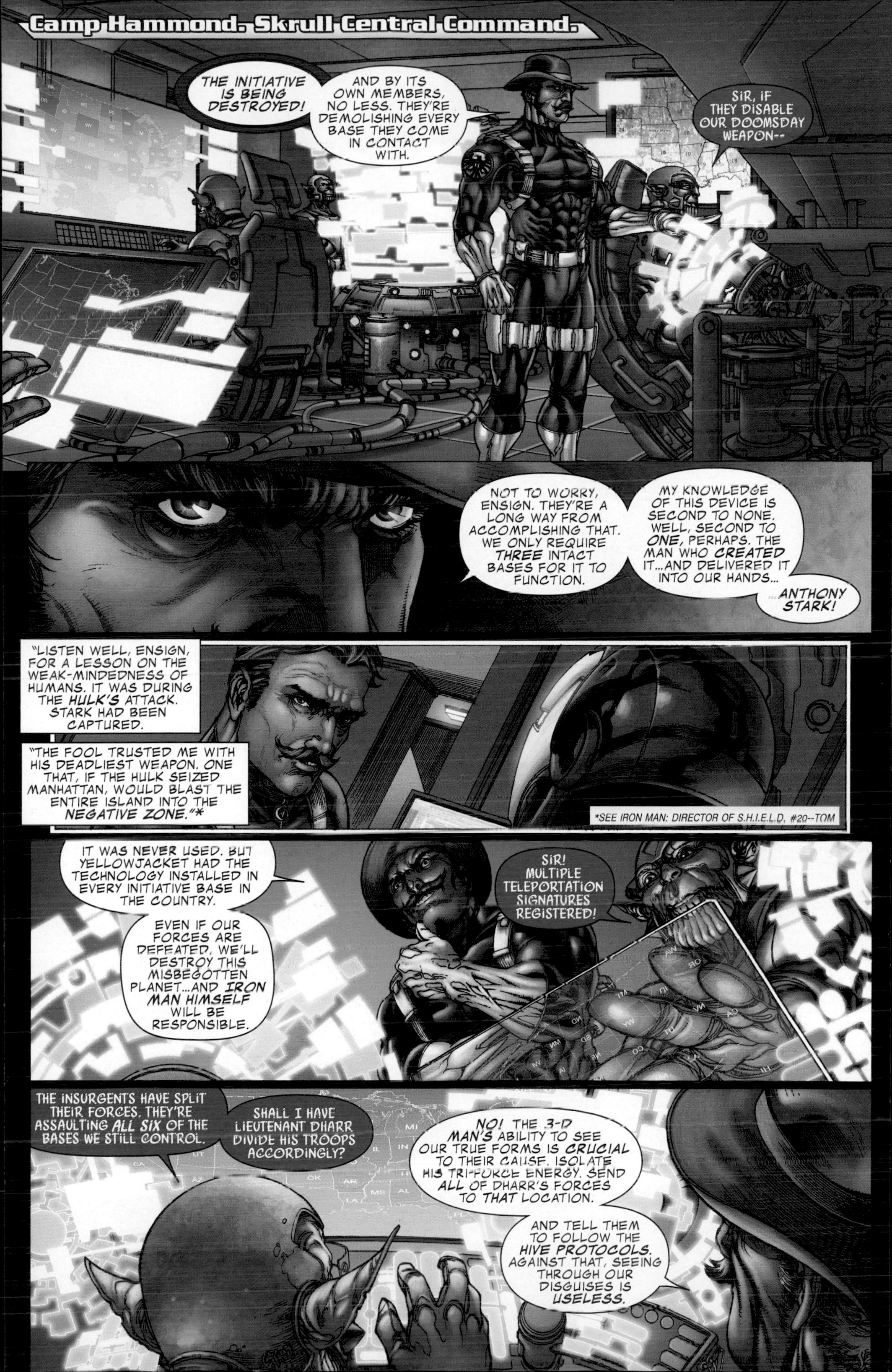
Camp Hammond. Skrull Central Command.
THE INITIATIVE IS BEING DESTROYED!
AND BY ITS OWN MEMBERS, NO LESS. THEY'RE DEMOLISHING EVERY BASE THEY COME IN CONTACT WITH.
SIR, IF THEY DISABLE OUR DOOMSDAY WEAPON--
NOT TO WORRY, ENSIGN. THEY'RE A LONG WAY FROM ACCOMPLISHING THAT. WE ONLY REQUIRE THREE INTACT BASES FOR IT TO FUNCTION.
MY KNOWLEDGE OF THIS DEVICE IS SECOND TO NONE. WELL, SECOND TO ONE, PERHAPS. THE MAN WHO CREATED IT...AND DELIVERED IT INTO OUR HANDS...
...ANTHONY STARK!
"LISTEN WELL, ENSIGN, FOR A LESSON ON THE WEAK-MINDEDNESS OF HUMANS. IT WAS DURING THE HULK'S ATTACK. STARK HAD BEEN CAPTURED.
"THE FOOL TRUSTED ME WITH HIS DEADLIEST WEAPON. ONE THAT, IF THE HULK SEIZED MANHATTAN, WOULD BLAST THE ENTIRE ISLAND INTO THE NEGATIVE ZONE."*
*SEE IRON MAN: DIRECTOR OF S.H.I.E.L.D. #20--TOM
IT WAS NEVER USED. BUT YELLOWJACKET HAD THE TECHNOLOGY INSTALLED IN EVERY INITIATIVE BASE IN THE COUNTRY.
EVEN IF OUR FORCES ARE DEFEATED, WE'LL DESTROY THIS MISBEGOTTEN PLANET...AND IRON MAN HIMSELF WILL BE RESPONSIBLE.
SIR! MULTIPLE TELEPORTATION SIGNATURES REGISTERED!
THE INSURGENTS HAVE SPLIT THEIR FORCES. THEY'RE ASSAULTING ALL SIX OF THE BASES WE STILL CONTROL.
SHALL I HAVE LIEUTENANT DHARR DIVIDE HIS TROOPS ACCORDINGLY?
NO! THE 3-D MAN'S ABILITY TO SEE OUR TRUE FORMS IS CRUCIAL TO THEIR CAUSE. ISOLATE HIS TRI-FORCE ENERGY. SEND ALL OF DHARR'S FORCES TO THAT LOCATION.
AND TELL THEM TO FOLLOW THE HIVE PROTOCOLS. AGAINST THAT, SEEING THROUGH OUR DISGUISES IS USELESS.

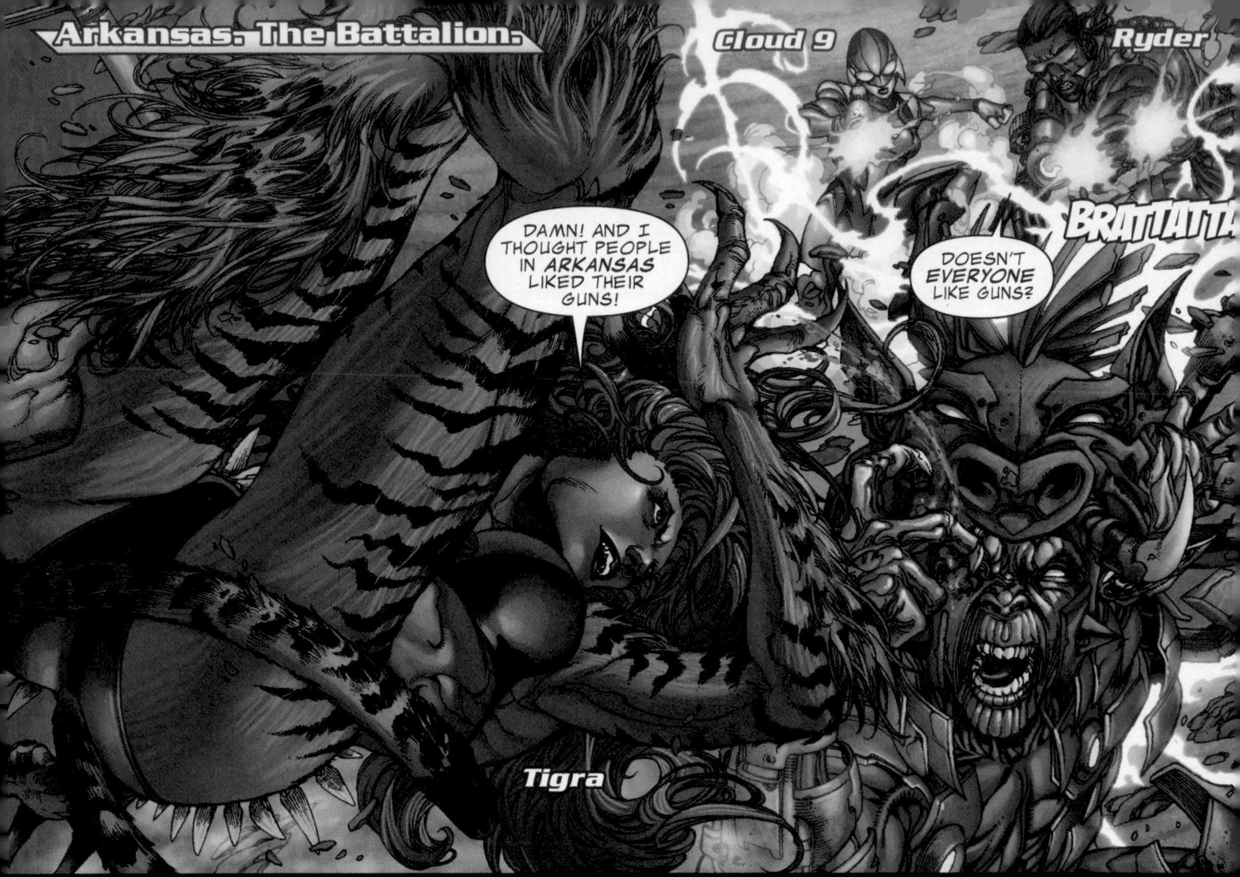
Arkansas. The Battalion.
Cloud 9
Ryder
DAMN! AND I THOUGHT PEOPLE IN ARKANSAS LIKED THEIR GUNS!
BRATTATTA
DOESN'T EVERYONE LIKE GUNS?
Tigra

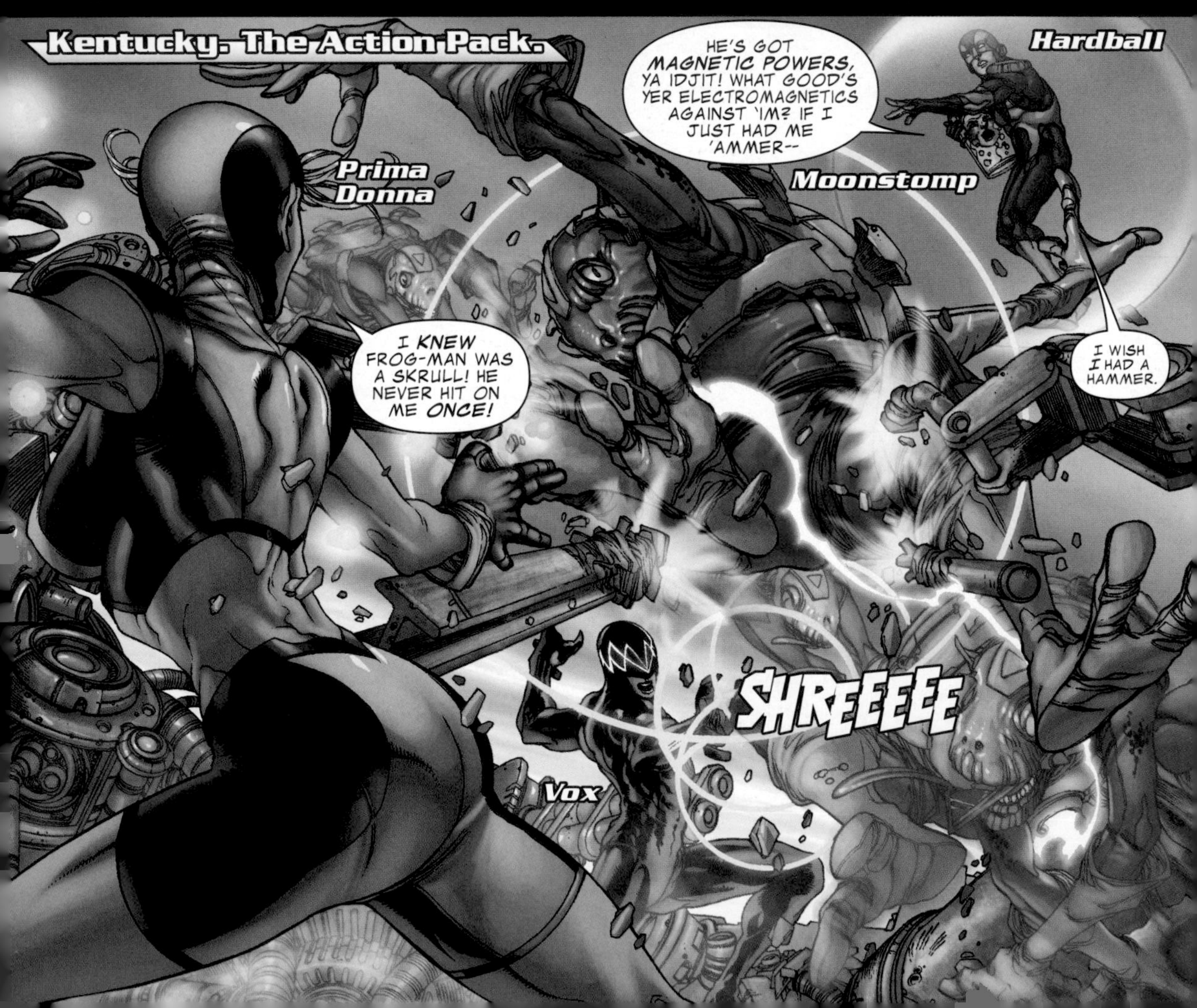
Kentucky. The Action Pack.
HE'S GOT MAGNETIC POWERS, YA IDJIT! WHAT GOOD'S YER ELECTROMAGNETICS AGAINST 'IM? IF I JUST HAD ME 'AMMER--
Hardball
Prima Donna
Moonstomp
I KNEW FROG-MAN WAS A SKRULL! HE NEVER HIT ON ME ONCE!
I WISH I HAD A HAMMER.
SHREEEEE
Vox

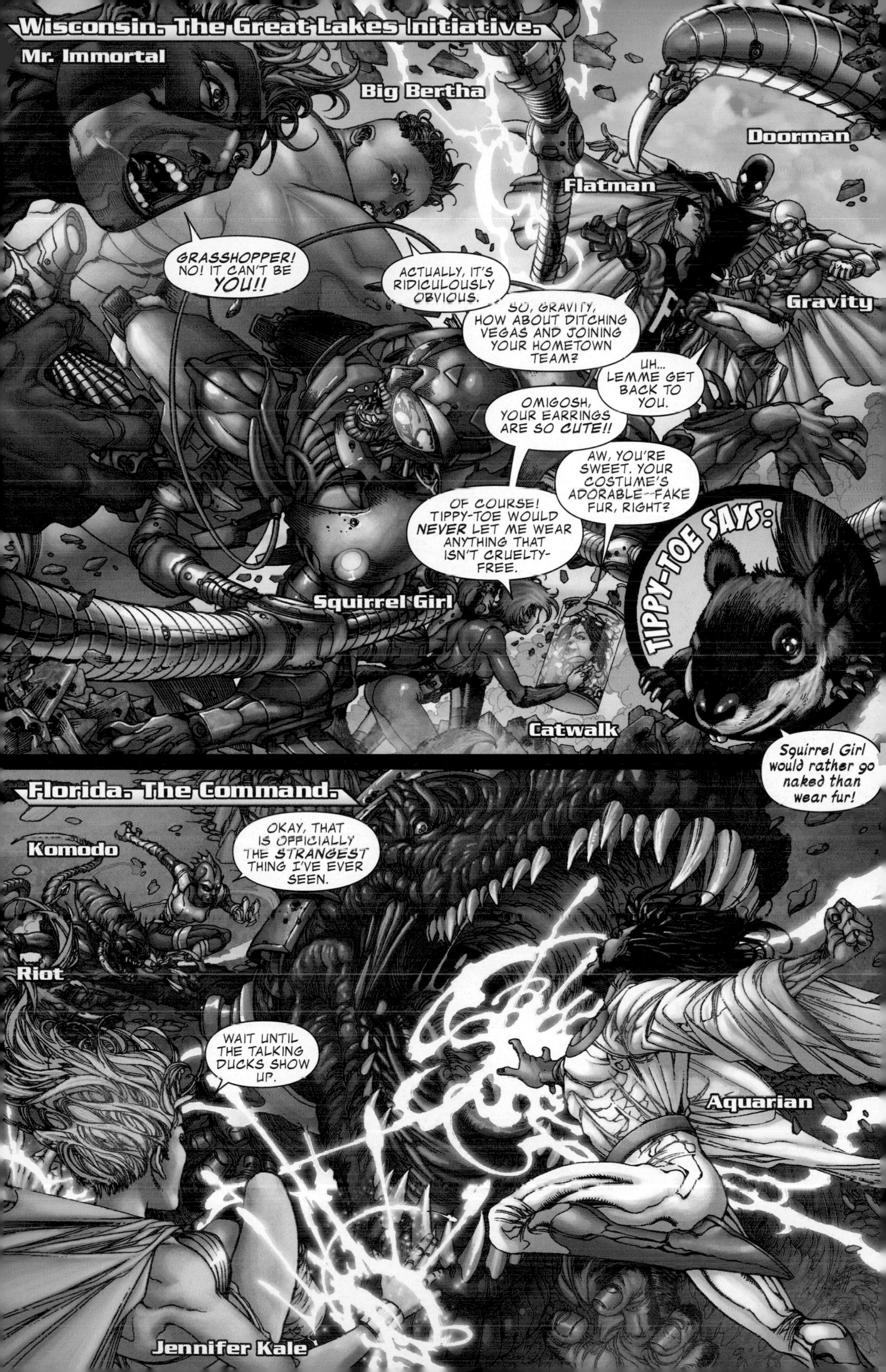

Wisconsin. The Great Lakes Initiative.
Mr. Immortal
Big Bertha
Doorman
Flatman
Gravity
GRASSHOPPER! NO! IT CAN'T BE YOU!!
ACTUALLY, IT'S RIDICULOUSLY OBVIOUS.
SO, GRAVITY, HOW ABOUT DITCHING VEGAS AND JOINING YOUR HOMETOWN TEAM?
UH... LEMME GET BACK TO YOU.
OMIGOSH, YOUR EARRINGS ARE SO CUTE!!
AW, YOU'RE SWEET. YOUR COSTUME'S ADORABLE--FAKE FUR, RIGHT?
OF COURSE! TIPPY-TOE WOULD NEVER LET ME WEAR ANYTHING THAT ISN'T CRUELTY-FREE.
TIPPY-TOE SAYS:
Squirrel Girl would rather go naked than wear fur!
Squirrel Girl
Catwalk
Florida. The Command.
Komodo
Riot
OKAY, THAT IS OFFICIALLY THE STRANGEST THING I'VE EVER SEEN.
WAIT UNTIL THE TALKING DUCKS SHOW UP.
Aquarian
Jennifer Kale

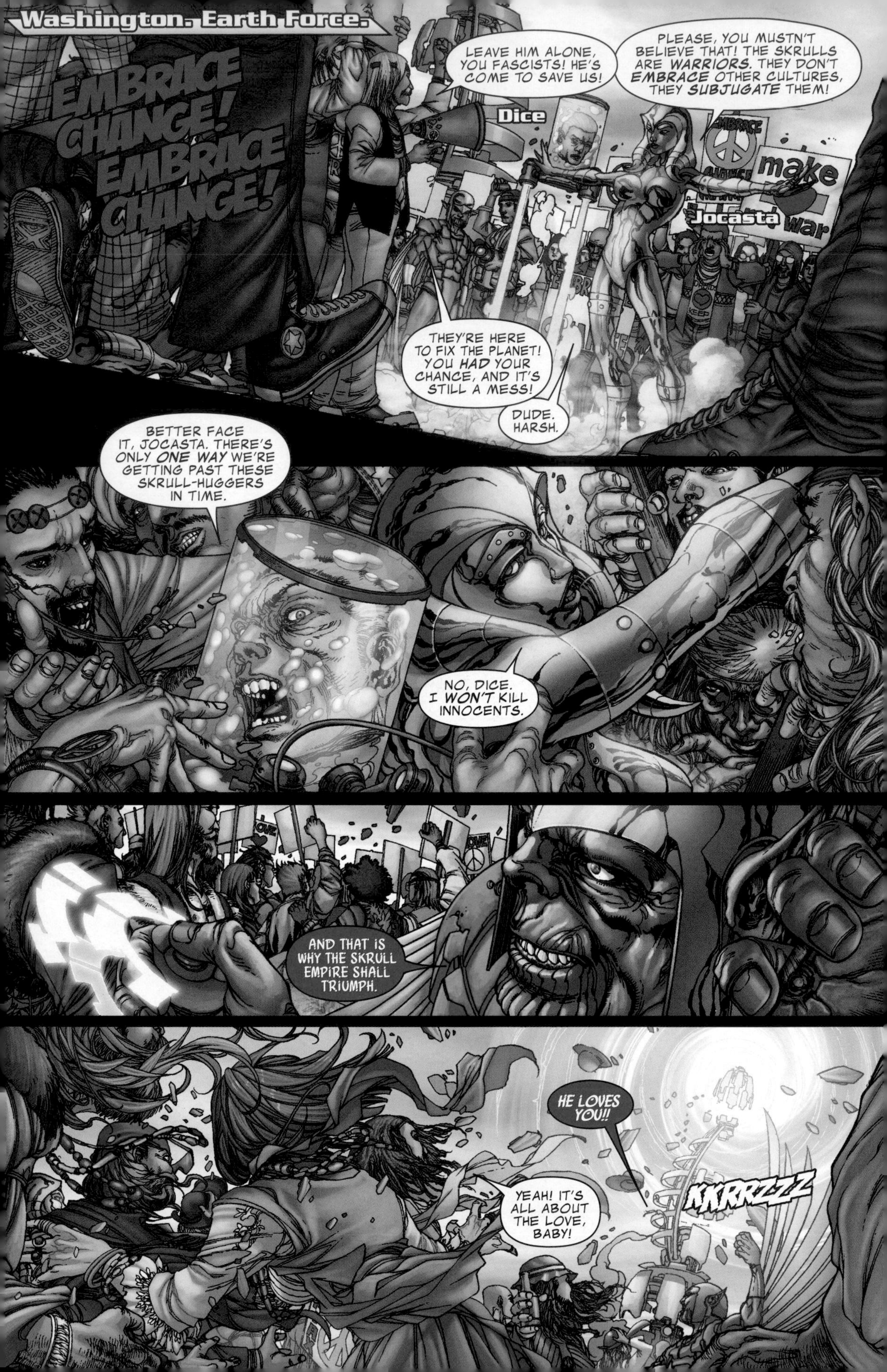

Washington. Earth Force.
EMBRACE CHANGE! EMBRACE CHANGE!
LEAVE HIM ALONE, YOU FASCISTS! HE'S COME TO SAVE US!
PLEASE, YOU MUSTN'T BELIEVE THAT! THE SKRULLS ARE WARRIORS. THEY DON'T EMBRACE OTHER CULTURES, THEY SUBJUGATE THEM!
Dice
Jocasta
make
war
THEY'RE HERE TO FIX THE PLANET! YOU HAD YOUR CHANCE, AND IT'S STILL A MESS!
DUDE. HARSH.
BETTER FACE IT, JOCASTA. THERE'S ONLY ONE WAY WE'RE GETTING PAST THESE SKRULL-HUGGERS IN TIME.
NO, DICE. I WON'T KILL INNOCENTS.
AND THAT IS WHY THE SKRULL EMPIRE SHALL TRIUMPH.
HE LOVES YOU!!
YEAH! IT'S ALL ABOUT THE LOVE, BABY!
KKRRZZZZ

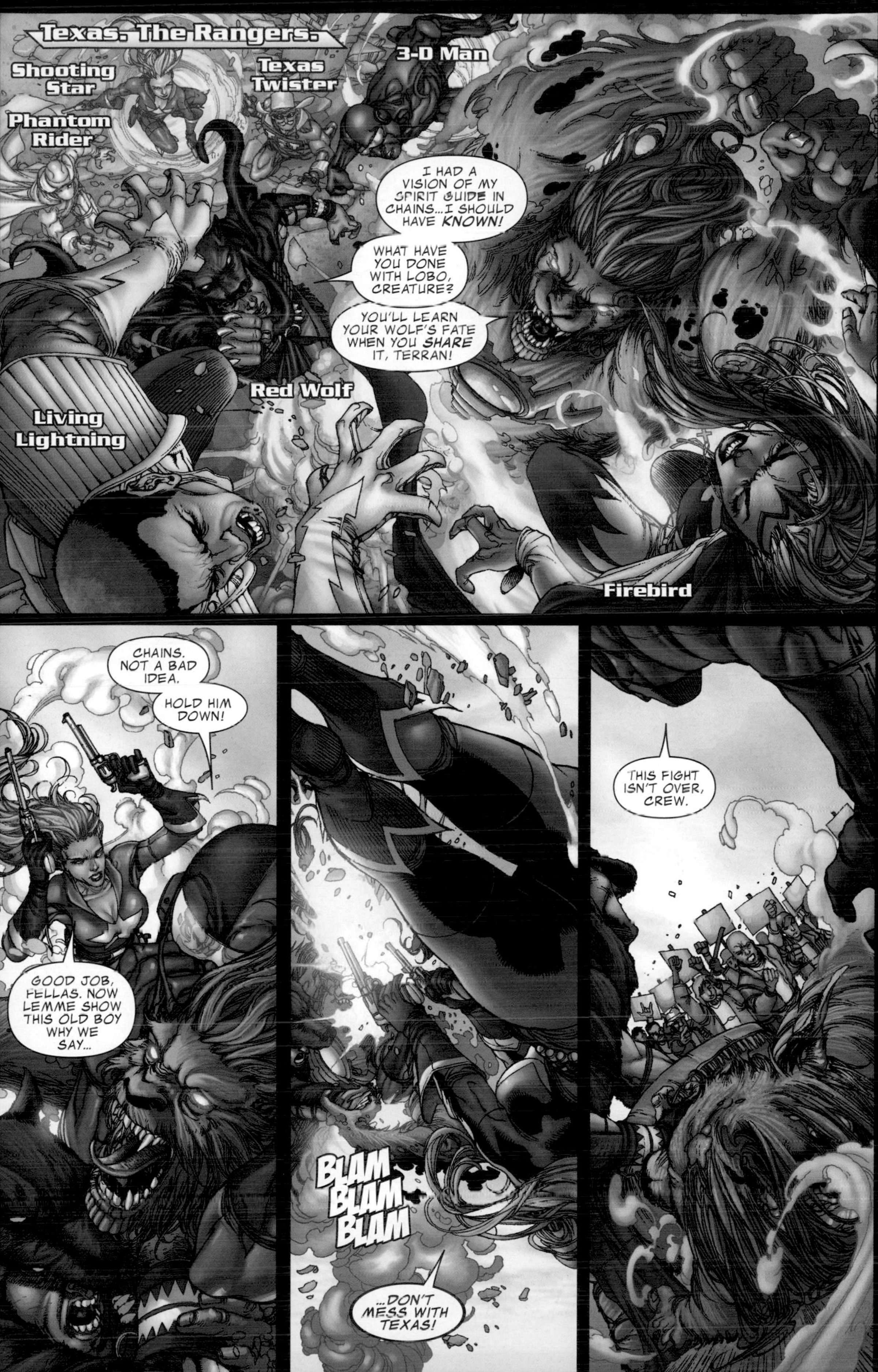
Texas. The Rangers.
Shooting Star
Phantom Rider
Texas Twister
3-D Man
Red Wolf
Living Lightning
Firebird
I HAD A VISION OF MY SPIRIT GUIDE IN CHAINS... I SHOULD HAVE KNOWN!
WHAT HAVE YOU DONE WITH LOBO, CREATURE?
YOU'LL LEARN YOUR WOLF'S FATE WHEN YOU SHARE IT, TERRAN!
CHAINS. NOT A BAD IDEA.
HOLD HIM DOWN!
GOOD JOB, FELLAS. NOW LEMME SHOW THIS OLD BOY WHY WE SAY...
BLAM BLAM BLAM
...DON'T MESS WITH TEXAS!
THIS FIGHT ISN'T OVER, CREW.

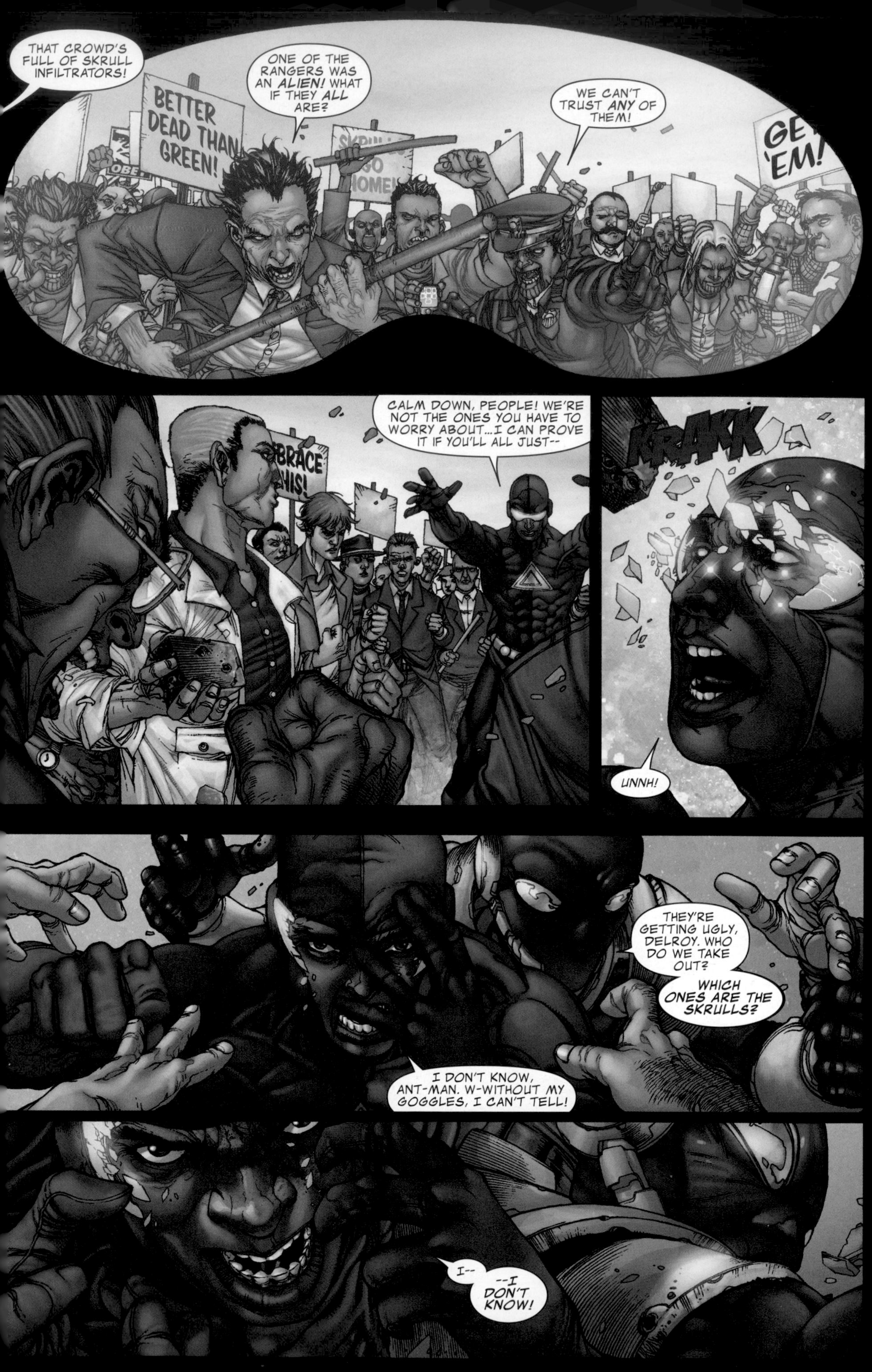
THAT CROWD'S FULL OF SKRULL INFILTRATORS!
BETTER DEAD THAN GREEN!
ONE OF THE RANGERS WAS AN ALIEN! WHAT IF THEY ALL ARE?
WE CAN'T TRUST ANY OF THEM!
GET 'EM!
CALM DOWN, PEOPLE! WE'RE NOT THE ONES YOU HAVE TO WORRY ABOUT...I CAN PROVE IT IF YOU'LL ALL JUST--
KRAKK
UNNH!
THEY'RE GETTING UGLY, DELROY. WHO DO WE TAKE OUT?
WHICH ONES ARE THE SKRULLS?
I DON'T KNOW, ANT-MAN. W-WITHOUT MY GOGGLES, I CAN'T TELL!
I--
--I DON'T KNOW!

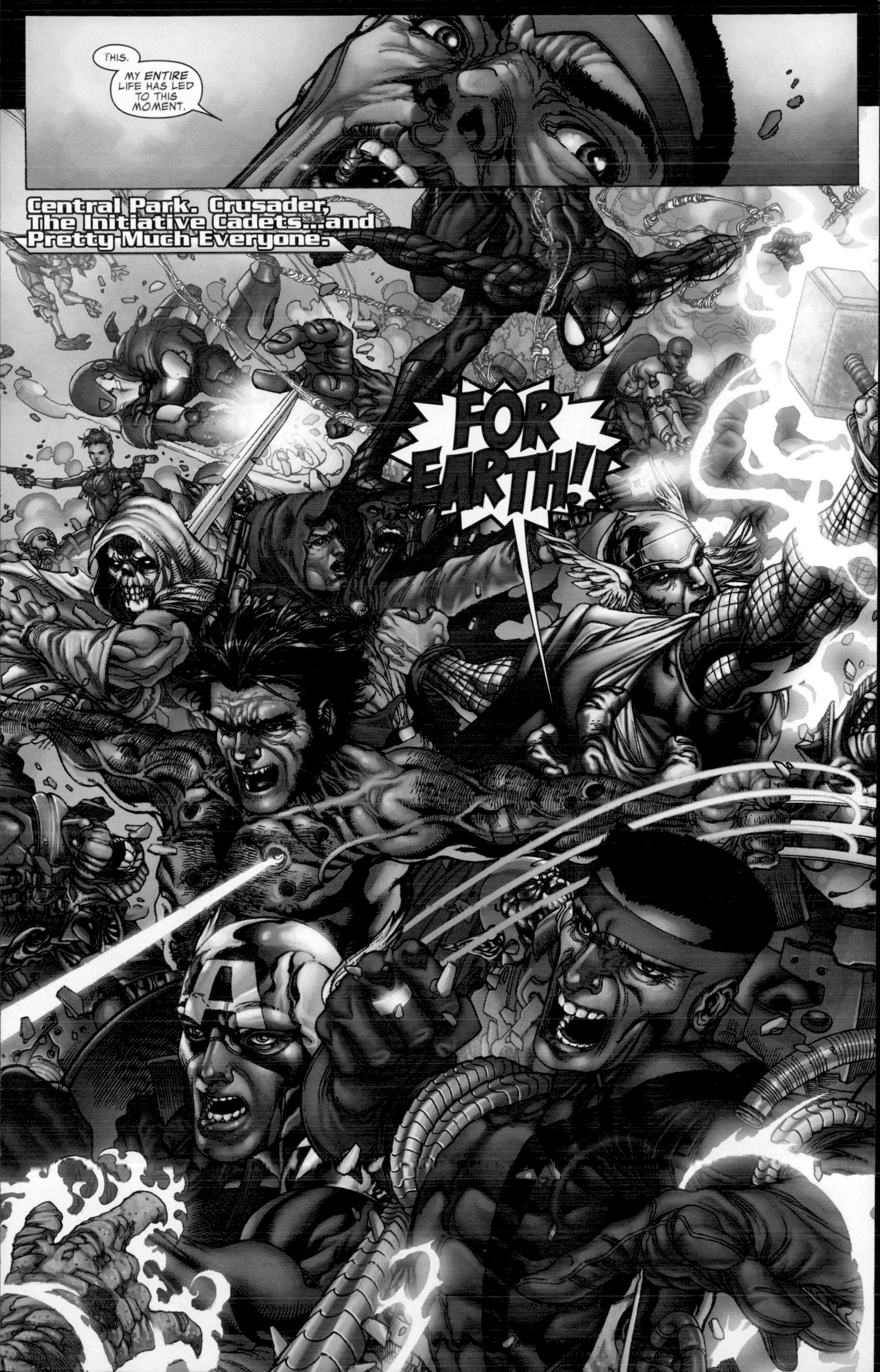
THIS.
MY ENTIRE LIFE HAS LED TO THIS MOMENT.
Central Park. Crusader, The Initiative Cadets...and Pretty Much Everyone.
FOR EARTH!!

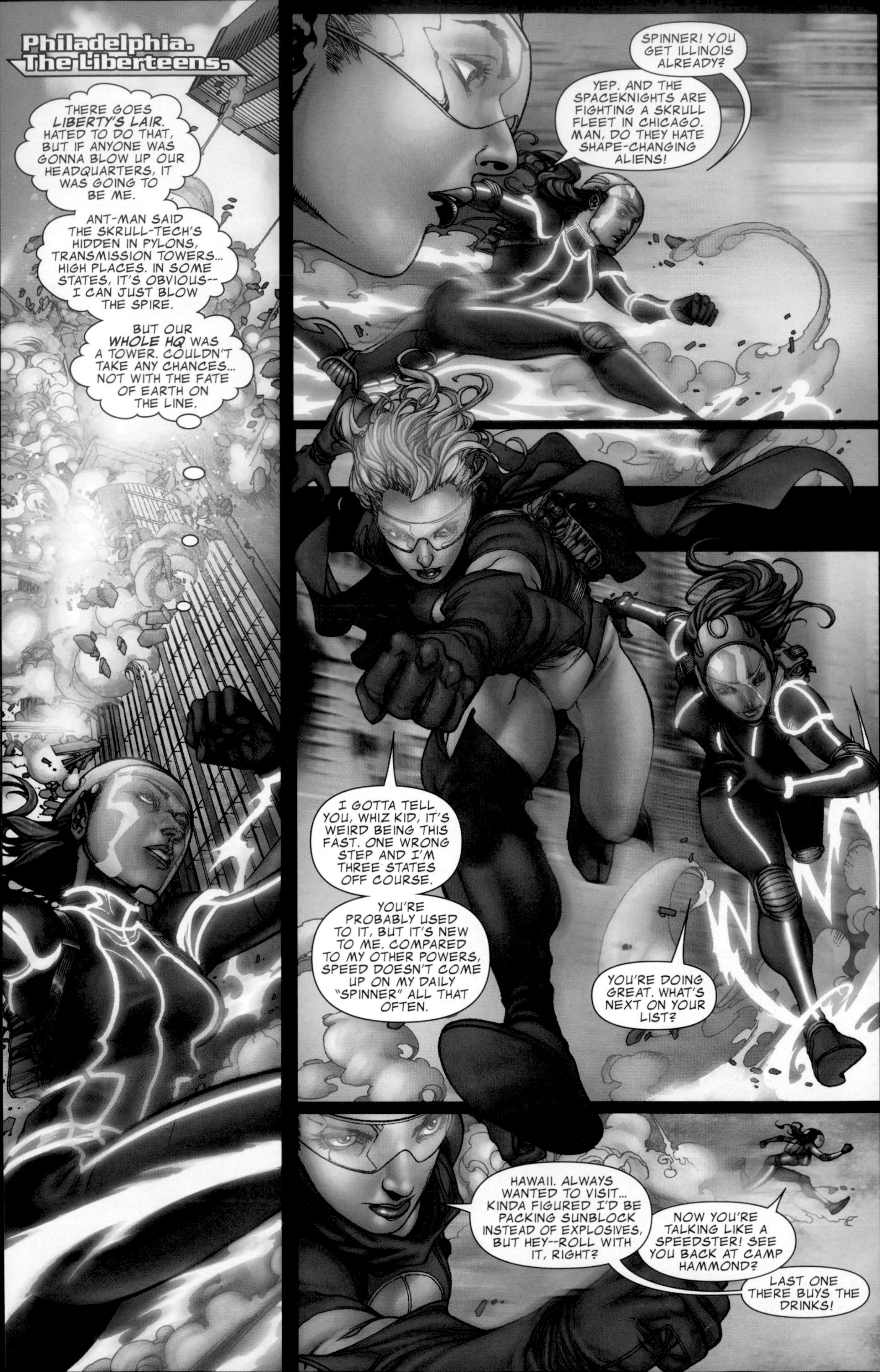
Philadelphia. The Liberteens.
THERE GOES LIBERTY'S LAIR. HATED TO DO THAT, BUT IF ANYONE WAS GONNA BLOW UP OUR HEADQUARTERS, IT WAS GOING TO BE ME.
ANT-MAN SAID THE SKRULL-TECH'S HIDDEN IN PYLONS, TRANSMISSION TOWERS... HIGH PLACES. IN SOME STATES, IT'S OBVIOUS-- I CAN JUST BLOW THE SPIRE.
BUT OUR WHOLE HQ WAS A TOWER. COULDN'T TAKE ANY CHANCES... NOT WITH THE FATE OF EARTH ON THE LINE.
SPINNER! YOU GET ILLINOIS ALREADY?
YEP. AND THE SPACEKNIGHTS ARE FIGHTING A SKRULL FLEET IN CHICAGO. MAN, DO THEY HATE SHAPE-CHANGING ALIENS!
I GOTTA TELL YOU, WHIZ KID, IT'S WEIRD BEING THIS FAST. ONE WRONG STEP AND I'M THREE STATES OFF COURSE.
YOU'RE PROBABLY USED TO IT, BUT IT'S NEW TO ME. COMPARED TO MY OTHER POWERS, SPEED DOESN'T COME UP ON MY DAILY "SPINNER" ALL THAT OFTEN.
YOU'RE DOING GREAT. WHAT'S NEXT ON YOUR LIST?
HAWAII. ALWAYS WANTED TO VISIT... KINDA FIGURED I'D BE PACKING SUNBLOCK INSTEAD OF EXPLOSIVES, BUT HEY--ROLL WITH IT, RIGHT?
NOW YOU'RE TALKING LIKE A SPEEDSTER! SEE YOU BACK AT CAMP HAMMOND?
LAST ONE THERE BUYS THE DRINKS!

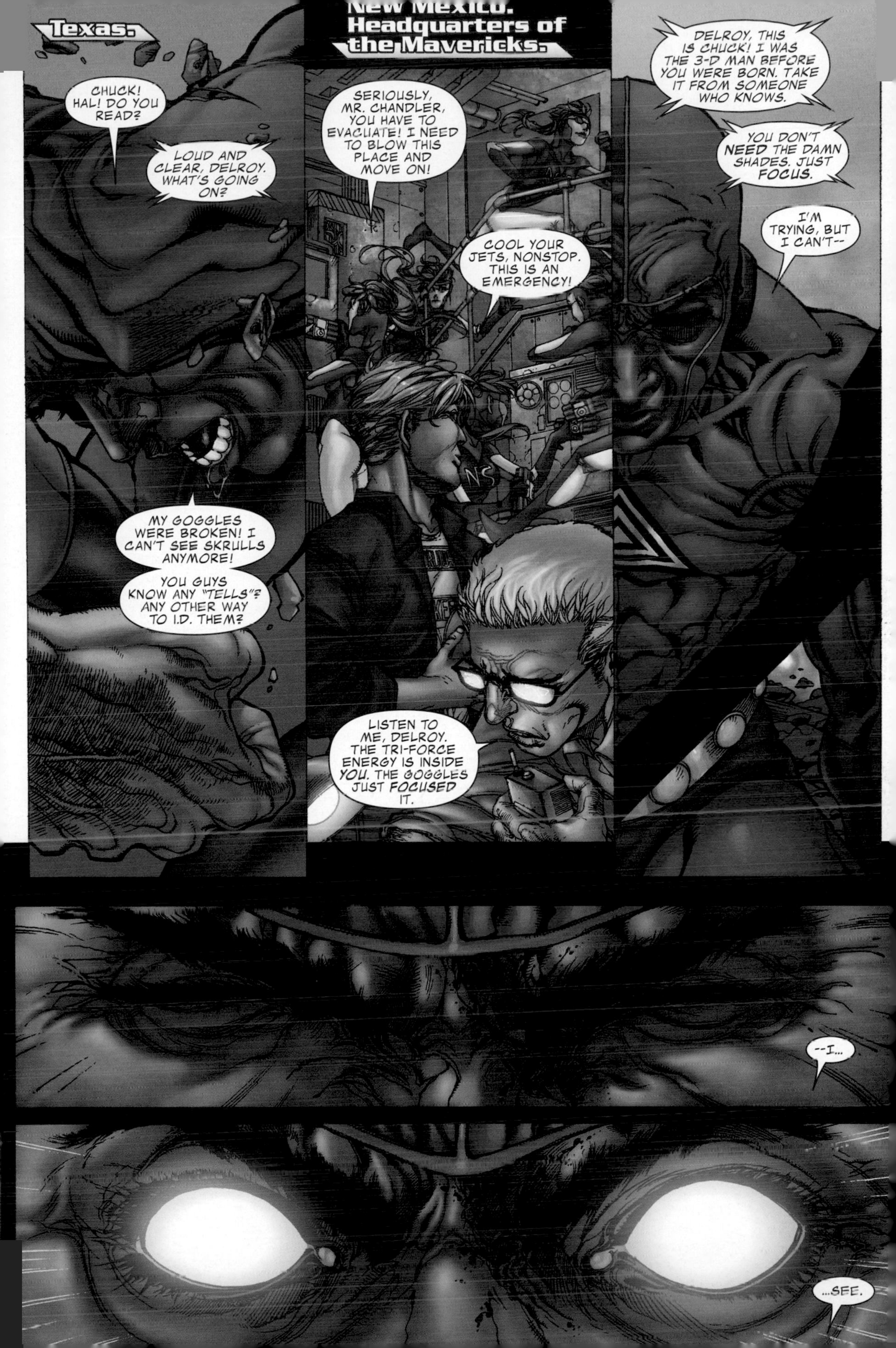
Texas.
CHUCK! HAL! DO YOU READ?
LOUD AND CLEAR, DELROY. WHAT'S GOING ON?
MY GOGGLES WERE BROKEN! I CAN'T SEE SKRULLS ANYMORE!
YOU GUYS KNOW ANY "TELLS"? ANY OTHER WAY TO I.D. THEM?
New Mexico. Headquarters of the Mavericks.
SERIOUSLY, MR. CHANDLER, YOU HAVE TO EVACUATE! I NEED TO BLOW THIS PLACE AND MOVE ON!
COOL YOUR JETS, NONSTOP. THIS IS AN EMERGENCY!
LISTEN TO ME, DELROY. THE TRI-FORCE ENERGY IS INSIDE YOU. THE GOGGLES JUST FOCUSED IT.
DELROY, THIS IS CHUCK! I WAS THE 3-D MAN BEFORE YOU WERE BORN. TAKE IT FROM SOMEONE WHO KNOWS.
YOU DON'T NEED THE DAMN SHADES. JUST FOCUS.
I'M TRYING, BUT I CAN'T--
--I...
...SEE.

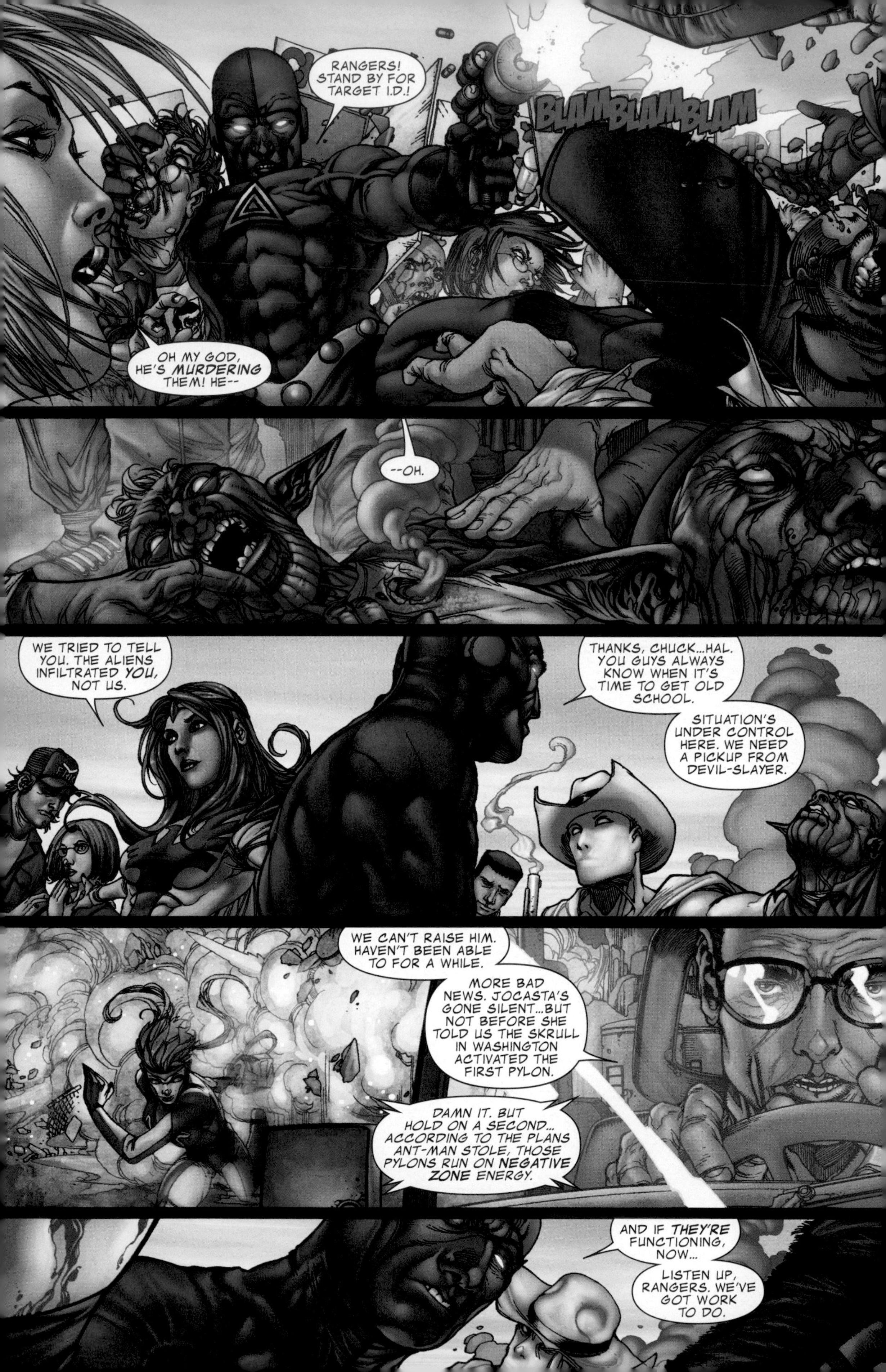
RANGERS! STAND BY FOR TARGET I.D.!
BLAM BLAM BLAM
OH MY GOD, HE'S *MURDERING* THEM! HE--
--OH.
WE TRIED TO TELL YOU. THE ALIENS INFILTRATED *YOU*, NOT US.
THANKS, CHUCK...HAL. YOU GUYS ALWAYS KNOW WHEN IT'S TIME TO GET OLD SCHOOL.
SITUATION'S UNDER CONTROL HERE. WE NEED A PICKUP FROM DEVIL-SLAYER.
WE CAN'T RAISE HIM. HAVEN'T BEEN ABLE TO FOR A WHILE.
MORE BAD NEWS. JOCASTA'S GONE SILENT...BUT NOT BEFORE SHE TOLD US THE SKRULL IN WASHINGTON ACTIVATED THE FIRST PYLON.
DAMN IT. BUT HOLD ON A SECOND... ACCORDING TO THE PLANS ANT-MAN STOLE, THOSE PYLONS RUN ON **NEGATIVE ZONE** *ENERGY.*
AND IF *THEY'RE* FUNCTIONING, NOW...
LISTEN UP, RANGERS. WE'VE GOT WORK TO DO.

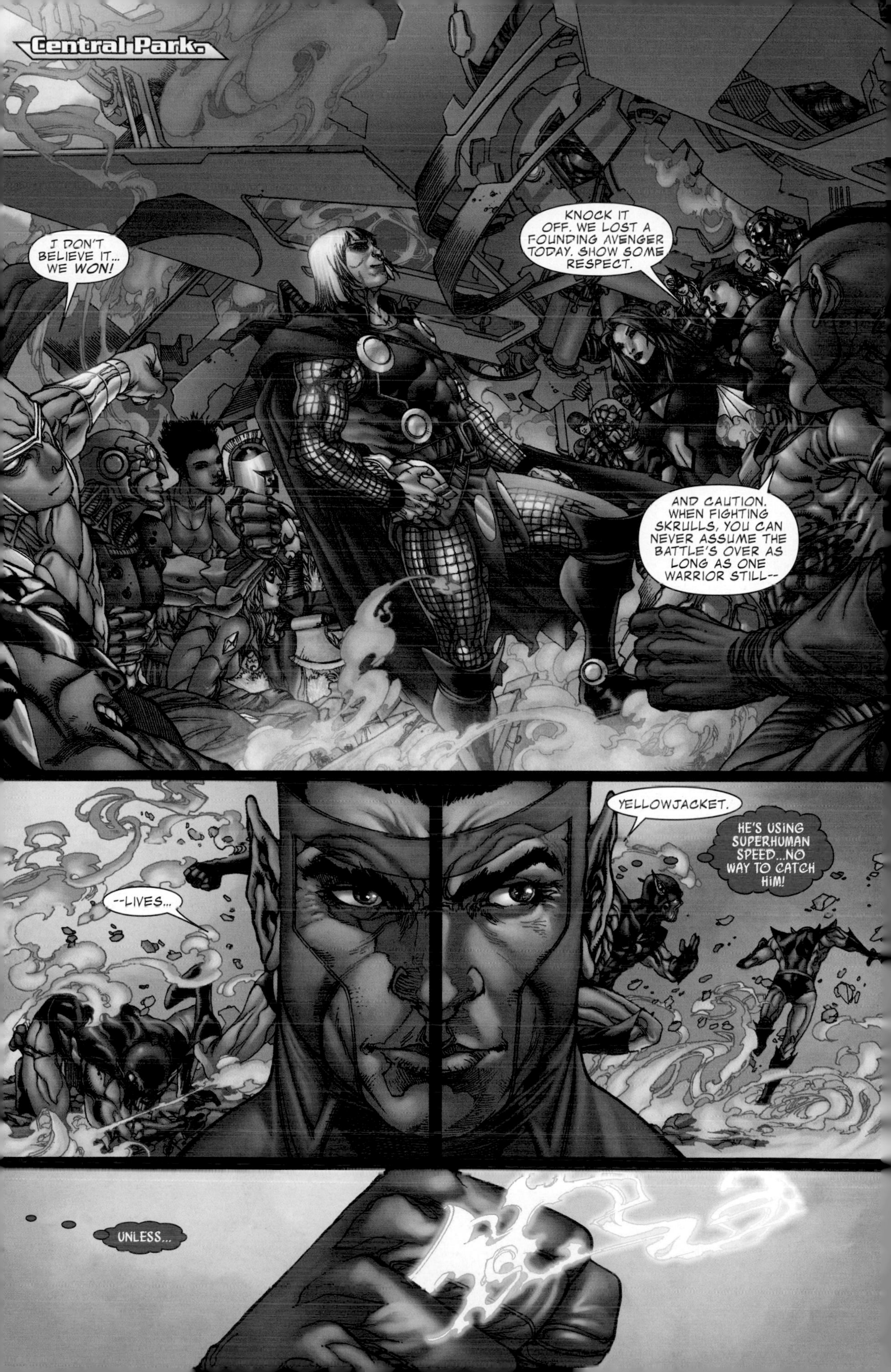
Central Park.
I DON'T BELIEVE IT... WE WON!
KNOCK IT OFF. WE LOST A FOUNDING AVENGER TODAY. SHOW SOME RESPECT.
AND CAUTION. WHEN FIGHTING SKRULLS, YOU CAN NEVER ASSUME THE BATTLE'S OVER AS LONG AS ONE WARRIOR STILL--
--LIVES...
YELLOWJACKET.
HE'S USING SUPERHUMAN SPEED...NO WAY TO CATCH HIM!
UNLESS...

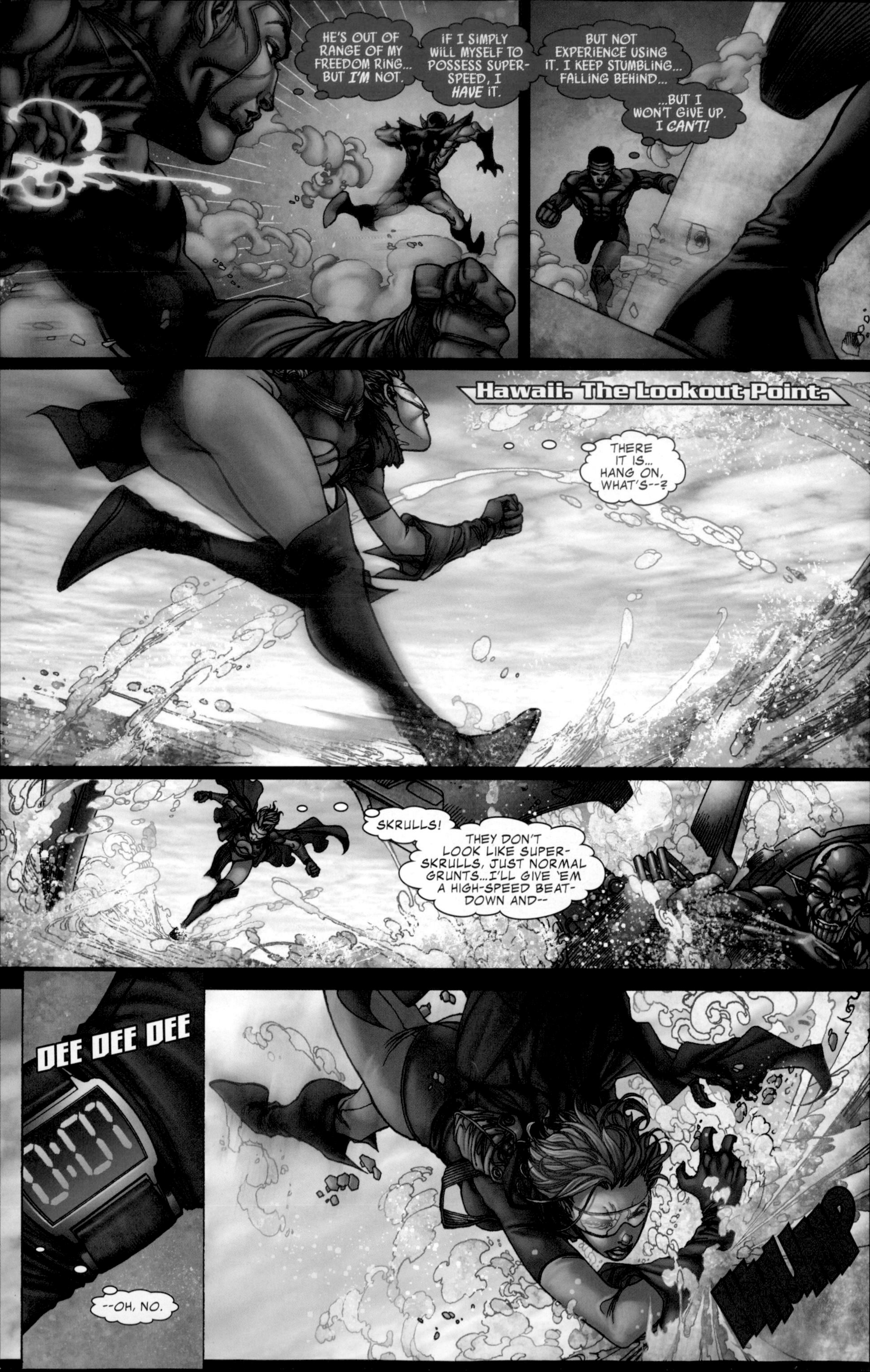
HE'S OUT OF RANGE OF MY FREEDOM RING... BUT I'M NOT.
IF I SIMPLY WILL MYSELF TO POSSESS SUPER-SPEED, I HAVE IT.
BUT NOT EXPERIENCE USING IT. I KEEP STUMBLING... FALLING BEHIND...
...BUT I WON'T GIVE UP. I CAN'T!
Hawaii. The Lookout Point.
THERE IT IS... HANG ON, WHAT'S--?
SKRULLS!
THEY DON'T LOOK LIKE SUPER-SKRULLS, JUST NORMAL GRUNTS...I'LL GIVE 'EM A HIGH-SPEED BEAT-DOWN AND--
DEE DEE DEE
--OH, NO.

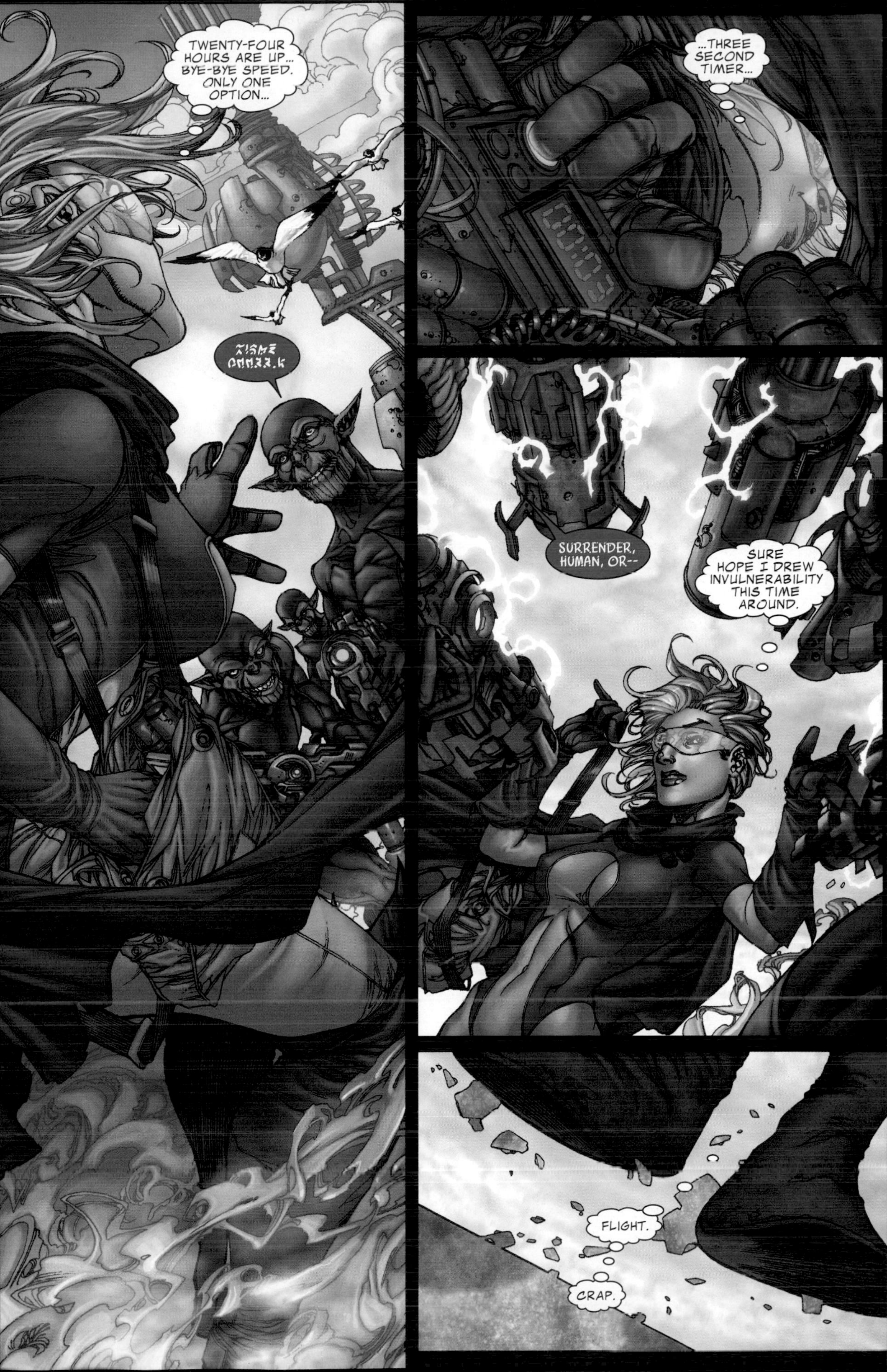

TWENTY-FOUR HOURS ARE UP... BYE-BYE SPEED. ONLY ONE OPTION...
...THREE SECOND TIMER...
SURRENDER, HUMAN, OR--
SURE HOPE I DREW INVULNERABILITY THIS TIME AROUND.
FLIGHT.
CRAP.

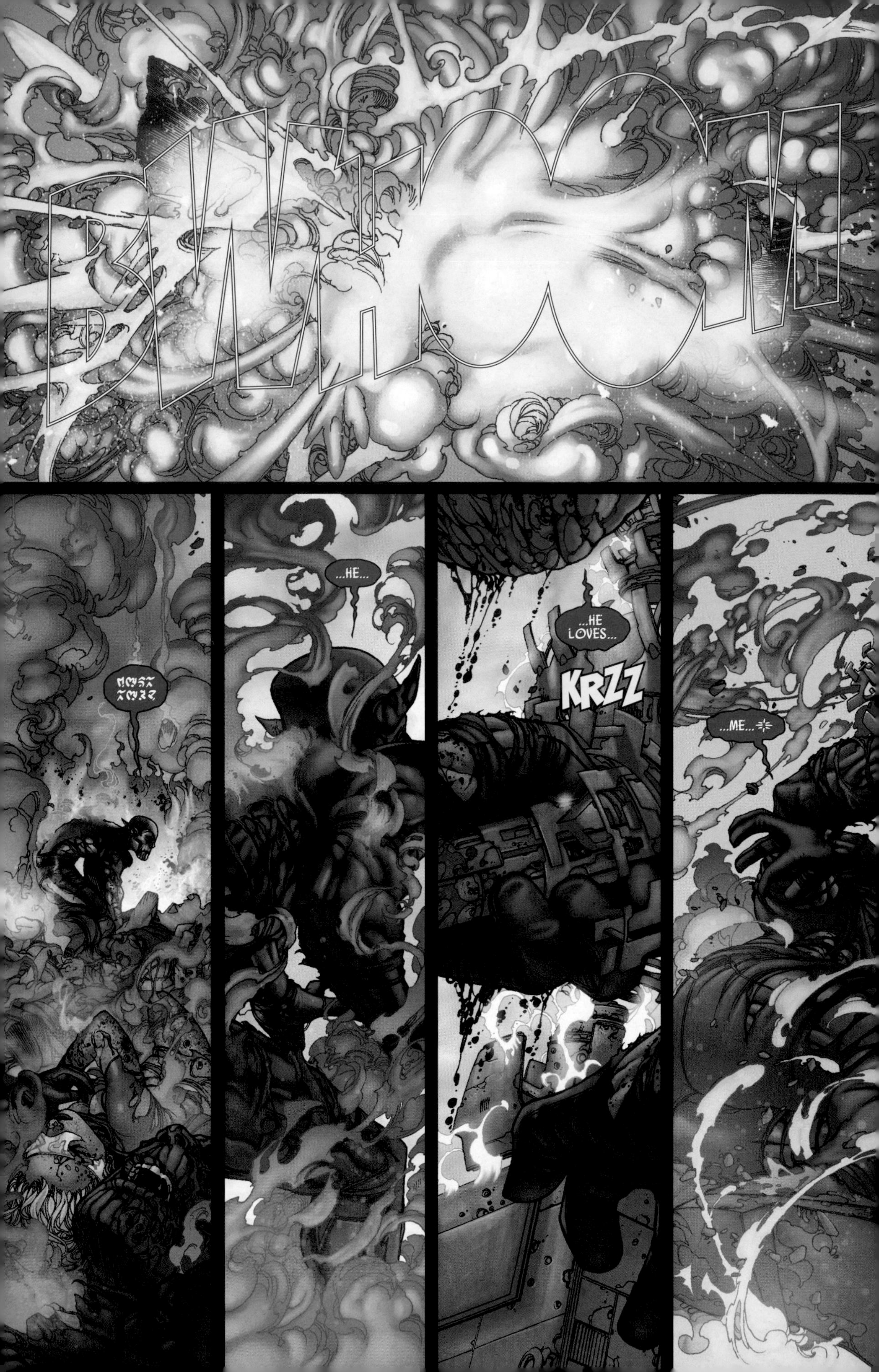

...HE...
...HE LOVES...
KRZZ
...ME...

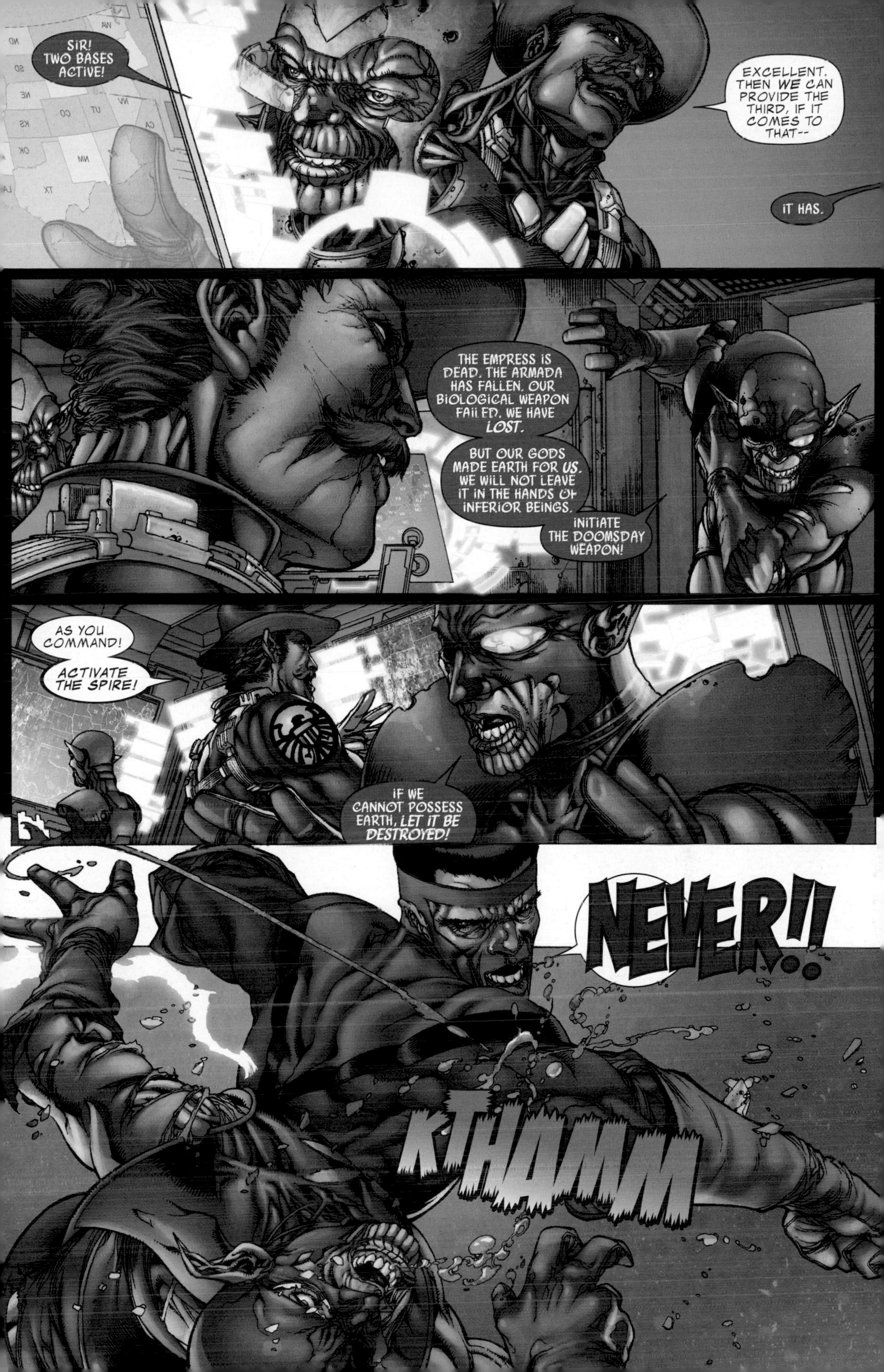
SIR! TWO BASES ACTIVE!
EXCELLENT. THEN WE CAN PROVIDE THE THIRD, IF IT COMES TO THAT--
IT HAS.
THE EMPRESS IS DEAD. THE ARMADA HAS FALLEN. OUR BIOLOGICAL WEAPON FAILED. WE HAVE LOST.
BUT OUR GODS MADE EARTH FOR US. WE WILL NOT LEAVE IT IN THE HANDS OF INFERIOR BEINGS.
INITIATE THE DOOMSDAY WEAPON!
AS YOU COMMAND!
ACTIVATE THE SPIRE!
IF WE CANNOT POSSESS EARTH, LET IT BE DESTROYED!
NEVER!!
KTHAMM

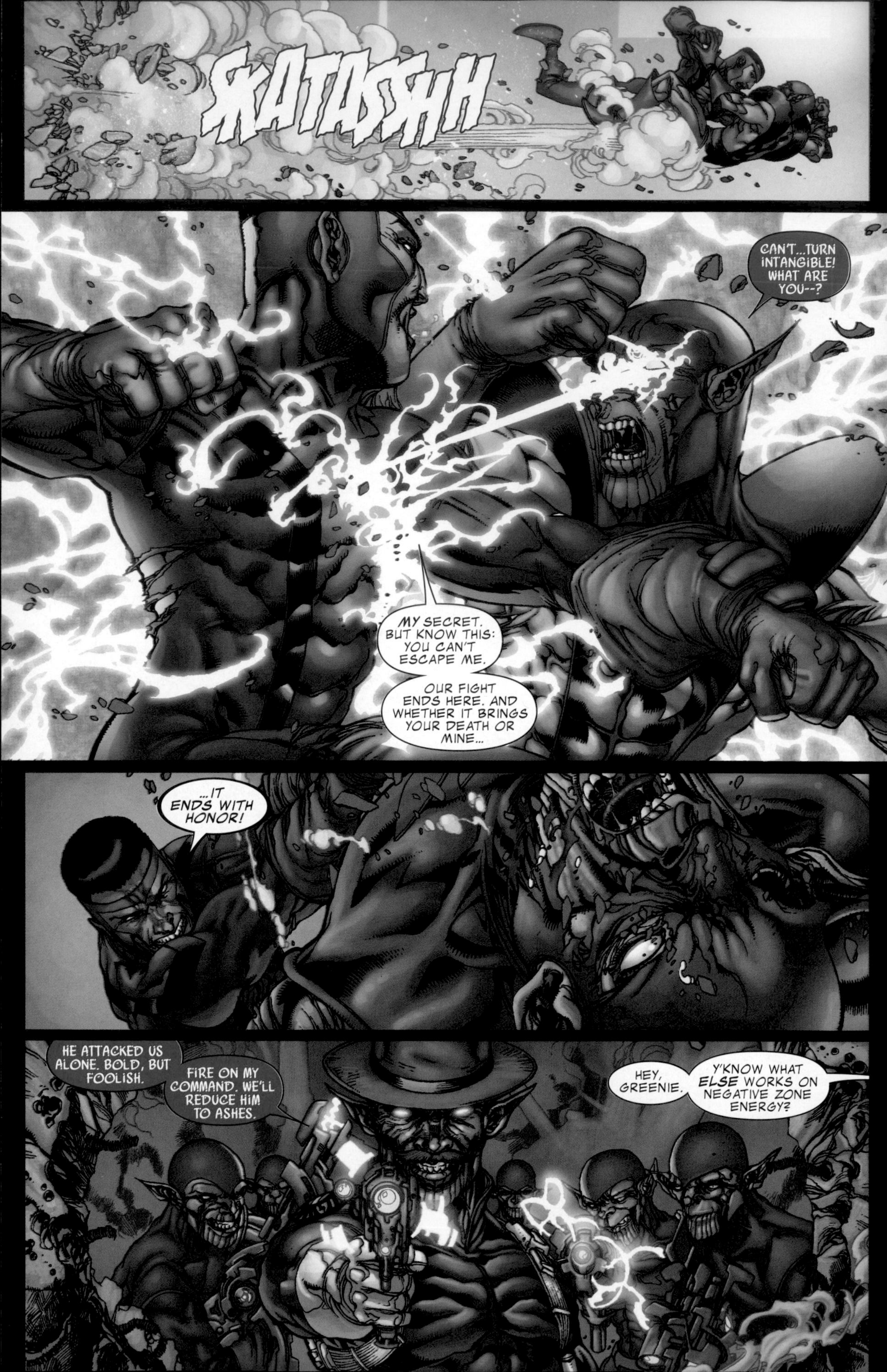

SKATASSHH
CAN'T...TURN INTANGIBLE! WHAT ARE YOU--?
MY SECRET. BUT KNOW THIS: YOU CAN'T ESCAPE ME.
OUR FIGHT ENDS HERE. AND WHETHER IT BRINGS YOUR DEATH OR MINE...
...IT ENDS WITH HONOR!
HE ATTACKED US ALONE. BOLD, BUT FOOLISH.
FIRE ON MY COMMAND. WE'LL REDUCE HIM TO ASHES.
HEY, GREENIE.
Y'KNOW WHAT ELSE WORKS ON NEGATIVE ZONE ENERGY?

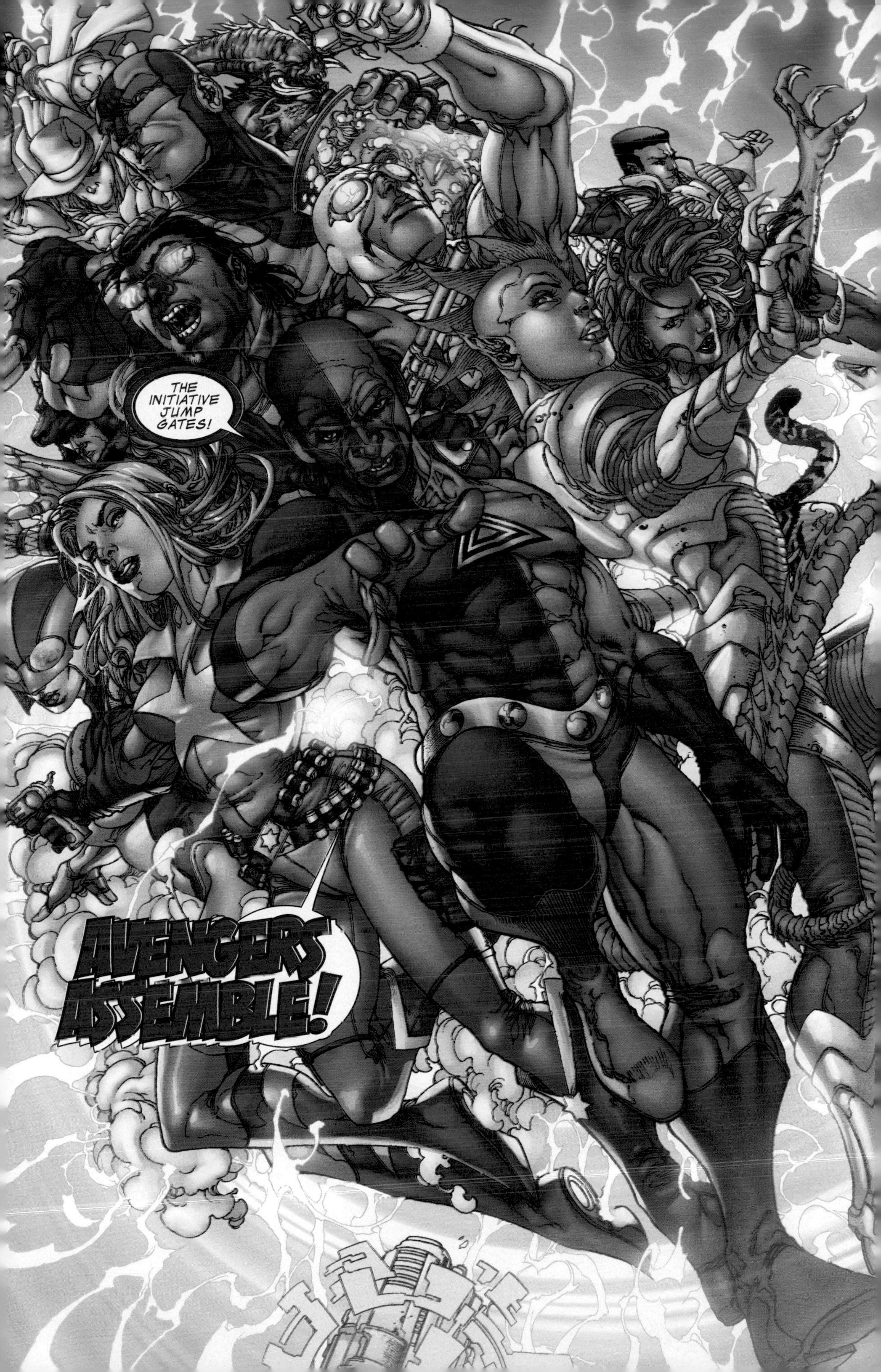
THE INITIATIVE JUMP GATES!
AVENGERS ASSEMBLE!

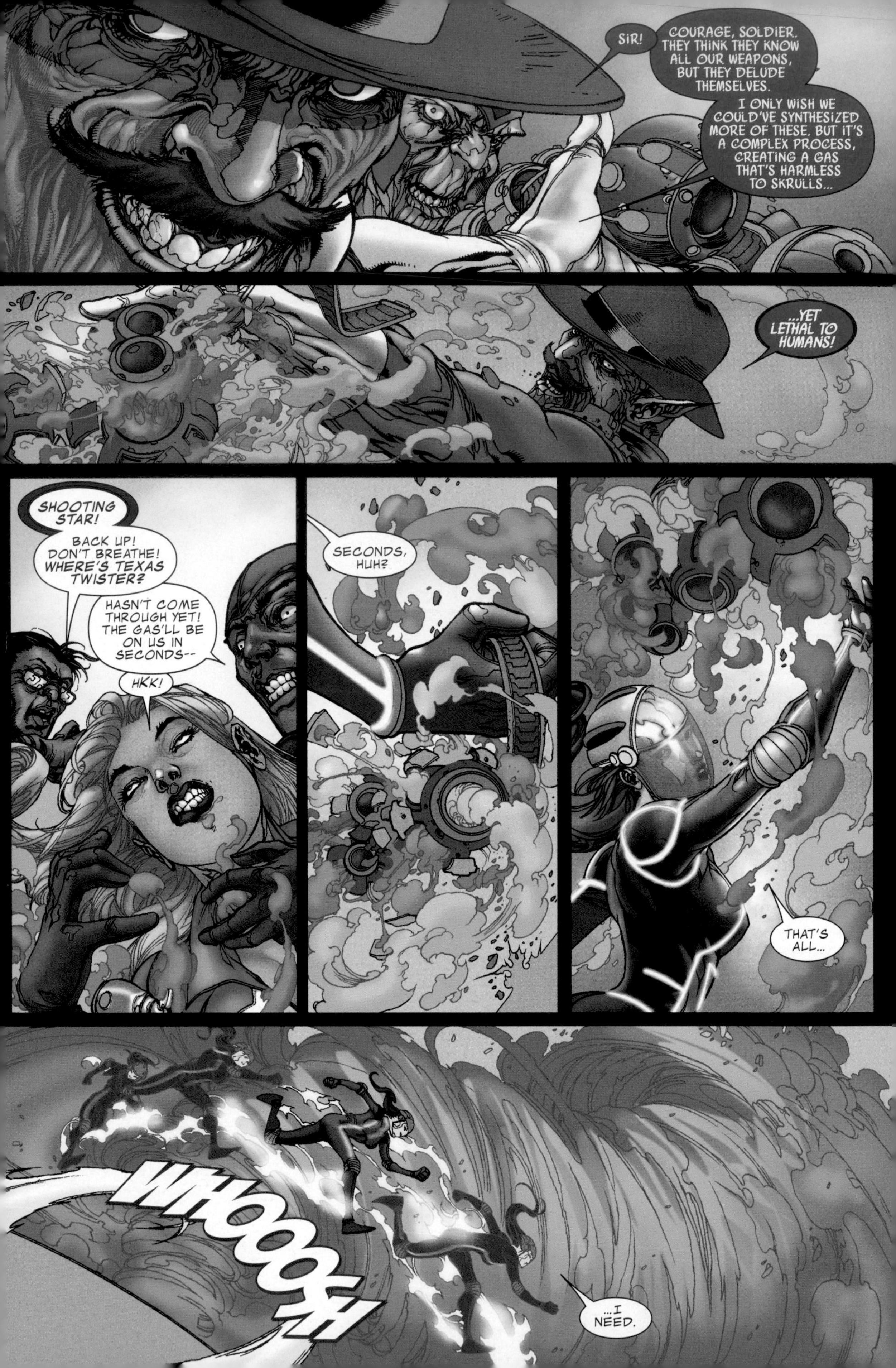
SIR!
COURAGE, SOLDIER. THEY THINK THEY KNOW ALL OUR WEAPONS, BUT THEY DELUDE THEMSELVES.
I ONLY WISH WE COULD'VE SYNTHESIZED MORE OF THESE. BUT IT'S A COMPLEX PROCESS, CREATING A GAS THAT'S HARMLESS TO SKRULLS...
...YET LETHAL TO HUMANS!
SHOOTING STAR!
BACK UP! DON'T BREATHE! WHERE'S TEXAS TWISTER?
HASN'T COME THROUGH YET! THE GAS'LL BE ON US IN SECONDS--
HKK!
SECONDS, HUH?
THAT'S ALL...
WHOOOSH
...I NEED.

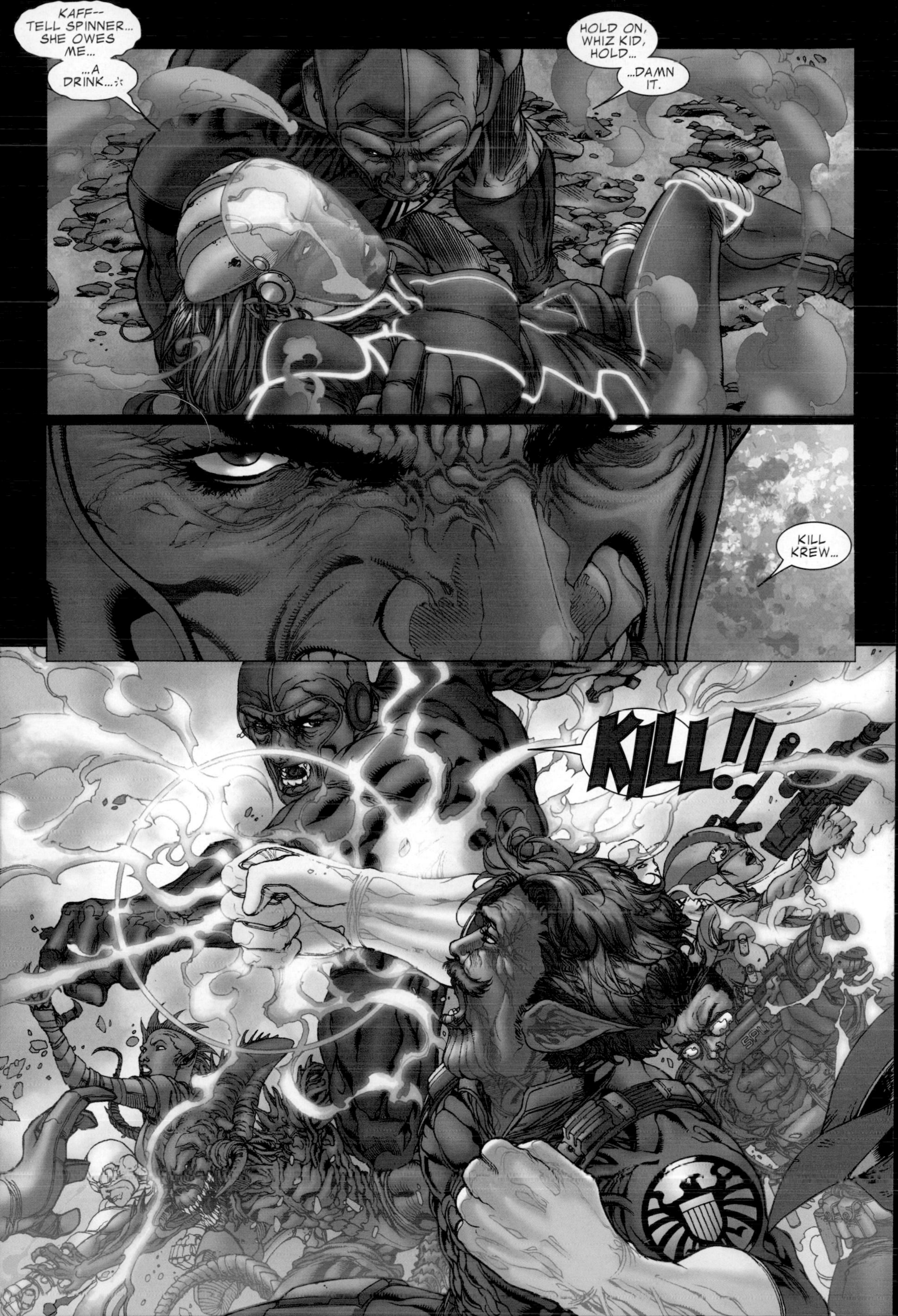
KAFF-- TELL SPINNER... SHE OWES ME...
...A DRINK...
HOLD ON, WHIZ KID, HOLD...
...DAMN IT.
KILL KREW...
KILL!!

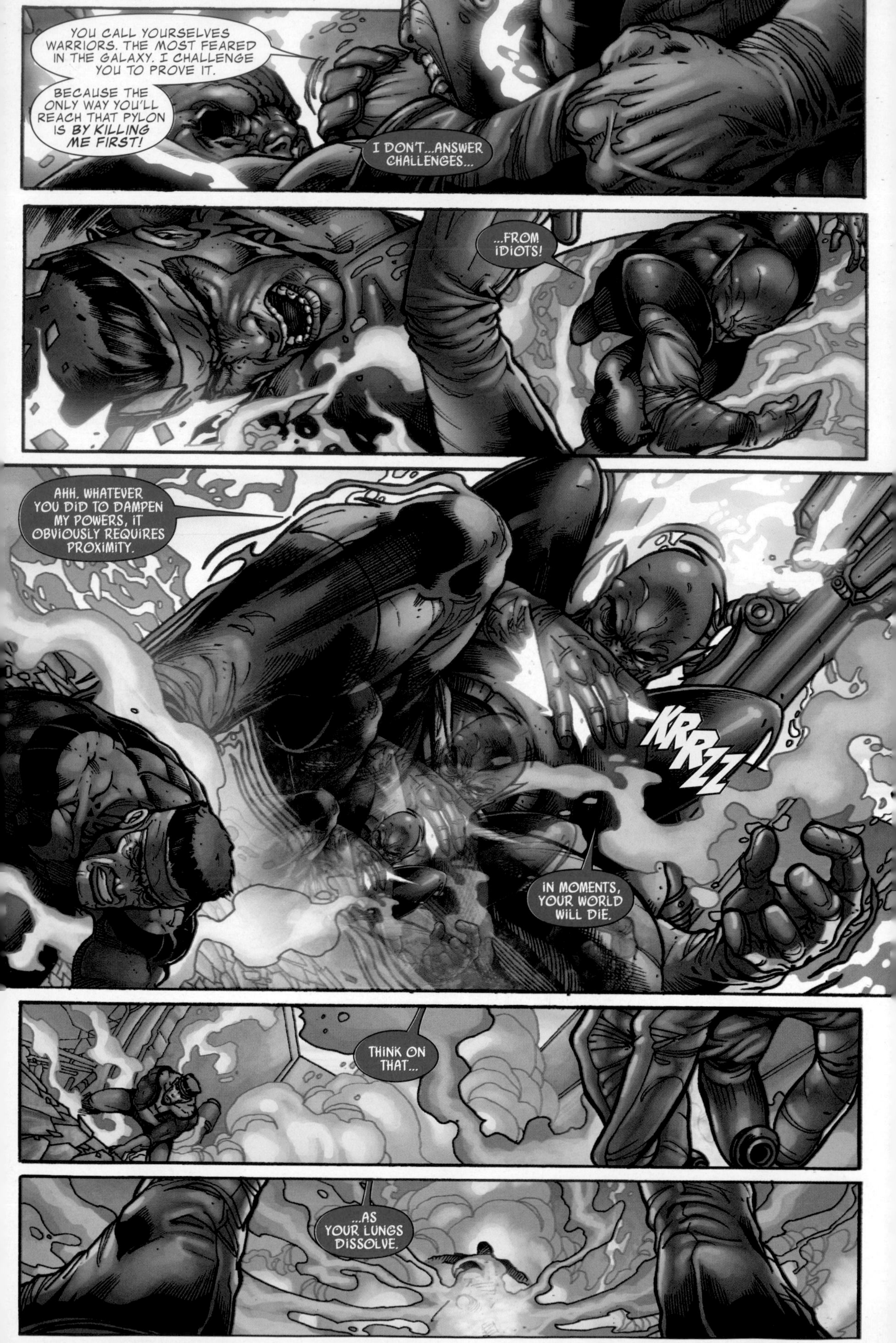
YOU CALL YOURSELVES WARRIORS. THE MOST FEARED IN THE GALAXY. I CHALLENGE YOU TO PROVE IT.
BECAUSE THE ONLY WAY YOU'LL REACH THAT PYLON IS BY KILLING ME FIRST!
I DON'T...ANSWER CHALLENGES...
...FROM IDIOTS!
AHH. WHATEVER YOU DID TO DAMPEN MY POWERS, IT OBVIOUSLY REQUIRES PROXIMITY.
KRRZZ
IN MOMENTS, YOUR WORLD WILL DIE.
THINK ON THAT...
...AS YOUR LUNGS DISSOLVE.

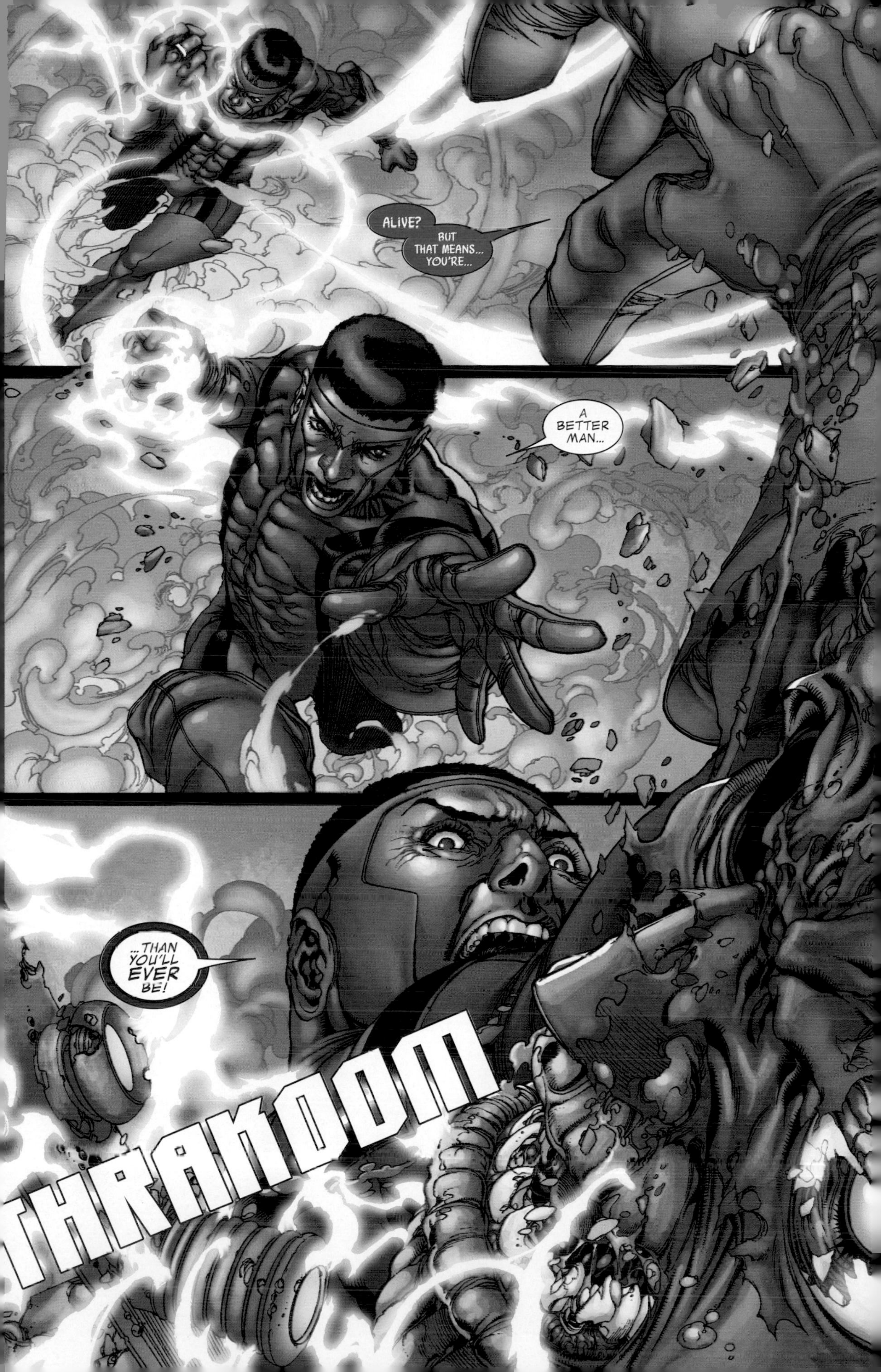
ALIVE?
BUT THAT MEANS... YOU'RE...
A BETTER MAN...
...THAN YOU'LL EVER BE!
THRAKOOM

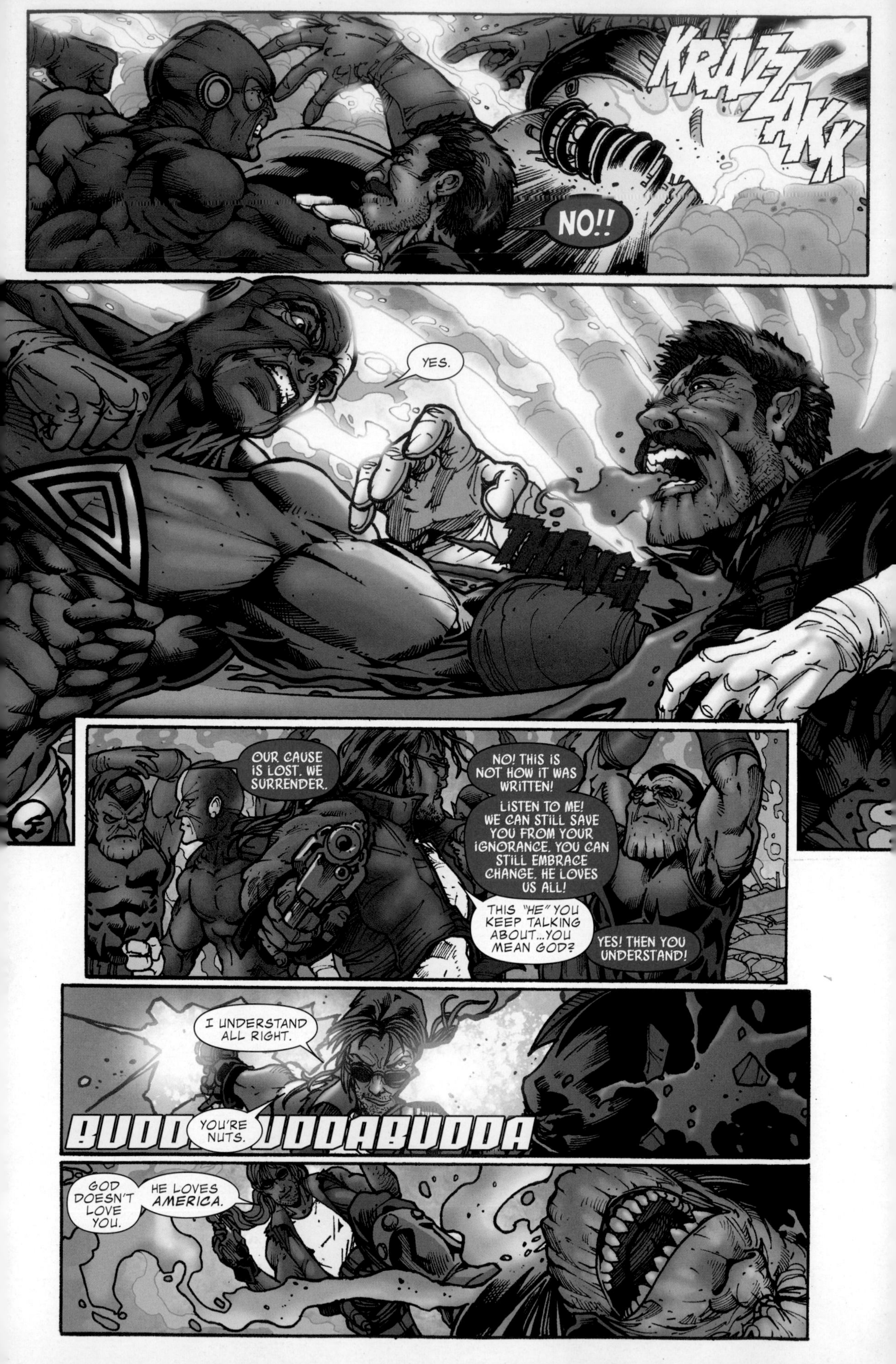
KRAZZAKK
NO!!
YES.
THWACK
OUR CAUSE IS LOST. WE SURRENDER.
NO! THIS IS NOT HOW IT WAS WRITTEN!
LISTEN TO ME! WE CAN STILL SAVE YOU FROM YOUR IGNORANCE. YOU CAN STILL EMBRACE CHANGE. HE LOVES US ALL!
THIS "HE" YOU KEEP TALKING ABOUT...YOU MEAN GOD?
YES! THEN YOU UNDERSTAND!
I UNDERSTAND ALL RIGHT.
YOU'RE NUTS.
UDDABUDDA
GOD DOESN'T LOVE YOU.
HE LOVES AMERICA.

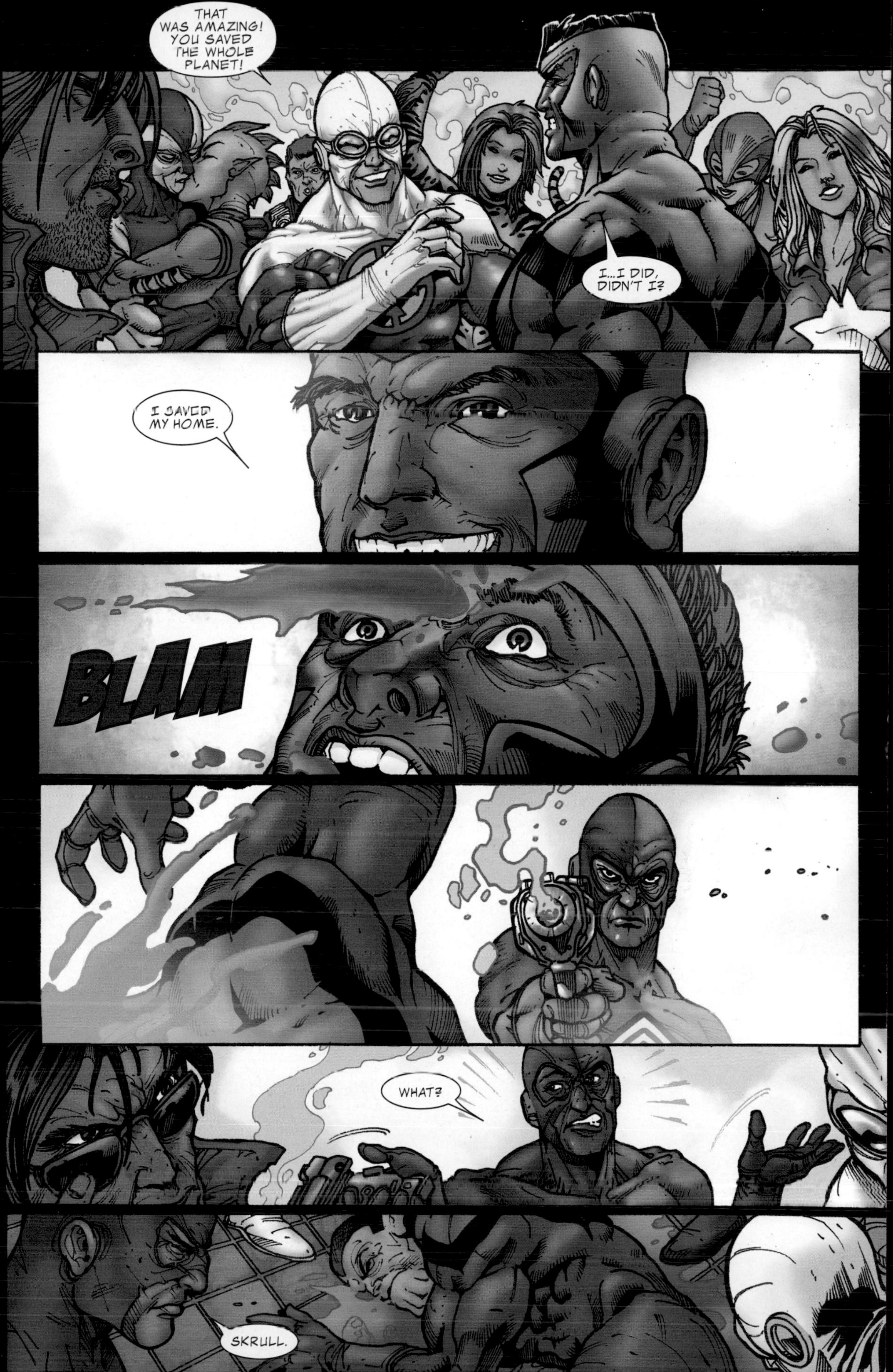
THAT WAS AMAZING! YOU SAVED THE WHOLE PLANET!
I...I DID, DIDN'T I?
I SAVED MY HOME.
BLAM
WHAT?
SKRULL.

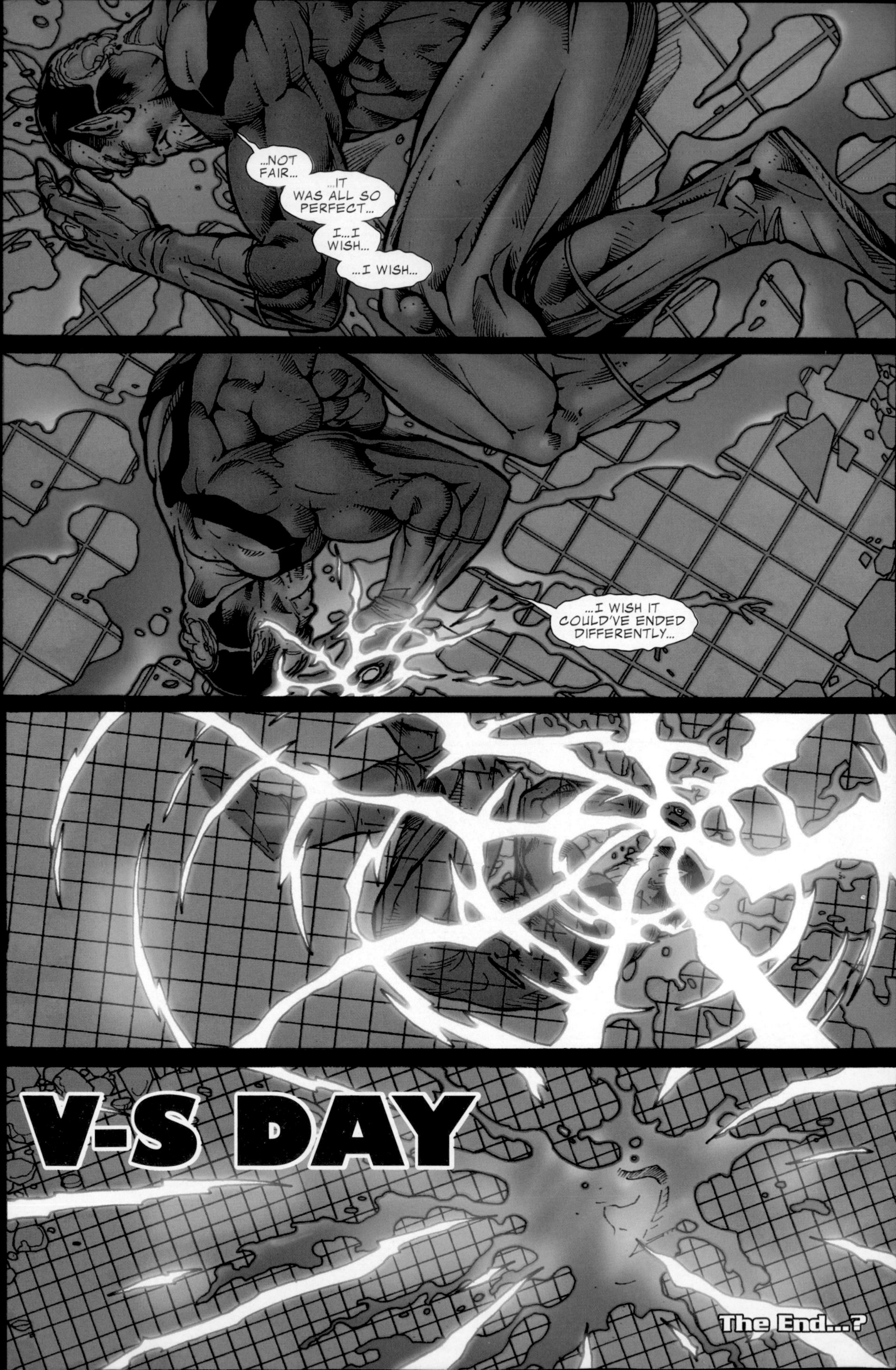
...NOT FAIR...
...IT WAS ALL SO PERFECT...
I...I WISH...
...I WISH...
...I WISH IT COULD'VE ENDED DIFFERENTLY...
V-S DAY
The End...?

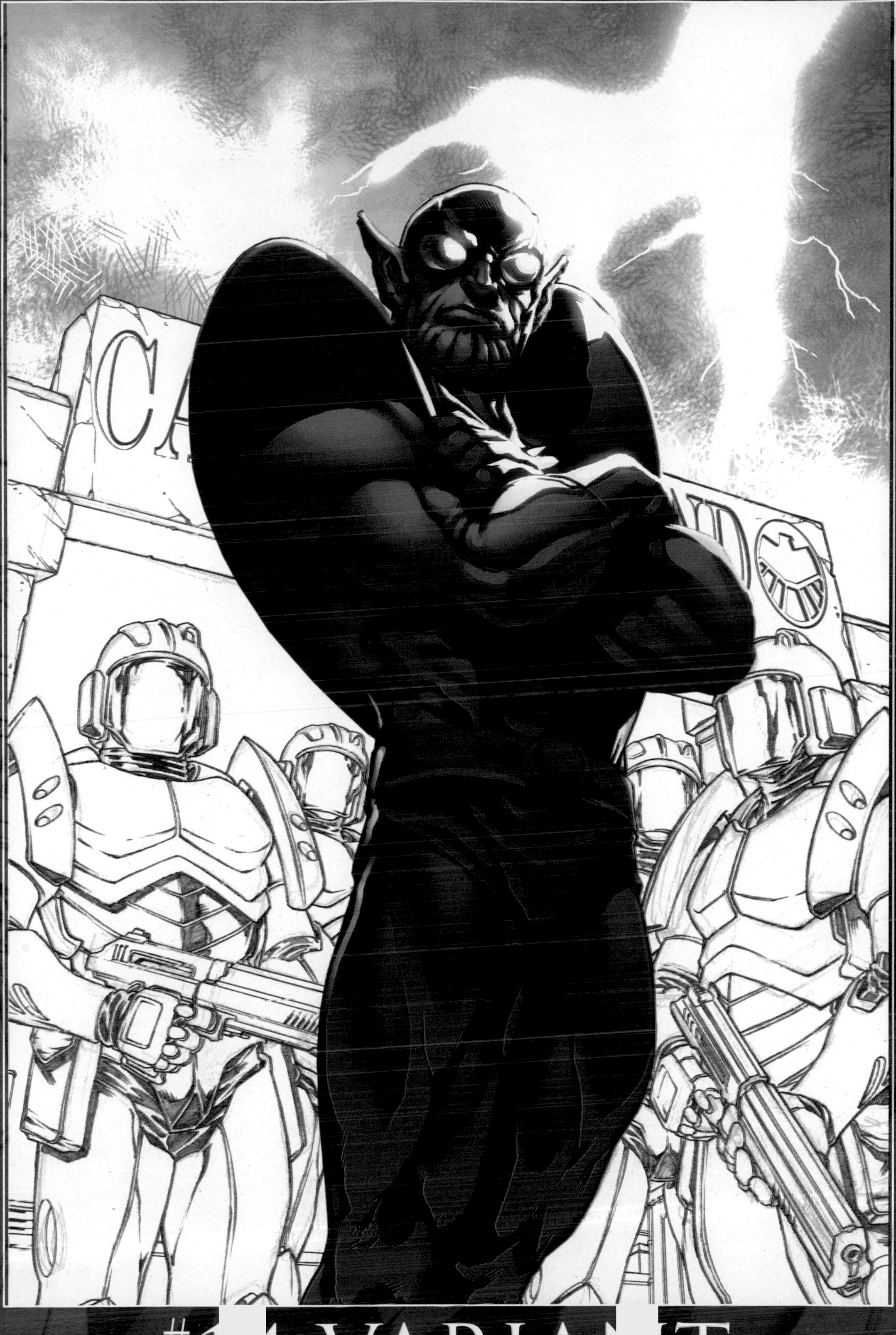

#14 VARIANT

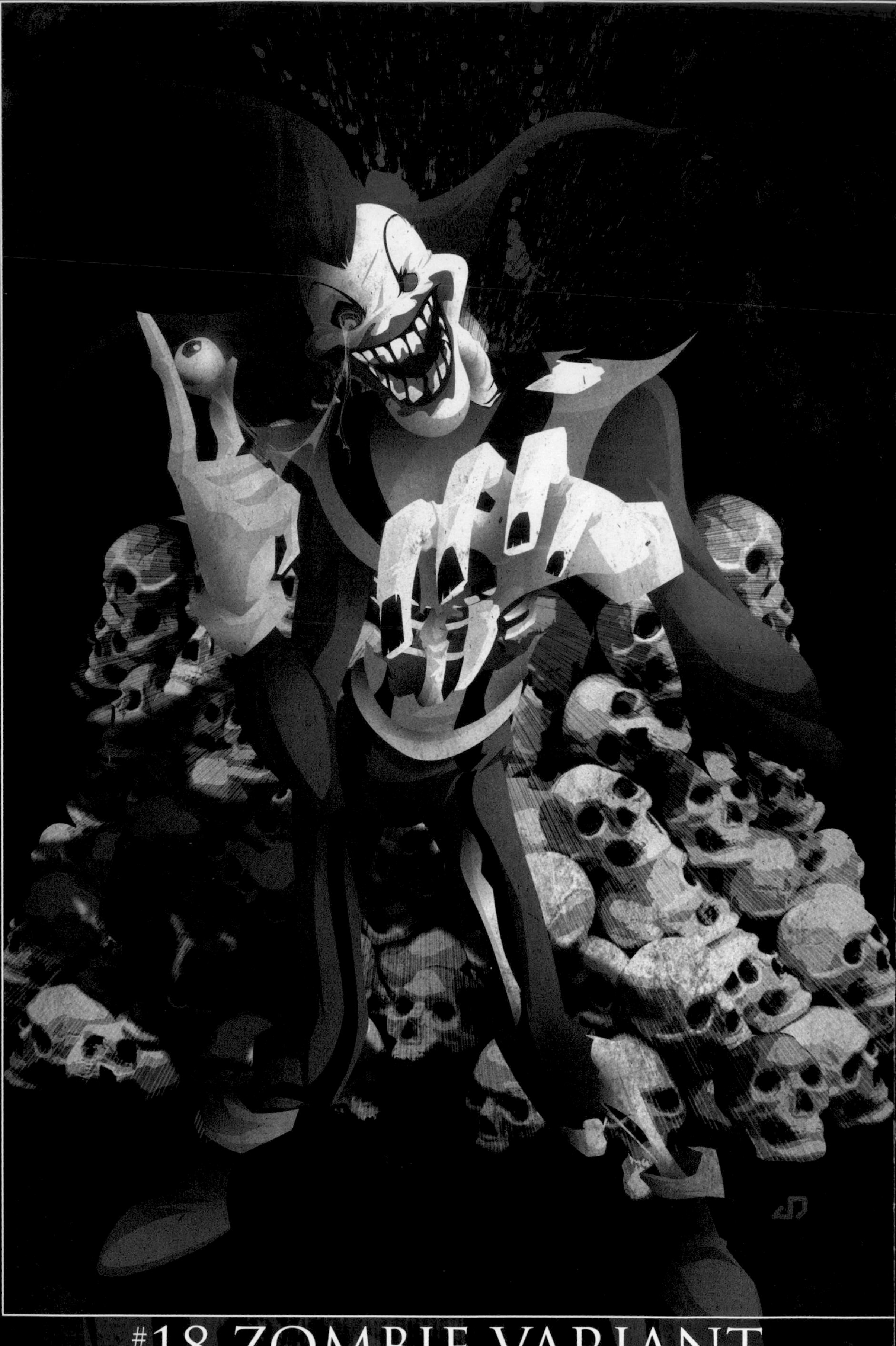

#18 ZOMBIE VARIANT
BY JUAN DOE

[redacted]HARACTER DESI[redacted]NS BY STEFANO CASELLI

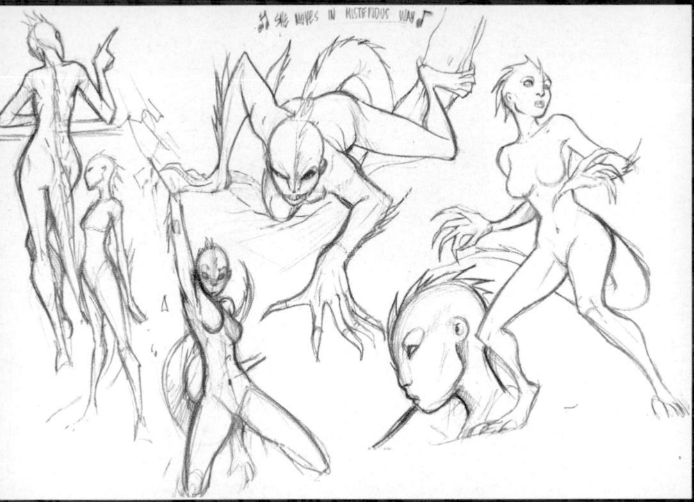
SHE MOVES IN MISTERIOUS WAY

KOMODO

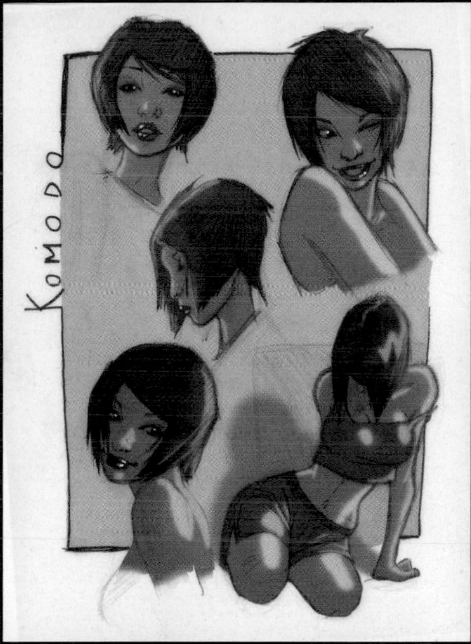
KOMODO

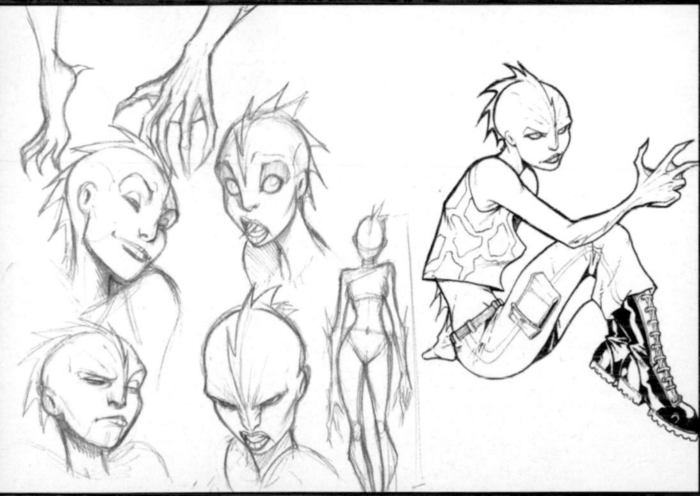

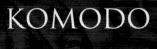

HARDBALL

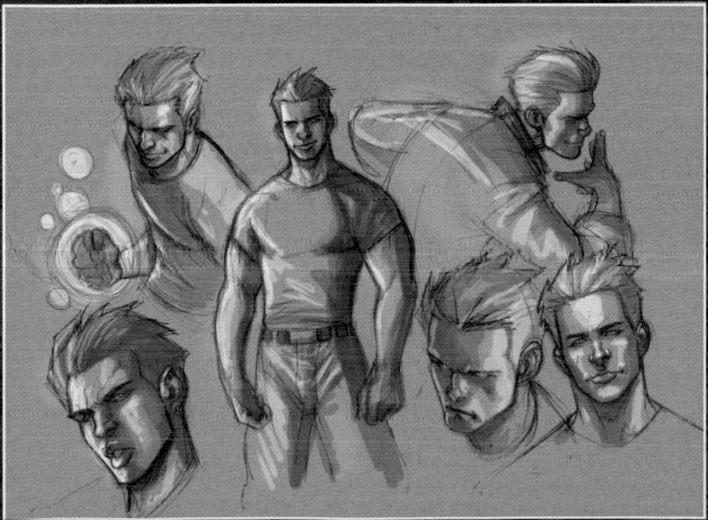

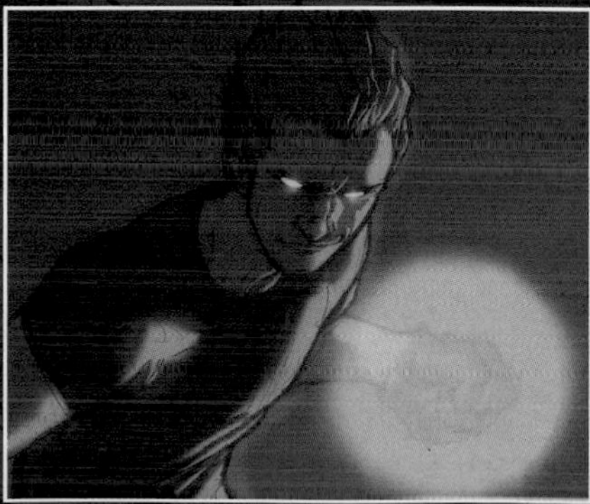

CLOUD 9

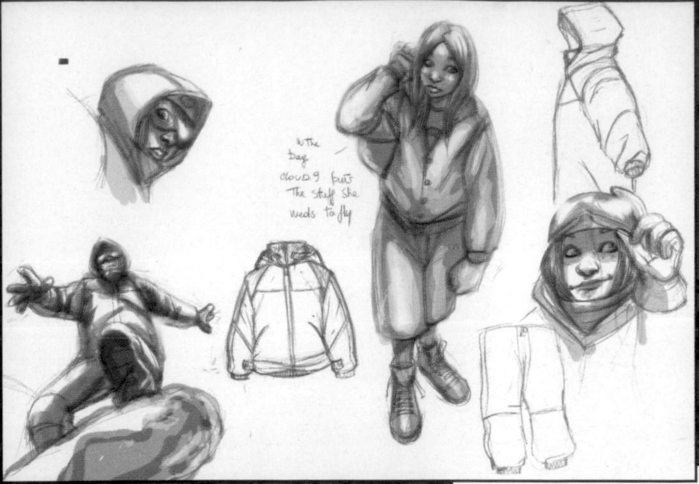
In The Day cloud 9 puts The stuff She needs to fly

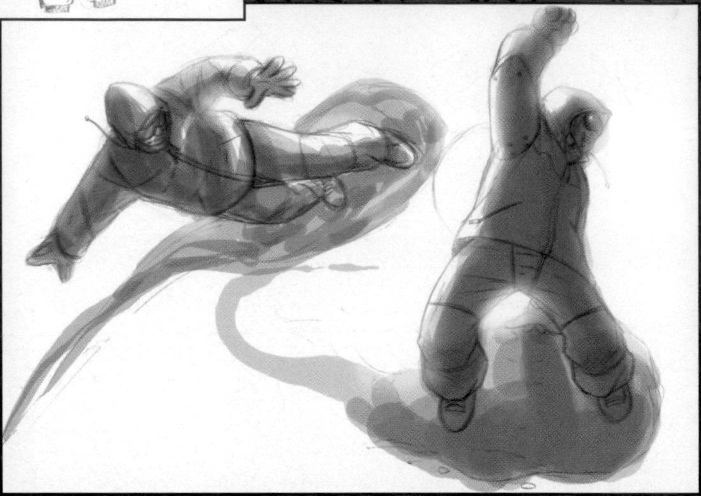

TRAUMA

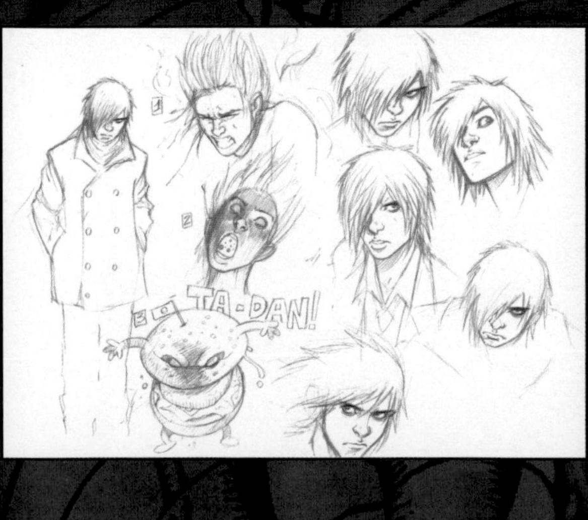
TA-DAN!

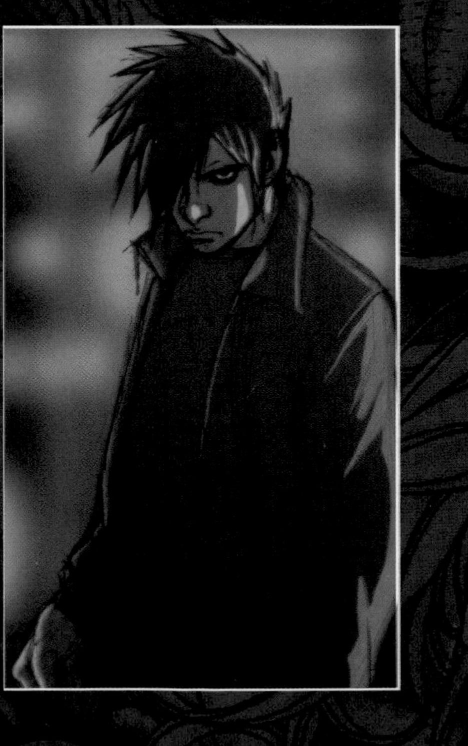

PROTON

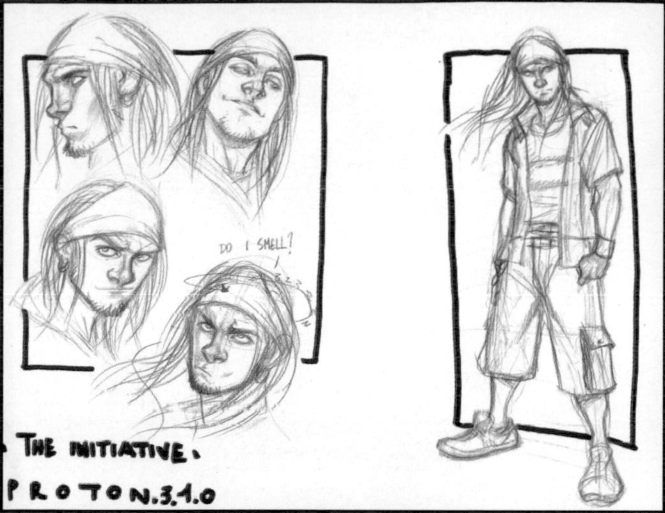
DO I SMELL?
THE INITIATIVE.
PROTON.3.1.0

THE GUANTLET

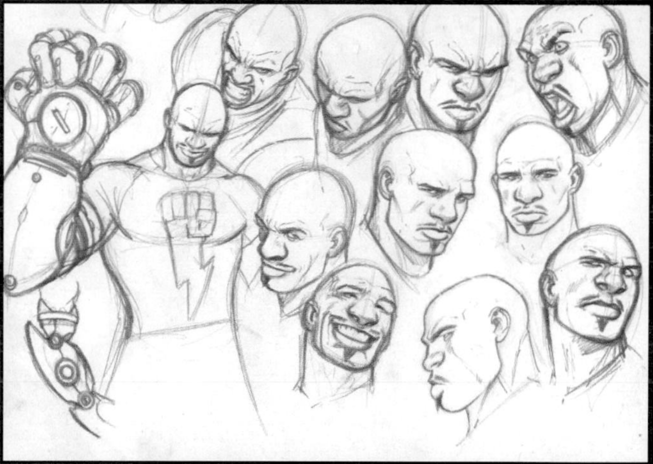

VOX, FROGMAN & PRIMA DONNA

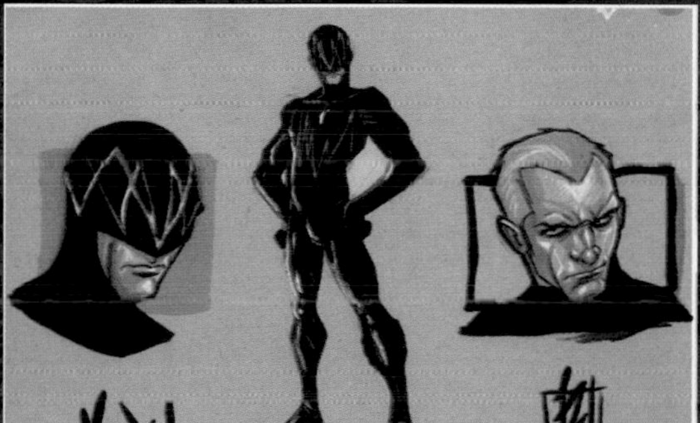
Vox!

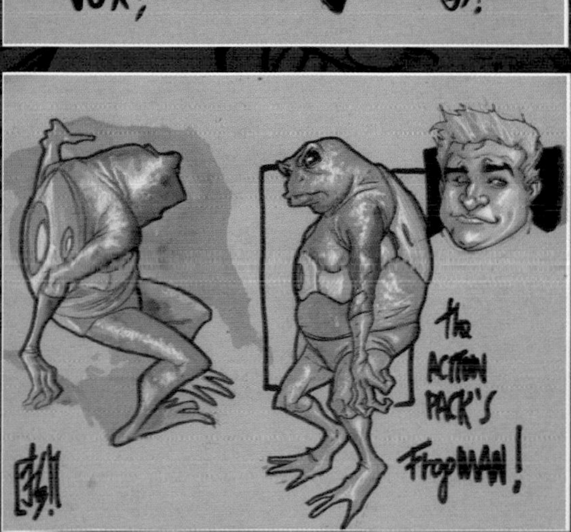
The ACTION PACK'S FrogMAN!

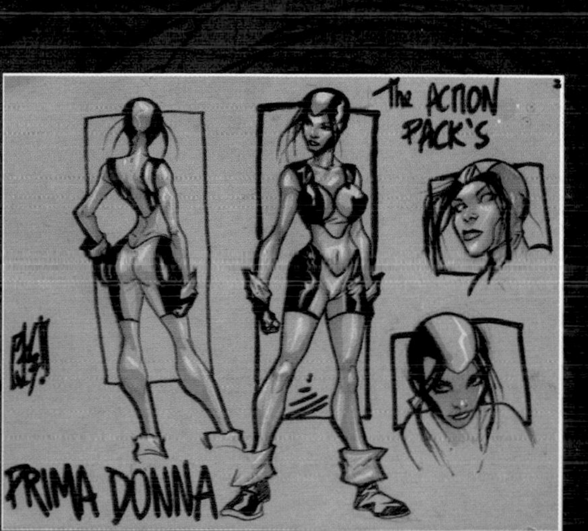
The ACTION PACK'S
PRIMA DONNA

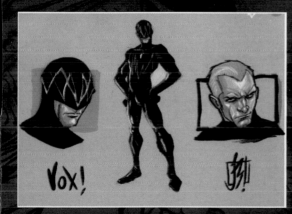

NEW CLOUD 9 COSTUME

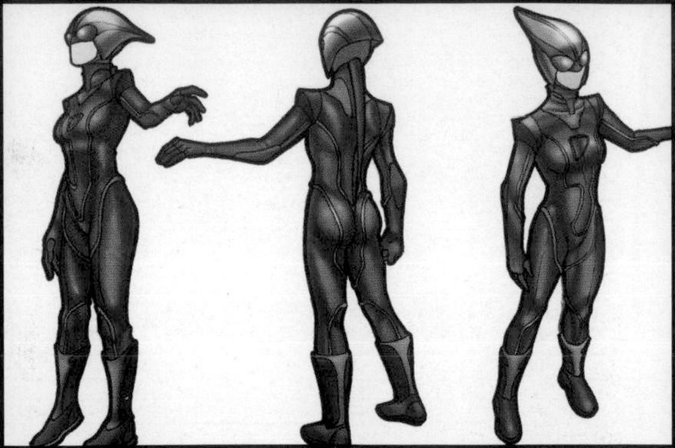

NEW HARDBALL COSTUME

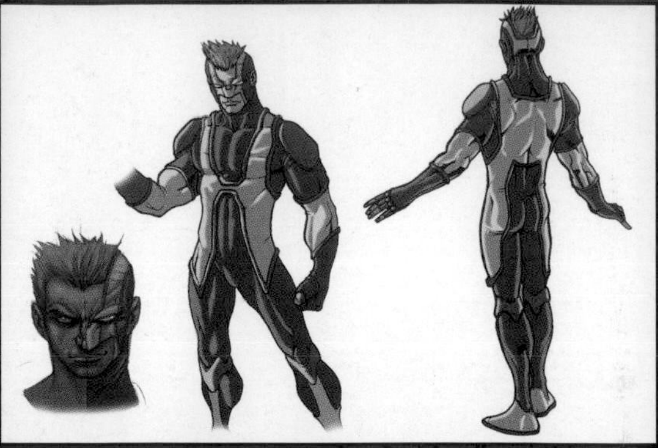

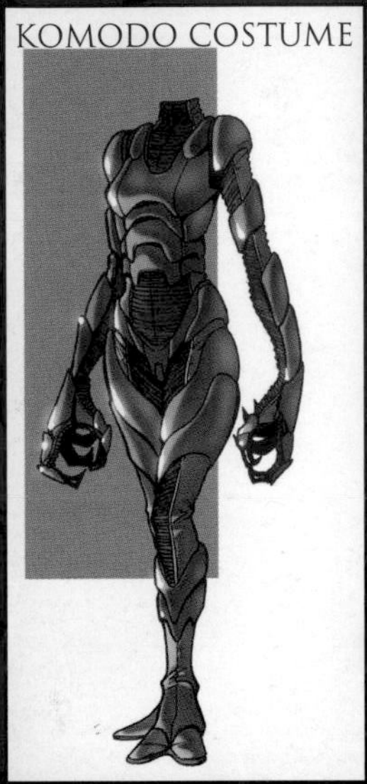
KOMODO COSTUME

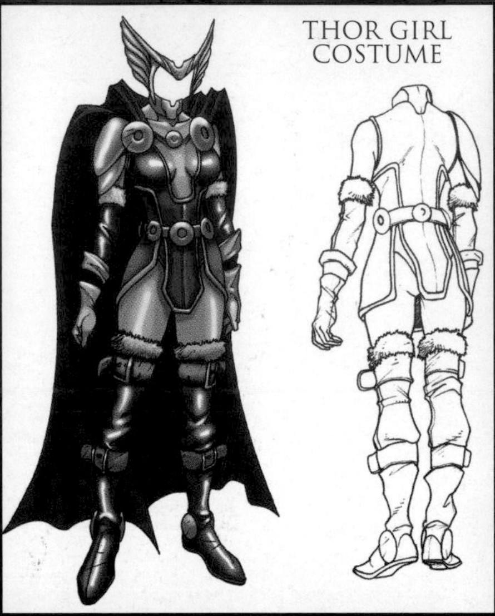
THOR GIRL
COSTUME

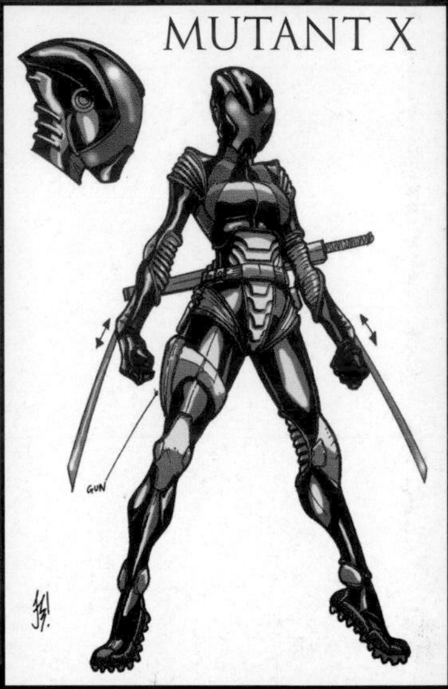
MUTANT X
GUN

CHARACTER DESIGNS BY HARVEY TOLIBAO

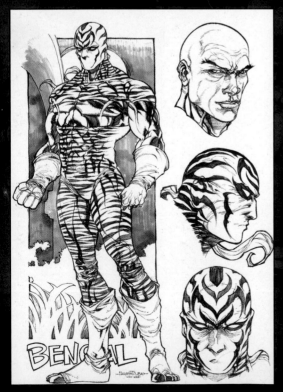

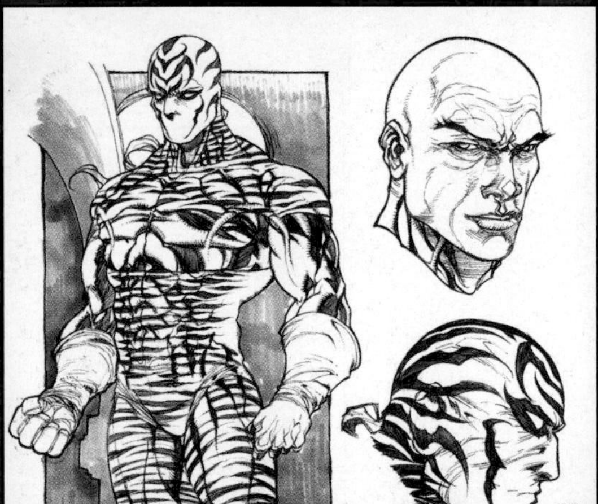
BENGAL

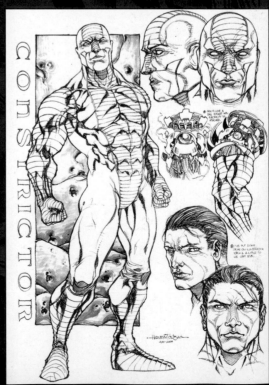

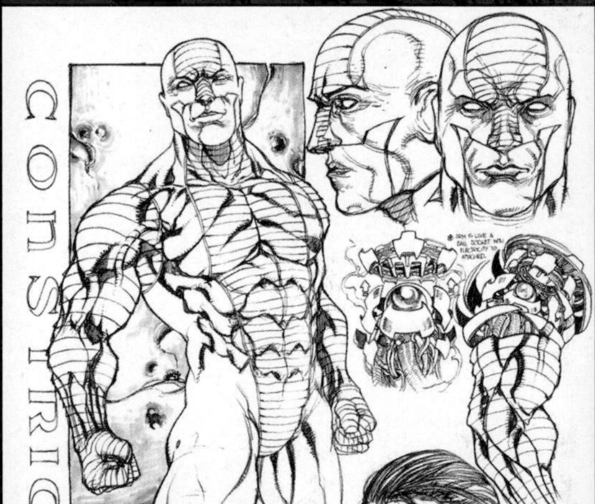
CONSTRICTOR

DATE DUE
